HOME
GROWING

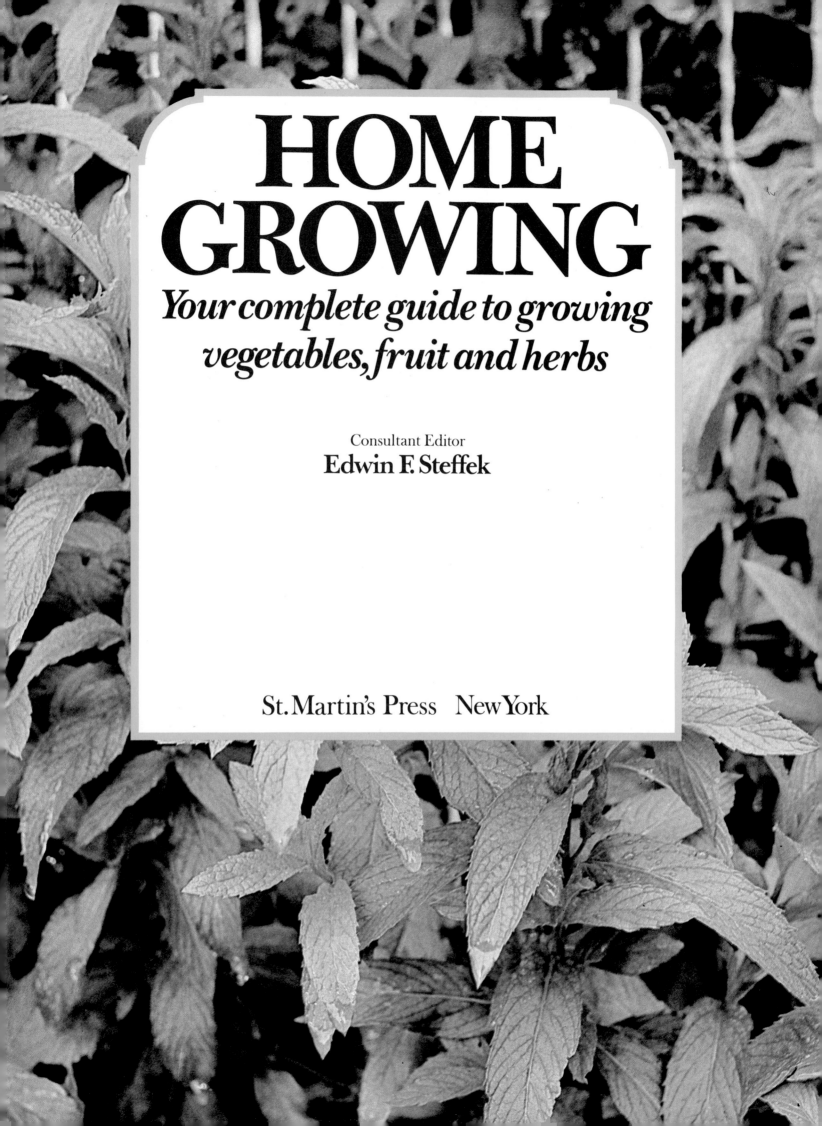

HOME GROWING

Your complete guide to growing vegetables, fruit and herbs

Consultant Editor
Edwin F. Steffek

St. Martin's Press New York

Contributors
Graham Andrews
Harry Baker
Ann Bonar
Guy Cooper
Peter Dodd
J.B. Duggan
Daphne ffiske
Brian Furner
Millar Gault
Nancy Mary Goodall
Cyril Harris
A.G. Healey
Joy Larkcom
P.J. Long
D. Macer-Wright
Cicely Mead

Ken Muir
Gay Nightingale
Horace Parsons
Peter Pashley
Ray Procter
Thomas Rivers
Keith Sangster
George Seddon
W.E. Shewell-Cooper
Donald Smee
D. Tostevin
James Trehane
John Warrington
Tony Webster
Richard A. Weeks
Ralph Whitlock
Jack Woodward

Editorial Staff:
Jean Wetherburn
Pepita Aris
Jonathan Elphick
Angela Errigo
Stella Hartwell
Elizabeth Holzer

Designed by:
Linda Palmer

Design Assistants:
Conal Buck
Keith Bloomfield

Picture research:
Ethne Rose

St. Martin's Press Inc.
175 Fifth Avenue
New York, N.Y. 10010

First published in the United States of America, 1977.
Not to be sold outside U.S.A. and its territories.

Printed in Great Britain

ISBN 0-312-38836-5

Library of Congress Catalog Number: 77-256

Library of Congress Cataloging in Publication Data
Main entry under title:

Home growing.

    Includes index.
        1.   Vegetable gardening.   2.   Fruit -culture.
I.   Steffek, Edwin F.
SB322.H65   635   77-256
    ISBN 0-312-38836-5

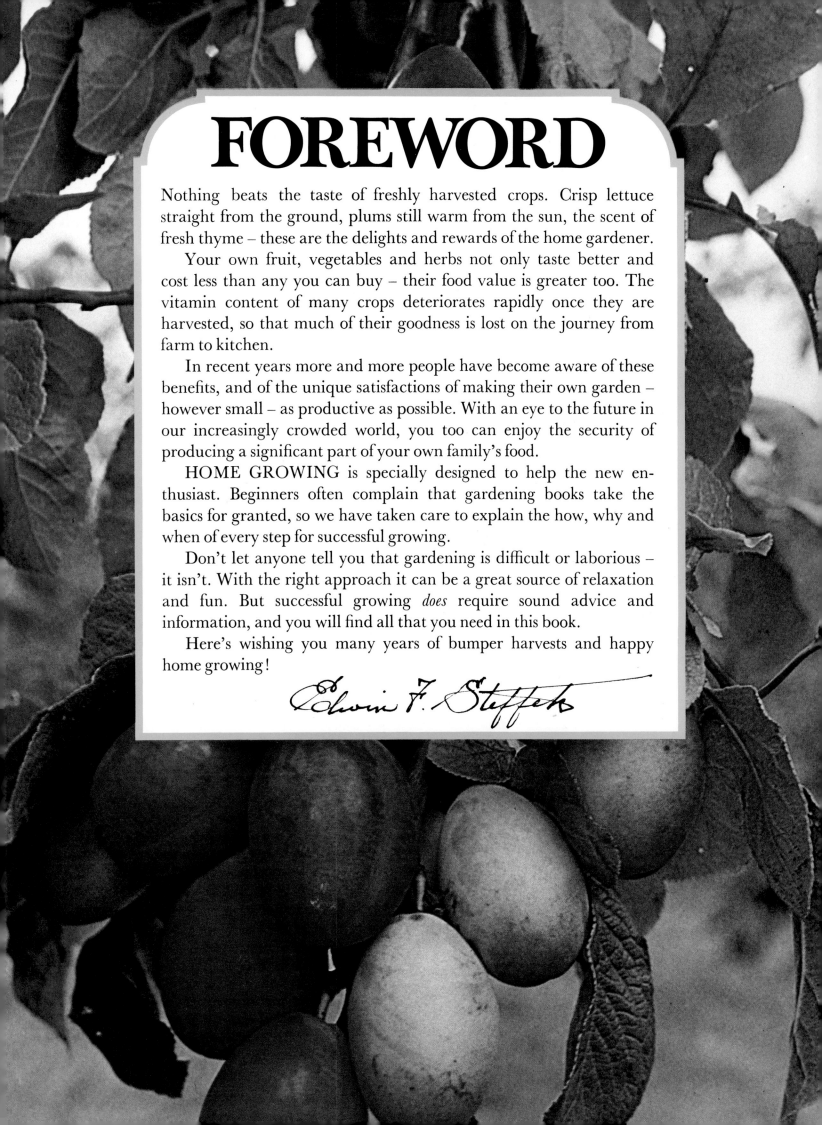

FOREWORD

Nothing beats the taste of freshly harvested crops. Crisp lettuce straight from the ground, plums still warm from the sun, the scent of fresh thyme – these are the delights and rewards of the home gardener.

Your own fruit, vegetables and herbs not only taste better and cost less than any you can buy – their food value is greater too. The vitamin content of many crops deteriorates rapidly once they are harvested, so that much of their goodness is lost on the journey from farm to kitchen.

In recent years more and more people have become aware of these benefits, and of the unique satisfactions of making their own garden – however small – as productive as possible. With an eye to the future in our increasingly crowded world, you too can enjoy the security of producing a significant part of your own family's food.

HOME GROWING is specially designed to help the new enthusiast. Beginners often complain that gardening books take the basics for granted, so we have taken care to explain the how, why and when of every step for successful growing.

Don't let anyone tell you that gardening is difficult or laborious – it isn't. With the right approach it can be a great source of relaxation and fun. But successful growing *does* require sound advice and information, and you will find all that you need in this book.

Here's wishing you many years of bumper harvests and happy home growing!

Edwin F. Steffek

CONTENTS

A to Z GROWING GUIDE...

BASIC GARDENING GUIDE...

A to Z
GROWING
GUIDE

Angelica

**Angelica has a special flavor
rather like vanilla-scented celery.
It has many culinary uses, most
popularly in its brilliant green
crystallized form.**

One of the largest and most handsome members of the *Umbelliferae* family, angelica (*Angelica archangelica*) was known as 'herb of the angels' in the sixteenth century. It is a biennial herb, generally dying out as soon as it has flowered and developed seeds in its second year of growth. The sweet-scented leaves spread out to form a magnificent plant, which may be as much as 2.1 m [7'] tall.

Cultivation

Angelica prefers semi-shady conditions and needs plenty of water. Ideally, a rich, moist soil produces the most flourishing plant. If soil is poor, rake in garden compost before sowing or transplanting.

Only fresh seeds germinate well, so be sure when ordering to ask specifically for seeds which have just ripened. Sow seeds in late summer or early autumn in finely raked open ground or boxes of potting soil. In either case germination temperature should be a fairly steady 15 to 21°C [60 to 70°F].

As soon as two or three true leaves appear, seedlings sown in boxes should be transplanted into open ground and watered in carefully. The young plants should be spaced about 45 cm [18"] apart so, if plants were started in the open, thin to this distance. When the plants are growing strongly thin again and allow a final planting distance of about 1.5 m [5'] between plants.

Water the growing plants regularly, taking great care not to submerge the crowns.

Keep the soil well dressed with a mulch. Except when young, the plant should not need much weeding.

Harvesting and after-care

Leaf stalks are best cut for use in early and mid-spring, before they become too fibrous.

Angelica often grows very tall. Its sweet-scented leaves can spread out to form a truly magnificent plant.

A sturdy plant when established, angelica needs no training or supports. In winter, when the plant dies down, it will withstand moderate frosts. If flower-bearing stems grow up from the base in the second summer, cut them out before seeding or the leaves will turn yellow and die.

The second summer, the plant should flower, then go to seed and die, if permitted. If you wish to extend the life of the plant cut off the flower heads as they appear. You can enjoy a crop of angelica for perhaps another five years. Alternatively, if you wish to gather seeds for a successive crop, allow a few weeks for them to ripen, then collect. Spread out and dry in the sun or a warm room for two or three days and sow as before. After harvesting the seed, dig up the plant and dispose of it, either by adding to the compost heap or by burning.

Using angelica

The best known way of using angelica is to crystallize the leaf stalk, preserving it for use in cakes, milk, steamed and baked desserts and sweetmeats. But it has several interesting uses as a fresh herb. The stalk, raw and grated, makes an excellent salad ingredient and adds flavor to seafood. Boiled and chopped, it can be added to poultry and vegetable stuffings. Boiled and puréed, the stalk enhances sauces, and braised angelica goes particularly well with game. The leaves can also be used in salads.

An elegant liqueur can be made from finely chopped angelica stalks and brandy. An infusion of angelica tea is good for the digestion and stimulates a poor appetite.

Apple

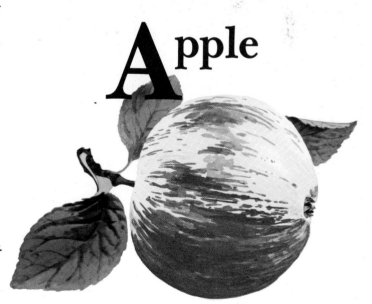

**This favorite tree bears numerous
crisp, juicy fruit.
According to variety, apples can be
eaten raw, cooked or pressed for juice
which is fermented to make cider.**

Today there are literally hundreds of apple varieties all descended from wild crab apple ancestors. They are all

Dwarf trees crop heavily and take up little garden space, so you can plant several varieties.

relatively hardy, flower in spring and bear fruit, according to variety, from midsummer to late autumn. From the

---

Apple
Malus pumila (fam. *Rosaceae*)
Hardy deciduous tree, with a useful life of about 50 years.
Size: from about 1.8 m [6′] tall for dwarf bushes to about 7.5 m [25′] for standard trees and up to 12 m [40′] for crab and cider apples.
Climate: cool to warm temperate.
Planting to harvesting time: dwarf trees on M9 rootstock start to produce fruit when 3 years old. More vigorous trees take a year or two longer.
Yield: dwarf bush trees may average about 14 kg [30 lb] a year, bush trees 28 kg [60 lb], mature cider trees may reach 500 kg [½ ton].

---

culinary point of view, they divide into four groups of which the first two are the most important. Cooking apples are sharply flavored and are therefore never eaten raw. They quickly form pulp when cooked. The second group is dessert apples, sweeter in flavor and mainly eaten raw. These may be cooked, when they will hold their shape. Cider apples are grown solely for their juice. This may be combined with a smaller proportion of juice from dessert apples to make a drink which may or may not be fermented. Crab apples are very tart and are used for jelly and preserves. Both the last two trees can be planted as pollinators for the other two types.

CHOOSING YOUR TREES

A combination of cooking and dessert apples suits most families best. Cooking apples sometimes tend to have a longer season and to keep better than the eating kinds, so a few carefully chosen varieties can keep a family supplied almost the whole year round, while bottled or frozen purée will bridge the few weeks between crops. Good cookers of either group may be more tolerant of less-than-perfect conditions.

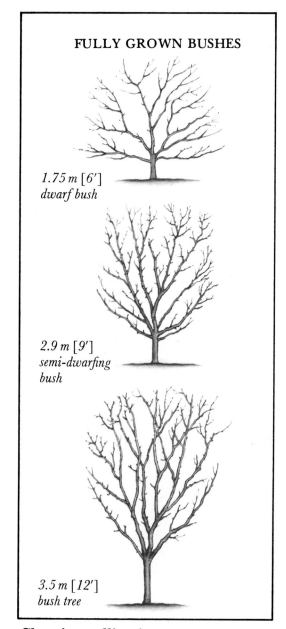

FULLY GROWN BUSHES

1.75 m [6′] dwarf bush

2.9 m [9′] semi-dwarfing bush

3.5 m [12′] bush tree

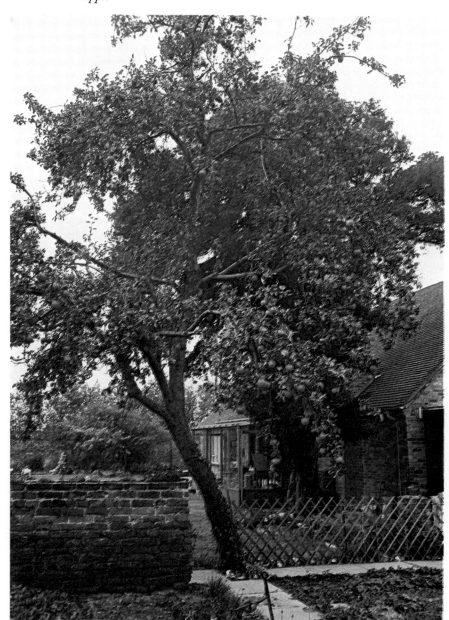

Cider apple standards eventually grow very big for fruit trees. They are both ornamental and useful.

Choosing pollination partners

Most apple trees benefit by having another variety in the vicinity, flowering at the same time, if they are to bear heavy crops of fruit, so you should plant a minimum of two. Some varieties are self-fertilizing but all give bigger crops if pollinated by another. The different apple groups usually pollinate each other. Throughout this section the text will suggest suitable pollinators for your apple. Your grower will advise you on varieties that flower at the same time and will pollinate each other.

Tree shapes

The simplest form of tree for the small garden or for limited space is the dwarf, which needs only a 1.5 m [5′] space. Old-fashioned standards or half-standards grow far too big for some home gardens or vegetable gardens and are best planted in the ornamental part of the garden where space is at a premium. It usually takes years before such trees come into full cropping. Most space saving are apples grown against walls or boundary fences, and instructions for such are given later. This can also serve a double purpose, being ornamental or disguising a bad view.

Rootstocks

Modern apple trees are formed by joining the apple variety to a separate root system or 'stock'. The fruiting habits of the resulting tree are that of the top, or scion, but the size is determined by the rootstock. The development of what are called dwarfing rootstocks now means that small but abundantly fruiting trees are available. By choosing your rootstocks you can select the variety you want at the size you want. The research was carried out at East Malling Research Station and at Merton in England and their root-stocks, referred to as M (Malling) and MM (Malling Merton), are used throughout the world.

Where space is very limited, you can plant a 'family tree'. These are trees with several varieties (usually three) grafted onto the same roots. Thus they will pollinate each other and you will have a choice of apple in even the smallest space.

Age of tree to buy

If you are going to train your apple on a wall or fence yourself, then you should buy a maiden or whip (one-year-old tree). Otherwise, buy a two- or three-year-old. It will bear fruit sooner. Do not let them bear more than a couple of sample fruit each during their first summer. You must give the roots time to reestablish; and do not buy older trees. They are older because they lack vigor.

CULTIVATION

A sunny site which is sheltered and frost-free at blossom time is necessary to ensure that insects can pollinate. Apples will grow successfully in most temperate areas. They will not grow in gardens waterlogged for long periods in wet weather, though a method of overcoming this is suggested below. In coastal areas salt-laden winds can cause damage and in places like Florida they do not get enough cold to rest properly.

Of course, some apples are more tolerant of heavy clay soil, high rainfall and indifferent drainage, and will put up with less sunshine than others.

The ideal soil is a medium loam, slightly acid and well-drained. If you can, prepare the soil for your apple trees in summer. Deep digging will improve surface drainage, while perennial weeds must be eliminated.

If you cannot prepare the soil so far in advance, leave it to settle for at least two weeks before planting if possible.

Test your soil with a simple soil-testing kit. If it is very acid, make it less so by applying lime. A neutral or slightly acid soil is more of a problem. Improve it by working in manure and use acid fertilizers such as sulphate of ammonia when necessary. Modern artificial fertilizers and foliar sprays can correct the lack of nutrients caused by too alkaline soil (often found in the Southwest).

You can improve both light, sandy or gravelly soil, as well as heavy clay ones, by working in liberal quantities of manure, garden compost, peat or leaf mold. Peat has no feeding value, but improves the consistency of the soil. If you are contemplating planting apples in an existing kitchen garden, be cautious. Where there has been a high level of feeding, tree growth will be stimulated to the detriment of fruit blossom. In this case plan a year's delay with no fertilizing, when you can go on growing vegetables.

When to plant the tree

You can plant at any time during the dormant season – when there are no leaves on the tree – provided the soil is neither frozen hard nor too wet to work freely. It is best to plant early in autumn so the tree can start to develop as soon as possible in spring or in early spring before the buds break.

Spacing

It is important to leave enough space between individual trees and also between trees and walls, fences, etc. For bush trees on M7 rootstock in soil of average quality, allow a radius of 2 m [7'] around each espaliered dwarf. If soil is rich, allow a radius of 2.8 m [9'].

For the smallest trees on M9 rootstock, allow a radius of 1.5 m [5']. For vigorous growers on dwarf M9 rootstock allow a radius of 1.75 m [6']. Three and four-and-one trees usually need a little more spacing, at least 4.25 m [14'], as

they are often more vigorous than other dwarfs.

Starting to plant

Plant the trees as soon as they are delivered, provided the soil in your garden is working well so that it is crumbly and not pasty. If the roots have dried out in transit soak them in water in a suitable container for about an hour or more. Trim any damaged roots back to a good one, making slanting cuts on the underside of the thicker roots.

If for any reason planting has to be delayed, heel the tree in temporarily in the open. Make a trench deep enough to bury the roots in, with one side of the trench sloping at an angle of about 45°. Lay the trees in this trench, against the sloping side, and return the soil over the roots. Cover them just up to the soil mark on the stem, which shows the depth the tree was previously growing in the nursery, and tread in lightly.

It is easier to plant trees if you have someone to help you. Dig the planting hole deep and wide enough for all the roots to be spread out fully in their natural growing positions.

Lay a stick across the planting hole to show you the ground level and ask your helper to hold the stem of the tree against this. Your aim must be that when you have finished planting the tree and treading down the soil, the tree will be at exactly the same soil depth as it was when growing in the nursery. The joint of the stock and the variety (top part) must not be below ground level, or the variety may put out roots, nullifying the dwarfing effect of the rootstock.

Staking

Dwarfs benefit from staking with preservative-treated wood. Drive two upright stakes into the planting hole so that they will be about 23 cm [9"] away from the tree. In light soil they should eventually be buried 60 cm [2'] below soil level, in heavy soil 45 cm [1' 6"]. After planting fix a cross-piece to the two stakes so that it comes to a little below the lowest branch, and fasten the tree to it.

Finishing planting

Put a spadeful of soil into the bottom of the hole, spread out the roots, sprinkle over a few handfuls of moist peat and start returning the soil.

If your soil is on the poor side, mix several handfuls of dried cow manure with the soil waiting to go back into the planting hole, but not in immediate contact with the roots. Your helper should wriggle the tree a little so the soil filters well between the roots. Tread the soil down to firm it as you go, but not too much if the soil is heavy.

Water with one 12 L [2¼ gal] bucket, and if there is no rain within a week, give it another bucket.

Create a shallow basin around the tree to contain waterings and surround the tree as far as the branches extend with a surface mulch (layer) of well-rotted compost, manure, leaf mold or damp peat, but do not let this touch the tree trunk, or it may rot the bark.

Support

Immediately after planting fasten the tree to its stakes. Use

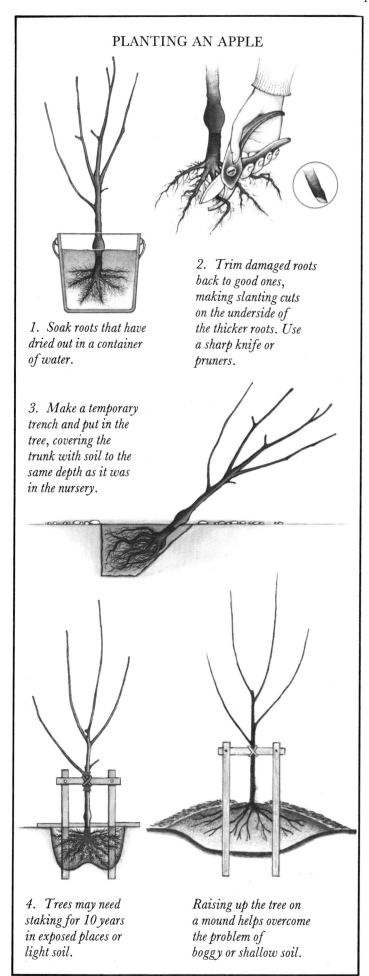

PLANTING AN APPLE

1. Soak roots that have dried out in a container of water.

2. Trim damaged roots back to good ones, making slanting cuts on the underside of the thicker roots. Use a sharp knife or pruners.

3. Make a temporary trench and put in the tree, covering the trunk with soil to the same depth as it was in the nursery.

4. Trees may need staking for 10 years in exposed places or light soil.

Raising up the tree on a mound helps overcome the problem of boggy or shallow soil.

an easily adjustable plastic tree tie or, failing that, wrap a piece of cloth around the tree to protect the bark and tie over it with cord. Finish by twisting the cord between the tree and stake to prevent chafing.

Inspect the tree's fastening frequently in early months because the soil will settle and it may be necessary to reposition the tie. The tree may be able to dispense with support in two to three years.

Planting in badly drained ground

Apple trees do not like perpetually wet feet. Deep digging and, wherever practicable, the improvement of drainage are the first steps. If you are still doubtful about the drainage, you can plant on a slight mound.

Instead of digging a normal-sized planting hole, make only a depression. Stand the tree in this, insert the usual stakes, and then remove topsoil from some other part of the garden and mound it up to the previous soil mark on the stem. The mound should be wider than the existing extent of the roots, to encourage them to grow out. Mulching should extend further than the branches and therefore each year you will have to topdress further out.

As the tree is on an individual mound, the roots will have to grow further before they encounter the inhospitable wetter layers. This method is also effective where shallow topsoil overlies chalk at a depth of about 45 cm [1′ 6″]. The disadvantage of mounding is that the tree is more vulnerable to drought, and generous watering is vital in dry periods, particularly in its early life. A mulch of garden compost will arrest surface evaporation.

Watering

The surface mulch will help to prevent evaporation and keep the soil moist during the first spring. This is a critical period for newly-planted trees and you must water freely and in adequate quantities in the first few summers if there is a drought.

Feeding

Apart from some dried manure mixed into the soil at planting, give no other food the first season. In succeeding late autumns or early springs, dress the ground around each tree, a little further out than the branches extend, with 38 g per sq m [$1\frac{1}{4}$ oz per sq yd] of sulphate of ammonia and 22 g per sq m [$\frac{3}{4}$ oz per sq yd] of sulphate of potash, raking the fertilizers into the surface.

Then every other year also rake in, at the same time, 54 g per sq m [$1\frac{3}{4}$ oz per sq yd] of superphosphate. If the harvest has been heavy an extra fertilizer dressing is beneficial.

Thinning

If you let an apple tree bear an exceedingly heavy crop in any one year, it may take a rest the next season. The big crop, too, is likely to be of undersized fruit.

Therefore, apples are thinned out to improve the appearance and size of the individual fruit. Fruit thinning is no less likely to be required on dwarf trees growing on M9 rootstock and trees trained as cordons and espaliers.

Some shedding of fruit occurs naturally in early summer, the so-called June drop, but the earlier you do any thinning the better for the tree. As soon as the fruitlets have 'set' (when a tiny but obvious fruitlet has replaced the blossom and you know a heavy crop is possible) take a thin pointed pair of scissors and cut out the king apple, the central fruitlet, from each cluster if you can reach them. Remove any blemished fruitlets and, having done that, continue thinning until only one or two fruits remain out of each original cluster. A fruit should never be closer than 10 cm [4″] to the next.

PRUNING THE TREE

The purpose of winter pruning is to build up a framework of robust main branches. Immediately after planting give the tree its first pruning. Hard winter pruning stimulates the wood growth and at this stage of the tree's career that is what you want. Make sure your shears are really sharp. If it is an unpruned maiden (one-year-old) tree cut it back to half its height, leaving three or four good buds.

Second year: If you have bought a two-year-old tree, it will only have three or four branches. If these are strong and long, cut each back halfway, making your cut close beyond a growth bud pointing outward. If, however, these first branches are not very long and look thin and wispy, you must be more drastic and cut off two-thirds of the length of each. Cutting back these first branches causes growth buds near the cut ends to develop.

Third year: By the tree's third winter each of the three or four primary branches will have made three or more secondary branches. Cut back the previous summer's growth by a third of its length if strong, by a half if thin and wispy.

Meanwhile, by this time some sideshoots (also known as laterals) may have grown from the secondary branches. If these laterals are badly placed to make new branches, cut each back to its fourth bud. Slice off, flush with the stem, any sideshoots springing from the trunk of the tree just below the main branches.

Fourth year: The four-year-old tree may be regarded as adult. From now on restrict winter pruning to the minimum necessary to build up a continuing supply of fruiting wood rather than extending the size of the tree. Crossing branches and cankerous and broken branches should always be removed.

Encouraging fruiting wood

If you do not prune a sideshoot, it may make fruit buds in its second year. These are bigger, fatter and rounder than growth buds and the year after will burst into blossom in spring. Each winter leave some sideshoots untouched to bear fruit.

If more sideshoots are needed, cut back some to the second bud from the base, but generally you should cut back the three-year-old sideshoots which have fruited to a 5 cm [2″] stump. Don't touch the tips of the branches once fruit-bearing has begun – unless a branch is growing in an undesirable direction and you want to replace the season's new extension growth with another one.

Under this system the tree will produce a good balance of fruiting laterals and vegetating ones to provide fruit later. Some varieties also form fruit buds at the tips of one-year-

old shoots. Leave such shoots intact.

TRAINING APPLES ON WIRES

Most economical of garden space is the cordon, where three different varieties can be grown in a 3 m [10′] row. Espaliers require a 4 m [14′] space and you must plant a pollinator. For training an espalier tree *see* PEAR.

Planting cordons

A cordon consists of a single stem bearing fruiting spurs. The tree is planted at an angle to restrict growth and to encourage early fruiting and an even production of buds on the stem.

If you have no suitable wall or fence, you can erect one as a garden divider, perhaps to separate the patio or lawn from the vegetable garden.

Put in sturdy posts about 2.1 m [7′ 6″] tall and about 3 m [10′] apart. Between these stretch three 0.25 m [$\frac{1}{16}$″] gauge galvanized wires at heights of 60 cm [2′], 1.25 m [4′] and 1.8 m [6′]. Use an adjustable fence strainer at the end of each wire to keep it taut. If possible, arrange the row to run from south to north.

For cordons use only one-year-old whips, if possible, and space them 75 cm [2′ 6″] apart in the row and, if you have more than one row, allow 1.8 m [6′] between rows. Plant them at an angle of 45°.

Immediately after planting, tie the cordon to a 2.4 m [8′] long bamboo cane which has previously been secured to the three horizontal wires at an angle of 45°. Three ties are necessary, using soft string, with the lowest tie near the bottom end of the cane and 5 cm [2″] above the union.

Pruning cordons

No pruning is usually necessary during the winter except in the case of tip-bearing varieties. With these, cut back the main stem only, by a quarter of the previous season's growth, and repeat this in subsequent winters.

The main pruning of cordons is carried out in midsummer in warmer districts and as much as a month later in cooler ones. Start when you see that sideshoots growing directly from the main cordon stem are maturing – that is, they are more than 23 cm [9″] long, the leaves have lost their early brightness and become a deep green and the skin of the shoot has stiffened and begun to look definitely bark-like for the lower part of its length.

At the base of such a shoot you will usually find a cluster of leaves. Disregard these, count three leaves from the base of the shoot and then cut close above the third leaf. Then there may also be growths springing from laterals made and pruned a previous year. Cut each of these back to the first leaf beyond the basal cluster.

If some of the new shoots are not mature, wait until they are and then prune them. If secondary growth occurs in late summer from near the point where you made your first cuts, prune such shoots back to one leaf or bud in mid-autumn.

When the cordon reaches the length of its cane, probably after about three years, unfasten the cane from the wires and bend the whole tree down about 5° and refasten the cane. This can be repeated again a few years later.

Apple blossom needs shelter from wind to aid pollination.

THINNING FRUITLETS

Cut out the central fruitlet in each cluster and then any diseased or smaller fruitlets.

WINTER PRUNING PROGRAM

If the nursery has not done so, prune the one-year-old tree to half its height leaving three or four good buds.

In the second year prune back strong growth halfway and weak growth by two thirds. Cut to an outward-pointing bud.

By the third winter, each of the 3 or 4 primary branches will have made about 3 more secondary branches. The leaders are the new growth from the tip. Laterals are secondary branches and both will grow fruiting spurs.

Cut back the previous summer's growth by a third of its length if strong and half if thin.

By the fourth year the tree is fully formed and shaped. Any further pruning will be in order to encourage fruiting.

PLANTING CORDONS AND SUMMER PRUNING OF LATERALS

line of break

scion

rootstock

wrong   **right**

This is the correct method of planting a cordon with the tree tied to a cane and the cane to the wires. Hold the tree at an angle of 45° while you plant.

The scion (tree top) should be planted leaning above the rootstock. Wrong way up, the tree could break off here from its roots.

pruning point

basal cluster of leaves

pruning point

last year's lateral

This is the correct way to prune the short spurs of the cordon in summer to encourage it to produce fruit buds.

Usually there comes a time when the mature tree stops producing further extension growth each summer but if it reaches the limit of space available before that happens, cut it back as necessary soon after new growth begins in the spring.

Except in the case of tip-bearing varieties, the leader should not normally be pruned until it must be checked for reasons of space. However, if the desired fruit-bearing sideshoots are scarce, stimulate the production of more by pruning the season's new extension growth of the leader by a third during winter. Individual buds in a bare length of stem can be encouraged by cutting a half-moon notch from the bark just above them.

At the other extreme, if after some years there are too many fruiting spurs and they are becoming crowded, cut some of these back and take some out entirely, doing this in winter or very early spring.

HARVESTING AND STORING

A dwarf on M9 rootstock should start to bear fruit in its second or third garden summer. This should give excellent crops of up to 28kg [60 lb] in good seasons, but you should probably count on its averaging less than half of this amount over the years. Very strong growers and those on rootstocks which are more vigorous than the dwarfing M9 will take longer before bearing.

When ready to pick, lift the apple in the palm of your hand and gently give it the slightest possible twist. If it is ready to pick it should come away quite easily. Handle apples carefully, because they bruise easily and this can spread rot among the stored crop. Cider and crab apples grown in grass may be allowed to drop off or, alternatively, you can spread sheets underneath and then shake the tree.

Cooking apples may be used before they are fully ripe, but their full flavour will develop with storage. Cider apples may be allowed to mature off the tree before being used. Then fully ripe, their flesh is easily bruised by thumb pressure. Pick and store apples as soon as they are ripe, otherwise they quickly deteriorate.

Apples require a well-ventilated, cool, slightly moist, dark storage place, just below 5° C [40° F]. You may be able to utilize a garden shed, garage, cellar or loft. All these places would normally be too dry for storing apples, but you can overcome this by storing the fruit in plastic bags.

Apples can be successfully frozen in several ways. They may be frozen uncooked—peel, core, cut into 1cm [½"] slices and drop into water to which salt or lemon has been added to avoid discoloration. Rinse before blanching. Open freeze and pack in plastic bags or rigid containers. Raw slices may be mixed with sugar at a ratio of 125 g [½ cup] sugar to ¼kg [1 lb] of fruit. Pack in plastic bags or rigid containers.

You can also freeze them in containers with a syrup made of 375 g [1½ cups] of sugar to ½ L [2½ cups] of water.

Apples may also be frozen after being baked. Simply cool, open freeze and wrap individually in foil.

Only store sound dry fruit and put different varieties in different bags. Use a lot of small bags, rather than a few large ones, so that any rot cannot spread far. Seal the bags, then snip off a fingernail-sized triangle from each bottom corner to admit a little air. Examine the apples periodically and use immediately any that begin to show soft bruising or brown spots; if left too long, these apples will be inedible.

Varieties:

Variety	Season	Comments
Baldwin	Winter	Old, biennial
Cortland*	Winter	Eating, cooking
Delicious	Winter	Good keeper
Early McIntosh	Summer	Eating, cooking
Golden Delicious*	Winter	Eating, cooking
Jonalicious	Fall	Eating, cooking
Jonathon	Winter	Eating, cooking
Lodi	Summer	Cooking (yellow)
Macoun*	Winter	Eating, cooking
McIntosh*	Winter	Favorite in East
Northern Spy	Winter	Excellent, slow starter
Red Delicious	Fall	Eating, cooking
Rhode Island Greening	Winter	Best cooker
Rome Beauty	Winter	Eating, cooking
Stark Earliest	Summer	Very early
Summer Delicious	Summer	Eating
Wealthy	Fall	All-purpose old Favorite
Whitney	Winter	Crab
York-A-Red	Winter	Eating, cider

Especially recommended as good varieties of apple for freezing.

PESTS AND DISEASES

Apples can be the victim of a number of pests and diseases: scab, mildew, caterpillars, aphids of various kinds, capsids, spider mites, coddling moths, apple maggots, brown rot and scale insects. These can all be controlled by a routine spray program.

For proper timing and approved materials to use, check with your local State Extension Service and follow their recommendations to the letter.

There are also a number of troubles that could occur and which will not be controlled by the spray program: canker, brown rot, woolly aphids, codling moth, bitter pit and birds.

Scab is a fungus disease producing black spots on leaves and fruit, which later cracks and may become infected with brown rot. It is worst in a wet spring and is treated with captan. Mildew produces white powdery patches on leaves and young shoots in spring, and infected flowers

VARIETIES OF DESSERT APPLE

Rhode Island Greening is an old favorite for pies and baking.

Rome Beauty, popular for both eating and cooking, is a good keeper.

Yellow and red-streaked Anoka is a hardy, August-ripening variety.

Northern Spy is slow to bear but is large, crisp and juicy.

Lodi, one of the earliest, is a yellow summer cooking apple.

Oriole, a new summer apple, is colored red over a yellow ground.

Roxbury Russet, Popular in bygone days, still makes excellent cider.

McIntosh is probably the most popular apple in the East.

Starking Delicious colors well and has good qualities.

Fireside, a Delicious type for coldest climates, is somewhat less colorful.

Golden Delicious has a pleasant flavor and is a good bearer.

Granny Smith, often imported, is both a dessert apple and a cooker.

turn cream in color and do not set. Remove infected shoots and spray with dinocap.

The white maggots of apple sawfly eat into the fruitlets and leave ribbon-like scars on resulting apples. Derris should be sprayed when most of the flower petals have fallen. Apple suckers feed on the undersurface of the leaves in the same way that aphids do and are controlled by the same insecticide. Capsid damage is mainly in the fruitlets. These develop pale scabs and become distorted in shape. Control as for aphids. Codling moth grubs are similar, but have a brown head; they go into fruit through the eye and eat the seeds and center of the apples from mid-summer.

Woolly aphids are covered with white fluff and commonly feed on the junctions of the branches. The bark cracks, which allows the entry of canker and other fungal diseases. Malathion sprayed in early summer, repeated two weeks later, or brushing with methylated spirits, will control the aphids.

Canker is a fungus disease of the wood of the branches, trunk and shoot, which causes trouble in humid climates. The bark flakes and dies where fungus enters through tree wounds. If it encircles the stem, the branch above it will die. Check with local authorities.

Brown rot infects the fruit, which then either drops, or remains mummified on the tree to infect next year's fruit. Fruit with brown skin or flesh should be destroyed as soon as seen, not stored.

Apricot

**Luxurious, orange-fleshed fruit, apricots grow on small trees and are therefore very suitable for the home garden.
They flourish in warm climates.**

The Romans, who introduced the apricot tree into Europe, named it *Praecocia*, meaning early, and this evolved into the word 'apricot'. It is one of the earliest fruit trees to flower. It is more tender than either the peach or the plum, to which it is related. In cooler temperate areas, unprotected blossoms are often damaged by cold and the tree needs shelter from early sun and good air drainage as well.

Suitable site and soil

For years the culture of apricots was confined to the milder regions. In the very coldest parts of the country you would be unwise to plant apricots except under glass; a cool, well-ventilated greenhouse will afford protection. A slightly heated greenhouse is suitable too, but the fruit will not be much earlier than the normal season—it is difficult to force apricots into fruiting early.

Because they bloom in very early spring, when some of the bleakest cold winds are experienced, the flowers have difficulty in setting, that is, becoming fertilized, so that fruit will form. Either that or a late frost will kill the blossoms and newly-set fruit. Consequently, apricots were traditionally grown in the milder areas of the West Coast and Northwest. Now, however, we have varieties better adjusted to culture in the Northeast. Among the best Eastern ones are Alfred, Farmingdale, Worley Peach, Veecot Goldcot and Curtis. For the Far West the best are Royal (Blenheim), Moor Park, Tilton, Perfection, Wentchee, Blenril and Earliril.

Buying the tree

Buy a one- or two-year-old tree.

While most trees will be grown in the conventional fashion, much like peach trees, an interesting innovation is an espalier, particularly a fan shape against a fence or on supporting wires. A conventional tree – as a minimum – needs 3.5 m [12'] square. If space is limited, try to purchase one on semi-dwarfing stock, which has a height of 2.5 m [8'] and a spread of 4.6 m [15'] according to soil conditions. However, a standard tree on vigorous stock will eventually grow to 3 m [12'] in height and 7.5 m [25'] in spread.

Apricots can be grown from seed by sowing the stones 7 cm [3"] deep and 60 cm [2'] apart. However, this could be an unrewarding task, as apricots do not grow true from seed, and you will wait for several years for the result.

Planting the tree

To prepare the site, fork the soil, adding a 10-12 L bucket of compost or peat per sq m [2-2½ gal per sq yd] plus dried manure at 125 g per sq m [4 oz per sq yd] or, better, a handful of superphosphate. Test the soil and if the pH

Apricot
Prunus armeniaca (fam. Rosaceae)
Hardy deciduous tree, with a useful life of up to about 50 years.
Size: 2.5-4.5 m [8-15'] tall.
Climate: cool to warm temperate.
Planting to harvesting time: two or more years for one- or two-year-old trees.
Yield: for mature, semi-dwarf tree 15-20 kg [35-40 lb].

shows acidity, add garden lime at 212 g per sq m [7 oz per sq yd] as a top-dressing. This dressing will gradually be washed into the soil by the rain.

Plant no deeper than 20 cm [8″]. Dig out a hole 15 cm [6″] deep and 1 m [3′] across. Prune back any damaged roots. Spread out the roots evenly in the hole. Place a spadeful of soil over each root and stamp this down firmly. Then fill the hole. When you have finished, the surface should be level. This allows for settling. If this is not done, there will be no depression to hold water during subsequent waterings.

Watering

Water liberally during dry weather especially the first year. Trees growing on slopes or in gravelly soil are particularly susceptible to drought, as are greenhouse trees, and lack of water may cause immature fruit to drop.

Feeding

Mulch the ground 2.5 cm [1″] deep all around the tree for 1 m [3′] or so using compost hay or straw. Wood ashes may be applied each spring early at the rate of 155 g per sq m [5 oz per sq yd]. These are raked in very lightly. Hydrated

lime may be applied every few years if a soil test indicates excess acidity.

Pollination

In cold areas during blossoming give the tree shelter on cold nights by hanging burlap or plastic sheets over it. Nail a support above the tree from which to hang your cover; it should not touch the flowers.

The fine pink flowers are self-fertile but in cool seasons they may need help to set. At midday when the flowers are fully open, stroke the centers of the blossoms with a fine paint brush – this will artificially transfer the male pollen from the anthers to the stigmas.

Thinning

When the fruit is formed and as big as peas remove about half of the smallest. Repeat the operation when they are the size of small walnuts, leaving the apricots spaced out evenly all over the tree 10 cm [4″] apart.

Pruning and training

An apricot should be pruned and treated in the same way

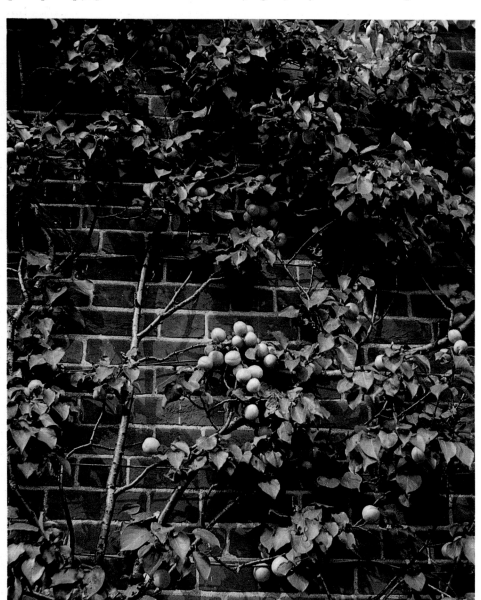

In the coldest parts of cool temperate areas, apricots should not be attempted, and even in milder parts they need the shelter of a wall facing the midday sun.

Apricots make small trees and can be grown in pots. Ensure good drainage and fill with potting mixture. Keep this moist in summer, drier in winter. Restrict pruning to the minimum that is necessary.

as a peach (*see* PEACH) in its formative years.

Fruit is produced on the shoots of the preceding year's growth and on short spurs carried on the older wood. Do not prune in the depth of winter, because of the danger of freezing. Early spring pruning permits removal of injured branches.

For a fan or other espaliered form, in midsummer cut back any vigorous current season's shoots to just above the fifth leaf from the base of the shoot. Leave untouched both weaker shoots and those required to extend the framework for a fan. After cropping, cut back the same pruned shoots to three leaves from a spur which will then bear fruit next year.

Pinch out unnecessary crowding shoots in the course of the summer when they are only 2.5 cm [1″] long. As soon as the fruit has been picked, any shoots badly placed for a fan can be removed and the branches re-tied to leave them evenly spaced over the support.

Harvesting and storing the crop

Fruit should be gathered when just ripe, usually in late summer. The top of the fruit, near the stalk, should be slightly soft. Be sure to pick very carefully to avoid bruising, as the fruit is extremely delicate. You should, first of all, always pick in the morning just as soon as the fruit is absolutely dry. If you have a cool room or storage area, you can extend the eating season by at least two or three weeks by making sure to pick the fruit when fully colored but still quite hard, letting it ripen slowly. Though it may be possible in some circumstances, it is very difficult to force the apricots to ripen earlier than they would otherwise, by additional heat in the greenhouse.

Pests and Diseases

Die-back is a damaging disease of apricots in temperate areas and is not easy to cure. If a branch does die, saw it off safely below the injury so that the wound is smooth. Paint the cut with a wound-sealing compound to prevent the growth of fungus; and destroy the cut branch. Also, paint any sizeable wounds with a commercial tree wound paint to prevent gummosis and its resulting cankers.

Brown rot and shot hole fungus are both controlled by the normal spray program. Your local State Extension Service can provide information.

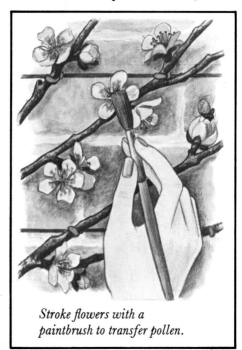

Stroke flowers with a paintbrush to transfer pollen.

In Mediterranean climates apricots are successful on bushes.

SHELTERING THE BLOSSOM

Blossom needs shelter on cold nights. Support a batten on the wall by two poles, and suspend netting or plastic from it. This should not be allowed to touch the flowers.

Artichoke

This strikingly handsome, thistle-like plant has arching, gray-green leaves and looks attractive enough to plant among shrubs or in a herbaceous border.

The globe-shaped flower buds consist of numerous edible 'leaves' or scales on a fleshy base. Always choose varieties with green globes, which are delicious and tender: purple globes have beautiful flowers but are not worth eating.

Suitable site and soil

The ideal position is sunny, well protected from wind and away from trees and hedges. If you are planning your kitchen garden on a rotation system, remember that artichokes must stay in the same place for several years and will develop into large, bushy plants.

Globe artichokes like a rich soil which is moist but well drained (not waterlogged in winter). Light sandy soil is best. If you have a heavy soil, break up the subsoil, then lighten the topsoil with ashes, coarse sand, peat or grit. These plants will give three good years of production only if they have a deep bed, rich in nutrients. To prepare poor soil for planting, apply some garden compost or well-rotted farm manure. Dig either of these in well during late winter or early spring, at a rate of about half a barrow-load per 5 sq m [6 sq yd]. A general fertilizer should be incorporated before planting; dig over the soil and distribute the fertilizer over the area to a depth of 10 cm [4″], at a proportion of 100 g per sq m [3 oz per sq yd].

Artichoke, globe

Cynara scolymus (fam. *Compositae*).
Hardy perennial with a useful life of four years.
Size: the bushy, herbaceous plants reach about
1-1.75 m [3′-5′] high, 1 m [3′] in diameter.
Climate: cool temperate to sub-tropical.
Planting to harvesting time: the plants crop in the
second year from offsets, in the third year from seed.
Yield: about 5 king heads and 10 side heads per
plant per season.

A crop of globe artichoke heads when ready for harvesting.

Propagate new plants by cutting offsets (sideshoots) about 25 cm [10″] high from the base of the plant in spring. Plant with a piece of root attached.

Both the main king heads and the smaller laterals are delicious to eat.

Lay leaf mold over the crowns of cut-down plants in the fall to protect them from frosts.

Sowing and planting

Artichokes can be grown from seed but the results are often erratic and it is better and easier to start with suckers, known as offsets, from a well-proven plant. Buy your off-sets in mid-spring. Plant firmly 10 cm [4"] deep, in rows at least 1 m [3'] apart, with 75 cm [2' 6"] between plants. Water well and mulch with garden compost or rotted manure.

If you wish to try seeds, sow after the last spring frost 1.5 cm [½"] deep and 30 cm [1'] apart. Care for seedlings as for offsets, thinning to 1 m [3'] apart when they grow too closely together.

Watering and feeding

Water the artichokes well and often through spring and summer, especially in dry periods. They must never be allowed to become dry at the roots.

In spring, a sprinkling of sodium nitrate, 15 g [½ oz] per plant, on damp soil provides a good start to growth.

Substitute ammonium sulphate on clay soils which are made even heavier by sodium salts. Fork garden compost between rows every spring.

In summer, apply a good liquid fertilizer at 10-day intervals. In this mid-season of vigorous growth, two weak doses of chelated iron (marketed under several names) are sometimes helpful. Lawn mowings spread around from time to time help retain moisture in the soil. Tall plants may need staking. Choose stakes strong enough to bear the full weight of the plant and insert them firmly. Tie the main stem to the stake, allowing room for the plant to sway naturally, otherwise flower heads may snap off.

Harvesting the crop

First year: there will probably be no big heads the first year, as the first main crop matures in the second year of growth. Some small buds will appear and should be pinched out at the first sign of formation to build up the basic plant and make it more productive for next year's harvest.

Second year: large terminal buds, known as king heads, should be picked for eating when firm. These will be about 10 cm [4"] in diameter. The leaves should be green, tightly packed and not yet opened for flowering. Each plant should produce at least five king heads. If the heads are left to mature to full growth they become inedible and the chokes open out into immense purple-blue thistles. Once the king head is picked, lateral (side) shoots then develp and smaller heads will grow, which can also be picked and eaten, after a ten-minute inversion upside down in warm, salted water.

Care after harvesting

After all the good heads are gathered, cut down the artichoke stems and most of the large leaves, except for a few leaves to protect the crown. If your area is liable to suffer frost or biting winter winds, protect the plants in mid-autumn with straw manure and a covering of bracken, wood shavings, a raked-up 10 cm [4"] covering of earth, or a mulch of compost of leaf mold. Remove these coverings after danger of hard frosts is over in the following spring. No row should be left to grow after it is more than four years old. Plant a new row of offsets each year so that the old rows can be dug up and replaced.

Propagation

To propagate new plants for the following season, take offsets from the base of an established parent plant when about 25 cm [10"] high in early or mid-spring. Use a sharp knife to remove the offsets and see that a piece of root is attached, to help growth. Plant offsets immediately after cutting them.

Pests and diseases

Artichoke hearts may be infected with a fungus disease called blight fungus which rots the petals. Remove infected heads as soon as seen.

Other problems which may occur include slugs, aphids and earwigs.

JERUSALEM AND CHINESE
Artichokes

**The Jerusalem artichoke (left)
and Chinese artichoke (right)
are both unusual and tasty
tubers which will grow in almost any
soil and give high yields for
very little gardening effort.**

The Jerusalem artichoke is a hardy vegetable native to North America. It is related to neither the globe nor the

Artichoke, Jerusalem
Helianthus tuberosus (fam. *Compositae*)
Perennial, treated as an **annual.**
Size: about 1.5-2.5 m [5-8'] tall.
Climate: temperate.
Planting to harvesting time: about 9-11 months.
Yield: about 1 kg [2 lb] per plant, with 5 plants per 3 m [10'] row.

1. Dress the soil with wood ash before planting, to remedy any potash deficiency.

2. Another way of planting out. Make drills 10 cm [4″] deep, 75 cm [2½′] apart. Set tubers 38 cm [15″] apart.

3. Tying-up to avoid wind damage. Use string to tie the plants to strands of wire between stakes.

4. At the approach of winter, cut off the dead stems and foliage fairly close to the ground.

5. Forking up. Take care not to spear the tubers, and be sure to clear the ground. Any remaining portions will grow next year, spreading like a weed.

6. In a severe winter, store tubers in dry peat or sand in a cool place. Rub off any soil and arrange them sandwich fashion in containers.

Chinese artichoke, being a member of the sunflower (*Helianthus*) group of the family *Compositae*. It is quite simple to grow and provides an excellent winter crop. The tall stem and broad leaves resemble those of the annual sunflower.

The swollen edible roots, or tubers, are knobbly with either 'white' (buff-colored) or purple skins. The 'white' type is better flavored and far more widely available. The tubers are about the size of a small potato tuber, extremely irregular in shape but usually with a rounded base and tapering to a long thin end.

Jerusalem artichokes are underrated vegetables perhaps because, in their raw state, they are rather unattractive. But properly prepared they have a subtle flavor and can be used in an interesting variety of dishes, from soups to desserts.

Suitable site and soil

Although these plants will grow in almost any position in the garden and in almost any type of soil, a sunny site is preferable and fertile, well-drained soil is the ideal. The tubers can be planted in early spring for harvesting the following autumn and winter. In a rotation system, however, it may be a better use of space to plant them in late autumn in ground which has been used for summer crops of peas, beans, potatoes or cabbages.

Planting

The tubers themselves are planted because, like potatoes, they bear tiny buds which will sprout into new plants. You should be able to obtain tubers from seed suppliers or grocers.

Use a garden line to mark out straight rows spaced 1 m [3'] apart. A trowel or a dibber may be used to make planting holes 15 cm [6"] deep at 60 cm [2'] intervals. Plant the tubers, cover them and fill in the planting holes. The tubers should sprout in about 2-4 weeks.

Care and development

In temperate regions, Jerusalem artichokes usually require little watering because rainfall provides sufficient moisture, but gives plenty of water in dry areas.

Prevent weed growth either by hoeing the weed seedlings in spring or by applying a mulch of straw or lawn mowings around the plants in early summer.

In sheltered areas this vegetable may be grown as a windbreak or as a screen to hide an unsightly view from the garden. In windy areas, however, gales can damage the plants severely. To prevent such damage, pinch off the top of the plants when they reach a height of 1.5 m [5']. Hammer stakes into the ground at either end of each row with additional stakes at 1.5 m [5'] intervals in the rows. Link the stakes together with two or three strands of wire and tie the plants to the wires with a soft garden string.

Harvesting the crop

When the stems and foliage die and turn brown in autumn, the tubers are ready to use. Stored tubers have less flavor than freshly dug ones.

They can be lifted at any time from late autumn to late winter so long as soil can be dug. The tubers are not loose, but are found growing tightly packed together.

Storing the crop

Where winters are severe and the ground may freeze solid, remove the tubers from the roots, rub off any soil and store them in dry sand or peat in a cool place.

Be sure that all the tubers have been cleared from the site after harvesting. If you are not replanting immediately, keep enough large tubers in store to use for planting the next crop.

CHINESE ARTICHOKE

This is a rare vegetable, and tubers for planting are not easy to obtain. It was introduced from China less than 100 years ago and was first grown in Europe at Crôsnes in France – hence its alternative name, crôsnes. Like the Jerusalem artichoke, it is grown for the sake of its tubers, which are long and tapered, with billowing rings. They need to be thoroughly washed before use. It is a low, bushy, undistinguished plant.

Cultivation

This crop needs a rich but not heavy soil. If necessary, lighten a heavy soil by an application of peat. Dig in a generous quantity of garden compost or farmyard manure the autumn before planting.

Propagation is by means of tubers, like potatoes. Plant in early spring, about 10 cm [4"] deep, and 25 cm [10"] apart, in rows 45 cm [18"] apart. Protect against late frosts by covering with sacks, straw or other materials. There is no transplanting.

Water lavishly, particularly in dry weather. Feed plants frequently – every week or ten days – with liquid manure. Chinese artichoke tubers are quite small – much smaller than those of the Jerusalem artichoke – and need coaxing to grow to a worthwhile size. Hoe frequently between the plants. Slugs are the main pest.

Harvesting and storing

In autumn you can lift the tubers and either use them immediately, or store them in damp soil. Alternatively you can leave them in the ground until required, making sure that you provide protection against frost. However you store your tubers, remember to retain enough for next season's planting. Once the crop has become established, it is difficult to eradicate without very thorough digging.

After cropping, dead stalks and leaves go on the compost heap. You can grow Chinese artichokes for several years on the same plot without deterioration in quantity or quality.

Chinese artichoke
Stachys affinis (fam. *Labiatae*)
Perennial, but treated as an **annual.**
Size: to about 45 cm [18"] high and 50 cm [20"] wide.
Climate: temperate.
Sowing to harvesting time: about 8 months.
Yield: 11 or 12 plants per 3 m [10'] row.

Asparagus

**Freshly cut spears of asparagus have
such an outstanding flavor that
the effort involved in growing
this luxury vegetable is very worthwhile.**

One of the oldest of cultivated vegetables, asparagus was grown by the Romans as early as 200 BC. Asparagus is a superb delicacy but it is becoming increasingly expensive to buy as a vegetable in some areas, which makes it all the more worthwhile to grow.

At least 12 flourishing asparagus plants are needed to provide a weekly portion for a family of four during harvesting. Young asparagus shoots are cut in spring and early summer when 0.5-1.5 cm [¼-½"] in diameter and 7.5-10 cm [3-4"] high. Any shoots that are not harvested grow to bear elegant, fern-like foliage.

Provided instructions are followed with care, growing good crops of asparagus is a rewarding project which should not present great problems. The main deterrent is the three-year gap between sowing and your first harvest. However, that gap can be bridged by buying one- or two-year-old crowns from a nursery. In this way you can have an established bed in a comparatively short time.

The seed bed

Young plants are going to stay where the seed is sown for a full year before being transplanted, so take care to select a sunny, sheltered site where the plants can grow undisturbed, and prepare the bed well. Make sure it is completely free of weeds, particularly perennials. The soil should be rich, with a good humus content – preferably well-rotted

---

Asparagus
Asparagus officinalis (fam. *Liliaceae*)
Perennial with a useful life of at least 20 years.
Size: grows in bush form to a height of about 1.5 m [5'].
Climate: temperate to sub-tropical.
Planting to harvesting time: from seed 3 years; from transplant 2 years.
Yield per plant (once established) is about 25 spears per year.

---

garden compost or farmyard manure. Autumn is the best time for preparation: the manure can then be well buried and the bed left rough during the winter.

Sow the seed in mid-spring, thinly in rows about 2.5 cm [1"] deep, with 45 cm [1' 6"] between the rows. Tubs, boxes or flowerpots can also be used as seed beds in a small garden. The seed should germinate within 7-21 days.

Keep the bed well watered and free from weeds throughout the summer. When the seedlings are about 15 cm [6"] high, thin out to about 30 cm [1'] apart.

In autumn, when the feathery foliage begins to turn yellow, cut the plants down to almost ground level. Some of them will probably be bearing berries. These are the female plants, which are not such good croppers as the males. If enough male plants are available the females can be rooted out and destroyed. If you are in doubt, mark the females so that the males can be transplanted first in the following spring. Pick up all berries and either burn the berry-bearing foliage or bury it deep in the compost heap.

The main bed

Preparing the main bed is without doubt the most important factor in growing asparagus successfully. It takes time and trouble but is essential. Remember that once the bed is established it will continue producing an annual crop for at least 20 years; 50 years is not unknown.

The ideal soil is a sandy loam. If your soil is too light, dig in plenty of garden compost or manure. If too heavy, treat with coarse sand and an application of lime (or gypsum in limestone areas), to break up its close texture. If heavy and waterlogged, grow the asparagus in raised beds. Work on the soil should begin in autumn.

Traditionally asparagus beds are 1.2-1.8 m [4-6'] wide. A bed 1.2 m [4'] wide takes two parallel rows of plants; a bed 1.8 m [6'] wide takes three staggered rows. Alternatively, if it suits your layout better, you can grow the plants 30 cm [1'] apart, in rows 90 cm [3'] apart.

It is a good idea to run a path on either side of the bed so that cultivation and harvesting can be carried out without treading on the soil, and without damaging the plants. In autumn dig in garden compost or well-rotted manure, and remove all weeds, especially perennials, from the site.

If the soil is extremely stony, waterlogged or otherwise unsuitable, the bed should be raised completely above ground level. For this you will have to construct a retaining wall all around, about 60 cm [2'] high, built with brick, concrete, stone or suitable wooden blocks. Fill beds with soil to the top of the wall, dig in a layer of garden compost or well-rotted manure, then build a mound of soil on top about 30 cm [1'] high in the center.

Setting out the transplants

Transplanting is done in spring. If you have grown from seed, you should be transplanting the one-year-old plants. If you are buying plants from a nursery make sure they are one- or two-year-old plants: do not be tempted to buy three-year-old crowns because they are far too old to

Asparagus is a delicious vegetable delicacy, and the taste of spears fresh from the garden is unsurpassed.

1. Placing asparagus crowns in a trench. Spread the roots out well.

2. Cover the roots with fine soil and gradually cover the crowns.

3. Fill the trench gradually during the first year, as the plant grows.

4. Harvesting the shoots, using a sharp knife, cutting at an angle.

A traditional asparagus bed will probably look like this: it is usually 1.2-1.8 m [4-6'] wide.

5. In autumn, all foliage should be cut down, almost to ground level.

Asparagus can be grown in raised beds if soil is stony or waterlogged.

Weed-free asparagus in the seedling stage. The beds should always be kept well watered, particularly during hot, dry weather, and they should also be weeded regularly and carefully during the growing season.

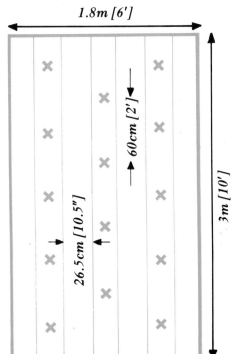

1.8m [6']

26.5cm [10.5"]

60cm [2']

3m [10']

survive the transplant shock and have little vigor.

In early spring dig trenches about 25 cm [10″] deep and wide, then put a little more garden compost or well-rotted manure and loamy soil along the bottom of the trench in the center to make a small ridge. If you have bought crowns – which should arrive from the nursery in mid-spring – get everything ready beforehand so that they can be planted immediately to avoid danger of drying out.

Allow 45-60 cm [1½-2′] between the plants in the rows. In fertile soils in warm climates allow 90 cm [3′] between plants. Asparagus roots are long and must be spread out well over the ridge. Cover the roots with fine soil, burying the crowns completely so that they are about 10 cm [4″] below the surface, and water well. Do not fill the trenches immediately; fill them gradually during the first year as the plant grows so that by the end of the year the land is flat, that is either level with the ground or the top of the curve of the raised bed. Build up the retaining walls if necessary.

Care and development

If one-year-old plants have been transplanted, a two-year waiting period now lies ahead. Even if two-year-old plants are used, they cannot be cropped in the first year and they will benefit in the long run from a two-year rest. But, meanwhile, there is useful work to be done on the asparagus bed.

The beds always need to be kept well-watered, particularly during hot, dry summers. Weeding must be carried out regularly throughout the growing season. With the advance of summer, any female plants retained will bear red berries. These berries should be removed – without damaging the foliage – as they only weaken the plants. In autumn, cut down all foliage almost to ground level and put it on the compost heap.

Harvesting the crop

The time invested in growing is repaid by the fact that only people who grow their own asparagus can ever hope to taste this delectable vegetable at its best. Ideally, asparagus should be cut only an hour before using. The succulent spring shoots are cut when they are 7.5-10 cm [3-4″] above the surface of the bed. Scrape the soil away and cut the shoot about 7.5-10 cm [3-4″] below the surface, taking great care not to damage adjacent shoots.

In the second year after transplanting, the first harvesting year, cut about three shoots only from each plant. These should be some of the earliest shoots; leave all the later ones, otherwise you will kill the plant.

In subsequent years, cut every shoot that appears for about two months but never after midsummer. Some of these shoots will be thin and straggly. They are good only for soup, but if allowed to grow they will use up resources that should go to the more vigorous shoots.

Care after harvesting

Stop cutting after about two months. After then, any shoots that appear should be allowed to grow to maturity so that the crowns are strengthened for the next year. The plants should be kept well watered, with occasional applications of liquid manure until winter. The foliage is cut back to within 2.5 cm [1″] of the ground in autumn (as in its first unproductive years), and a top-dressing of farmyard manure, garden compost or seaweed applied. This not only feeds the plants but also helps to protect them from any winter storms and severe frosts.

Before spreading the layer of manure, clear off any remaining weeds from the site and lightly fork over the surrounding soil.

Pests and diseases

Asparagus has one fairly common specific pest: the asparagus beetle (*Crioceris asparagi*). This beetle has reddish wing-cases bearing a double black cross. Its grubs are gray, with black heads and legs. Both beetles and grubs (of which there may be several generations in the course of a summer) feed on the shoots and foliage of the plants, and can seriously weaken them. Apply an insecticide, such as derris or pyrethrum or Sevin, preferably in powdered form wherever the insects are observed. Several applications may have to be made at intervals throughout the summer. In autumn the debris cleaned from the bed should be burned, as the pests can survive the winter in the dry hollow stems.

In autumn the debris cleaned from the bed should be burned, as the pests can survive the winter in the dry hollow stems.

Other pests which affect asparagus are slugs and snails and earwigs. For these scatter a snail and slug bait between the plants.

Asparagus Pea

The square-shaped pea pod is eaten whole and has a delicate flavor similar to that of asparagus.

This unusual vegetable is native to Sicily. Quite different in growth and appearance from the common garden pea, the asparagus pea makes a low, spreading plant which bears reddish-brown flowers. Asparagus peas are easy to grow, and are becoming very popular with gardeners who appreciate delicately flavored vegetables. The pods must be eaten while they are young and tender, otherwise they become very stringy.

Cultivation

Plant in an open site which receives plenty of sunshine, in light sandy soil. If possible, give the ground a dressing of rotted farmyard or stable manure or garden compost, which should be dug in during the winter months. If these are not available, rake into the surface a well balanced, complete fertilizer at the rate of 90 g per sq m [3 oz per sq yd] about ten days before sowing.

Make a V-shaped drill about 5 cm [2″] deep, space the seeds about 10 cm [4″] apart in the row, allowing 40 cm [15″] between rows. In warmer areas seed can be sown any time in mid-spring, whereas the early part of late spring is preferable in colder areas. To ensure a continuous supply of peas, make a second sowing about 3-4 weeks after the first one.

As soon as the young seedlings break the surface of the soil, hoe through the soil as close as possible to the plants to kill off any weed seedlings and to promote healthy growth of the plants. Repeat when necessary during the life of the plant. If the soil has been well prepared, no further feeding during growth should be necessary. Unlike the garden pea, this plant does not produce tendrils, and support is not required.

Harvesting the crop

Pods should be ready to pick about 12-13 weeks after sowing, in mid to late summer, according to climatic conditions prevailing during growth. It is essential to gather the pods when very young and tender, the ideal being about 2.5-3 cm [1-1¼″] long and certainly before the 'peas' in the pod have reached any size. After harvesting pull up plants and add to the compost heap.

Pests and diseases

None.

Asparagus pea
Lotus tetragonolobus, synonym *Tetragonolobus purpureus* (fam. *Leguminosae*), also known as winged pea or Goa bean.
Hardy annual.
Size: grows to about 30 cm [1′] high.
Climate: temperate; will not withstand extreme heat or frost.
Sowing to harvesting time: 12-13 weeks.
Yield: 14 kg [30 lb] on average per 3 m [10′] row.

Aubergine

See **EGGPLANT**

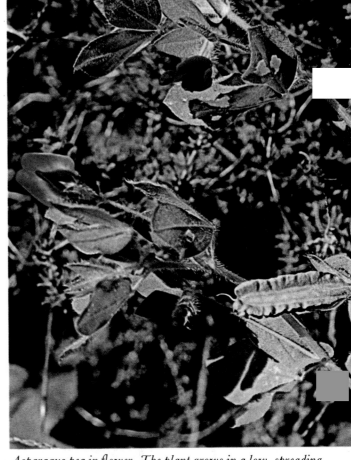

Asparagus pea in flower. The plant grows in a low, spreading formation. The young, tender pods are an unusual and delicately flowered vegetable.

Balm

Balm is very easy to grow and is one of the first herbs to appear in the spring. Its strong, fresh lemon scent attracts bees to the garden.

Balm (*Melissa officinalis* – which translated means 'bee plant') grows in clumps with erect branches, nettle-like leaves and small, tubular, white flowers. The green-leaved variety is used in cooking to give a sweet, lemon flavor and for making a refreshing tea.

Cultivation

Balm is native to the Mediterranean but will grow in almost any location, resisting both moderate frosts and high temperatures. It prefers fairly rich, moist soil and in dry, light soils benefits from a little shade. In cities, balm can be grown in pots, tubs or window boxes, but must be kept well-watered. A pot of balm will also grow well indoors on a sunny windowsill and is a useful fresh herb for flavoring food in winter.

It is best to start balm from a young nursery plant in mid-spring or mid-autumn. Balm has invasive roots that may need restraining in a herb garden. A common and reliable method is to plant the herb in a bottomless container, such as a bucket without a bottom or part of a drainpipe, which has been sunk into the ground and filled with good soil. This will prevent the roots spreading into neighboring plants.

If you cannot get young plants, sow the seed in a shallow drill about 1.5 cm [$\frac{1}{2}''$] deep and thin the seedlings, which appear after three to four weeks, to 30 cm [1'] apart.

An established balm plant will set a lot of seed and this can be a nuisance in a herb garden. Keep a watch for unwanted seedlings and weed them out as they appear.

Harvesting and after-care

Pick leaves for immediate use as required throughout the spring, when they are most tender. After the plant flowers

An attractive bush of lemon-scented balm. This easily grown herb can also be raised in pots.

in early summer the leaves begin to grow tough. Mid- to late summer is the best time for harvesting the leaves for drying. Dried balm should be kept in a dark screw-cap jar and stored in a dry, dark place.

Cut the stems down to the ground in autumn, and in exceptionally frosty areas protect the balm plants with straw. To propagate new plants, you can divide and replant the roots in autumn or spring. Space the root sections 30 cm [1'] apart in soil that has been dug over and treated with compost.

Basil

Basil originated in tropical India and is still regarded by Hindus as a herb sacred to the gods Vishnu and Krishna. Excellent in cooking, basil's spicy-flavored leaves can be used fresh or dried.

Although basil (*Ocimum basilicum*) comes from tropical Asia, it will grow outdoors in temperate climates. Bush basil (*Ocimum minimum*) is a smaller, more compact, slightly hardier type which is more suitable for cool climates.

Cultivation

Ideally, basil should be grown in a warm, sheltered position facing the midday sun. In very warm climates it benefits from semi-shady positions. Basil prefers light, rich, well-drained soil. Before sowing dig the soil and add some well-rotted garden compost, peat or leaf mold.

Sow the seed 20 cm [8"] apart in mid-spring. In a cool region you may wish to start the seed under glass. Sow two or three seeds spaced apart in a 5 cm [2"] pot filled with good potting mixture. Maintain a fairly constant 15°C [60°F], when germination should take about 14 days, then gradually get the seedlings used to cooler temperatures until they are planted outside in late spring. Plant the whole root ball of the seedling without breaking it up.

In late summer pinch off the flowers and stem tips to

33

encourage a leafier plant, water in dry weather and hoe lightly to deter weeds.

Harvesting and after-care

Cut the leaves freshly as needed throughout summer. Take leaves for drying, just before the plant flowers in late summer. Hang them upside down in a dark, warm place and when they are dry crumble the leaves and store in a tightly-sealed jar for use through the winter.

After harvesting, pull up the plant and add it to the compost heap. Before doing so you may take cuttings to propagate a supply of new plants. These should be potted and usually produce roots after a few days. Bush basil grows very well in pots and is a useful winter herb. Dig up the selected plants in late summer and pot them up individually using 10 cm [4″] containers.

Using basil

Basil is considered invaluable among herbs in Italy, where it is used extravagantly, and in India, where it is a common ingredient in curry dishes, but it is less familiar elsewhere. It is especially suited to any tomato dish, but also gives a special flavor to cheese, egg and fish dishes. Unlike most herbs basil actually becomes stronger in flavor in cooking, so it should be used more carefully in cooked dishes than in salads and sandwiches.

Bay

Bay is the only tree whose leaves are used as a culinary herb. The ancient Greeks knew it as laurel, a symbol of glory and honor for poets and heroes.

Bay (*Laurus nobilis*) is a handsome, dense evergreen tree with smooth, pungent, dark green leaves and in late spring it produces small yellow flowers, followed by glossy black berries. The leaves may be used in cooking either fresh or dried and are one of the ingredients in the classic French *bouquet garni*.

Cultivation

Choose a sunny, sheltered site, allowing about 1.8 m [6′] clearance all around. A few weeks before planting in mid-spring, dig some well-rotted garden compost or manure into the soil.

When ordering your bay, try to obtain a three-year-old, well-rooted tree with healthy, dark, shiny foliage and about 1 m [3′] high. Water the plant in its container before planting.

Dig the planting hole deep enough to cover the roots to the original soil line on the stem, and wide enough for the roots to spread out well. Return a little soil to the hole, carefully remove the tree from its pot and place it in the hole. Fill in with soil, shaking the plant gently so that the soil can settle naturally between the roots and continue to fill the hole gradually. Firm the soil all the way around at intervals until the hole is full, then tread it in firmly, fill in again if necessary and rake the surface lightly.

Water occasionally during the first few years, especially in hot weather, and during dry spells spray the leaves with water in the cool of the day. Protect from frost in the first few years by surrounding with plastic bags or burlap where winters are mild. In colder areas grow in a tub and store in a cool place indoors in winter. Weed by hand to avoid damaging surface roots. If pruning, cut outer shoots in mid-spring.

Take off the leaves sparingly during the first few years so that the new growth is not weakened. Thereafter, pick the leaves as required. Always leave the young foliage. Where collecting for drying, clip the leaves singly.

Propagating

Bay cuttings can be taken in late autumn. Choose firm sideshoots 7.5-15 cm [3-6″] long and pull them off gently with a strip of the main shoot. Trim this heel neatly and place the cutting in damp, sandy compost under glass in a shady position. When it has rooted, after about 12 to 18 months, pot it in a 7.5 cm [3½″] pot and return to frame or greenhouse. Keep moist and shaded and plant the following spring.

Growing in containers

Bay is a good choice for container growing. The restricted root area of the container limits the size of the tree and makes it a decorative plant for doorsteps and patios. There are three traditional shapes for container-grown bay – pyramid, 'mop-head' and bush – the first two of which are pruned to shape by the nursery. The trees are frequently sold when they are about 1.5 m [5′] high and in 25-30 cm [10-12″] containers.

Bay flourishes in pots and will grow in its original container for about six years after its purchase. After that time, or when the roots show through the drainage holes, get a container about 5 cm [2″] larger than the original.

Bay makes a most attractive and useful pot plant.

Before repotting, water the plant well. Fill the base of the new container with pieces of broken clay pots for drainage and repot the plant in a good standard potting compost. Firm the soil down very thoroughly to retain moisture. Water and take extra care to make sure the compost does not dry out at all during the next few weeks.

Bay grows best outdoors, but can be grown in a conservatory or cool greenhouse. Water the plant well and often in dry weather, but never during light frosts. A well-established tree can be left outside during a mild winter, but take it indoors to an unheated place or cover with protective sheeting during frosty weather.

In late spring or early summer, prune the tree lightly to shape by clipping individual shoots. Feed in summer with liquid fertilizer and replace the top layer of potting soil to a level of about 2.5 cm [1″] each year, in early spring.

Pests and diseases

Watch for scale insects that look like little brown blobs and live on the underside of leaves and on the stem and trunk. These commonly infest bay trees grown in containers and those taken into a greenhouse for the winter. Cover the surface of the soil with sheeting or newspaper and scrape the insects off very gently with the blunt edge of a knife onto the covering. Then spray the whole tree thoroughly with an insecticide and repeat 10 to 14 days later.

BEANS

Beans grown for human consumption fall into three main categories, snap or green beans, which includes yellow or wax beans, dry beans and shell beans. There are many regional and national variations in the names given to the different types.

Snap beans are picked when green and the pods are cooked whole with the beans inside. French beans, also known as string beans and kidney beans, belong to this category and are all bush beans. Closely allied are climbing or pole (or runner) beans, which are also picked while still immature and cooked whole and differ from snap beans only in growth habit. Shell beans are those which are allowed to ripen on the plant and are then harvested, dried and processed. They are matured beans without pods and are usually stored for winter cooking and baking. These include such kinds as the red-streaked Dwarf, French Horticultural or Haricot beans (occasionally used as green shell beans or in their pods like snap beans while still young), red kidney beans and White Marrowfats.

Lima beans are picked when green and the beans are taken from the pods to be cooked. Also known as butter beans, limas grow as both climbers and bush plants.

For cultivation *see* BROAD BEAN, LIMA BEAN, FRENCH BEAN, RUNNER BEAN and SOY BEAN.

Bean Sprouts

Ready to eat in as little as six days, the new sprouts of these beans require little effort to grow and are an extremely nutritious vegetable.

Bean sprouts and seed sprouts are exceptional vegetables, with a number of unique features. The seeds can be planted or sown at any time of the year; they can be ready to eat in three to six days from the sowing date; they will grow in any climate, needing neither soil nor sun, and you do not even need a garden. They are highly nutritious, being particularly rich in vitamin C.

Because they are so quick and easy to grow, bean sprouts and seed sprouts are an inexpensive source of fresh vegetables all year round. Excellent in salads or as a substitute for lettuce during winter, bean sprouts and seed sprouts are much used in Chinese cooking. They make an attractive and tasty base for many cooked dishes, especially rice dishes like curry and risotto, and can be used in breads or cooked with other vegetables. Cook quickly to prevent loss of their valuable nutrients.

Types of bean sprouts

The most popular types are mung beans and adzuki beans. Mung beans, or Chinese bean sprouts, are the best known and are a familiar ingredient in many popular Chinese dishes. Mid-green in color with white sprouts, mung beans may be used raw or cooked when they are 5 cm [2″] high. Adzuki beans are also from the Far East. They have

---

Bean sprouts
Phaseolus aureus, mung bean, also known as Chinese bean sprout, green or golden gram; *Phaseolus angularis*, adzuki bean; both fam. *Leguminosae*.
Size: mung sprout, about 5 cm [2″] long; adzuki sprout, about 2.5 cm [1″] long.
Climate: grow indoors anywhere.
Sowing to harvesting time: 3-6 days.
Yield: mung sprouts, about 225-275 g per 25 g [8-10 oz per 1 oz] of seed; adzuki beans, about 125-175 g per 25 g [4-6 oz per 1 oz] of seed.

1. The easiest way to wash the seeds is in their growing container. Pour about 5 ml [2 teaspoons] of seeds into the jam jar.

2. Pour cold or tepid water into the jar to cover the seeds.

3. Place your hand over the top of the jar and shake vigorously.

As the seeds sprout, their goodness grows. Mung beans will be ready to eat after three to five days or when they are 5 cm [2"]; they deteriorate if left longer.

4. Secure muslin lid over neck of the jar with an elastic band

5. Drain off the water and then repeat the process 2 or 3 times.

6. The jar can be placed anywhere out of direct light. The seeds germinate to give sprouts at a temperature of 13° to 18°C [55° to 65°F].

been grown for centuries for their crunchy texture, nutty flavor and their filling bulk. They have an attractive, rich mahogany-red color with white sprouts, and are also suitable for use raw or cooked. They are eaten when 2.5 cm [1″] high. Other types are triticale, alfalfa and fenugreek, each with its own distinctive flavor.

Jam jar growing

The simplest, cheapest and most effective method of growing bean sprouts is the glass jar method. All that is needed is a jam jar or a similar glass container, a rubber band and a piece of muslin. The muslin should be large enough to fit comfortably over the jam jar opening and be secured with the band.

Take about 5 ml [2 teaspoons] of the seed and rinse it thoroughly. This is most easily done by placing it in the container, filling the container with cold or tepid water and shaking vigorously. Drain, then repeat the rinsing and draining several times. This initial saturation aids germination.

Do not exceed the suggested amount of seed when you first start to grow bean sprouts. By the time they are ready to eat they will have increased their volume as much as tenfold. Too many will fill up the jar and push out the top. Secure the muslin lid and leave the container on its side to allow the remaining water to drain off.

Repeat the rinsing and draining process twice a day, in the morning and evening. The beans need to be kept constantly moist, but not really wet otherwise they may go moldy. Place the jar anywhere out of direct light – in a corner, on a shelf or in a cupboard. They need a temperature of between 13° to 18°C [55° to 65°F].

As the seed sprouts, the fats and starches in it are changed into vitamins, sugar (which provides quick energy) and proteins, which make the sprout more digestible, less fattening and even more nutritious than it was as a seed.

Less than a week to harvest

Mung beans will be ready to eat within three to five days, or whenever they have reached about 5 cm [2″] in height. By then they will have increased eight or ten times over their weight as a seed, and many times over in volume. If they are left in the jar any longer they will continue to grow, lose their crispness and begin to discolor.

Adzuki beans are ready within four to six days, or when they have reached about 2.5 cm [1″] in length, when they will have increased their weight by four to six times as much as the bean.

Continuous cropping

Bean sprouts are filling; the crop from one jar gives four serving portions if the bean sprouts are prepared as a separate vegetable, and many more if they are served as part of a dish.

If you do not eat the shoots all at once they will keep a few days in the vegetable compartment of a refrigerator. But fresh foods always lose some of their vitamin content the longer they are kept. It makes sense to grow only what you can eat immediately and keep a fresh supply of beans growing, rather than storing them.

Beetroot

As well as the well-known red beet, there are also varieties with yellow and white roots. Beets are either eaten cold in salads or can be served as a hot vegetable.

The most common type of beet is round (also called globe or ball) and deep carmine-red. There are two other shapes – oval (known as intermediate or tankard) and long, and two other colors. Long beets are rarely grown today and then only as a stored crop for winter eating. They are the least sweet and succulent varieties.

The advantages of the yellow and white types, which are round in form, is that they do not 'bleed' in salads. The green foliage of both types can be cooked as spinach.

Suitable site and soil

Beet is part of the root-crop in a rotational system, and should be grown on land in the vegetable plot which was well fed with compost the previous season. It needs plenty of light and a well-drained soil.

Dig heavy soil in late autumn and leave rough. Dig light soil in spring. Remove all weeds and their roots. If you plan to make successional sowings later, dig the soil to a depth of about 17.5 cm [7″]. Before sowing, rake the soil level and remove any large stones or debris. A very light soil should then be firmed slightly and raked again.

Sowing

Sow in mid to late spring when the soil is warming up.

Beet
Beta vulgaris (fam. *Chenopodiaceae*), also known as beet.
Half-hardy biennial, grown as an **annual.**
Size: plants about 30 cm [1′] tall, swollen roots between 2.5 cm [1″] and 9 cm [3½″] in diameter, according to form and variety and picking time.
Climate: cool to warm temperate.
Sowing to harvesting time: round and intermediate types 8-10 weeks; long types about 19 weeks.
Yield: round and oval types, about 40 roots per 3 m [10′] row; long beets about 20 roots per 3 m [10′] row.

There are several types of beet; most common is the round (globe or ball type. Another is oval (intermediate or tankard). Long beet, with a tapering end, is seldom grown now. The other two round types, distinguished by their colors, yellow and white, are ideal for use in salads as they do not bleed into the other ingredients.

Plant seeds 2.5 cm [1"] apart in rows 30 cm [1'] apart. Germination takes place within 1-2 weeks.

Thin out round and intermediate seedlings when 2-7 cm [1-3"] tall with spacing of 10cm [4"].

Thin out long beet seedlings when 15 cm [6"] tall with a spacing of 15 cm [6"]. Protect from birds.

Water plants regularly, especially during dry weather, and hoe between plants, removing weed seedlings by hand.

Seeds are usually sold as clusters, each containing four or five seeds (a few exceptions come as one single seed). Plant each cluster about 2.5 cm [1"] apart, in rows 30 cm [1'] apart. The seeds should germinate within 1-2 weeks of sowing. Thin out the seedlings when they are between 2-7 cm [1-3"] tall for round and intermediate varieties, and 15 cm [6"] for long beet, giving a spacing of 10 cm [4"] and 15 cm [6"] respectively. Protect from birds.

Care and development

Keep the plants supplied with adequate water at the roots, especially during periods of drought, to maintain steady growth, and prevent cracking and toughness.

Start hoeing between the rows as soon as the seedlings show. Remove weed seedlings growing close to the beet plants by hand since the hoe may damage the roots.

Harvesting and storing the crop

Round and intermediate beets are ready to start pulling up when they are 2.5 cm [1"] in diameter. Pull them here and there in the rows to leave space for the rest to grow larger. Continue pulling more beets as and when needed. Dig up long beets in mid-autumn and store.

All beets may be stored; choose a dry day to harvest for storing. Shake each root to remove adhering soil. Twist off the foliage at about 5 cm [2"] from the crown, i.e. the top of the beet. Sandwich the beet in single layers between 2.5 cm [1"] layers of peat or sand in boxes. Store the boxes in a cool place such as a garden or toolshed, garage or cellar. If kept at a temperature of about 10°C [50°F] the beet should remain in good condition for six months.

Container-growing

Choose round varieties for container-growing. Large tubs are most suitable but if using pots the smallest useful size is 30 cm [1']. Sprinkle seeds thinly over a standard seed starting mixture and cover with 2.5 cm [1"] of the mixture. Water well, using a fine rose on the watering can. Thin the seedlings to allow each plant enough room to develop, leaving only eight plants in a 30 cm [1'] pot. Water frequently in warm weather.

Growing under a cover or frame

Choose round varieties of beets for growing under covers or in frames. Tunnel-like arrangements are suitable for one single row; wider ones may take two or three rows spaced about 17.5 cm [7"] apart. Sow thinly in early spring in seed drills 2.5 cm [1"] deep, about 17.5 cm [7"] apart. Thin the seedlings to 5 cm [2"] apart. Ensure that they are never short of water.

After germination, provided that the days are not excessively cold, open the frames or protectors slightly to admit air. Close when night temperatures fall below about 10°C [50°F]. Remove the glass panels or covers entirely on days when temperatures average about 16°C [60°F], but replace in the evening if frost threatens. Remove the covers when the weather is warmer (usually 4-6 weeks after sowing). Once established beets are relatively cold-hardy.

When ready to harvest twist foliage off 5 cm [2"] from crown.

Round varieties of beet are the best sort for container growing. Water well and thin seedlings to allow plants room for development.

Pests and diseases

The deficiency disease known as speckled yellow may occur if the soil lacks manganese, causing the leaves to go yellowish between the veins at first and then brown. This can be controlled by watering with a solution of manganese sulphate at 30 g per 12 L [1 oz per 2½ gal]. Some aphids, particularly blackfly and greenfly, may also infest the plants. This is not frequent and a routine pyrethrum spray will take care of them.

Blackberry

This fruit is composed of numerous drupelets, each containing a seed. They are suitable for cooking or for eating raw. They grow on canes, which may be smooth or thorny.

Wild blackberries, also known as brambles, are found in hedges and copses throughout Western Europe and North America. Varieties which are cultivated in the Northern Hemisphere are often a pest in the Southern. Because blackberries come true to seed (as well as reproducing by rooting canes) scores of species are known.

Blackberry
Species of *Rubus* (fam. *Rosaceae*), in Europe derived from *R. fruticosus*, which has itself been subdivided into many species, in America for crosses of *R. alleghaniensis*, *R. argutus* and *R. frondosus*.
Hardy perennial cane usually prickly, with a cropping life of about 15 years.
Size: 1.8 m [6′] in height and up to 4.5 m [15′] wide when trained.
Climate: cool to warm temperate.
Planting to harvesting time: two years.
Yield: about 2.25-4.5 kg [5-10 lb].

The dewberry, with black fruit similar in appearance but composed of fewer and larger drupelets, and ripening earlier than the blackberry, is closely related. In Europe the name is given to *R. caesius*, in America to trailing native species, chief among them *R. canadensis*. Some varieties are cultivated.

Because *Rubus* berries interbreed so easily, crosses between the different sorts of blackberries and with raspberries have been separated, and the cultivation of these hybrid and/or sport berries is covered under LOGANBERRY.

Although wild blackberries are delicious, they tend to be small and hard to pick because the brambles have sharp thorns and quickly form impenetrable bushes. In the garden therefore, the improved blackberries are trained to make picking easier. Some modern varieties are thornless, which are easier to handle but less vigorous.

Garden varieties produce larger fruit and more abundant crops than wild ones, and the fruiting period is longer. The berries are borne on canes of the previous year's growth, in dark purple or black clusters.

The pinky white flowers are self-fertile and are produced in succession. This means that blackberries will fruit in cold regions where other earlier-flowering fruit fails to set (form fruit from the flowers).

Suitable site and soil

Blackberries will crop adequately without much care. They are often the solution for the problem corners because they will crop in shade or facing north, or in frost pockets. Flowers continue to appear for an extended period and these will set, even if earlier ones are killed. A bigger, more regular crop will be obtained in a sunny site sheltered from wind and frost.

Canes may be trained against a wall or shed, or on wires supported by posts. A row on a slope should run up and down, not across, or it may trap cold air.

Well-drained medium loams are ideal; light soils need additional organic matter. A limestone soil is least suitable. Acid soil should be treated with lime. On poor soil choose a more vigorous variety.

Eradicate all perennial weeds before planting, because blackberries have a 15-year life. Dig in organic matter to about 45 cm [1½′], adding roughly 2.5-6.5 kg per sq ml [5-15 lb per sq yd].

Training wires and fences

If wire fences are to be erected to save space and make picking easier, do this before planting. Use metal or treated wooden posts 2.3 m [7′ 6″] tall, with 1.8 m [6′] above ground, carrying four 25 mm [⅛″] plastic coated wires 30 cm [1′] apart, starting 90 cm [3′] above the ground. Length will depend on the number of canes. The wires will bear the full weight on the canes, so the post should be propped with a strut; or run a guy-rope from the top of the post outward to a well-secured peg.

On a wall, fence or shed the same intervals should be used and the wires well secured.

Planting

The best time to plant is late autumn. Very vigorous varie-

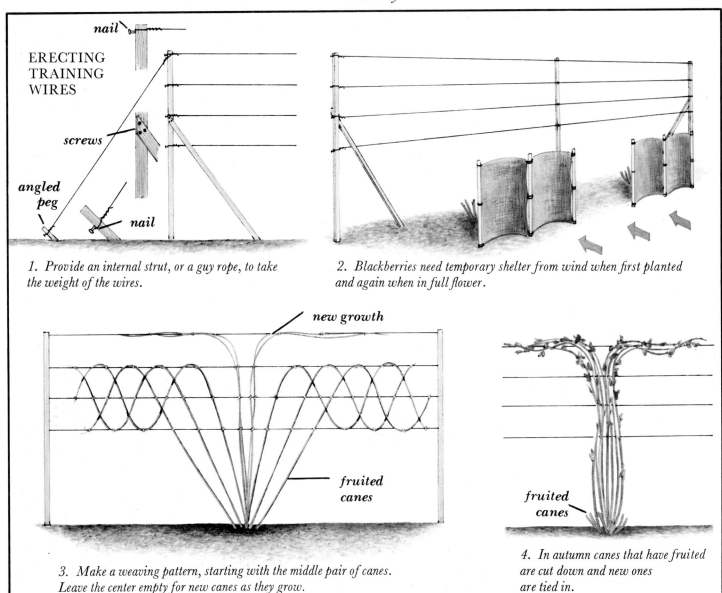

ERECTING
TRAINING
WIRES

nail

screws

*angled
peg*

nail

*1. Provide an internal strut, or a guy rope, to take
the weight of the wires.*

*2. Blackberries need temporary shelter from wind when first planted
and again when in full flower.*

new growth

*fruited
canes*

*3. Make a weaving pattern, starting with the middle pair of canes.
Leave the center empty for new canes as they grow.*

*fruited
canes*

*4. In autumn canes that have fruited
are cut down and new ones
are tied in.*

ties may be planted up to 3.5-4.5 m [12-15'] apart between rows and up to 4 feet apart in the rows, the weaker and thornless varieties closer.

Dig the planting hole 10-12.5 cm [4-5"] deep. Cut off broken roots and set the plant in with the roots spread out naturally to their full length. The crown should be level with the soil surface. Crumble the soil over the roots, firming it gently and fill the hole. After planting, cut down the canes to 23 cm [9"].

Providing shelter

Provide temporary protection from strong winds until plants are established, and again when in full flower. Sacking, plastic sheets or snow fencing may be erected on poles in front of the plants.

Training

Blackberries do not need much attention during the growing season. The first summer only a few canes will grow, and these will not fruit. Wearing stout gloves against prickles, gradually tie them in. The fruiting canes are woven between the bottom and the third wire (*see diagram*), leaving the center empty for the new canes.

Choose the two canes nearest to the center. Take them up to the next-to-top wire and attach them one on either side, leaving the center empty with a 75 cm [2' 6"] space between them. Now weave them down to the bottom wire and up again, working outward from the middle, tying the cane along its length, and taking care that all the curves are gentle. Now take the second pair of canes up to the next-to-top wire, about 23 cm [9"] outside the first pair, then repeat, and so on, until all the canes are tied in.

Sometimes the main canes and sideshoots outgrow their space. If so cut them back in late winter, the main canes by about 60-90 cm [2-3'], the sideshoots to within a hand-span of the main stem.

In the second summer, when these canes are fruiting, new canes will be produced. Tie these vertically up the middle and, when they reach the top wire, spread them out on either side and tie them along the top wire to control any movement. These canes will bear next year's crop.

Watering

The best method is a perforated hose laid along each side of the row in turn. In a normal year, watering increases yield; during a drought it is vital to ensure that canes pro-

CANE LAYERING

shallow indentation with soil above

bent wire peg

To layer, peg down a new season's shoot in early summer, letting the tip emerge. It will quickly root and can be cut off.

Blackberries are suitable for shady corners, and can be trained for easy picking on walls, fences and garden sheds.

duce both fruit and new growth. Without adequate moisture, fruit will mature at the expense of new shoots and hence next year's crop.

Feeding
Topdress in early summer every year with garden compost 2.5 cm [1″] thick. If this is not available use a complete fertilizer and mulch with straw, lawn clippings, etc.

Harvesting the crop
Fruit is produced on the previous year's wood, so there is no crop the first year. Picking starts in late summer with early varieties, when the berries are fully black. Pluck off berries with the plug, the white center of the fruit. Pick every few days to encourage more fruit to ripen.

Pruning and after-care
After cropping has finished, cut out the canes which produced fruit, either completely or to the strongest new sideshoot low on a cane.
Wearing heavy gloves untie the new canes, and disentangle them if need be. Lay them out singly on the ground and sort them into two groups. It is usual to retain only 8-10

Dewberries (top) are sweet and black. They are similar to blackberries but their canes have a trailing habit. Blackberries (above) grow best in rich loam but once planted they need little attention. Thornless varieties have been developed to make picking and handling easier. Pick every few days in order to encourage more fruit to ripen. Continuous picking encourages continuous growth.

canes on each plant. These are then tied in the pattern previously described. Any winter die-back can be removed in early spring by cutting the dead tip back to a bud or sideshoot. Destroy all prunings.

Propagation
Blackberries are easily increased by cane layering, which simply means pegging down a new-season shoot near the tip in early or midsummer until it makes independent roots. Make a hole a hand-span deep and lay the end of the cane in so the tip shows but the stem just behind it is buried. Peg the stem down with a piece of bent wire. The new plants should be well-rooted by the late autumn, when they can be cut off and planted in their permanent positions. Cut back the parent canes to ground level.

Pests and diseases

Blackberry dwarf disease is spread by aphids. Instead of producing a few strong canes, infected plants grow a lot of very short new shoots which never grow. Diseased plants must be destroyed. If crown or other gulls or borers appear merely cut off the affected portions several inches below the injury and burn.

Blackcurrant

**These delicious dark-juiced berries
are the richest in vitamin C of
all the garden fruit.
The flavor is sharp and the fruit
is cooked before being eaten. The
leaves are also useful for flavoring.**

Blackcurrants are an easy soft fruit to cultivate and require a moist climate. Wild species of blackcurrant occur all across the temperature zone and temperate north almost to the Arctic circle. *Ribes americanum* is closely related to the cultivated species. Though the plant itself will withstand frost, the blossom is borne in early spring and prone to frost damage. Unfortunately their culture is forbidden in white pine areas because of the white pine blister rust, and they are little cultivated in the U.S.

Unlike other soft fruit bushes which are grown on a single stem like a miniature tree, blackcurrants are encouraged to be shrubby, with several main shoots rising from below

---

Blackcurrant
Ribes nigrum (fam. Saxifragaceae)
Hardy deciduous shrub, with a useful life of 15 years.
Size: about 1.5 m [5'] high and across.
Climate: cold to warm temperate.
Planting to harvesting time: two years.
Yield: 4.5 kg [10 lb].

---

soil level. It is the tallest of the soft fruit bushes. Both leaves and stem have a strong smell when crushed. The fruit begins to ripen after midsummer and cropping from different varieties continues for about two months.

Suitable site and soil

Choose the warmest, most sheltered spot available because the flowers are prone to frost damage. A place in full sun is best, though they will tolerate partial shade. Shelter from wind is vital to allow insects to pollinate the flowers (*see* the diagram in BLACKBERRY).

Blackcurrants are more tolerant to indifferent drainage than most other fruits, but the very best results will be obtained in a deep, loamy well-drained soil.

A slightly acid soil is best, and a soil test should give a pH value of between 6 and 7. If it is less than 5.5, scatter garden lime at the rate of 180 g per sq m [6 oz per sq yd].

Dig the ground over a couple of months before planting – preferably in late autumn. Pay special attention to weed eradication, as perennial weeds can be a great nuisance later on. If possible, dig in manure or compost at this time. If neither is available, add leaf mold or peat at the rate of a wheelbarrow-load per 1.5 sq m [2 sq yd]. Blackcurrants like plenty of nitrogenous fertilizer. Extra plant food will be provided by forking into the surface a dressing of general garden fertilizer at 122 g per sq m [4 oz per sq yd].

Planting

Most families will probably find that about four bushes are sufficient. A range of varieties, although not necessary for cross-pollination, will spread the picking season and provide some insurance against a single frost causing crop failure.

Planting can be done anytime during early spring when the soil is not frost bound or wet. Buy two-year-old plants and, if possible, make sure they are from certified healthy stock. Plant the bushes 1.8 m [6'] apart. Dig a planting hole large enough for you to spread out all the roots fully in their natural direction. An established blackcurrant has a number of main stems. To encourage this growth habit, the bush should be planted between 2.5-5 cm [1-2"] deeper than it was in the nursery. Firm the soil back around the roots.

Immediately after planting, cut down every shoot to within 2.5 cm [1"] of the ground, to just above the first or second visible growth bud. Though this means you will get no fruit the first year, it will ensure that the bush develops a good root system. It also encourages the bushes to form a good crown below ground.

Watering

Start early in the growing season if the weather is at all dry. Watering is essential, as blackcurrants need more moisture than comparable fruit. Mulching with manure in early spring will help reduce water loss through evaporation.

Feeding

Blackcurrants thrive on heavy manuring. First, in early spring every year, scatter and rake in 30 g per sq m [1 oz per sq yd] of sulphate of ammonia and 15 g per sq m [½ oz per sq yd] of sulphate of potash over the bed. Where the

PLANTING AND PRUNING

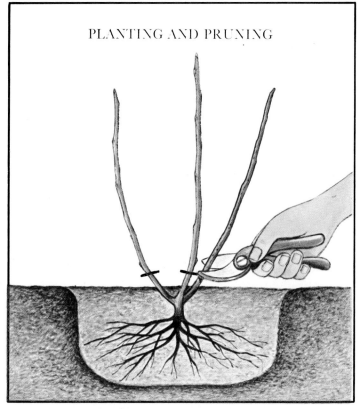

Blackcurrants are planted lower in the ground than the original soil mark. This, and pruning after planting, encourages new shoots from below soil level.

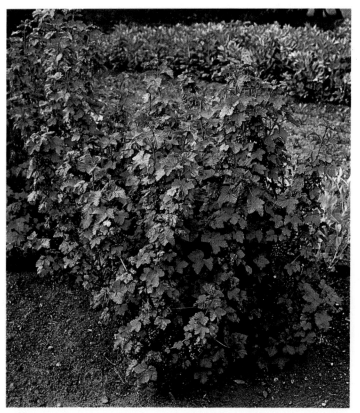

Blackcurrants grow taller than all the other soft fruit bushes. They need heavy quantities of both nitrogenous feed, water and moisture-retaining soil, to do well.

pruning points

Pruning from the second year is to encourage new wood, as this bears the most fruit the following year, and to build up a good bush shape. Prune to the ground, or to a low-growing shoot, and ignore new growth at the tip of old wood.

PRUNING FROM THE SECOND YEAR

new shoots

old shoot

Low-growing branches, crossing branches and those which are diseased are cut out first, followed by branches in the center of the bush, to let in light and air. Finally a proportion of old wood is cut to a low shoot, or removed entirely.

soil is acid, use nitrate of soda instead of sulphate of ammonia. Then mulch the bed with manure or compost at the rate of a wheelbarrow-load to every 2.5 sq m [3 sq yd]. If no manure is available, double the quantities of fertilizers and mulch with moist peat.

Frost protection

The greenish-white flowers are borne in drooping bunches like grapes, and appear in early and mid-spring. Cover the bushes at night with burlap or any sort of cloth if frost is expected.

Pruning

Little pruning will be necessary in the winter after planting, though you can cut any weak growths back to the first bud above ground level.

In the second season you should prune immediately after your first harvest. Blackcurrants bear most of their fruit on the new shoots produced the previous summer, so the aim in pruning is to encourage the growth of strong new wood from the base of the plant. Most of the new shoots will be retained, as well as a proportion of the older wood which also bears a quota of fruit and produces more young wood. First, cut away low-growing shoots which hang down to the ground, any which are dead or obviously diseased, and any which are crossing or awkwardly placed. If the center of the bush is crowded, next remove some of the shoots there to let in light and air.

Finally, remove about a fifth of the older wood that remains. Make your cuts above a good new low-growing shoot or close to the ground to encourage new growth lower down and ignore promising growth at the tips of these shoots.

In subsequent years old wood with sideshoots on it will be cut right to the ground.

When the bushes are well established, after about four seasons, you should remove about a third of a bush each winter, following these rules. If growth is very vigorous remove less; and if it is weak and needs stimulating remove more.

Harvesting and storing the crop

Blackcurrants reach maximum cropping capacity after four or five years. They are ready to eat when deep black. For speed strip them straight off their stalks using a kitchen fork, but berries plucked in a bunch are less likely to get moldy and will keep five days.

Propagation

Blackcurrants are easily increased by hardwood cuttings taken in mid-autumn from healthy bushes. Never take cuttings from diseased bushes to replace those about to be destroyed.

Cut off shoots of ripening wood about 20-25 cm [8-10"] long just below a bud. Put them about 15 cm [6"] deep in the ground with two buds or so showing and, unlike red currants and gooseberries, retain the buds under the soil. Space them about 20 cm [8"] apart. The following autumn you may take and transplant the cuttings to their permanent positions.

Pests and diseases

Reversion is a serious disease, so-called because bushes revert within about three years to the form of the wild species. Fruit-bearing deteriorates and eventually ceases. There is no cure, although you can help guard against it by buying disease-free stock. As soon as you have identified reversion, burn affected bushes, roots and all, and plant new healthy stock in a different site.

The virus is carried by a gall mite. Thousands of mites grow within a single bud which swells up prematurely to an abnormal size. In spring the buds open and the mites migrate to the developing shoots. Pick off and burn swollen buds as soon as you see them. Some varieties are more susceptible than others to attack. As soon as you see big buds suspect an attack of reversion.

Unfortunately, there is no way of destroying the pests inside the buds. Spray with a 3% solution of lime-sulphur just before the flowers open and repeat after three weeks. A strong lime-sulphur spray causes leaf scorching and reduction of crops in some varieties. This spray will also protect against American gooseberry mildew.

First check for signs of disease just before the blossoms open, when the buds are like little bunches of grapes. Healthy flowers are covered with tiny downy gray hairs. Infected buds have fewer hairs, so that they appear a much brighter pink. Some varieties, however, are more hairy than others. In midsummer look for signs of leaf reversion. In a healthy blackcurrant leaf there is a definite cleft between the bottom edge of the leaf's basal lobe and the stem of the leaf. In an infected leaf this angle becomes much less pronounced and the leaf is flattened straight across. Also, in a healthy leaf you will find that the top lobe in the center of the leaf has five or more main veins on either side of the central rib and at least 14 serrations along each edge. A reverted leaf will have fewer than five main veins and less than 12 serrations. Compare leaves of the same varieties if you can. The brown spotting blackcurrant leaf spot, a fungus disease, can severely weaken growth. Spray with zineb or thiram immediately after flowering and three more times at four-weekly intervals.

Birds will eat your ripening fruit if you don't prevent them. If you cannot grow it in a fruit cage, cover the bushes with netting or rayon web while the fruit is ripening, and in some areas you will need to protect the buds also.

American gooseberry mildew may inflict blackcurrants. It will appear as a dense, white powdery fungus on the undersurface of leaves, and on shoots in spring and later on berries. On the shoots it will show as brown and felty. You should cut out any infected shoots as soon as seen, back to healthy growth, and spray with dinocap or a systemic fungicide, repeating as the manufacturers instruct. Remove infected berries and take particular care to prune out felted shoots in winter and burn them. Birds, capsids and aphids are also pests and should be discouraged by a winter spray-of tar oil at 5%. Spray again in summer if they appear, with malathion. Most serious of all is the susceptability of blackcurrants to white pine blister rust, of which it is the alternate host. Do not grow in white pine country for the sake of both plants.

Blackcurrants are very easy to
increase. Take hardwood cuttings
in mid-autumn and insert them
in the ground, retaining the
buds below ground level.

Left: Blackcurrants reach maximum
fruiting after 4-5 years, and
continue bearing for 15 years.
For speed strip the fruit
straight into a collander.

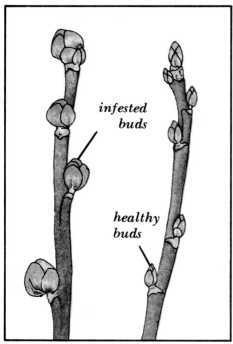

Gall mites, carriers of incurable
reversion virus, invade the buds
in spring, causing them to swell
up to an unnatural size. There
is no way of stopping them growing
inside the bud. Pick off and burn.

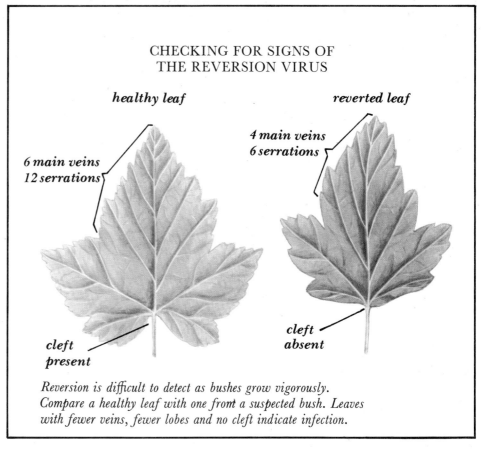

CHECKING FOR SIGNS OF THE REVERSION VIRUS

Reversion is difficult to detect as bushes grow vigorously.
Compare a healthy leaf with one from a suspected bush. Leaves
with fewer veins, fewer lobes and no cleft indicate infection.

Blueberry

Sweet-tasting and full of juice, blueberries grow in bunches on woody bushes. Though they contain many seeds, these are unnoticeable when eaten. They are good for canning, pies and tarts.

Blueberries grow well on rather poor ground, where other fruit would not flourish. Light, acid, sandy soil suit them well and if your garden is on the edge of wild land you might well make good use of reclaimed land by growing this delicious fruit.

The high-bush blueberry is ornamental as well as useful, with a brilliant autumn leaf color. The shrub produces long new growths from the woody crown each year, as well as fruiting sideshoots from last year's wood. The flowers, which smell like cowslips, appear in mid-spring. They are white and urn-shaped and hang downward in clusters. They open in succession for some weeks which helps to diminish frost damage.

Other types of blueberries

There are a number of sweet edible species of the *Vaccinium* genus, and also sour ones including the cowberry, *V. vitis-idaea*, and cranberry, *V. macrocarpon*, most of them native to America.

The European wild bilberry (also called blaeberry or whortleberry), *V. myrtillus*, produces edible fruit on a shrub up to 45 cm [1′ 6″] high. The fruit are small and are produced singly, unlike the American blueberries which are borne in clusters and are therefore easier to pick.

Another small shrub, up to 20 cm [8″] high, is the American

Blueberry
Derivative of *Vaccinium corymbosum*, *V. australe* and *V. lamacrkii* (*Ericaceae*), all high-bush types.
Hardy deciduous shrub with a useful life of 30 years.
Size: 2 m [7′] high, rather less wide.
Climate: cool to warm temperate.
Planting to harvesting time: two years.
Yield: 4.5 kg [9 lb] per bush.

V. angustifolium, the low-bush blueberry, with small sweet fruit. It grows in colder areas than the high-bush blueberry, where it is protected in winter by the snow covering it.

The rabbit-eye blueberry, *V. ashei*, is a tall semi-deciduous shrub up to 5.5 m [18′], which will grow freely on poor, dry, less acid soils. It likes a warmer climate, which the high-bush blueberry will not tolerate and is grown in the South.

Suitable site and soil

The blueberry needs a period of winter cold to crop successfully and is therefore limited to places where frost occurs. Sites which often suit it are grassland or other poor land not usually suitable for cultivation. Wherever rhododendrons grow successfully, you can try this fruit-bearing shrub.

The ideal site is flat or sloping land in full sun with an open aspect and free air circulation to dry the heavy fruit clusters. Like blackcurrants, blueberries should be sheltered from the wind, though their bell shape helps protect them from frost.

Do not grow blueberries with other fuit, even to use the same fruit cage. Most other fruits require lime and manure, but the blueberry will not tolerate them.

The best soil is light sand, high in peat content, as moisture retention is important. The soil should be acid and if it is not, blueberries should not be attempted. A soil test should give a pH of 4 to 5.2. If it is 6, sulphur may be added at 60 g per sq m [2 oz per sq yd]. The shrub needs good drainage. Soils on which water stands after heavy rain should be ridged.

If a tract of wild land is being incorporated into the garden for the first time, the renting of a cultivator will save much tiring work. This will turn in and bury heavy growths, which will then create an ideal rooting medium. This preparation is ideally carried out in the summer months when the weather is at its driest and warmest.

Planting

A single blueberry can be planted and the flowers will set (form fruit), but crops will be increased if you plant two or more varieties together. Buy two-year-old bushes, which will be about 30 cm [1′] high. Plant early spring in most areas, spaced 1.8 m [6′] apart. The bush makes a slow start, but it has a long life.

If the soil lacks organic matter, spread sphagnum peat 7.5 cm [3″] deep evenly over the area and dig it in.

Dig a hole big enough to contain the natural spread of the roots and place the plant in it to the same depth as its nursery planting. Crumble the soil back over the roots until the hole is filled. Mulch around the bush with sawdust, then sprinkle over 60 g [2 oz] of a complete acid fertilizer such as is used for azaleas, camillias or hollies. After planting tip the shoots to remove any flower buds; it should not be allowed to fruit in the first year.

Watering

A well-mulched soil should need no extra watering in areas

Blueberries may be the answer to poor sandy soils, particularly the edge of wild land. They will grow wherever rhododendrons are successful, and their red leaves in autumn are very ornamental.

The British bilberry. This species is less productive than its American relative, the blueberry.

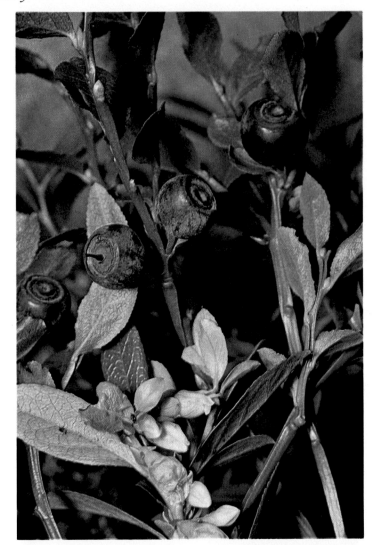

that receive well-dispersed rainfall of 75 cm [30″ or more] a year. Watering will be necessary where summers are continuously hot and dry. The leaves will turn red prematurely when short of water. Tap water (which may be too alkaline) can safely be used for infrequent watering.

Feeding and soil improvement

In winter mulch the ground 5-10 cm [4″] deep with sawdust. This helps retain moisture and stimulates growth. Extra nitrogen must be added to help rot down the sawdust; otherwise it would take nitrogen from the soil as it decomposes. You can wait until spring to spread 45 g [1½ oz] sulphate of ammonia or 60 g [2 oz] of dried blood and 30 g [1 oz] of sulphate of potash per sq m [yd] on top of the sawdust.

In early summer spread a further 45 g [1½ oz] of sulphate of ammonia or 60 g [2 oz] of dried blood, and if necessary water, in. Do not make the two applications together. If sawdust is not available, use pulverized fir bark or peat (though this has no nutrients) and for the latter omit the sulphate of ammonia and dried blood applications. Do not use spent mushroom soil or any dried animal manures.

Weeding

If weeds get into the mulch, they are likely to be perennial, and herbicides should be used. Watch out especially for blackberry seedlings among the bushes, introduced by birds. If they are not removed quickly, they are likely to become impossible to eradicate.

Pruning

Growth is in two stages. First, sideshoots grow from below the flower clusters formed the previous year. These pause in early summer and then grow again to form flower beds. Then in midsummer new shoots thrust from ground level from the woody crown and by late autumn these may be 1.8 m [6′] high with the top 25 cm [10″] covered with flower buds.

Real pruning begins in the third winter after planting, when the original branches of the young bush have become dry and twiggy.

Fruit is carried on the previous year's shoots. These may either be new long growths from the crown, or sideshoots on the growths of the year before that.

Each winter cut the oldest of the stems which have borne crops. Cut them to the base, or to a strong low sideshoot if there is one. This encourages strong new growth and heavy cropping. After a dull cold summer, prune back any green soft growth from the tip to tough brown wood.

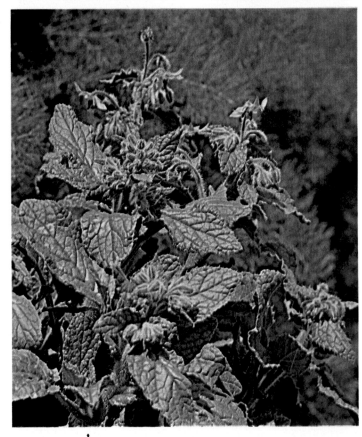

Harvesting and storing the crop

The first small crop may ripen the second summer after planting. Blueberries should reach their maximum cropping after about four to eight years.

The clusters should be picked over four or five times, starting in midsummer. Berries should be rolled off with the thumb and finger, dropping their stalks in the process.

Pests and diseases

Blueberries are attacked primarily by birds and rodents. Reddened, curled leaves may be caused by rose bloom disease. Spray with a good fungicide beginning when the leaves are young. If 'witches' brooms' appear, cut them out.

Varieties

Among the preferred varieties of highbush blueberries we have: Berkeley, Blue Ray, Bluetta, Dixie, Pemberton, Coville, Darrow, Late Blue, Concord, Blue Crop, Collins, Jersey, Weymouth and Earli Blue.

During a dry spring water the plants well until they are established. Hoe lightly between plants to keep the soil friable, or crumbly, and weed-free.

Using borage

Fresh leaves may be added to salads or to give an exhilarating lift to summer drinks and punches. Pick the young leaves from the lower stems before the flower heads show in midsummer. The flowers are also delicious in salads, both for decoration and for their cucumber flavor.

Clip the seed-head before the seeds have a chance to self-sow to save them for sowing the following year.

Borage

Borage is a sturdy plant with a fresh, cucumber scent and the most beautiful, intensely blue flowers. Both the leaves and flowers are edible.

Borage (*Borago officinalis*) is a hardy annual which grows to about 30-75 cm [1-2½'] high. Its heavily-veined, deep green leaves and hollow, rounded stems are very rough and prickly. The abundant blue, star-shaped flowers attract bees and produce plenty of seeds for subsequent sowing. In sheltered gardens in truly warm areas it can flower through the winter, and will only succumb to a bad frost.

Cultivation

Borage grows well in a sunny or shady position, whether in bank or border, rockery or herb garden, and in any type of soil. It is also suitable for growing in containers about 12.5 cm [5"] in diameter, filled with potting soil.

Before sowing fork the soil deeply so that the tap root – the long primary root – can grow down freely. Sow in early spring, covering the seeds with about 2.5 cm [1"] of soil. When the first pair of true leaves are well-developed thin the seedlings to 30 cm [1'] apart and make the soil firm around the remaining plants.

Borage is an attractive herb and easy to grow. Its leaves give a delicious flavor to drinks and salads.

Broad Bean

This bean comes in three types – long-podded, short-podded and dwarf. Though usually shelled for cooking, the pods can be eaten whole when young.

The broad bean is one of the oldest of cultivated vegetables. It belongs to the vetch group of the family *Leguminosae*, which includes several species grown as fodder for cattle and horses. The varieties grown for human consumption, however, have been developed for a more delicate flavor and are very nutritious.

The broad bean is hardy and easy to grow. Each seed sown sends up several succulent, square-sectioned stalks, usually

---

Broad Bean
Vicia faba (fam. *Leguminosae*) also known as English or fava bean.
Hardy annual.
Size: plants grow to about 60-90 cm [2-3'] tall.
Climate: temperate.
Sowing to harvesting time: 14 weeks for spring sowing; 24 weeks for autumn sowing.
Yield: 5 kg [11 lb] per 3 m [10'] double row.

---

to a height of 60-90 cm [2-3'], though there are a few dwarf varieties. Its gray-green leaves are large and rather fleshy; the white and black flowers are borne in clusters from the stem and have a strong, pleasant scent. One group of broad beans has short, broad, flat pods with about 6 seeds inside. These are the Windsors, sown in spring. Several varieties have green beans, which keep their color when frozen and are therefore grown for that purpose. Another type has very long pods – as much as 38-50 cm [15-20″] with 9 or 10 seeds in each. The pods hang down from the stem. These beans, known as Longpods, may be sown in autumn, and show an inch or two of shoot above ground before the first winter frosts. The chief variety in this section has white beans in its pods. The broad bean is a cool climate crop. It must be sown so that it produces its crop before the arrival of very hot weather. Beans sown later in spring, in the hope of getting a succession of crops throughout the summer, seldom do well.

Suitable site and soil

Broad beans, when fully grown, will be like a fairly dense hedge up to 1 m [3'] high across the garden, so when planning their site keep in mind the needs of the crops that will be next to the beans. Some crops will appreciate the shade and protection, but others will not. Arrange the rows so that they run north-south to ensure that plants growing on either side of the beans get sunlight for some hours during each day.

Broad beans like a rich, deep and fairly heavy soil but will tolerate almost any type. They do best in ground manured for a previous crop, rather than on freshly-applied manure or garden compost. They do not like an acid soil, which can be corrected by an application of lime.

There is no need to fuss with broad beans. If the soil is naturally rich or has been manured for a previous crop, just dig it deeply and thoroughly. If the soil tends to be acid, work in garden lime, at the rate indicated by the result of a soil test.

Sowing

Broad beans are large seeds, so they are sown individually. One method is to draw a shallow, flat-bottomed drill, about 6.5 cm [2½″] deep and about 10 cm [4″] wide, across the garden plot. Place two rows of beans in the drill with the rows about 7.5 cm [3″] apart and the beans spaced about 5 cm [2″] apart in each row. Ideally the seeds should be arranged so that each one is opposite a gap in the opposite rank but this is not absolutely essential. Cover with soil, using a draw hoe, make the soil firm by treading on it and rake it over.

Most gardeners leave a space of 45-60 cm [1½-2'] between each double row drill, but broad beans have a low germination rate – no more than 75% of the seeds usually grow – so it is a better use of space to plant a second double row only 10-15 cm [4-6″] from the first. It is very unlikely that severe overcrowding will result. The effect is to make a hedge of broad beans 30-45 cm [1-1½'] wide across the garden. With this arrangement it is impossible to walk between the ranks for picking, but all the beans are within easy reach if you walk first along one side and then the other.

The bean seed will germinate at almost any temperature above freezing point. The normal period from sowing to germination is from 1 to 2 weeks. Broad beans can tolerate moderate or even severe frosts, down to –7 to –9°C [20-15°F], provided they are not too prolonged. However, those sown in autumn should not be put into the soil too early (late autumn is ideal) or they will make a vigorous initial growth and then bend over at the first frost, with possible damage to the stems.

The seedlings are quite distinctive – they are among the largest seedlings in the vegetable garden. They have sharp-pointed, bright green leaves when they first emerge. No thinning is required.

Transplanting

Once planted, broad beans are seldom transplanted. The seed has a low gemination rate, however, and because occasionally unfavorable weather produces a failure, many gardeners provide an insurance by raising a small stock of bean seedlings in pots, in a frame or in the greenhouse. They are used to fill the gaps in the ranks in early spring.

Care and development

As the broad bean usually completes its life cycle before the onset of severe summer droughts, it will probably not need much watering. However, in the event of a drought, water generously.

The crop will be making its maximum growth when weeds too are growing strongly, so they need frequent hoeing. Tall weeds often take advantage of the cover provided to grow persistently within an inch or two of the bean plants and these should be pulled out by hand.

The broad bean is not a climbing plant; it will not twine itself around a pole, as a runner bean will, and has no tendrils to hook onto a support like a pea. It is, however, shallow-rooted and tends to flop over as it approaches its maximum height or in windy weather. There are two ways of combating this tendency. One is to earth up the bases of the plants, gathering the soil around them with a hoe. The other is to stick a row of twigs alongside each rank.

Pollination is carried out by bees. When the flowers have just begun to bloom, many gardeners pinch out the top shoot of the plant. This encourages larger and earlier bean pods and, as the top shoot is a favorite place for aphids to congregate, also reduces their attacks.

Harvesting

Harvesting is a matter of individual taste. Some people like well-matured broad beans, leaving them on the plants until the pods are turning bronze and are well-filled with hard beans. Most, however, prefer them fresh and young, picking the pods as soon as they can feel sizable beans inside. It is also possible to pick the pods before the beans inside

A row of broad beans supported by stakes. As the plant is shallow-rooted, it tends to flop over when reaching its maximum height. Stakes or strong twigs alongside each row help to combat this, and are particularly useful in very windy weather.

Sow in double rows, with staggered spacing, to avoid crowding.

Pick out the top shoots to encourage earlier and bigger pods.

Spray against aphids – remember the underside of leaves too.

Bean pods reaching maturity. The lowest clusters of beans will mature first. At this point it is possible to cut off the top shoots of the plants and cook the leaves in the same way as spinach.

have properly developed and cook them whole in the same way as pole beans.

For spring-sown crops, the normal time from sowing to harvest is about 14 to 16 weeks. Autumn-sown crops take longer – about 24 to 28 weeks. The pods should be picked by splitting off the pod from the main stem with a quick downward movement of the hand. When the lowest clusters of beans, which mature first, are beginning to form, the top shoots of the plant may be snipped off and – if clean and not already attacked by aphids – cooked like spinach.

After-care

Generally, broad bean plants are disposed of as soon as they have finished bearing crops, about midsummer. The space they occupy in the garden is then ready for other crops. It is best to plant brassicas in the soil – a good crop rotation, because brassicas benefit especially from the nitrogen that broad beans release.

Because of the nitrogen-producing bacterial nodules on its roots, the broad bean plant, like other leguminous plants, enriches the soil for the next crop. When clearing the ground after a crop, therefore, dig in the plants' stems, roots and leaves – chopping them up into short lengths if necessary.

Growing under glass

The broad bean is so hardy that glass is only used to bring on a reserve to fill in the gaps in outdoor rows. Broad beans can also be planted or sown in pots or flats in cold frames in midwinter in warmer areas to be ready for transplanting in early spring. When this procedure is followed, it is as well to sow one bean per pot and to transplant very carefully, with a minimum disturbance of the roots.

Pests and diseases

The most important and troublesome pest that attacks the broad bean is the aphid. This juice-sucking insect saps the life of the plant and fouls the leaf surface with sticky honeydew. The earliest broad bean crops usually bear their pods before the aphids attack, but the later ones are often heavily infested.

Pinching off the top shoot of the plant is an effective deterrent, as that is the favorite place for the aphids to congregate. Derris and malathion are effective against the pests, but the later crops may have to be dusted or sprayed several times. Spray in the evening after pollinating insects have finished working. Bear in mind that many aphids are tucked away in crevices on the underside of leaves. Experiments in companion plantings have revived the old farmer's belief that summer savory sown among the broad bean ranks can keep aphids away.

Chocolate spot (*Botrytis fabae*), may appear on the leaves of late broan bean crops. It is not usually very serious and, as it chiefly attacks weak plants, as good a treatment as any to encourage strong growth. Lime helps to prevent an

Harvesting the beans – split the pods from the stem with a sharp downward twist.

attack on acid soils and, if the plants are thought to need an extra feeding, a fertilizer rich in potash can be given.

If beetles or their larvae attack in force, spray with Sevin or malathion.

Varieties

Broad beans are not widely grown and only a few are readily available, such as: Broad Windsor Long Pod, Frostproof, Express and Masterpiece.

Broccoli

The head or 'curd' of the large-headed broccoli is a closely packed mass of flower stems and buds, tightly enclosed by leaves.

Broccoli is a cold climate crop, despite the tenderness of the seedlings. Like most cabbages, the plant will survive hard frosts in mild areas but in harsh conditions the flower head may be damaged and so is generally given some protection. In common with most other garden brassicas, broccoli has been evolved from the wild cabbage.

Broccoli comes in two shapes, the loosely packed sprouting broccoli (*see* SPROUTING BROCCOLI) and the compact, large-headed broccoli covered here. The large-headed broccoli has been evolved from the sprouting, but in appearance it is more like a cauliflower. It has a compact white head and is occasionally listed in seed catalogues with cauliflower. There are also purple-headed varieties.

Large-headed Broccoli
Brassica oleracea botrytis (fam. *Cruciferae*).
Hardy biennial plant, grown as an **annual.**
Size: 60-90 cm [2-3′] high and 20-45 cm [8-18″] in diameter.
Climate: cool temperate.
Sowing to harvesting time: 9 months to a year.
Yield: 2.7 kg [6 lb] per 3 m [10′] row.

All the tiny, independent flower heads of sprouting broccoli have been merged into one. The head is knobbly and consists of several rounded sections, unlike the cauliflower which has one compact crown forming a single smooth dome. The cauliflower head is set in a loose frame of upright leaves, but the inner frame of broccoli leaves fits tightly around the flower head and folds over it in winter.

Planning a succession of crops

Between them cauliflowers and broccoli are always in season where winters are mild. Early broccoli mature in late autumn or early winter; mid-season varieties come to harvest right through the winter, in such areas though frost holds up their development. The later varieties crop the following spring and the last crop is almost in midsummer and can coincide with the earliest cauliflowers.

Suitable site and soil

Broccoli likes a sunny site. Ideally, there should also be some shelter from wind, but very protected spots in low-lying country encourages frost to collect. In these cases a position where wind prevents intense frost is better. Do not choose a site that was used the previous year for any other brassica crop, as your broccoli may get club root and the cabbage root fly. Choose a different site for all brassicas each year.

Improving your soil

Like all brassicas, broccoli prefers a rich, heavy soil – it also needs good draingage. If possible, broccoli should be grown after a crop for which the ground was previously manured, otherwise dig in manure or garden compost at the rate of 3 kg per sq m [6 lb per sq yd] early in the autumn before planting. This will give the soil time to consolidate, which is very important to ensure compact heads.

If the soil is at all acid, apply sufficient garden lime, so that a soil test gives a pH of just over 7. A very acid soil is unsuitable for growing broccoli.

Sowing

Where a succession of varieties is possible, sowing is done from early to late spring for cropping the following autumn to spring. Broccoli needs a long growing period so that it can establish itself before the cold weather comes. For the earliest crops, sow seed thinly in drills about 1.5 cm [½″] deep and 15 cm [6″] apart under a frame in early spring. Seed can also be sown the same way outdoors in mid or late spring. Germination takes 7-12 days. Thin when the seedlings are large enough to handle.

Planting

The ground should be trodden down well before planting to ensure that it is thoroughly firmed. When the young plants have grown four or five leaves they can be transplanted. If they are left longer than this the head will be poor. They should be hardened off before planting in their permanent positions, from late spring to midsummer.

Plant the seedlings fairly deep in the holes made with a dibber, so that the base of the leaves is only a finger's breadth or so above the surface of the soil. The plant will

1. *Sowing in a frame for early crops. Seed should be sown thinly in drills, in early spring.*

2. *The seed should germinate in 7-12 days. Thin out the seedlings when large enough to handle.*

3. *Before planting, tread the ground well.*

4. *Winter protection: pushing plants into a shallow trench, made by scraping the soil away on one side.*

5. *Cover the roots and stems with soil again.*

Right: the inner frame of leaves of the compact, large-headed broccoli fits tightly around the head in winter.

6. *Another method of winter protection to prevent the curd from freezing and thawing – cover the heads with dry straw in times of hard frost.*

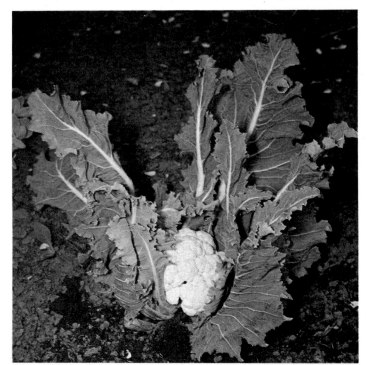

finish up with a heavy superstructure and needs firm anchorage. Push the dibber into the soil alongside the plants at an angle towards them. This will firm the soil up against the roots and also produce a hole for watering in dry weather.

Plant in rows 60-75 cm [2-2½'] apart, with about 60 cm [2'] between plants. In dry weather, take extra care with transplanting. Dig a hole for each plant, fill with water and press the soil firmly around the roots as soon as the plant is inserted. Or the roots may be dipped in a bucket of mud just before planting.

Care of plants

While broccoli will not stand having permanently wet roots, it should never be allowed to get dry during the summer and especially after planting. A light mulching will help to keep the soil moist without waterlogging. Providing the ground was well fed as advised, there will be no need to feed during the growing season. Hoe around the plants frequently to keep down weeds.

Protection in winter

Some winter protection may be necessary where it can be grown at this time. Remove the soil from the roots on the side away from the midday sun, then push the plants gently onto their sides so that they face away from the sun. Cover the roots and stem with soil again. This prevents alternate freezing and thawing of the curd. Alternatively the heads may be covered with dry straw in times of harder frost.

If the curds are showing, they may be covered by breaking the midrib of some of the leaves and bending them over.

Harvesting and storing the crop

If you can grow a succession of broccoli, your first harvest will be in late summer and may continue through the autumn and winter to the beginning of the following summer.

Varieties which come to maturity in winter, or which have to survive the winter to expand in the following spring and summer, are less reliable. They may be badly checked by severe weather and a proportion of the crop destroyed.

Large-headed broccoli should be picked when the enclosed leaves unfold, revealing the curd. For the early and late crops, wait until the unfurling process is complete. In winter it is often advisable to forestall frost damage by cutting broccoli early.

Large-headed broccoli may be pulled out of the ground and the leaves trimmed off with a sharp knife. Or it may be cut on the site, slicing through the stalk to leave the outer leaves on the stem and the inner leaves, which are edible, around the curd.

If too many heads are maturing together, the surplus may be pulled up with the roots and soil still attached, and hung upside-down in a cool, dark cellar or shed. Cover the curd with tissue paper and store for up to three weeks.

Care after harvesting

Once the heads have been cut the crop is finished. The ground may now be finally cleared. Surplus leaves and the fleshy part of the stalk may be dug in or composted if you are sure they are free from disease or pests, but the roots and stem are very woody and should be burnt, to prevent spread of pests and disease.

Pests and diseases

Broccoli is susceptible to all the pests and diseases common to other brassicas (*see* CABBAGE), but in some areas it can also suffer from a deficiency disease called whiptail, caused by a shortage of molybdenum in the plant. The leaves become badly malformed, being reduced to only the midribs with an edging of leaf. Any curd which develops is small and leafy; seedlings will be yellow, with the leaves turning inward. It appears on acid soils, so liming is advisable, which will make the soil neutral to alkaline.

If these same symptoms occur when the plant is young, it may be due to a check in growth, caused by cold, dryness or too much fertilizer too soon, and not necessarily the result of whiptail.

Varieties

Broccoli varieties available include: Spartan Early, Premium Crop, De Cicco, Calabrese, Green Comet, Waltham, Cleopatra and Green Mountain.

Brussels Sprouts

This popular vegetable belongs to the cabbage family. The tiny compacted 'sprouts' grow all the way up the stem.

Like most of the other brassicas, Brussels sprouts have been developed from the wild cabbage *Brassica oleracea*. The stem of the plant is crowned by a head of inward-curling leaves. From the crown almost down to the base of the stem are leaf axils, or joints, and careful plant breeding has ensured that tight little cabbage-like heads are produced in these right up the stem. Each of these miniature cabbages is called a sprout. The buds in the leaf axils of most brassicas do not form until the second season of growth but Brussels sprouts develop theirs during the first year.

The natural tendency of the plant is for sprouts to form first near the base of the stem. After these have been picked those further up the stem grow bigger, and so a succession of picking can be made from the same plant. For many years plants were developed to produce greater quantities of larger sprouts. Commercial growers, however, began to select varieties which produced a mass of medium to small sprouts of uniform size which all came to maturity at the same time.

It is helpful to bear this in mind when choosing varieties. For general kitchen use the gardener will probably prefer the larger plants which produce a succession of sprouts throughout the winter. If, however, the sprouts are chiefly grown for freezing, a variety used by commercial growers might be more suitable.

The picking season can be further extended by using a range of varieties bred to produce sprouts which mature early or late in the winter. The harvesting season is from early autumn to early spring if the climate is sufficiently mild.

Brussels sprouts are a cool-climate crop. They are hardy and will withstand considerable frost, but they do not like extreme heat. A hot dry summer seems to inhibit their capacity to produce tight sprouts in the following autumn. Throughout the germination and growing periods, the plants need a temperature at least a little above freezing point. When they are mature and cropping, they will stand quite severe and prolonged frosts. The plants will not grow during such extreme conditions but they will remain alive and will resume growth when the frost is past.

Suitable site and soil

Brussels sprouts are nearly always transplanted into their final positions as young plants. For the seedbed any available plot of fairly fine soil will do. The seedlings will be there for only a few weeks. They may also be cultivated in boxes or pots or in cold frames.

When deciding where to plant, remember that Brussels sprouts plants grow tall and that they are in position for a long time. If possible, arrange the rows so that other plants on either side get a share of sunlight. Remember to choose a plot that has not been occupied by brassicas the previous year to avoid the build-up of pests and diseases. Sprouts are rather top-heavy plants, so try to choose a site which gives some wind protection.

Brussels sprouts will grow in almost any type of soil, though

---

Brussels sprouts
Brassica oleracea gemnifera (fam. *Cruciferae*)
Hardy biennial, usually grown as an **annual.**
Size: to about 90 cm [3'] tall.
Climate: temperate
Sowing to harvesting time: about 28-36 weeks.
Yield: 6 plants per 3 m [10'] row, each producing about 1 kg [2 lb] of sprouts.

---

they do not like overly acidic conditions. Preferably, choose a site that was manured for a previous crop or, in the autumn before planting, dig the site deeply and work in a heavy dressing of well-rotted farmyard manure or garden compost. This will allow time for the soil to become firm, very important if 'blown' sprouts (open, leafy ones) are to be avoided. If you have not manured the land the previous autumn, apply a top-dressing of a complete fertilizer in spring at the rate of 90-125 g per sq m [3-4 oz per sq yd], to improve the soil.

Sowing

As with all brassicas, the seeds of Brussels sprouts are small and round. In the open ground they are sown in drills about 1.5 cm [½"] deep and as close together as is convenient, about 15 cm [6"]. For a main crop, this sowing should be made in mid-spring, and the seeds should be sown thinly. Germination should take place within 7-12 days of sowing.

Planting

When all danger of frost is past in late spring or early summer, the plants should be moved to their final bed. It is essential to allow plenty of space for Brussels sprout plants. Allow 75-90 cm [2½-3'] between rows, and 45 cm [1½'] between each plant in the row.

The Brussels sprout plant is rather shallow-rooted, and its roots have to support a tall, heavy-headed superstructure. So it is important to plant deeply. At transplanting time the plants will be from 10-15 cm [4-6"] high, and they should generally be planted so that their lower leaves are resting on the soil. Try to choose a day just after rain has fallen and water the holes before planting. Make sure the plants are firmed in well to anchor the roots and encourage the development of tight 'buttons', or sprouts.

The plants should be allowed to remain in the seedbed, without pricking out, until the time for the main transplanting. Some gardeners transplant part of the crop but leave plants about 45 cm [1½'] apart in the rows in which they were sown. This can be satisfactory but the plants left in their original site are seldom as good as those which have been transplanted. The transplanting seems to benefit the plants; they grow stronger and produce an earlier crop.

Buying transplants

Rather than taking the trouble to sow seed and grow seedlings, many gardeners prefer to buy their plants at the transplanting stage. While not so common as cabbage, Brussels sprout plants are sometimes available at markets and garden shops, and a delay of a day or two between pulling the plants and replanting them usually does no great harm.

Early crops

As sprouts require a long growth period and, as the last frost sometimes comes late in spring, many gardeners try to bring on an early crop under glass. The soil temperature for germination needs to be 10° to 13°C [50° to 55°F]. The seed is usually sown in boxes, in an unheated greenhouse or conservatory, or in a cold frame.

In areas which have a mild enough winter the seed is some-

1. Make a planting hole about 10 cm [4″] deep, using a dibber.

2. Unless the soil is moist, fill the dibber hole with water.

3. Push the dibber into the soil near the plant to firm the roots.

4. Fill the hole beside the plant with water when the weather is dry.

5. Test for firmness of planting by pulling at one of the leaves.

6. Draw up soil around the stems to anchor them 1 month after planting.

7. Break off the yellowing lower leaves of the plants in autumn.

8. Protect the sprouts with wire or plastic netting from attack by birds.

9. Gather the sprouts by starting at the bottom and working your way upward.

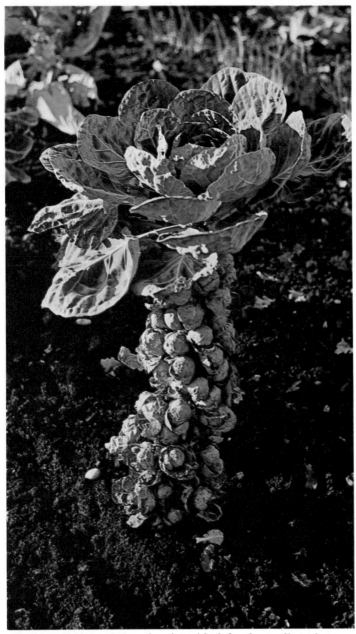

Sprouts of this semi-dwarf variety, ideal for the small garden, can be harvested as early as mid-autumn.

Chop up the stems of the sprouts plants and, if free from pests and diseases, put them on the compost heap.

times sown in sheltered borders in autumn and protected by temporary arrangements of glass or plastic against any winter frosts, ready for transplanting early in spring.

Early sowings of Brussels sprouts are transplanted twice. As soon as the seedlings show the first pair of leaves they are pricked out, or transferred from seed boxes to pots or trays which, like the seed boxes, also need the protection of glass or plastic. The seed boxes, pots or trays should contain a fine soil or potting mixture. Transplant the seedlings about 5 cm [2″] apart in every direction. An advantage of using boxes is that they can be placed outside the greenhouse or frame on mild days to allow the plants to harden off. If the transplanted seedlings are growing in open ground under Hotkaps or other covers, they may be removed on mild days.

Care and development

Remember that sprouts need plenty of water when they are young, so keep them well watered. Also water well in dry weather, so that they can grow without check.

A mulch of garden compost or farmyard manure will help to keep the soil moist and supply a little more plant food. Too much nitrogen while growing results in 'blown' sprouts later, so any addition of complete fertilizers should be done with caution, and preferably in the light of experience. Summer care consists mainly of keeping the surrounding soil free from weeds. The hoeing involved is also beneficial to the plants as it keeps the soil aerated, but hoe lightly across the surface to avoid damaging the shallow roots.

Harvesting the crop

As the crop reaches maturity – 28-36 weeks after sowing, depending on variety – the lower leaves of the plant will start to yellow. Cut or pull them off. They come off easily if pulled downward. The sprouts mature from the bottom of the stem, though sometimes the bottom few are too poor for use. Split each sprout off from the stem with a sharp downward tug. After the lower ones are removed, those higher up will grow more quickly.

At this stage the tops of the plants can be cut off and cooked as a cabbage. Once this is done, remaining sprouts will mature quite quickly. Some gardeners who want all their sprouts early and small for freezing cut off the top several weeks before the crop is ready for picking. Most of the sprouts will then mature at the same time.

If more sprouts are grown than can be used in the course of a season, the sprouts themselves will unfold and form flower stems and heads in spring in sufficiently mild areas. Some gardeners leave a few plants for this very purpose. The young shoots, picked as they are expanding, make delicious spring greens at a time when vegetables are scarce.

Care after harvesting

Almost every part of the Brussels sprout plant is used. The sprouts and crown are both eaten and all that is left is the stout, woody stem. This will rot in time but should be chopped up with a sharp spade to aid decay. It can be dug into the soil but is probably best incorporated in the compost heap, if free from pests and disease.

A Brussels sprouts crop is quite a heavy drain on soil, which will benefit from a generous manuring before being used again.

Growing in containers
Brussels sprouts can be grown in boxes, tubs, barrels or other containers in a small garden. Each plant requires a large container about 30 cm [1'] deep and quite wide. Even just one is worth growing for its high yield – about 50-75 sprouts.

Pests and diseases
The pests and diseases of all brassicas are the same; *see* CABBAGE for those attacking Brussels sprouts.

Varieties
Among those generally available are: Jade Cross, Long Island improved, Early Morn, Green Pearl, Indra and Topscore.

Cabbage

Cabbage is a vegetable of great value, for varieties suitable for sowing in different seasons make it possible to grow a fresh supply much of the year.

A biennial grown as an annual, the cabbage was evolved from the wild cabbage which grows in many coastal regions of northwestern Europe. It is anchored in the soil by a shallow root and consists of a rather short woody stem and an edible head, or heart, of tightly packed leaves surrounded and enclosed by looser, coarse leaves. Different varieties provide crops all year round.
The first Savoy was developed in the area of France known as Savoy in the Middle Ages. This cabbage-like plant, which is actually more closely related to the Brussels sprout, is hardier than true cabbages.

TYPES OF CABBAGE
There are two main ways of classifying cabbages – one is

according to shape and the other is by their season of use. The shape simply means whether the head is pointed or round. The season of use refers to harvest time: spring cabbages (climate permitting) are sown in late summer or early autumn for harvesting the following spring; others (summer and autumn cabbages, including red cabbages) are sown in very early spring and harvested in summer while the third group (winter cabbages and Savoys) is sown in late spring and early summer for harvesting in autumn or winter where the climate permits.
Most of the autumn and winter varieties are round-headed, while virtually all the spring cabbages are pointed. Young spring cabbages, harvested in early spring before they have developed hearts, are called 'spring greens'.
Red cabbages are always round-headed and are usually sown in spring for autumn harvesting.
Savoys are treated much as winter cabbages. The different varieties are highly specialized in that they mature at different times – the range is wide enough to provide crops ready for harvesting in every month from late autumn to early spring. If you live in a city, however, it would not be a good idea to grow Savoys, for the deeply crimped leaves soon become ingrained with dust, soot and other pollutants. Each group of cabbage needs a different type of treatment, though there are some general rules for growing all types of cabbage, as there are for growing all types of brassicas. The cardinal rule for brassicas is never sow or plant them in a plot that contained a brassica crop the previous year.

Spring cabbages
Sown in summer, spring cabbages are moved in autumn to a permanent bed – e.g. a plot which has just produced a crop of potatoes or peas. Protect the crop with covers during the winter, if necessary.

Summer and autumn cabbages
To prepare a permanent bed for summer or autumn cabbages, which are sown in spring, dig the ground deeply the previous autumn and work in a heavy application of farmyard manure or garden compost. At the same time,

---

Cabbage
Brassica oleracea capitata (fam. *Cruciferae*)
Biennial, grown as an **annual.**
Size: 22.5-45 cm [9-18"] high and 15-60 cm [6-24"] wide.
Climate: cool temperate to sub-tropical.
Sowing to harvesting time: 11-13 weeks for red and autumn cabbages, 18-22 weeks for winter cabbages, 26-30 weeks for mature spring cabbages.
Yield: about 10-12 cabbages, each 0.5-1.4 kg [1-3 lb] per 3 m [10'] row.
Savoy
Brassica oleracea bullata major (fam. *Cruciferae*)
Size: to about 20 cm [8"] high and 50 cm [20"] wide.
Climate: cool temperate.
Sowing to harvesting time: about 11-13 weeks.
Yield: about 6-7 Savoys per 3 m [10'] row.

Savoys are much hardier and distinct from other types of cabbage.

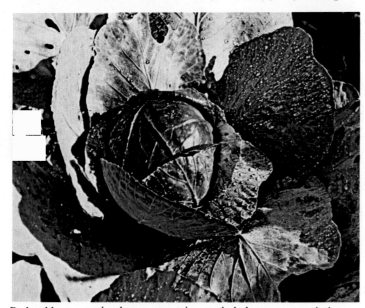

Red cabbages need a longer maturing period than green varieties.

Most varieties of spring cabbage have pointed heads.

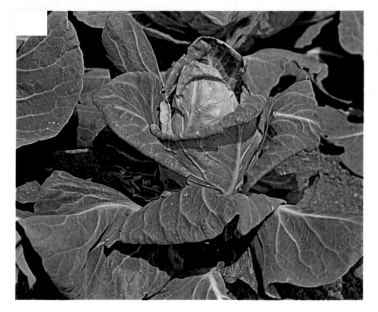

apply lime if the soil is acid. Alternatively, if you cannot afford to let the land lie fallow, grow a crop – such as leeks – that needs generous manuring.

Winter cabbages

In more temperate regions, winter cabbages can be planted after any crop, such as early peas or broad beans, which is harvested in late spring and for which the ground was well manured in the previous autumn. In cooler areas where the growing season is shorter, however, it is not possible to grow another crop beforehand on the same land.

Most of the details of cultivation are the same for winter cabbages as for the summer varieties, but the land must be well enough drained so that it does not become sodden in winter. You should allow at least 45 cm [1½′] of space between each plant, the larger varieties requiring 60 cm [2′] in each direction. It is a good idea to 'earth up' the cabbages to enable them to withstand strong winter winds – pile up soil around the stems.

Winter cabbages need less nitrogen and more potash than summer cabbages, and a tomato fertilizer may be used for this crop instead of the usual general fertilizer.

You can also give the soil an extra dressing of sulphate of potash, at the rate of 60 g per sq m [2 oz per sq yd], which will help them stand up to hard weather and soot, where available, at the rate of 1.3 kg per sq m [2½ lb per sq yd], which gives the plants a healthy dark green color.

Red cabbages

These need a longer period of maturing than the green varieties. To have red cabbages ready for harvesting in late summer, sow seed in the open in the early spring, transplant the young plants as soon as possible and water well if the weather is dry. For winter harvesting, sow the seed a little later and put the young plants under or in a cold frame in winter months if need be.

Remember that if the plants are exposed to severe frost they may be damaged. General methods of cultivation for red cabbages are the same as for the green types.

Savoy cabbages

These are hardier than the other types of cabbage, and can be grown well on poor soil. Savoys have a distinctly different texture and flavor from other cabbages, and make a welcome change. You should grow relatively few plants in rich soil, as they can grow to a huge size.

Collards

Collards, or coleworts, are dwarf cabbages, about the size of a lettuce, which can either be cut as spring greens in early spring, allowed to mature to mid-late spring, or sown in early spring when they produce excellent miniature cabbages. They have the advantages of being rather hardy and of reaching the edible stage very quickly. Popular in the South.

(Facing page) *Plant cabbages so they will just touch each other when mature, without being overcrowded.*

1. *Prepare the seedbed by raking the soil to a fine consistency.*

2. *Make a tiny trench, or drill, in the bed, using the side of the hoe.*

3. *Sow seeds in the drill, 1.5 cm [½″] deep, about 8 seeds per 30 cm [1″].*

4. *Cover the seeds with a thin layer of fine soil or peat, using a trowel.*

5. *Smooth and firm the surface of the seedbed with the back of the rake.*

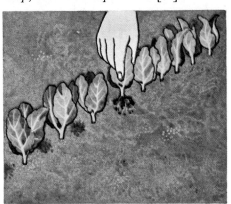

6. *Thin the row of young cabbage plants to about 30 cm [1′] apart.*

7. *Water the ground well before transplanting the young plants.*

8. *Dig a hole with a trowel, fill it with water and firm in the plant.*

9. *Water the young cabbages liberally as they grow.*

10. *To harvest headed cabbage, cut the head out with a sharp knife, leaving the large outer leaves on the stump. In time shoots will appear which produce greens.*

CULTIVATION

There are three main sowing periods for cabbages. The first is in late winter or very early spring, to provide crops for early summer harvesting. The second is the maincrop, sown outdoors in mid-spring, for autumn and winter harvesting. The third is from mid-to late summer, to provide a crop for the winter which can then be harvested the following spring.

Sow the earliest crops indoors under glass, either in seed boxes in a greenhouse or a cold frame. Sow the other crops in a fine seedbed outdoors.

Suitable site and soil

Cabbages grow best on a medium light soil, though they can be grown well on most types of well-drained soil that retain a reasonable amount of moisture. Prepare the soil well in advance of sowing.

Sowing Techniques

For starting outdoors, sow in drills (tiny trenches) about 1.5 cm [½"] deep at the rate of about 8 seeds per 30 cm [1']. Thin out alternate seedlings when one cabbage-like leaf shows. Under glass, sow the seed thinly or prick out seedlings at the two-leaf stage, to give the plants room to develop. The same spacing applies as for outdoor plants.

Planting

Generally speaking, cabbages are transplanted to their permanent beds when five or six leaves have appeared and the stems are the thickness of a pencil. If left too long in their seedbed growth will be stunted, so be sure to transplant at the proper time.

Assuming you prepared the permanent bed in advance, the soil should be moist at the time of transplanting. Dig a small hole and fill it with water. Place the plant roots in it before the water soaks away, then firmly press the soil around the root using a trowel, a dibber or your hands.

The final spacing should be 30-45 cm [1-1½'] for spring cabbage; 30 cm [1'] between plants and 45 cm [1½'] between rows for summer cabbage, and 45 cm [1½'] between plants and 60 cm [2'] between rows for the main fall crop.

Watering, feeding and weeding

Never allow cabbages to become dry. Water liberally during dry weather, and during the growing period feed occasionally with a liquid feed. Give spring cabbages a dressing of nitrogenous manure and hoe it in well to give the plants a good start at the end of winter.

Hoe around the plants frequently, not only to control weeds but also to aerate the soil and to deter insect pests from laying eggs near the crop. Break off any outer leaves that start to turn yellow.

Harvesting and storing

The cabbage is ready for harvesting when the head is hard. Cut the stem with a sharp knife, a little above the base of the lowest leaves, and remove the outer leaves which are much too coarse for eating.

Spring cabbages are often harvested, as spring greens, in late winter or very early spring, before the heads are properly formed. The fully formed cabbage is picked, as its name suggests, early in the spring.

Red cabbage is usually harvested in autumn.

Mature, hard, round-ended cabbages, stripped of their outer leaves, can be kept in a cool shed for several weeks. This applies especially to red cabbages. Spring cabbages do not keep long once they have been harvested.

After harvesting

Once the cabbages have been cut, the crop is finished and the ground may be cleared. Dig the surplus leaves into the soil. Burn the stems or chop them up well and add them to the compost heap, if free from pests and diseases. The stems of cabbages harvested in autumn and winter are sometimes left in the ground to shoot again in spring where the climate is mild enough, thus providing another welcome source of spring greens.

Varieties

Among the recommended varieties for the U.S. area: Earliana, Premium Flat Dutch, Ruby Ball, Savoy King.

Pests and diseases

Cabbages can be attacked by the following troubles: clubroot, yellows, cabbage-root maggot, root knot and cabbage worm. These will also invade other brassicas and are specific to these crops.

Clubroot is a fungus disease which infects the roots and is soil-borne. The roots become swollen and distorted, and rot; the leaves become blue-green and wilt. The disease can be spread on tools, shoes, machinery and infected roots left in the soil; it is worst on acid soils and wet, badly-drained sites. Control consists of liming the soil to make it neutral or slightly alkaline, improving the structure so that water drains away, and rotating the crop. Infected roots should be removed completely and burned; soil should be rested for at least five years.

Yellows usually appear within two to four weeks after transplanting, if at all. The best control is the use of resistant varieties. Next is the use of disinfected seed.

Cabbage-root maggot causes wilting of the young plants, because the small white maggots eat into the main root. Trouble can occur first in late spring, and continue all summer as successive broods hatch. Since the eggs are laid on the soil surface close to the plants, squares of tarred felt with a central hole or flat plastic collars placed around the plants on the soil will prevent this, otherwise dust the soil with diazinon.

Root knot is caused by nematodes or eelworms, microscopic creatures that bore into the roots and cause irregular swellings. They are more troublesome in the South than in the North. Long rotations that starve out the creatures are best, coupled with interplanting with marigolds, which science has proven harmful to the nematodes. Soil sterilization is not practiced for home-owners.

The worst pest, however, is the common white cabbage butterfly, whose green larvae bore into the heads. Spray or dust with whatever insecticide local restrictions permit.

Calabrese

SEE **SPROUTING BROCCOLI**

Cantaloupe

SEE **MELON**

Cape Gooseberry

The fruit is a juicy little golden ball enclosed in a 'Chinese lantern' which protects it from birds and insects. It needs a fairly warm climate.

Cape gooseberries or physalis have a sweet to sharp taste and are eaten raw as dessert or cooked in chutneys and curries. A confection is made by folding back the calyx and using this to dip the berries in fondant.

Though they are associated with South Africa, the berries originated in Peru, and were named for the Cape of Good Hope. In sub-tropical climates it will give quite large crops in relatively poor soil. Although it is a perennial replanting every year gives better yields. The plant is a member of the tomato family and needs similar conditions, as it is very sensitive to frost. It forms a bushy but rather sprawling plant which benefits from support.

Suitable site and soil

In a cool temperate area choose a site in the full sun, which is sheltered from the wind. A well-drained sandy soil is ideal. Treat poor soil with well-rotted manure at the rate of a 10 L (2 gal) bucket per sq m (yd). Do this at seed planting time, which will give it time to break down. A general fertilizer, at the rate of 45 g per sq m (1½ oz per sq yd) about two weeks before planting out, can be used instead.

Sowing and planting

Sow the seed in early spring in a greenhouse in a peat-based commercial seed mixture. Sow them 0.5 cm [¼]″ deep in 5 cm [2″] pots. Place a sheet of glass over the seeds to increase humidity. A temperature of 18°C [65°F] is needed. (Outdoor sowing is possible, but slower.)
Seeds sprout after 10-14 days. Early pricking out is essential when the seedlings are about 1.5-2 cm [½-¾″] high, putting them into 7.5 cm [3″] pots, which should then be kept in the greenhouse. If seedlings are planted out at this time, the plant will produce too much growth and will not fruit early. Transplant to permanent positions in the open when there is no more risk of frost. Allow 1 m [3′] between them. From mid-spring, you can plant out under protectors.

Care and development

Stake the plant with a 1.25 m [4′] bamboo cane at the time of planting, and tie it with soft string. Overwatering reduces fruiting. The leaves may be allowed to turn dull gray-green, but do not let the plant wilt. Feeding encourages luxuriant growth at the expense of fruiting. Feed only after the plant shows its first flowers, at the rate of 60 g per sq m [2 oz per sq yd] with a general fertilizer. Commercial tomato feeds are suitable as they are low in nitrogen. The root system is shallow, therefore hoe carefully to remove weeds. If the plants reach 30 cm [1′] high without producing any sideshoots, the growing tip of the plant should be pinched out. Later on tips of sideshoots can be removed to keep the plant within bounds, and sub-sideshoots completely removed.

Cape gooseberry
Physalis peruviana edulis (fam. *Solanaceae*)
Herbaceous perennial, often grown as an **annual.**
Size: 1.5 m [4-5′] out-of-doors, 2.5 m [8′] under glass.
Climate: warm temperate to sub-tropical.
Planting to harvesting time: minimum 4 months, 7 months as a half-hardy annual.
Yield: 1-2 kg [2-4 lb].

A member of the tomato family, the Cape gooseberry requires support and should be staked with a 1.25 m [4′] bamboo cane when planted out. A row can be staked out like raspberries with posts and wires stretched between them. Do not plant in rotation with tomatoes or potatoes.

The 'Chinese lantern' of the Cape gooseberry protects the fruit from birds and insects. Though Cape gooseberries are ready to pick when golden-brown, they reach their flavor peak a few weeks later.

The Cape gooseberry should be grown on a site which is in full sun and sheltered from the wind. It will crop well on poor, sandy soil, the main requirement for its success being good drainage and adequate watering.

Growing in the greenhouse

If you have sufficient heat in your greenhouse to keep out frost, the plant may be grown as a perennial. Crops in the second year are substantially larger, as they get an early start. Repot your transplants into larger 20-25 cm [8-10″] containers containing a mixture with a high proportion of sand. Don't use old tomato soil, which might carry over pests and diseases.

Cut the plant down to about 25 cm [10″] at the end of the season. Winter watering should only just keep the soil moist, to reduce the risk of root rot. Do not water from above after pruning as gray mold (*botrytis*) can develop. The following spring pollination must be aided by shaking the plant when the flowers are open.

Train plants on a trellis or with a system of wires: erect two 1.8 m [6′] wooden poles – making sure the poles are far enough apart to accommodate the plants when full grown. Tie two wires horizontally, between the two poles, one 60 cm [2′] and the other 1.2 m [4′] above ground level. Tie each plant onto the wires where they cross.

If the plant is to be staked, it may be necessary to pinch out the growing tips when 4-6 fruits have set, otherwise it will grow too tall.

Growing in a warm climate

The Cape gooseberry is not very fussy about its site. The main requirement is adequate drainage and provision for watering in the dry months. It will crop well on poor sandy soil; on rich silty soil the plant grows prolifically at the expense of fruiting.

Fertilize the site as before, and plant out seedlings when about 10 weeks old and a height of 30 cm [1′]. Allow 45 cm-1 m [1½-3′] between plants, depending on soil fertility. A row of Cape gooseberries may be staked like raspberries (*see* RASPBERRY) with posts and wires at 75 cm [2½′] and 1.25 m [4′]. Water thoroughly after transplanting and, if there is no rain, water at 2-3 week intervals until well established. Though a perennial, plants are usually treated as annual because mortality rates from root-rots and virus diseases increase during the second season. Cape gooseberries should not be planted in rotation with tomatoes or potatoes, due to eel worms and other problems.

Harvesting

Fruit is ready to harvest when the calyx changes color to golden-brown and acquires a papery texture. The fruit will hang for several weeks when ripe, though this may not be practicable in some areas where birds attack the crop. Pick the fruit complete with calyx. If the fruit has been grown outdoors in a temperate climate, gather all berries showing a hint of yellow when a severe frost threatens. These will continue to ripen in a sunny position. In warmer climates first pickings are in autumn, or when the calyx changes color, and continue at 1-2 week intervals. The fruit develops its flavor peak 2-3 weeks after assuming its deep golden color.

Storing the crop

Storage time depends on humidity. In cool climates drying the husk is essential, by spreading the fruit in a single layer on a warm windowsill or greenhouse. They can then be kept a few weeks in a dry atmosphere at 10-15°C [50-60°F]. Do not dehusk them until they are needed. In a warm climate they will keep up to five months.

Pests and diseases

In a temperate climate there are no problems because the fruit has natural protection from its husk. If Cape gooseberries are grown in the greenhouse, aphids and whiteflies can be a nuisance; if they occur, spray with a commercial insecticide. In a sub-tropical climate cut-worms, red spider mites, caterpillars, the potato tuber moth, root-rots and virus diseases cause problems.

Capsicum

SEE **PEPPERS**

Caraway

Caraway is an aromatic plant most often grown for its seeds, which are used in cooking, baking, confectionery and flavoring liqueurs.

Caraway (*Carum carvi*) is a biennial in the *Umbelliferae* family and in its first season will produce feather shoots about 20 cm [8″] high, like carrot tops. In its second season it will grow to 60 cm [2′] and produce white umbels, ribbed umbrella-like flower heads.

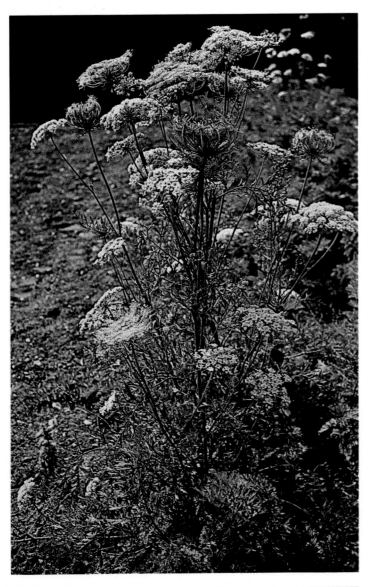

Producing an aromatic seed which has a wide range of uses in the kitchen, and is best known in rye bread, caraway is an undemanding plant to cultivate.

The name caraway is thought to derive either from the Gaelic word 'caroh' meaning ship, or 'karawya', the Arabic word for seed. Caraway seeds are recorded in Egyptian and Roman days; and in Elizabethan times, the seeds were served, either in a dish by themselves, or with roast apples, after a meal to help digestion and reduce flatulence, or gas. They were also added to herb bags, along with flower petals and other fragrant herbs and spices.

The fragrant seeds are the most useful part of the caraway plant. Dried, they are best known as a seasoning in rye bread, but are also particularly suitable for flavoring cream cheese, cooked brassicas, such as steamed Brussels sprouts or sauerkraut, and are common in German, Austrian and Jewish dishes. The young leaves may be used in soups or salads and the taproots may be eaten like parsnips. Oil of caraway is used in making the unique liqueur called Kümmel.

Found wild in Europe, North America and India, caraway is undemanding, unaffected by either dry weather or frost, and can be grown either in- or outdoors in a herb garden, window box, tub or other container.

Cultivation

Caraway will grow satisfactorily in semi-shady conditions but it does not need much water and should never be planted in soil that tends to stay damp. The best soil for it is fine, sandy and well-drained. Heavy soil should be treated with a mixture of sand and peat.

Sowing can be done outdoors in mid-spring or late summer, putting the seed thinly in drills 45 cm [1½'] apart. Seeding to germination is approximately three weeks, and the seedlings should be thinned to a final spacing of 30 cm [1'] between plants.

Since caraway produces a long taproot, it is not advisable to transplant it. When growing in containers, therefore, two or three seeds should be sown in the container in which it is to grow, and the weakest seedlings discarded as soon as possible. Seedlings sown in the spring will not flower until late spring the next year. Seedlings sown in the autumn will reach maturity the following midsummer.

During the very dry spells, the plants should be kept damp by light watering every two or three days. The plants need no special feeding or support, but tend the ground around the plants regularly to make sure that it is kept completely free from weeds.

Harvesting and after-care

The leaves should be cut sparingly 8-10 weeks after planting out. The seeds are ready for collection when the stems start to discolor and the fruit is dark green. The roots can be used once the seed heads have been collected. The seed heads should be removed from the plant with care, put into paper bags and kept in a dry place until the seeds fall. The seeds should be put in an opaque airtight container; dampness impairs their flavor. Stored in this way they will keep their pungency for at least a year.

Caraway seeds are ready for harvesting when the stems begin to discolor and the fruit goes dark green. If they are left the seeds will fall and be lost in the garden. The heads should be kept in paper bags until the seeds loosen.

Cardoon

An aristocratic vegetable for the adventurous gardener, the cardoon is a large, handsome thistle-like plant which yields delicious stems after blanching.

The cardoon is a hardy, herbaceous plant, a native of southern Europe that was introduced to Britain in the late 16th century. Its botanical name *Cynara cardunculus* comes from the Greek *kynon*, a dog; its abundant spines are rather like dog's teeth. The cardoon is similar in appearance to its close relative the globe artichoke (*C. scolymus*), but it is hardier. It is often grown solely for its appearance at the back of a flower border, where it towers majestically over the other plants.

The flower buds of cardoons can be eaten exactly like those of globe artichokes, but they are much smaller; if picked when very young, they can be cooked and eaten whole. Usually, however, it is the stems that are eaten, after blanching in the same way as celery.

Suitable site and soil

Cardoons need plenty of sunlight and warmth for ordinary growth, but to produce lush leaves you must also water them generously in dry weather. They need a rich soil; in dry soils they are best grown in a trench, but in heavy, wet soils they can be grown normally.

Sowing under glass

If the ground is cold, you should sow the seeds in pots under glass in mid-spring. Sow three seeds to each 7.5 cm [3″] pot and later thin to one seedling per pot. Plant the young cardoons outside in their permanent positions in late spring. Alternatively, raise young plants from seed

Cardoon
Cynara cardunculus (fam. *Compositae*)
Perennial, usually grown as an **annual.**
Size: to 1.8 m [6′] or more high.
Climate: cool temperate to sub-tropical.
Sowing to harvesting time: 24-34 weeks.
Yield: 6-7 plants per 3 m [10′] row.

sown in early spring in a heated greenhouse or propagator.

Sowing outdoors and thinning out

If sowing outdoors in a permanent position, the ground should be warm. Prepare trenches 30 cm [1′] deep and 45 cm [1½′] wide, as for celery, with 7.5 cm [3″] of well-rotted manure or good garden compost mixed with soil at the base of the trench. Allow this material to settle, when there should be a hollow for retaining water.

Sow the seed in the trench in mid to late spring in groups of 3-4 seeds at 45 cm [1½′] intervals, and 2.5 cm [1″] deep. Place an inverted flowerpot over each little group of seeds to prevent mice or other animals from eating them. If you are sowing more than one row of cardoons, the trenches should be 1 m [3′] apart so that you will have enough room for cultivation later.

As soon as the seeds have sprouted, remove the flowerpots covering them. When the seedlings are big enough to handle (at about 5 cm [2″] high), thin them out from 3 or 4 seedlings per group to a single one, leaving the strongest.

Care and development

From late spring to early autumn, water your cardoons well; when the weather is very dry, flood the trenches. Prevent the soil from becoming a solid mass and remove all weeds by hoeing regularly. At the end of midsummer, give the plants a mulch of moist horticultural peat or garden compost. Throughout late summer, feed them weekly with diluted liquid fertilizer.

When the plants have reached 30 cm [1′] high, push a stake into the ground alongside each plant and tie the leaves lightly to it.

Blanching

To blanch cardoons, remove all dead or yellowing leaves in late summer to early autumn, bunch all the leaves together and tie them together at their tops with twine. Then wrap long strips of thick brown paper 15 cm [6″] wide around the plant, starting at the bottom; alternatively, you can bind the plants with strong black plastic film. Leave several centimeters (inches) of the leaves free so that the plant can still make its own food. Next, pack soil around the tied-up plants to exclude all light. An alternative method of blanching requires no 'earthing-up'. You should thatch the plants with layers of straw 10 cm [4″] thick to cover them completely. The straw can be tied at the top and turned over on one side so that it resembles an old-fashioned nightcap. This method, although more painstaking, gives quicker results than the previous one: the cardoons should be ready to eat in four weeks or less, instead of six to eight.

Instead of blanching your cardoons at the end of late summer, you may prefer to wait until winter and eat them when there are few other fresh vegetables available. If frosts set in before you have started blanching, you should cover the plants with a mulch of straw or other light material, removing this in the morning. If blanching has not been completed when winter arrives in earnest, dig up the plants with as much soil as possible on their roots and move them to a storage room such as a shed, cellar or

1. *To blanch, tie each plant lightly to a 60 cm [2″] cane when it is about 30 cm [1′] high.*

2. *To avoid cutting your hands on the leaves, gather them with two sticks and some string.*

3. *Bunch all the leaves together and tie them at the top with raffia, soft strings or twine.*

4. *Wind strips of brown paper around stem upwards from soil level, leaving the leafy tops exposed.*

5. *It is important to pack earth or soil around the tied-up plant to stop all light from getting through.*

An alternative method to earthing-up is to thatch with layers of straw 7.5-10 cm [3-4″] thick.

Black plastic sheeting can be used in place of brown paper for blanching. The thatching method, however, produces cardoons to eat in just 4 weeks or less instead of the 6-8 taken with the earthing-up technique.

garage; heap soil, sand or peat over the roots and keep them moist. Provided you follow these instructions, they should remain in good condition for several weeks.

If the storage place is completely dark, you can remove the wrappings – otherwise leave them on until you are going to use the cardoons.

Pests and diseases

There are few troubles, apart from damage by slugs or snails.

Carrot

Carrots are one of the easiest vegetable crops to grow, provided the soil has been well prepared. They are rich in vitamin A and, harvested young, sweeter and more tender than market crops.

Carrots are herbaceous biennials, grown as annuals. The swollen 'taproots' of the most cultivated varieties of carrot are orange, but some types do produce white, yellow or even purple roots.

There are three main types of carrot: the finger-sized, shorthorn or 'stump-rooted' type ideal for an early or forced crop; the medium-length, thin-ended type with a cylindrical, tapering root, suitable for both storage and immediate use, and the long tapering type which makes a good late-maturing crop and is particularly suitable for exhibition growing.

Suitable site and soil

Carrots prefer a deep, light loam and a sunny or partially shaded aspect. Early crops grow best in full sun. Maincrop varieties can be grown on well-prepared, heavier soil. Soil conditions are all-important because the carrot is a root vegetable and must penetrate and build up its structure within the soil. Carrots require a deeply dug bed of friable (crumbly) soil about 45 cm [1½'] deep, rich in finely-divided particles of humus. The bed should have been manured in the previous growing season. If manure, garden compost or similar materials are introduced into the structure of the carrot bed in the season of sowing or during the immediate preparation of the bed, some of the crop will tend to be malformed, the roots being forked into two or more branches. Large stones can also result in crooked roots.

On a plot where crops are being grown in a rotation system, carrots should, ideally, be grown in the previous year's pea bed.

Preparing the soil

Carrots grow best in sandy loams, but even heavy soils can be adapted for growing them by thorough digging and the incorporation of humus-forming manure or garden compost, provided this is done well in advance of the growing season. Leaf mold can be introduced while you are digging the bed. You should sift the soil thoroughly with a garden sieve to remove all stones and large lumps of soil and work plenty of moist peat into it. The reason for adding peat is that carrots like a well-drained soil but not a dry one. The peat helps to bind loose, fast-draining sandy soils and also encourages better drainage and crumb structure on heavy soils that need lightening.

Leave the surface of the carrot bed rough until a week or ten days before sowing. Rake it level and create a good tilth (a fine crumbly layer) to ensure maximum germination. After raking immediately work in a handful per sq m (sq yd) of a good general fertilizer to give the seedlings a good start. Rake the fertilizer well into the surface of the bed.

When you have raked the bed level, position a line of string between two stakes across the bed to mark out the row of carrots. Run the corner of a hoe or rake along the line to cut out a V-shaped furrow at least 2.5 cm [1"] deep. Rows should be 23 cm [9"] apart for early crops, and 30 cm [1'] for maincrops.

Sowing

Maincrops are sown from mid-spring to midsummer, the later the better, to avoid attacks from carrot fly. Early crops are sown in early spring.

Carrots prefer warm soil and grow best in the early days of the season. If you sow too early, however, before the cold

---

Carrot
Daucus carota (fam. *Umbelliferae*)
Herbaceous biennial, grown as an **annual.**
Size: 23 x 4 cm [9 x 1¼"] for long-rooted varieties, 12.5 x 6.5 cm [5 x 2½"] for stump-rooted types.
Climate: cool temperate.
Sowing to harvesting time: early or forced crops are ready for pulling after about 9-11 weeks, maincrop after 14-18 weeks.
Yield: about 90 g [3 oz] of roots per plant.

Rich in vitamin A, carrots should be harvested when young and tender and eaten soon for the best flavor.

weather has cleared, there is a danger of seed failure. If the weather is bleak at the time you planned to sow, use Hotkaps or polyethylene mini-tunnels to protect the seedlings. In fact, they can go onto the seedbeds three weeks before sowing to warm the soil; after sowing they can be replaced to give the seeds a good start in their early growth. Sow carrot seed either in pinches between finger and thumb or by carefully shaking the seed into the drill direct from the packet with the hand held just an inch or so above the drill.

After sowing, replace the soil by gently covering the drill, using the back of the rake. A better but more painstaking method of doing this job is to place your feet on either side of the V-shaped drill in which the seed is lying at a depth of about 2 cm [¾"]. Then shuffle forward along the row with the toes pointing outwards and the heels pushing soil into the row. This action safely covers the carrot seed and at the same time gives the row a gentle firming. After covering the seed, rake the soil level by lightly pulling the rake down the row – never across it. Raking across the row would disturb or actually displace some of the seeds. Germination normally occurs from 14-18 days after sowing.

When sowing carrot seed the rule is to sow as thinly as possible, thus avoiding waste and the backbreaking task of thinning out. The most painstaking method for a successful crop is to sow the seeds singly, but a less time-consuming method is to mix a little dry horticultural sand with the seed in the packet. Alternatively, mix radish seed with the carrot seed. The radishes are soon ready for harvesting and this is an easy way of thinning the carrot row early on.

Thinning and general care

The essential task of thinning, by pulling out the smallest seedlings in each cluster, should begin when the greenery is about 2.5 cm [1"] or more high.

The best time to thin your carrots is after a rain shower; the water loosens the bed and makes the seedlings easy to lift. The first one or two thinnings will be tiny, but the last one or two in the early crop can be used in the kitchen. The early crop should have a final distance of 5 cm [2"] between each root, the maincrops are thinned progressively to a final spacing of about 10 cm [4"].

You should remove discarded seedlings from the area immediately. From time to time during these thinning operations, scatter a very light dressing of general fertilizer around the rows and allow the rain to wash this food into the soil; if it is dry, water it in. Keep the weeds under control, and do not allow the crop to run short of water, otherwise the roots split.

Harvesting and storing the crop

Once they have reached the desired size, short-rooted early varieties can be harvested from midsummer and harvesting can continue for several weeks. Maincrop varieties should be harvested beginning in early autumn.

Choose a dry day at the end of the season to lift the crop. Use a garden fork pushed into the soil well away from the vegetables to avoid damaging their skins. After lifting, cut off the foliage near the crown and put it on the compost heap. They are now ready for use or for storing.

Choose sound roots for storing and use during winter. Carrots can be stored outdoors in a hole filled with dry sand and covered with straw or in a ridge, like potatoes. To store indoors, place the carrots in boxes of sand, soil or peat in a frostproof cellar or shed. On the other hand, carrots can be dug through most of the winter if covered with a heavy mulch.

Frame cultivation

Forcing varieties of carrots can be grown to mature at times when bought carrots are expensive.

The hotbed for out-of-season carrots can be a helpful novelty. It should be a mild one, consisting of a basic layer of straw and rotted manure mixed with rotted leaves. Stack up this mixture until it is about 15 cm [6"] deep. Turn it over and moisten it every day for about a week to encourage fermentation, then flatten it and cover it with about 15 cm [6"] of good garden loam. Scatter seeds of a stump-rooted carrot variety thinly onto the soil, work them in below the surface with a hand-fork, and firm the bed with a wooden board. Water frequently, give ventilation when the weather allows it, and cover the frame with sacking or other protection on frosty nights; do not allow the night-time temperature to fall below 7°C [45°F], if possible, to encourage growth.

Consign the first carrot thinnings to the compost heap; subsequent thinnings, to about 5 cm [2"] apart, can be used in the kitchen.

Pests and diseases

The greatest pest, particularly in the Northwest is the carrot-rust fly, which is attracted by the pungent smell of the carrot foliage, and finds small areas of disturbed soil near the rows ideal places to lay its eggs. The small, pale yellow maggots that emerge from the eggs then burrow into the roots and may devastate the crop. Wilting, reddened foliage is usually the first symptom above soil level.

The chief carrot-rust fly attack usually occurs in the late spring; so if you can delay sowing the crop until the end of early summer it should be possible to miss this pest altogether. The second generation of adult flies does not start laying its eggs until well into late summer, but the maggots that hatch from these eggs hardly ever cause any damage to the crop.

Since thinning the young plants unavoidably releases the smell of the foliage, sowing the seed as thinly as possible in the first place is a great help in reducing the possibility of attack. Do this in the evening when the fly is less likely to be around, and destroy the thinnings. Never use a hoe to thin out young crops; this damages the foliage even more.

Some veteran gardeners sow parsley between the carrot rows because the scent of parsley is said to counteract that of the carrot leaves and so distract or deter the fly. In the same way a rag soaked in kerosene can be pulled along the rows occasionally to introduce a camouflage scent. Other troubles that may occur are wireworm, eelworm and aphids. In all cases, check with your local State Experimental Station for a list of locally approved controls.

Ball-shaped carrots are ideal for shallow soil.

Long tapering varieties for a late-maturing crop.

The medium-sized cylindrical types of carrot are good both for storage and immediate use.

1. *Hoe regularly between the rows of seedlings to remove any weeds.*

2. *Thin the seedlings to 2.5 cm [1″] apart after watering thoroughly.*

3. *Firm in and water the remaining seedlings to deter carrot-rust fly.*

4. *Sprinkle general fertilizer between the rows of carrots and water.*

5. *Water the night before, then young carrots can easily be pulled by hand.*

6. *Use a fork to lift mature carrots which can be stored in early autumn.*

Store carrots between layers of dry sand in a box in a frostproof shed. Cut off tops and pack evenly. They can also be stored outside covered with straw or in a ridge.

Cauliflower

Although more difficult to grow than other brassicas, this popular vegetable is well worth the effort.

The cauliflower is a highly specialized member of the brassica tribe. Generations of selective growing have developed the stalks of the opened flower-buds to form a compact head or 'curd'.

The plant produces a short, woody stem, 7.5-15 cm [3-6″] high, crowned by a cup of leaves which encloses the curd. When the leaves unfurl to disclose the entire top surface of the curd, the cauliflower is ready for cutting. There are many varieties, ranging from those which mature in early summer to those which are ready in late autumn. In the latter part of the year the range overlaps with heading broccoli. These are also called winter cauliflowers.

Suitable site and soil

Like other brassicas, cauliflowers are usually transplanted, so they need two sites. The seedbed can be any bed of fine soil, or a box of potting soil. Work on the permanent bed should be done in autumn. The site should be sunny and sheltered from wind, but must not contain hollows that trap frost. The soil should be either double-trenched or dug to a sufficient depth to take a good layer of rotted farmyard manure or garden compost in the bottom. The lighter the soil, the more organic matter it needs. It may also be reinforced by a dressing of about 125 g per sq m [4 oz per sq yd] of a complete fertilizer worked into the soil about a week before planting. Correct any soil acidity by an application of lime well before planting, at a rate determined by the result of a soil test. Land or garden lime may be applied with the manure.

As with all brassicas, avoid using a plot on which a brassica crop was grown in the previous year. Cauliflowers are even more susceptible than most other brassicas to the pests and diseases encouraged by continuous cropping.

Cauliflower
botrytis (fam. *Cruciferae*)
Biennial, usually grown as a **half-hardy annual.**
Size: Head 7.5-38 cm [3-15″] across; stalks 7.5-15 cm [3-6″] long; leaves 45-60 cm [18-24″] high.
Climate: cool to warm temperate.
Sowing to harvesting time: 18-24 weeks.
Yield: 0.5-1 kg [1-2 lb] per plant; 5-7 plants per 3 m [10′] row.

The spreading leaves of the summer cauliflower, the 'true' cauliflower. The winter type is a kind of broccoli.

A freshly-cut cauliflower. Harvest cauliflower while the head is still firm and compact.

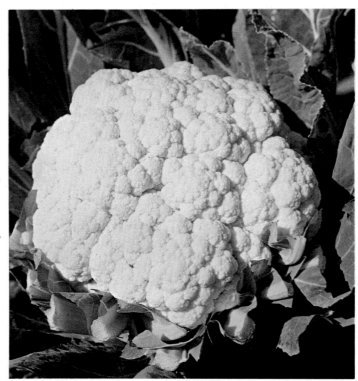

Sowing

Cauliflowers are divided into groups, according to the time of harvesting:

Group 1 contains the earliest cauliflowers, which are intended to be harvested in late spring and early summer. They may be dwarf cauliflowers, only 30 cm [1'] or so high. They should be sown under glass from late autumn to mid-winter where the climate is mild enough, and will require a constant temperature of 10-15°C [50-60°F]. They produce a minimum of small, pale leaves that give little protection to the curd, which is pure white and of a delicate flavor. Group 2 contains the regular earlies in most climates and consists of varieties for starting indoors or in hotbeds and putting out a few days after early cabbage. They may be dwarf as well, but not as small as those in Group 1, and the leaves are rather larger and darker. They should be sown in boxes, pans or pots under glass at the same time as Group 1 cauliflowers. A second sowing may be made outdoors in early spring, although this should be protected by covers against night frosts and chilly daytime weather. These plants should come to maturity a month or two later than those brought on under glass.

Group 3 contains the maincrop, consisting of a number of larger, hardier varieties of cauliflower, for harvesting from late summer to mid-autumn. Sow in an outdoor seedbed in mid-spring, giving some protection against night frosts if necessary. Sow in drills about 1.5 cm [½"] deep, in rows 23-30 cm [9-12"] apart and set out in late June or early July. Group 4 consists of a number of dwarf, very hardy varieties; originating in Australia and introduced in Britain and the United States in recent years. Sown at the same time and in the same manner as those in Group 3, they come to maturity rather later and will tolerate a moderate amount of autumn frost. They have compact, high quality, uniform curds protected by tightly incurling leaves.

The small, round cauliflower seeds tend to be expensive, so try to sow them economically – ideally about 2.5 cm [1"] apart. Sowing time to germination is from 1-2 weeks. With those sown under glass, prick out the little plants into boxes, pans or even small pots when they reach the two-leaf stage. Allow 5 cm [2"] between plants in each direction. Alternatively, you can use smaller pots, but it is especially important to put only one plant in each pot, to allow for healthy, hardy growth.

Planting out

Transplant to the prepared outdoor bed when the plants have about five leaves and protect with Hotkaps if there is a danger of severe frost.

Take great care to avoid shock to the plants when transplanting them, as this is one of the main reasons for small or non-existent heads. In times of drought, water both the plants and the prepared bed before transplanting. Keep a ball of soil intact around the roots of each plant during the transplanting. It is as well to work with a trowel rather than a dibber. In warm, sunny weather, dig a small hole in the soil, fill it with water, insert the plant roots, and press soil firmly around them.

Buying cauliflower plants for transplanting is less satisfactory than for other hardier types of brassica – cauliflowers suffer much more from the slightest check.

Care and development

The secret of success with cauliflower is rapid and continuous growth. From transplanting time onward they need copious watering. Even though the soil may be very rich as a result of its preparation it can do with even more feeding in many cases. There are several methods. One is to mulch the soil around the plants with rotted farmyard manure or garden compost three weeks after planting, drenching it with water afterwards. Another method is to work a top-dressing of a nitrogenous fertilizer, such as

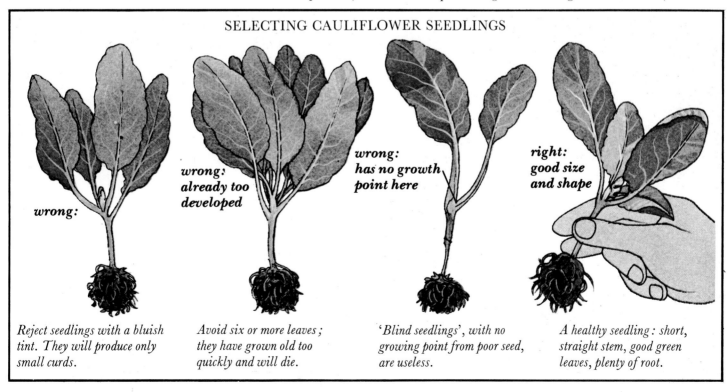

SELECTING CAULIFLOWER SEEDLINGS

wrong:

wrong: already too developed

wrong: has no growth point here

right: good size and shape

Reject seedlings with a bluish tint. They will produce only small curds.

Avoid six or more leaves; they have grown old too quickly and will die.

'Blind seedlings', with no growing point from poor seed, are useless.

A healthy seedling: short, straight stem, good green leaves, plenty of root.

1. *Before planting out seedlings at the four-leaf stage, dip roots into pesticide paste to avoid club root.*

2. *Keep a ball of soil around the root when transplanting, and in warm weather fill the holes with water before inserting the seedling. Take care to avoid any shock during the operation.*

3. *Dust with insecticide to guard against pests.*

4. *Water gently around the seedlings, using a rose on the can. Water the soil not the plants.*

5. *Fold back the inner leaves over the curd to protect it from direct sunlight.*

6. *Tie the leaves in position over the top of the curd with raffia or with a rubber band.*

7. *Harvest before curd opens. Cut horizontally with a sharp knife, leaving a few leaves around curd.*

8. *One storing method is to hang upside-down in a cool, dark place, spraying with water every night.*

ammonium sulphate or nitrate of soda into the soil around the plants with a hoe, again followed by a generous watering. This should be done five weeks after planting. Alternatively, the nitrogenous fertilizer may be dissolved in water and the solution used for watering the plants two or three times at regular intervals during the growing period.

As cauliflowers, especially the small varieties, are not strongly competitive plants, they should be thoroughly weeded throughout the growing period. A heavy mulch does have the effect of suppressing weeds for a time.

Harvesting the crop

One advantage of choosing your seed from seed catalogues instead of buying plants from nurseries is that you can make a selection of varieties which will extend your harvesting period.

A cauliflower is ready for cutting when the upper surface of the curd is fully exposed, and the inner leaves no longer cover it. If left in the ground longer, the head expands and loses its compactness. Cauliflowers can be held back if too many are maturing at once. Gather up the leaves and tie them together over the curd so that they cover it, using a piece of garden twine, a rubber band or raffia. This should take care of the plant for a week or more. Breaking the ribs of some of the leaves and bending the leaves over the curd will delay maturing for a few days. Another method is to pull up the plant complete with its roots, and hang the cauliflower upside down in a cool shed, away from strong light, spraying it with water every night. This will keep the plant fresh for up to three weeks.

When harvesting cauliflower, cut through the stem with a sharp knife, leaving sufficient leaves attached to the curd to form a 'frame' around it. Cut in the early morning, when the plant is freshest – ideally with dew on it. Cauliflowers can also be frozen successfully. With the addition of a cheese sauce, these frozen cauliflowers can provide almost instant and highly nutritious one-dish meals.

After-care

Unlike some brassicas, the cauliflower will not produce worthwhile shoots after its head has been cut. Clear the remains of the crop as quickly as possible, either burning the surplus leaves, stems and roots or putting them on the compost heap if they are free from pests and diseases. Chop up the stems and roots first.

Varieties

Early Snowball and Igloo.

Pests and diseases

All the pests and diseases common to brassicas attack cauliflowers, but two additional troubles affect cauliflowers and broccoli in particular.

Whiptail is a disorder in which the leaves become distorted to thin, whiplike thongs and the curd may be deformed, or not form at all. It is caused by a lack of the element molybdenum in the soil, usually as a result of continuous or too intensive cropping. Molybdenum is a 'trace' element, that is, one that is essential for the healthy growth of plants but which is needed only in minute amounts. The remedy for

this deficiency is to give the plot a rest from brassicas, to allow the soil to replenish its molybdenum resources. The natural process may be aided by applying a solution of sodium molybdate at the rate of 30g [1 oz] dissolved in 8 L [2 gal] of water to every 8.4 sq m [10 sq yd].

Another deficiency disease is caused by lack of the trace element boron. This causes browning and sometimes stunting of the curd, a hollow stem and distorted leaves. It is best dealt with by applying a light dusting of borax, but keep it light, since an excess can kill most plants.

Celeriac

Celeriac is a swollen root which tastes very much like celery. It is delicious eaten as a cooked vegetable or in salads, either raw or blanched.

Both celeriac and celery are cultivated crops that have evolved from wild celery, which grows in marshy meadows and ditches near the sea in northwestern Europe. But while celery has been developed for the sake of its stem, celeriac is grown for its root and is sometimes called turnip-rooted celery. Celeriac is not nearly as well known a crop, having been developed mainly in Germany and introduced elsewhere only in recent years. It has an aroma and taste similar to that of celery and it is used for flavoring soups, fish stocks and other dishes, as well as for serving

Celeriac
Apium graveolens rapaceum (fam. *Umbelliferae*).
Hardy biennial, grown as an **annual.**
Size: about 30 cm [1′] tall; edible roots are about 7.5-10 cm [3-4″] round.
Climate: temperate.
Planting to harvesting time: 24 weeks.
Yield: 8 to 10 plants per 3 m [10′] row.

1. *For indoor sowing, first prepare a seed tray and firm down compost.*

2. *Sow the celeriac seeds thinly and evenly in the seed tray.*

3. *Cover the newly-planted seeds with finely-sifted compost.*

4. *Water the surface of the compost lightly using a rose on the can.*

5. *Cover with black plastic and put in a warm, dry place to germinate.*

6. *After germination, replace with an inflated clear plastic bag.*

7. *Plant (but not bury) 30 cm [12"] in shallow drills 40 cm [16"] apart.*

8. *After plant has grown remove sideshoots from swollen root.*

9. *Scrape the soil away with a hoe so that at least half the root is exposed.*

10. *Earth up the root in mid-autumn to protect against the frost, until it is lifted.*

Though the shoots of celeriac can be eaten like celery, the plant is usually grown for its tasty root.

as a cooked vegetable or grated raw as a salad.

Suitable site and soil

Choose a fairly sunny, sheltered plot. Celeriac likes a reasonably rich soil, though not excessively so. The soil should be well-drained and, ideally, celeriac should be planted on a site which had a generous application of farmyard manure or garden compost in the previous autumn, well dug in. However, do not be discouraged if the soil does not match up to the ideal; celeriac will grow in most soils, provided they are not dry or very wet.

Sowing and planting out

Celeriac seed requires a soil temperature of 15°C [60°F] for germination. In most temperate climates this is reached in mid-spring, but celeriac requires a long growing season and it is advisable to sow the seed in boxes in a cold frame, indoors or in a heated greenhouse in early spring.

Sow about 0.5 cm [¼"] deep and cover lightly with soil. When the seedlings are big enough to handle, which will be shortly after they have reached the four-leaf stage, prick out into boxes with about 5 cm [2"] between seedlings. The seedlings should be gradually hardened off during the spring by opening the window or removing the glass or plastic covering – for a few hours around midday in sunny weather at first, and then for longer periods until protection can be dispensed with entirely.

Transplant seedlings into the permanent bed in late spring, putting them in rows that are 30-38 cm [12-15"] apart, with the plants about 30 cm [1'] apart in the rows. At this stage, the plants will already have slightly swollen root-bulbs. Plant with these at about surface level – above rather than below – and handle carefully to avoid any unnecessary disturbance to the roots.

Care and development

Water the young plants frequently after transplanting, and also during drought, but do not saturate. When nearly mature, the need for water lessens, and they can withstand a moderate drought with an occasional watering, but the final size will be decreased.

For most of the summer the crop requires little attention, except to be kept free from weeds – use the hoe frequently. Towards the end of summer sideshoots will start to sprout from the root. These should be removed. Scrape away soil around the root so that at least half of it is exposed, but in mid-autumn earth up the root to protect it from frost until lifting.

The leaves can be used as celery. It is more usual, however, to take just one crop – the roots.

Harvesting and storing

Lift the roots as required beginning in mid-autumn. They will tolerate moderate frost if left in the ground during winter. Do not lift for storing until hard frosts make it absolutely necessary, because the roots retain their flavor better if left in the ground. However, in very cold districts, they should all be lifted at the end of autumn and stored in boxes of sand or soil in a dry shed for use at any time during winter and early spring or covered with a heavy

mulch to permit digging a large part of the winter. Remove all the leaves except the small ones in the center before storing. There is little clearing up to be done after harvesting. The rather sparse foliage may be consigned to the compost heap or dug into the soil.

Pests and diseases

The same pests and diseases attack celery and celeriac, including the fungus disease celery leaf-spot, the larva of the celery fly and the carrot fly larva.

Celery

Winter celery needs time in preparing trenches and blanching, but the summer varieties are self-blanching. Both types are delicious eaten raw or cooked.

Celery has been developed from the wild celery, a plant fairly common in meadows and roadside ditches in maritime areas in many parts of the world. It has been bred mostly in Italy (first by the Romans) for its tall, thick stalks or 'sticks' which, blanched or not, are used both

---

Celery
Apium graveolens (fam. *Umbelliferae*)
Biennial, grown as an **annual.**
Size: 30-50 cm [12-20"] high, 7.5-10 cm [3-4"] in diameter.
Climate: temperate.
Sowing to harvesting time: 6-8 months; mature plants may be left in ground for several more months and lifted as required.
Yield: 12-15 plants, each 0.7-1 kg [1½-2 lb], per 3 m [10'] row.

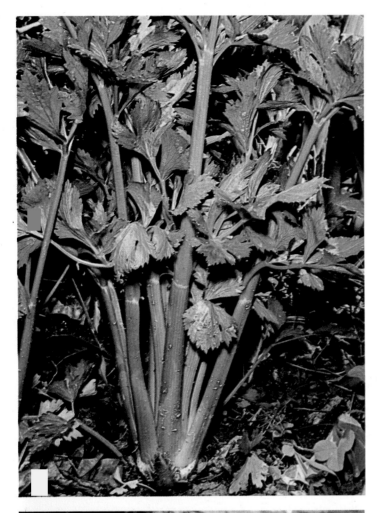

'American green' is one of the unblanched varieties of summery celery and, by far, are of the most popular types grown. These are transplanted earlier than winter celery, set out in blocks on a flat bed.

as a salad and a vegetable, also for flavoring soups and meat dishes. However, celery did not begin to be commonly grown in the rest of Europe until well into the nineteenth century.

Celery has been considered a specialist's crop, largely because of the labor and skill thought to be involved in trenching and blanching. In fact, these operations are not particularly difficult or time-consuming. For those who wish to avoid them, however, there are now self-blanching varieties of celery. There is also an increased demand for green celery by the public.

The winter varieties are quite hardy. The mature plants will tolerate moderate frost and, indeed, this seems to improve their flavor. In severe weather, however, any plants left in the ground should be protected by covering them with soil and then straw, hay or burlap. The summer varieties are less hardy than the winter ones, and they mature earlier.

Suitable site and soil

Celery does not grow well in shade, so choose a sunny, open location. The soil should be very rich, having been treated with farmyard or other organic manure in the previous autumn rather than immediately before planting. Deep, easily worked soil, moderately free from stones, is ideal. Avoid any soils which are definitely prone to waterlogging and also those such as light, sandy ones which dry out too quickly.

Sowing

Celery seed requires a temperature of 13-16°C [55-61°F] for germination. It is possible to wait until the outdoor temperatures rise to this level in spring, but you may prefer to gain a few weeks by sowing indoors in a greenhouse, or under frames or protective covers.

Sow in potting soil in a propagator, in a seed-tray or peat pots in a heated greenhouse in early spring, usually 10-12 weeks before setting out time, which is rarely before June 1st in northern states, because low temperatures can cause bolting (run to flower). The seed is very small and it is easier to sow if you mix it first with a little moist sand or vermiculite. Sow it 2 cm [¾"] deep and cover lightly with sifted compost. Water carefully and allow to germinate in darkness. Seed is treated with chemicals so do not use leftover seed as a herb in the kitchen.

Celery may take a long time to germinate – from 10 days to well over three weeks, depending on the temperature. The seedlings have the distinct celery scent and leaves with serrated edges. When they are large enough to handle, prick them out (except those in peat pots) into trays or boxes of potting soil, setting them out at 5 cm [2"] apart.

The succulent leaf-stalks of winter celery have a strong flavor, whether eaten raw in salads, or as a cooked vegetable. Green leaf tops make delicious soup.

1. *Dig trench 30 cm [12″] deep by 38 cm [15″] wide and lay down manure. Return soil short of ground level.*

2. *Plant in a single row 30 cm [1′] apart, then water. Remove sideshoots and wrap newspaper around stems.*

3. *Earth up when about 30 cm [12″] high. Earthing up should continue until the trench becomes a ridge.*

Catch-cropping summer celery: plant in blocks with lettuce (raised indoors from seed sown before celery).

4. *To harvest, first scrape back the soil.*

5. *Thrust fork well down to avoid damaging stems.*

For white summer celery, erect framework of stakes and sacking or plastic. Move this in as plants are taken.

Instead of sowing indoors, you may sow outdoors in fine soil under protectors or in a frame and thin the seedlings to 5 cm [2"] apart. In both cases, harden them off gradually by placing the seed-trays outdoors on sunny days, or by removing the protectors or opening the frames for a few hours each day.

Planting out winter celery

Plant out in late spring or early summer. Winter celery should be planted in previously prepared trenches. These should be about 38 cm [15"] wide by 30 cm [1'] deep and 90 cm [3'] apart. They can be dug at any time during the previous winter or early spring. Before planting, clean them out, removing the soil that has been disintegrated by frost and has fallen into the bottom of the trench. Fork over the bottom of the trench and put in a 10-15 cm [4-6"] deep layer of rotted farmyard manure or garden compost. Cover this with 7.5-10 cm [3-4"] of soil. Transplant the celery plants into the soil at the bottom of the trench in a single row, at a spacing of 30 cm [1']. Plant them firmly and water well.

Care and development

Water the plants frequently – never allow the soil to become dry. Applications of liquid manure will be beneficial, but avoid splashing the leaves. You may also give light applications of a dry balanced fertilizer, but work these well into the soil with a rake or hoe, and water in. If the plants throw out any sideshoots, remove them.

Blanching

When the plants are about 30-38 cm [12-15"] high, begin earthing them up. Choose a fine day, when the ground is fairly dry. First, tie the stems together just below the leaves, loosely with raffia, string or a rubber band. Then rake the loose soil from the edges of the trenches down into the trench around the bases of the plants, until it is about halfway up the stems.

Carry out further earthing-up operations at intervals of 2-3 weeks. Press in the soil quite firmly around the plants, but not too hard. Continue with the earthing-up process until only the leaves are showing above the soil. Your celery trench will then have become a ridge.

When earthing up celery, you should be very careful to prevent soil from penetrating into the spaces between the stems. Once this has happened, it is almost impossible to get the sticks completely clean in the kitchen. Tying the stems together and forking in the soil with care should prove satisfactory. A better method is to tie newspaper or cardboard around the plants before earthing them up, or shortly after transplanting, encourage the plants to grow through earthenware drainpipes. The blanching process will continue right through late summer and well into autumn.

Summer celery

With self-blanching varieties, a trench is unnecessary. These varieties are usually sown a week or two later than the others, as they are more inclined to bolt (run to flower); they will therefore be ready a little later for transplanting. Prepare the soil as for winter celery, digging in plenty of garden compost or well-rotted farmyard manure, but do not dig trenches; summer celery is grown on a flat bed. Set out the young plants in a 'block' arrangement not in rows, spaced 23 cm [9"] apart each way. The white varieties of summer celery, although often called 'self-blanching', do in fact need to be shaded from the light for complete blanching. By growing them in blocks, the outer plants cast shade on the inner ones and so blanch them. Erect a framework around the plants, and cover it with burlap, hardboard or black plastic sheeting to keep the outer plants blanched. The green varieties of summer celery do not need blanching at all.

Harvesting, storing and after-care

Lift winter celery as required, during autumn and winter. Light frost improves the flavor. Start at the end of a row and walk along it, lifting each stem carefully to avoid damaging the next in line. The bigger the plant, the crisper it is likely to be. The summer varieties are normally ready, earlier than the other, from the beginning of late summer onwards. As you harvest the white types, move the framework up to the next plants in the block to keep them blanched. You can leave winter celery in the ground until you need it. Cover the plants with straw or bracken in very cold or rainy weather. Summer celery is not frost-resistant and should be used as soon as it is ready.

After harvesting, put the leaves, outer stems and roots on the compost heap, and level the ridges. The soil is already well enriched for succeeding crops, but avoid replanting with carrots which are a member of the same family, to prevent a build-up of pests and diseases.

Pests and diseases

The chief pest of celery is the celery fly (*Philophylla heraclei*). The eggs hatch into tiny, leaf-mining maggots which tunnel into the leaf tissues of the plant during late spring, producing transparent blotches which turn pale brown and eventually shrivel the leaf. A second attack may occur in summer. Handpick badly affected leaves, and spray the remainder in spring and summer with malathion. Carrot fly larvae occasionally attack the roots of the plants (*see* CARROT) and, if celery is not thoroughly earthed up slugs can find their way into the heart and cause considerable damage.

The most troublesome fungus disease is celery leaf spot (*Septoria apii-graveolens*), prevalent in wet summers. Small brown spots appear on the leaves and may spread rapidly. Seed advertised as 'thiram-treated' should produce plants resistant to leaf-spot. If an attack develops, remove infected leaves promptly and spray the remainder with Bordeaux mixture or other fungicidal compound containing copper. Give the plants an extra application of a potash-high fertilizer.

Soft rot makes the centers of the plants soft, brown and slimey. Once the plants are affected they cannot be cured. The disease enters through wounds caused by pests, careless cultivation or severe frost. Virus diseases may also cause trouble; if these occur, the only course is to destroy the affected plants.

Cherry

These yellow, red or nearly black stone fruits can have a sweet or tart flavor and are eaten raw or cooked according to variety.

Cherries belong to the same genus, *Prunus*, as the peach, plum and apricot. They bloom early and need a sheltered site. They also require a period of winter cold to crop well. They do not thrive where summer temperatures are high, though sour cherries tolerate heat better than sweet cherries.

Fruiting cherries are divided into two species, the sour *Prunus cerasus* which need cooking, and the sweet *Prunus avium*, which can be eaten raw. The Duke cherries are a cross between the two, useful for both dessert and cooking, but their fruit is inferior to the best of the other two groups.

Sweet cherries

Sweet cherries are not suitable for a small garden as they form big trees, up to 14 m [46'], or considerably more, high

---

Sweet Cherry
Prunus avium (fam. *Rosaceae*)
Hardy deciduous tree, with a useful life of 50 years or more.
Size: 10-15 m [33-50'] or more high, 15 m [49'] across.
Climate: cool to warm temperate.
Planting to harvesting time: up to 6 years.
Yield: 100 kg [220 lb] per tree.

Sour cherry
Prunus cerasus (fam. *Rosaceae*)
Hardy deciduous tree, with a useful life of 50 years or more.
Size: 4 m [13'] or more high, 6 m [20'] in diameter.
Climate: cool to warm temperate.
Planting to harvesting time: 2 to 3 years.
Yield: 15-20 kg [33-44 lb] per tree.

---

and wide. Tree sizes and shapes vary greatly within the group, when they are usually sold as standards or half-standards. Birds are a great problem as the tree size makes them difficult to net. They flower before apples, from mid to late spring, and are therefore susceptible to frost. To do well they need a sheltered site open to the sun. They are also particular about soil.

Sweet cherries benefit from a pollinator, so it helps to plant two different varieties flowering at the same time, and in compatible pollination groups, to ensure that the fruit sets satisfactorily.

The fruit is generally heart-shaped and varies in color from nearly yellow to black. They are the earliest top fruit to mature, cropping from midsummer. In nursery catalogues sweet cherries are often divided into two groups by the color of their juice. 'Black' varieties have dark red juice and 'white' varieties have colorless juice. They can be further subdivided into Heart cherries with soft tender flesh, and Bigarreau with firm breaking flesh.

Sour or 'pie' cherries

Sour cherries are easier to cultivate than sweet cherries. Both are demanding as to soil, but sour cherries will thrive on a heavier soil. They also tolerate a greater degree of cold – they flower after sweet cherries – and so are more likely to miss the frost.

Unlike sweet cherries the sour ones are self-fertile, so a single tree will set fruit. They make smaller trees than sweet cherries. A Morello, one of the best varieties, may form dense bushy growth, often wider than it is high.

Most of the varieties are red, but the Morello turns almost black when left to ripen on the tree. Sour cherries come into bearing more quickly than sweet, and the crop of the mature tree is of a more manageable size.

CULTIVATION

The crucial consideration for cherries is drainage. Plums and apples will tolerate a degree of poor drainage but the cherry will yield poorly. Heavy soils are therefore best avoided as are dry sandy soils which will, in a drought, give small fruit and the minimum of flesh. Look to see if there are ornamental cherries in your area and how well they are doing as these need similar conditions to sweet and sour cherries.

A warm site is ideal, sheltered from prevailing winds. Frost at flowering time can be a problem and trees should be protected. In cool temperate areas, therefore, avoid valley bottoms and frost pockets. A slight slope with room for cold air to drain away at the bottom is ideal.

The soil should be well drained but capable of retaining water; a medium loam is therefore best. A soil test should show either a slight acidity or neutrality, a pH reading of 6.0-7.0.

Buying the tree

A stone sown in the garden will not produce as good a tree as recommended varieties, and may take as long as 15 years to fruit.

Sour cherries are self-fertilizing and can be planted singly. Morellos will pollinate sweet cherries if they are flowering

Montmorency is the best known of the American cherries.
It is very popular for use in pies and tarts.

Sour cherries are successful wall-trained, and are one of the few
fruits that will tolerate a sunless wall.

The Merton Bigarreau sweet cherry, one of the mid-season
varieties developed this century, is a heavy cropper with a fine
flavor. Sweet cherries are very particular about soil. They make
large trees, so you need plenty of room to grow them
successfully.

A mid-season white variety of sweet cherry, Napoleon is a good regular bearer which does well as a trained tree.

Morello is the best of the sour cherry types, and is self-fertilizing, so you need plant only one.

concurrently. However, it is essential for sweet cherries to have a pollinator. They divide into several pollination groups. One group contains what is known as universal donors, which will pollinate any other variety, but varieties in the remaining groups will only pollinate those of another group. The two you choose must also flower together, so check carefully.

Buy certified virus-free trees if they are available. These offer some protection against disease, and they grow and crop better.

Cherry trees are budded or grafted onto rootstocks. The best is the East Malling Mazzard F 12/1, while a tree on *Prunus avium* rootstock is always preferable. A semi-dwarfing rootstock Colt is being introduced.

Planting

Early spring planting is best. If the tree arrives too early, it can be heeled in (*see* APPLE) to wait for suitable conditions. If the roots are dry when the tree arrives, soak them in water. Before planting, trim any damaged roots and remove entirely any dominant downward-pointing root.

If you are planting more than one sour cherry, allow 6 m [20′] between them. Plant standard sweet cherries 7-10 m [23-33′] apart, depending on the vigor of the variety and plant trees on semi-dwarfing rootstock 5-7 m [16-23′] apart. Cherries are very susceptible to some weedkillers so remove all persistent weeds by careful digging. If they are to be planted in grassland, 3 sq m [10 sq ft] should be cleared around the tree position.

Dig a hole big enough to take the root system when fully spread out. Fork over the bottom and add a 10 L [2-gal] bucket of rotted manure, or the same quantity of moist peat. Plant the tree at the same depth as in the nursery, with the union with the rootstock (a slight swelling) 7.5 cm [3″] above the soil level. Hold the tree upright while you replace the soil, shaking it gently to settle soil around the roots. Firm each layer well before putting in the next.

Following planting and a good watering, dress the soil around the tree with two buckets of rotted manure or a mulch of straw. If the land is very dry or there is a prolonged rainless period after planting, regular watering of the young tree may be necessary, but otherwise the mulch should help to retain sufficient moisture.

Care of the tree

It is not wise to stake cherry trees, as any rubbing that occurs between the tie and the tree can lead to infection through the wound. If branches have to be tied, this should be done with a length of plastic tubing, which does not wound the branches. Cherry roots are vigorous and penetrate deep down into the soil. After the first watering when the tree is planted, watering is only necessary under drought conditions in the first few years.

Mulch around each tree in spring, before the soil dries out, with manure at the rate of a 10 L [2-gal] bucket per sq m [yd]. In addition trees on most sites will benefit from a spring application of 30 g per sq m [1 oz per sq yd] of a complete fertilizer. Every third year supplement this with 20 g per sq m [$\frac{2}{3}$ oz per sq yd] of superphosphate.

Keep a minimum of 3 sq m [10 sq ft] clear around the tree by hoeing. If the cherry rootstock produces suckers, these should be cut off where they are attached to the roots with a sharp knife. Once the tree reaches maturity, at ten years or more, grass may be grown up to the base of the tree, though this should be mown regularly.

TRAINING AND PRUNING

All cherries can be grown as standards. A new form for both types is the central leader pyramid, and the cherry may be trained in the same way as a pear (*see* PEAR).

When young, standard sweet cherries are pruned like apples to shape the head, but subsequently they need almost no pruning, as fruiting spurs are freely formed on older wood. After the shaping of sour cherries, pruning continues in order to encourage the production of new wood, which bears fruit the following year.

It is essential to remember never to winter prune cherries in the coldest areas. There, they should only be pruned in early spring, just before the leaf buds burst open. All the cuts should be made very smooth, without snags, and the larger ones painted with tree paint.

Pruning sour cherries to encourage fruit

In addition to any shaping, sour cherries may benefit from a light pruning after harvesting. They fruit on the previous year's growth, so the aim is to encourage new side-growth and gradually remove old shoots, when these are not needed for the shape of the tree. Prune back to a new sideshoot.

HARVESTING AND PROTECTION

Birds are a major pest of cherries; they may attack the buds in winter and consume and spoil fruit in summer. Net the tree with a 2.5 cm [1"] mesh plastic net. Stand on a stepladder and throw it over while someone helps you adjust and tie it in below. Sweet cherries do get too big to net effectively. Individual sprays can be protected with plastic bags but, by then, the crop is usually large enough to spare a part of the fruit.

Fruit ripens on the tree to develop flavor, so protect against birds.

For sweet cherries several picks at two or three day intervals are required. Cut through the stalks with blunt-nosed scissors and handle the cherries by the stalk. Take care not to damage the tree spur. A stepladder will be useful when you pick the higher branches. Pad it, however, to avoid scraping the bark. Sweet cherries can split if there is rain just before harvesting, so if rain threatens it may be better to harvest partially unripe fruit.

Pests and diseases

The principal diseases of cherries in the United States are brown rot, black knot (a cankerous trouble), mildew and leaf spot. Among the insects which can be troublesome are aphids, curculios, San Jose scale and Japanese beetle. For

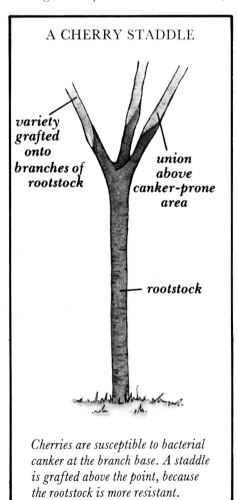

A CHERRY STADDLE

variety grafted onto branches of rootstock

union above canker-prone area

rootstock

Cherries are susceptible to bacterial canker at the branch base. A staddle is grafted above the point, because the rootstock is more resistant.

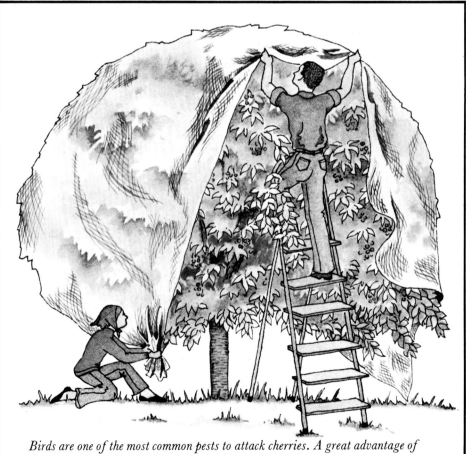

Birds are one of the most common pests to attack cherries. A great advantage of growing the smaller sour cherry is that a net can be thrown over the whole tree and be secured underneath for protection.

these and other less troublesome pests, obtain a locally approved spray chart from your own area Experimental Station or Extension Office. This will provide information about approved materials and local timings.

Varieties

Among the recommended varieties for cultivation in the United States are: (sweet) Bing, Black Tartarian, Napoleon; (sour) Early Richmond, Montmorency.

Care of the tree

Remember that trees trained against walls are always more susceptible to drought.

TRAINING AND PRUNING

Sour cherries are usually grown as bushes and can also be successfully fan-trained, but sweet cherries are really too vigorous for this form.

Because of the risk of infection the very minimum of pruning is recommended.

Training a sour cherry as a fan

For this popular European method, you will need a wall 2.5 m [8'] high and 6 m [20'] across. Wire the wall horizontally with 3 mm [⅛"] gauge wire at a spacing of 30 cm [1'] each. The best form is that used for peaches, with the central leader pruned out entirely and the fan built up from two opposite diagonal branches (*see* PEACH).

Training bushes

For a sour cherry bush, buy a maiden (one-year-old) and prune it off in the spring about 1 m [3'] from ground level, just above a good bud. This will induce lateral branches to grow out in subsequent years. No further pruning will be required for four to five years, with the exception of cutting out branches which rub each other, or any canker.

Bacterial canker (*Pseudomonas mors-prunorum*) is the most serious disease of cherries in Northern Europe, and the most frequent cause of death among the stone fruits. The bacteria gain entry through wounds and the scars left by leaves falling in autumn, and the disease develops during the winter to kill the bark and young growth, producing raised, cracked and flaking bark from which gum is often produced. If these cankers surround a stem or branch the portion above the canker will die the following summer; it may produce leaves but only of a pale green or yellow colour. The disease first appears on the foliage; sometimes buds are killed in spring, or 'shot-holes' appear on the leaves. Therefore trees should never be pruned in winter, and in late summer should be sprayed with Bordeaux mixture, repeated twice at three-weekly intervals.

The cherry fruit fly is a major pest in most cherry-growing countries outside Northern Europe. When it is sighted in spring, spray with derris or malathion 2-4 times at 10-day intervals.

Bacterial canker, the main European disease of the cherry.

1. *Saw below cankerous growths.*

2. *Make two cuts to avoid splitting.*

3. *Trim the stump to the line of the trunk with a pruning knife.*

4. *Cover scar with bitumen tree-wound paint.*

Chervil

A pretty plant which is one of the easiest herbs to grow, chervil provides sweet, fragrant leaves for flavoring throughout the year.

Chervil (*Anthriscus cerefolium*) is a hardy annual herb in the *Umbelliferae* family which grows to 30-45 cm [1-1½'] high and up to 30 cm [1'] in diameter. Its delicately feathery, bright green leaves make it an attractive plant to grow, and it does equally well in a garden or container – indoors or out.

Chervil has often been compared with parsley in both appearance and taste, but many gourmets find it superior in both respects as the flavor is slightly more peppery than parsley, with a hint of anise. It is most often used as a garnish, but the fresh leaves can be made into soup and, either fresh or dried, they are a subtle flavoring for potato dishes, salads, sauces and bouquets garnis.

The curly-leaved chervil is the most popular variety. There is also a smooth-leaved chervil, but this is not nearly as strongly flavored. When ordering your seeds, therefore, try to obtain the curly type.

Cultivation

Chervil grows best in semi-shady conditions. In full sun the plant flowers too quickly, which destroys the flavor of the leaves. It grows in any well-drained soil.

The herb may be sown successively at monthly intervals from early spring to early summer and again in early autumn. Sow the seed on top of the soil and rake the surface lightly. Germination takes place within 7 to 10 days.

If you plant more than one row, allow 30 cm [1'] between each. Thin the seedlings first to 15 cm [6"] and then to 30 cm [1'] apart.

Keep chervil well watered at all times. It needs no special feeding and it should produce a completely green bed which requires virtually no weeding.

Harvesting and propagating

The production of flowers in summer impairs the flavor of the leaves. For this reason the leaves should be clipped off when the plant reaches its full height, before the flowers form. If you make successional sowings in the spring, you will have a steady supply of young chervil leaves through the summer months. Then, if seeds are sown again in autumn, the leaves should stay green and be available for picking throughout winter and spring in the milder climates.

Propagation should always be from fresh seed as it does not remain viable for more than a short period. If you wish to propagate your own crop, let two or three of the curliest-leaved plants produce their white umbels of flowers and go to seed. Gather the seeds when ripe.

Storing the crop

Fresh leaves should be used immediately after picking because they wither very rapidly. Otherwise they may be dried. Unlike most herbs, which are simply hung upside-down to dry, chervil dries most successfully with a short, sharp blast of heat. Put the leaves in a basket or tray and place this over a low heater at night. By morning, the leaves should be crisp. Rub them together to a fairly fine texture and put them into an opaque, airtight container.

Chicory

Chicory, commonly known as endive in the United States and Europe, grows easily. The first season's leaves are eaten like spinach; the inner leaves produced by forcing during the second season are blanched and eaten as 'chicons' or 'witloof'.

Chicory, native to northwestern Europe, is known as endive in the United States and Europe and as chicory (which we use) in Britain, from its Latin name. It has dark green, dandelion-like leaves. The flowers are pale blue, about 2.5 cm [1"], and borne on tall, branched fibrous stems. Gardeners do not normally see the flower unless they want to obtain the seed. Improved varieties of wild chicory are much used in pasture for cows and sheep; and

The salad type of chicory is grown for both its heart and leaves, ideal for an early summer vegetable.

one European variety is cultivated for its roots which, when ground, are added to some blends of coffee.

Chicory is grown primarily for its blanched inner leaves or 'chicons' which provide welcome winter and early spring salad. They can withstand quite severe frosts down to −7°C [20°F] or even lower when fully mature. The leaves will die back in winter, but the roots will remain alive through periods of hard frost.

Sugarloaf or Sugarhat chicory is quite distinct. In autumn it produces a very close head of inwardly curled leaves, rather like Chinese cabbage in appearance, which will withstand moderate frost. Unlike the other varieties, it is not lifted in autumn and forced indoors but should remain where it is, providing a very acceptable winter salad, when other salad greens are scarce.

Suitable site and soil

An open site with not too much shade is ideal. The soil should be rich and 60 cm [2'] deep, and not waterlogged. Shallow or stony soils cause the roots to fork. In autumn dig deeply and apply rotted farmyard manure or garden compost so that it is completely absorbed during winter. A week or two before sowing, work in garden lime, if a soil test shows the soil is at all acid.

Sowing and planting

Sow in early summer in drills 1.5 cm [½"] deep and 30-38 cm [12-15"] apart, in soil worked to a fine tilth. When the plants are large enough, thin to 23-25 cm [9-10"] between each one.

Do not transplant; the plants should remain where sown for the entire summer. The roots reach their maximum growth in autumn, when the leaves start to die down.

Cultivation

Chicory does best when kept well watered and growing strongly. If the soil has been well manured beforehand, no additional feeding should be necessary. Vigorous growth will smother many of the smaller weeds, but use the hoe to remove larger weeds.

Harvesting the crop

A bonus crop may be taken from some varieties by cooking

Chicory flowers are very striking but will only be seen if the plant is allowed to go to seed.

Chicory (Endive)
Cichorium intybus (fam. *Compositae*)
Perennial, grown as a **biennial.**
Size: leaves grow to a height of 25-30 cm [10-12"] in the first year (when harvested); chicons (blanched shoots) 12.5-23 cm [5-9"] long.
Climate: cool temperate.
Sowing to harvesting time: 26-29 weeks from sowing to lifting the roots, which are then stored and forced at intervals during winter and spring.
Yield: 12-15 plants, each 125 g [4 oz], per 3 m [10'] row.

---

1. *To store chicory roots cut 2.5 cm [1"] above surface. Pull and trim.*

2. *Store roots in moist sand in a box and keep in a cool, dry place.*

3. *To force, cover roots in 23 cm [9"] of moist peat in a black plastic bag.*

4. *Inflate bag to keep top and sides off crowns; secure with string and tag.*

5. *Stand in a warm place and open plastic to check progress after 2-3 weeks.*

6. *Block hole in converted pot. Then pot and set roots 6.5 cm [2½"] apart.*

the leaves as spinach. During the summer either take a few leaves from a number of plants, in order not to weaken any one of them, or reserve certain plants for this purpose.

Sugarloaf or Sugarhat chicory will form tightly packed hearts in autumn and may be cut for salad as needed. When cutting, remove the soil down to the point where the heart joins the root; this will probably be 2.5 cm [1"] or so below the soil surface. Cut off the heart with a sharp knife, or pull up the plant and trim afterwards. The root of Sugarloaf chicory is not lifted and stored, as with other varieties. Chicory roots may be lifted in autumn and stored in boxes, or they may be left in the soil until shortly before being required for forcing. The former is the more satisfactory method, for roots left in the ground may start to sprout prematurely in mild weather or be impossible to dig from frozen soil.

Storing

The ideal method of storing is in boxes of moist sand. The roots are lifted and trimmed back to about 20 cm [8"] in length. The leaves are cut off to within 2.5 cm [1"] at the crown, which should have a diameter of about 7.5 cm [3"] at the top. The roots are then placed in closely packed horizontal layers, with moist sand between each layer. The boxes are stored in a cool, dry place free from frost. Any roots left in the ground will produce flower stems in the second year and should be saved only for producing seed. Otherwise consign the plants to the compost heap.

Forcing

About three weeks before the first chicory shoots, or 'chicons', are required for the table, take out the required number of roots and set them upright 5-7.5 cm [2-3"] apart in barrels, tubs, pots or some other container. Fill the container with damp sand or light soil. Quite good results can also be obtained by using moist horticultural peat, or moist potting soil. The crowns of the roots should be 2.5 cm [1"] or so below the surface of the soil.

Put the containers in a reasonably warm shed or cellar and cover them with boxes, black plastic, burlap or anything else that will keep them completely dark. The roots need a temperature of about 10°C [50°F] to start producing shoots. Give the sand an occasional sprinkling of slightly warmed water to keep it just moist, but do not, under any circumstances, overwater.

The chicons will emerge, white and spearlike, and will be ready to cut when about 10 cm [4"] above the surface of the soil. The crowns are below the surface, so pull up the root and cut off the chicon afterwards. The aim is to get a complete chicon, not one that disintegrates into separate leaves as soon as it is touched, and this can be achieved by cutting immediately above the crown. Use the chicons as soon as possible.

A second crop, smaller and poorer, may sometimes be taken by replacing the roots in the same container.

Pests and diseases

Chicory is remarkably free from the pests and diseases which attack other vegetables. The only trouble that is likely to occur is slugs. Scatter slug bait if needed.

Chinese Cabbage

**This crisp, crunchy cabbage
is more like a cos lettuce than
other cabbages. It can be eaten either
cooked or raw.**

Chinese cabbage, also known as Bak-choi, looks more like Romaine or cos lettuce than a cabbage. A distinctive feature is the thick, white central midrib of the leaves, and a network of prominent white veins, radiating from it, which gives the leaves a beautiful marbled look. Most varieties available have leaves that form a compact conical-shaped heart weighing 1.5 kg [3 lb] or more. In some varieties the leaves tend to form an open rosette rather than a heart. The leaf color ranges from a very delicate light green to dark green.

The leaves have a crunchy texture and a very delicate flavor, quite unlike that of ordinary cabbage. Very similar is Pe-tsai, or mustard greens (*Brassica pekinensis*), which resembles a large cos lettuce. It may be grown and used in the same way as Chinese cabbage.

Chinese cabbage is most useful in autumn and early winter when other fresh vegetables, particularly any suitable for salads, are getting scarce. It is very fast growing and is often ready for eating within nine to ten weeks of sowing. One of its drawbacks is that it is by nature a short-day plant, and tends to bolt, or run to seed, rather than forming a heart, if it is sown early in the year when the days are getting longer. For this reason, although it can be sown in a cool temperate climate any time from mid-spring, it is

---

Chinese cabbage
Brassica chinensis (fam. *Cruciferae*)
Half-hardy annual.
Size: 38-45 cm [15-18″] high and 30-38 cm [12-15″] across.
Climate: temperate.
Sowing to harvesting time: 12-16 weeks.
Yield: 10 plants per 3 m [10′] row.

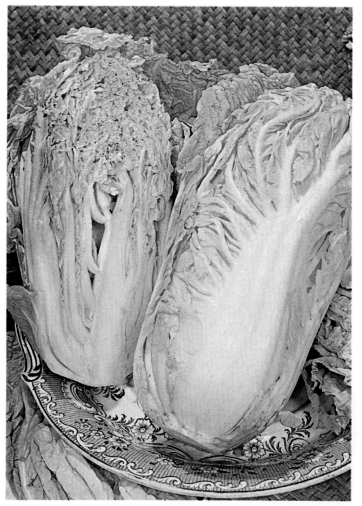

A freshly-cut 'Bak-Choi'. The plant is ideal for autumn salads when conventional green salads are scarce.

In order to blanch the heart of a Chinese cabbage, tie the leaves with raffia at both the top and bottom.

93

advisable to postpone the first sowing until early summer. For a succession, two subsequent sowings can be made in mid- and late summer.

Suitable site and soil

Chinese cabbage does best on a rich soil that retains moisture and is not too acid. It will tolerate light shade. It may be treated as a second crop, sown after an early summer crop, such as early potatoes, broad beans, peas or lettuce, has been cleared. No special soil preparation is necessary – just clear any weeds, and rake down the soil to a fine tilth. Avoid cramping Chinese cabbage. Plant it where the air can circulate freely to help prevent the leaves rotting, as they are prone to do in a prolonged damp autumn.

Sowing

Sow the seed thinly in rows at least 38-60 cm [15-24″] apart. Sowing individual seeds about 2.5 cm [1″] apart is a little more time consuming, but does make thinning later far easier.

If you are sowing in hot dry conditions, make sure the soil is thoroughly moist before sowing. Either water the ground very well beforehand, or draw out the drill; water the drill itself very carefully – a small-spouted can is best for this – until it is almost muddy. Sow the seeds in the drill, and cover them with dry soil from either side of the drill. This dry soil acts as a mulch, prevents the moisture beneath from evaporating, and ensures that the seeds get off to a good start.

Care and development

Chinese cabbage is a plant that needs moisture if it is to grow satisfactorily, so if the weather is very dry, watering may be necessary. An occasional very heavy watering is far more beneficial than intermittent light watering and, after watering, it is best to mulch the soil with a 5-7.5 cm [2-3″] layer of organic matter such as lawn mowings, spent mushroom compost or garden compost. This preserves the moisture in the soil and enables the Chinese cabbage to make steady growth even in a prolonged dry spell.

Start thinning as soon as the seedlings are large enough to handle, thinning in stages until they are 30-38 cm [12-15″] apart, depending on the variety. The only other care necessary is to keep the ground weed-free. The main pests are slugs, flea-beetle and gray mold.

Harvesting

The main season for summer-sown Chinese cabbage is early to mid-autumn. After this the quality of plants left in the open ground depends entirely on the weather. In dry, mild weather they can stand in good condition into winter, but in harsh or wet weather they deteriorate rapidly and may not last through the autumn. For this reason it is worth covering them with glass, if possible, in mid-autumn to protect them and prolong their useful season.

When required for use Chinese cabbage is usually lifted whole, though it is possible to take off a few leaves at a time, leaving the plants in the ground. Chinese cabbage can either be eaten raw in salads like lettuce or cooked.

Chinese Gooseberry

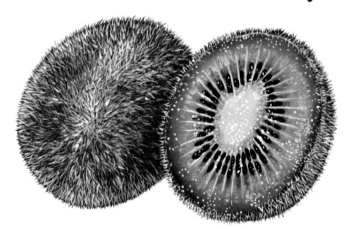

This hairy red-brown fruit with greenish flesh is larger and juicier than a gooseberry. The taste is slightly tart but it is eaten raw. It contains three to five times the vitamin C of a lemon.

This vigorous vine originated in Southeast Asia where it is known as the 'tree of health'; though it is very hardy when dormant, the spring growth and first flowers are frost tender. It will not crop properly in cooler climates or locations because it needs warmth to ripen the fruit. In the Mediterranean climate of the Southern Hemisphere it has been particularly successful. The plant is often grown solely for its decorative appearance. The new leaves are heart-shaped 15-23 cm [6-9″] long and 20 cm [8″] across; there is a cream and yellow variety *aureovariegata*, and a related ornamental species, *A. kolomikta*, has green, cream and pink leaves. The shoots are covered with dense reddish hairs and the flowers are borne in clusters on short stalks from the leaf axils. They appear in late spring and are 4 cm [1½″] across, fragrant, clematis-like and creamy white at first, turning to buff yellow in midsummer. The berries are the size of a hen's egg and contain numerous black seeds. Only female plants bear fruit, but a male plant must be planted with it for pollination.

Suitable site and soil

The plant can be grown successfully in cool temperate

Chinese Gooseberry
Actinidia Chinensis (fam. *Actinidiaceae*), also called kiwi fruit.
Hardy deciduous climbing vine with a cropping life of at least 20 years.
Size: vigorous varieties up to 9 m [30′] long.
Climate: cool to warm temperate.
Planting to harvesting time: 2 years.
Yield: mature vine 4-5 kg [8-10 lb].

Solid support is needed to hold weight of vines. Buy 2.5 m [8'] creosoted posts and insert them 45 cm [1½'] into the ground with a 1.8 m [6'] span across a garden path. Space 3.6 m [12'] apart. On top lay lengthwise 4 m [13½'] posts about 25 cm [4"] square. Slimmer poles 25 cm × 12 cm [4" × 2"] are fixed securely on top. Run wires lengthwise down the structure at 60 cm [2'] intervals. Plant female plant on one side. Train by regular pruning and tying in so it occupies the whole of the top. The male is planted the other side and trained lengthwise.

male plant kept pruned

3.6m [12']

1.8m [6']

2.2m [7']

female plant trained over top

wires to support laterals

path

PERGOLA CONSTRUCTION FOR CHINESE GOOSEBERRY

Prune established plants in early winter – above the last bud which bore fruit the previous summer.

Though Chinese gooseberries have 30 times the vitamin C of apples, they are often grown for ornamental use.

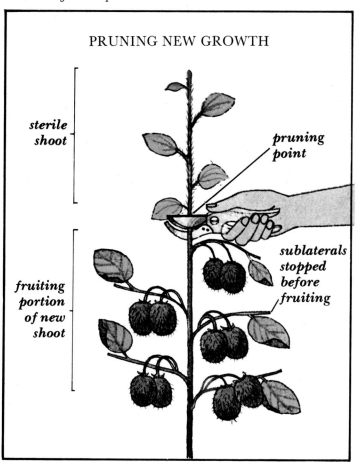

PRUNING NEW GROWTH

sterile shoot

pruning point

fruiting portion of new shoot

sublaterals stopped before fruiting

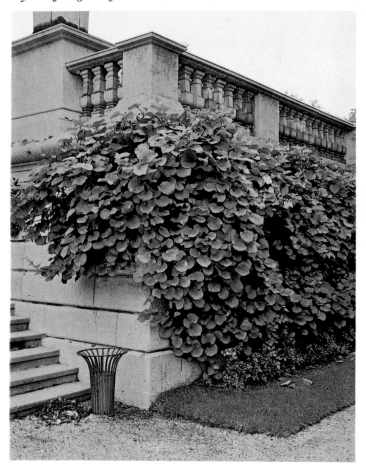

areas in sheltered sites; a wall facing the midday sun is best as the fruit is late developing and sun into the autumn months is vital for success. Low-lying areas and sites that are exposed to prevailing winds should be avoided. The Chinese gooseberry should be planted against a wall or fence, to which you have fixed supports. A trellis or wires spaced 30 cm [1f] apart are suitable and it will twine around them.

In a warm temperate climate the plant can be grown on a durable arch or pergola. It is slightly less tender than citrus fruit, though it should not be exposed to wind. The pergola should be sufficiently sturdy to support the weight of both stems and fruit. A system of wires, such as that described in BLACKBERRY, is also suitable.

Chinese gooseberries thrive on well-drained soil; a deep sandy loam is best as they dislike wet. Add bulky organic manures, garden compost or peat to the site, 12 L [2½ gal] per plant, some weeks before planting.

Cultivation

Though vines can be propagated from seed sown 0.5 cm [¼"] deep under glass in mid-spring, this is inadvisable. You will have to wait several years till the plants flower to determine their sex, while varieties do not come true to seed. You will do better to buy rooted cuttings of a plant of each sex from a nursery.

Set the plants 5.5-7.5 m [18-24'] apart depending on variety. Fork 0.5 kg [1 lb] of a good organic fertilizer into the bottom of the planting hole.

Once growing they require very little attention. On lighter soils a regular supply of water is needed if fruit is to grow to full size, especially during periods of drought. An annual top-dressing of rotted farmyard manure or other organic material in late winter is all that is needed to feed the plant.

It is only necessary to prune established plants. This is done in early winter and consists of pruning above the last bud which bore fruit during the preceding summer. In the following spring this too will develop into a branch, which will bear fruit the same year on the first 3-6 buds. The following winter it should be pruned in the same way. If the vines get into too great a tangle, and to keep the center open, you may prune hard; new shoots will arise along the length of the plant. There is no need to let the male plant grow to the same size as the female. It may be kept hard pruned to 2 m [8'].

Growing under glass

In cold areas or locations, the plants are best grown under glass, in potting mixture in large containers 30 cm [1'] across, which will help constrict growth. The climber must be given some support, such as a trellis or a string system such as that for cucumbers (*see* CUCUMBER). The female flowers will have to be hand-pollinated (by the method described under APRICOT). Give the plants liquid feed at regular intervals during the summer months.

Harvesting and use

After the flowers have set the first fruits begin to appear in midsummer and grow rapidly. Worthwhile crops are pro-

duced in about four years, maximum production is reached at about seven, though less vigorous varieties are slower. The fruit should be gathered in late autumn when the leaves begin to fall, and allowed to ripen indoors in a warm room. The fruit can then be kept in the refrigerator for several weeks. To peel the fruit, soak in warm water for a few seconds.

Chives

The hollow green leaves of chives are eaten for their delicate flavor, as an addition to other dishes.

Chives, *Allium schoenoprasum*, are the most delicately flavored of the onion family, *Amaryllidaccao*, and unlike the more familiar relatives are not grown for their bulb. Their "grass" is chopped up and added to salad, sauces and cooked dishes or mixed with cream cheese, although the small, bulbous root can also be eaten.

Growing wild across the Northern hemisphere, they will tolerate most soils and conditions, often growing all year round. The purple flowers and heads make the plant an attractive edging to the herb or vegetable garden and are very decorative in early summer. Chives can vary in height between 15 cm [6"] and 45 cm [18"], but the small varieties have the best flavor. Giant varieties are more suited to being grown for ornament.

Cultivation

The best site for chives is a warm border with partial shade, but they will grow in most positions. Profuse leaf growth is encouraged by providing a site of medium loam, enriched with leaf mold or well-rotted manure. Seed can be sown from early to late spring in the open ground or you can start in early spring with bulbs.

Chives started from seed are sown in shallow drills where the plants will continue growing. When the seedlings are up, thin them to 15 cm [6″] apart, or transplant the sturdier ones to a well enriched bed.

If bulbs are being planted, press them firmly into the soil, 22 cm [9″] apart, with their tips level with the soil surface, They become established quickly and grow into clumps. each having a large number of bulbs at the base. At this stage they should be lifted, preferably by mid-spring, split up and replanted. Clumps can also be lifted after the flowering period. Divided, replanted and kept watered, these will provide a good supply of young leaves in late summer. The flowers should not be allowed to go to seed.

Harvesting and maintaining

Cut the foliage with scissors, always leaving some "grass" to continue growing. No winter protection is needed but if foliage is wanted during the off season a glass-topped box, closed at each end, placed over the crop, will maintain or encourage fresh growth in late autumn or late winter. A clump can be grown for winter use, in a sunny window box or indoors in 10 cm [4″] pots. Chives need little attention once established in firm, humus-rich soil and if replanted to avoid overcrowding they seldom fall prey to pests and diseases.

Chive flowers make a decorative border but do not allow them to go to seed. Cut off buds to increase foliage.

Chive bulbs should be planted in early spring. Press firmly into prepared ground with the tips at soil level.

Harvest the chives with a pair of scissors. To maintain supply through late summer leave some foliage to grow.

Citrus Fruits

Oranges, lemons, tangerines and grapefruit are the most common citrus fruits. Each has a bitter rind enclosing juicy flesh. Citrus fruits are eaten raw, used to flavor a variety of dishes or to make drinks.

Citrus trees probably originated in Southeast Asia, the East Indies and India, and were comparatively slow to reach the Mediterranean. When Columbus took the orange to America it was a relatively new fruit. The best quality is grown in areas with a Mediterranean-type climate, such as California and Florida. Citrus fruit tolerates high temperatures – well over 38°C [100°F] – but responds better to regularly alternate cool and warm periods. During the dormant period most will tolerate a certain amount of frost. Below 10°C [50°F] they experience some check in growth, but a sudden hard frost is disastrous and even a lesser frost can damage ripening fruit.

Citrus flowers are produced chiefly on new growth, either singly or in clusters in spring. They are about 2 cm [$\frac{3}{4}$''] across and are very fragrant. Lemons, however, flower throughout the year in warm habitats. Pollination is by insects, though fruit is also produced without fertilization. While the fruit is forming, it contains a high percentage of citric acid, which is replaced by sugars as maturity is reached, up to 90% of the eventual juice content. The pulp is contained inside a white pith of varying thickness.

TYPES OF CITRUS

The lemon, *C. limonia,* is a small tree or spreading bush which droops more than the other citrus trees. It has irregularly placed branches and stout spines. It is widely grown in areas with a Mediterranean climate, but is intolerant of cold and very sensitive to changes in temperature. Under natural conditions it will blossom almost continuously, though it produces too many flowers for them all to set. The big advantage, however, is that ripe fruit is available throughout the year.

The fruit is greenish to yellow 7.5-12.5 cm [3-5''] long, with a knob at the bottom. The acidity of its fruit is a virtue in the kitchen, where it is often used for flavoring. Though frost has a damaging effect on fruit on the tree, lemons need less heat to ripen than the orange.

The lime, *C. aurantifolia,* another small tree with green fruit up to 4 cm [$1\frac{1}{2}$''] wide, is grown instead of the lemon in tropical areas. **The citron,** *C. medica,* is a slightly larger tree, bearing fruit shaped like a lemon or pear which can be up to 20 cm [8''] long. Of this group of acid fruits, the lemon is the best choice for the home gardener.

The sweet orange, *C. sinensis,* makes a round-topped tree

> **Citrus fruit**
> Sweet orange *Citrus sinensis,* sour or Seville orange *C. aurantium,* mandarin or tangerine *C. nobilis deliciosa,* lemon *C. limonia,* grapefruit *C. paradisi,* lime *C. aurantifolia* (fam. *Rutaceae*)
> **Nearly hardy evergreen trees** with a useful life of 80-100 years and 30-40 years in a pot.
> **Size:** lemons are the smallest at 2.5 m [8'], grapefruit the largest reaching 12 m [40'], oranges grow to 7.5 m [25'], tangerines are smaller at 4.5-6 m [15-20'].
> **Climate:** warm temperate and sub-tropical.
> **Planting to harvesting time:** 2 years for lemon and grapefruit, 4 for orange if conditions are favorable.
> **Yield:** a pot tree will give about 3 dozen fruits, lemons 45-65 kg [100-150 lbs], oranges 65-110 kg [150-250 lb], grapefruit 110-135 kg [250-300 lb].

---

with regularly arranged branches and slender spines. It is more resistant to cold than the lemon and nearly hardy. It is the hardiest of all citrus trees except the tangerine. The navel orange has a second, very much smaller fruit inside the peel at the end of the main fruit. The blood orange, *C. melitensis,* is a variety of the sweet orange with red juice.

The Seville, bitter or sour orange, *C. aurantium,* is similar in appearance to the sweet orange. Though the pulp is sour, it is celebrated as the raw fruit for orange marmalade.

The tangerine (originally tangierine – from Tangiers), mandarin orange, *C. nobilis deliciosa* grows on rather smaller trees than the orange. The fruit is bright orange or reddish, usually with many seeds but sometimes seedless, and peels very easily. It is the hardiest of the citrus.

The calamondin or Panama orange, *C. mitis,* which fruits when only 60 cm [2'] high, is becoming popular as a house plant. Its tiny fruits are sour and best used for marmalade.

The grapefruit, *C. paradisi,* was once considered an improved form of the shaddock or pummelo, *C. maxima* (syn *C. grandis*). It grows into a large tree and the fruit comes in clusters like grapes, which gives it its name. The tree is very sensitive to cold, especially when young. The peel is yellow and the flesh creamy or pink; the fruit is 15 cm [6''] across. The tangelo and ugli are hybrids with tangerines.

The kumquat, *Fortunella japonica,* is not a true citrus but is a closely related shrub or small tree growing up to 2.5 m [8'] high, with dark glossy leaves and small orange-like fruit 2.5-4 cm [1-1$\frac{1}{2}$''] across. They have slightly acid pulp but a sweet spicy peel and as a result are eaten whole, either in syrup or as marmalade. Kumquats have the advantage that they will grow in colder areas than true citrus fruit.

Poncirus trifoliata is much used for citrus root stocks, as it increases their resistance to frost. It has been crossed with the sweet orange to produce the citrange, which is hardy in mild parts of the cool temperate area. This tree is also grown for its ornamental appearance, as the fragrant white flowers are up to 6.5 cm [2$\frac{1}{2}$''] wide. The fruit, which are orange to yellow, are golf-ball size with aromatic and subacid pulp.

CULTIVATION

Citrus fruit are grown outside in warm temperate areas. It is necessary to avoid frost spots when fruit on the tree may be damaged, and some shelter from prevailing winds should be provided, particularly for young trees. In cool temperate areas citrus fruits can be successfully cultivated outdoors in summer, provided they winter indoors away from frost. This characteristic led to a large number of 'orangeries' being built in Northern Europe from the eighteenth century onwards. A minimum of 5° to 7°C [40° to 45°F] should be maintained and sudden change of temperature avoided. The trees should be planted in tubs or pots. Once filled the pots are fairly heavy, so the most convenient, and easiest, way to move them is to have wheels attached to the bottom of the final container.

Citrus are fairly tolerant as to soil, but it must be deep with good drainage. A light to medium loam that is slightly alkaline is best. Heavy soils will be improved with the addition of manure or garden compost and some coarse

(*Above*) Limes grow on small trees. In the tropics they replace lemons for drinks and most kitchen uses.

(*Right*) Valencia oranges, a popular variety of sweet orange, ripen late and have a long fruiting season.

(*Right*) Tangerine trees resist cold better than other citrus fruits.

(*Below*) A lemon tree has spines and a rather straggly, irregular shape.

1. *For seeding, plant single pips 1.5 cm [½″] deep in 7.5 cm [3″] pots.*

2. *Pips produce several seedlings; pick off the less vigorous ones.*

3. *With clay pots, soak in a bucket of water to prepare for potting.*

4. *First put in a layer of broken clay pottery to a depth of 4 cm [1½″].*

5. *In hot weather the plant should be sprayed every evening.*

6. *Regular watering will prevent the roots from drying out.*

7. *Empty stale earth, leave root ball and repot with fresh potting soil.*

8. *If tree is pot-bound stretch out roots and clip back to two-thirds their length with clippers.*

9. *As the tree grows, place it in tub with castors. Mulch should be added but the stem left clear.*

10. *The Versailles caisson, with sliding sides, enables the earth to be changed without repotting.*

sand. In warm areas grass should not be grown under the tree.

Raising citrus fruit from seed

Growing citrus from seed is not such a gamble as it is with other fruit. They produce polyembryonic seeds, which means that more than one plant may grow from each seed. If you discard the least vigorous seedlings, the selected seedlings should come reasonably true to type. Plant lemon or orange seeds 1.5 cm [½″] deep in sandy soil in early spring, singly in 7.5 cm [3″] pots. They need a temperature of 13-15°C [55-60°F] to germinate, which takes about three weeks. Leave the seedlings for two years in these pots then transplant them into 10 cm [4″] pots. In the fourth spring transplant again into a bigger pot.

The main disadvantage of seed sowing is that they are slow to fruit – cropping may be delayed ten years. However, trees raised from seedlings are slightly more hardy than those raised vegetatively, and they are all very long-lived.

Buying a tree

Commercial trees are two to three years old and usually budded onto rootstocks of various types. The sweet orange, *C. sinensis*, gives good trees, cropping well, but is susceptible to root rot. The sour orange, *C. aurantium*, resists this and is good for drought and exposed areas. It has proved the most popular in California. There, the rough-skinned variety of the lemon, *C. limonia*, has proved best; this is good for soils with a high sand content. *Poncirus trifoliata* is more hardy than the others and has been used to try to develop a tree that will withstand cold. The type of stock does not much affect the quality of the fruit, so the stock is chosen according to local conditions.

Planting out

Spacing depends on the height of the species chosen. The diameter should be the same as the height; for example the lemon grows to 2.5 m [8′], so you should allow 2.5 m [8′] space.

Many nurseries supply trees in plastic or metal containers; these may be left a few days before planting if they are watered. Trees with bare roots must be soaked for an hour or so and then planted quickly. The roots of citrus dry very rapidly, and if possible they should never be left without moist wrappings.

Prepare the site about a month in advance by digging in rotted organic matter. Dig a hole 60 cm [2′] deep and wide and plant, firm and water your citrus like other fruit trees (*see* APPLE).

Watering

Roots must not be allowed to dry out. Evergreens are particularly vulnerable to lack of water; and drought while fruit are ripening makes them pithy and juiceless. The trees will benefit from a daily syringe with a fine spray of water in the evening in hot weather.

Feeding

Crops from a mature tree are heavy so this drain on the tree must be made good. Manure or garden compost may be applied twice a year, at the start of the growing season and halfway through it, at the rate of four 12 L [2½ gal] buckets a time. Failing this, from about the sixth year, give them sulphate of potash at the rate of 30 g per sq m [1 oz per sq yd] for the area covered by the tree; the amount will therefore increase with tree size. Where manure is used, give half these quantities.

Citrus trees suffer from deficiency diseases, that is, a lack of the trace elements which are essential to growth. These can be replaced by foliar feeding, so you should seek local advice.

Pruning

Bought trees will have a formed framework so little pruning is required. Pinch out the growing tips of trees grown from seed at three years to keep them bushy. Too crowded or crossing branches are cut out to keep the tree reasonably open. In warm areas it is essential to keep a cover of foliage, as strong sun on the woody parts will cause damage. Water shoots arising inside the tree, usually on the upperside of the branches, which quickly outgrow the supporting branch and therefore ruin the shape of the tree. These should be removed when young unless they are required to fill a gap. Lemons are pruned more than other citrus fruit, as they are inclined to be straggly, and are prone to water shoot development.

In the greenhouse

In cool temperate areas citrus trees need wintering under glass and can be raised there entirely. The main requirement is for light and for a minimum temperature of about 4° to 10°C [45° to 50°F]. The lemon will stand a night temperature of 4°C [40°F], the orange likes a daytime temperature of 10°C [50°F]. In early to mid-spring the temperature should be allowed to rise to 21°C [70°F], and in the summer when the tree may be moved into the garden or patio until early autumn, a temperature of 27°C [80°F] is clearly desirable.

Choose a container with drainage holes and put a layer of drainage material at the bottom. Fill with a good potting soil or equal parts by volume of loam, sharp sand, peat, or leaf mold or manure. Add 30 g [1 oz] of superphosphate, or 15 g [½ oz] if you have used manure.

Pot cultivation offers a convenient method of keeping an orange tree small. Use the smallest pot that will take the roots of the new tree. At three years old it may be transplanted into a 25 cm [10″] pot and three years later into a larger one, and so on to a maximum size of 60 cm [2′].

Fresh compost should be given to the tree each year, or at least biennially; the tree is repotted at the end of every winter even when there is no need for change in pot size. Water it, then lay the pot on its side. Do not disturb the soil around the roots, but remove all the rest and replace with new. During this operation any long root curling around the pot can be pruned to two-thirds its length. When the tree has been moved into its final pot or tub, more shifting is abandoned, and it is mulched annually with rotted manure or garden compost.

Watering must be regular in summer, though in winter the tree may be allowed to get almost dry. Liquid feed can

Before they fruit citrus trees produce fragrant flowers, like the blossom of the Ruby Red grapefruit shown here.

be given in summer while the fruit is swelling. Spray the leaves with clear water daily in warm weather and once a week in winter. On warm days when the tree is still under glass, ensure that it is adequately ventilated. ↘

Harvesting

The best quality fruit – and the best to store – is that which reaches a good size before coloring, though oranges may be ripe when green. A steady temperature above 18°C [65°F] is needed. Healthy trees produce very heavy crops of fruit. Except for lemons and limes, most citrus fruit are left on the tree until mature. Fruit are not likely to ripen all at once, and the picking season is therefore spread over many weeks. Though the skin appears tough, it is susceptible to damage and mold will result. Use pruners to separate the fruit from the tree. Lemons should be stored at 16°C [60°F] until ripe.

Propagation

Semi-ripe cuttings of new sideshoots 7.5-10 cm [3.4"] long can be rooted with the help of a mist propagator or a plastic tent and rooting hormone. They may take in under a month but it could be eight months before they root. Rooted plants may then be potted and gradually hardened off before planting out about a year after rooting. These cuttings are unlikely to be as vigorous as plants which have been budded from a nursery, or as those produced from seed, and they may be more susceptible to certain diseases.

Pests and diseases

Scale insects, whitefly and aphids are likely to attack the trees. Canker is a bacterial disease affecting the bark and also producing spots on the leaves. Since the pests, troubles and timings vary greatly from region to region, it is best to consult your local Extension Office or State Experimental Station. If you are growing citrus as ornamentals, you will obtain reasonable control with malathion and a clean-up spray of summer oil in May or June.

Attacks by moths and fruit flies may be severe in some areas. Again, check local restrictions or regulations regarding their control or erradication.

Inside, scale can normally be cleared away by a soap and water washing. Check with local authorities.

Collards

SEE **CABBAGE**

Coriander

Coriander seeds are used whole or ground in curries, chutneys and desserts. Young leaves are used as a garnish, in salads and for flavoring fish.

Coriander (*Coriandrum sativum*) is a hardy annual herb 45 cm [1½'] high in the *Umbelliferae* family which is grown mainly for its slightly orange flavored seeds. Whole, they may be added to rice dishes, curries and chutneys and used in pickling fish. Ground, they are excellent in curry dishes, and go well with roast pork and baked ham. The powder can be sprinkled on custards and used in Eastern pastries, and cakes such as gingerbread. Coriander is one of the flavorings in gin and may be added to a hot rum toddy.

Before coriander goes to seed, the young leaves may replace parsley as a garnish and be added to salads, curries and fish.

The plant is an attractive bright green with round, upright stems, deeply divided shining leaves and small delicate white flowers, sometimes tinted mauve, which appear in early summer. These are borne in umbels of five to ten flower stalks, springing from a common point like the ribs of an inside-out umbrella. Before the seeds are ripe in late summer the plant develops a disagreeable smell. The name coriander comes from the Greek *koris* meaning a bug – its odor was thought to be like that of bedbugs. As they ripen this disappears and they become pleasantly aromatic.

Cultivation

Coriander is extremely easy to grow and, although it prefers light, warm, rich soil, it will grow almost anywhere. Propagation is from seed, which is rather slow to germinate. It can be sown in drills 1.5 cm [½"] deep and 30 cm [1'] apart either in late autumn or in spring. It can also be sown under glass in early spring in a temperature of 15°C [60°F] for planting out in late spring. When the seedlings are established, thin out the rows so that the individual plants are at least 20-23 cm [8-9"] apart. All that is needed in the way of care is to keep them free of weeds and, for the best results, to water when the weather is extremely dry and warm.

Harvesting and storing

Classically, coriander is reaped with a sickle, but for small quantities scissors or shears will do. The seeds tend to fall the moment they become ripe, so watch out from the beginning of late summer and harvest them quickly when they turn beige. Tie the seed-heads in bunches and dry them in a warm, dark, airy place over sheets of paper to catch the seeds. Store in opaque, airtight jars.

Corn

SEE SWEET CORN

Corn Salad

This extremely hardy plant grows well in a dry, sandy soil and will provide a welcome supply of salad during the winter months.

Corn salad is at its best at the blank and bleak end of the salad calendar – mid to late winter. The slightly earthy taste of 7.5 cm [3″] long leaves is reminiscent of cos lettuce and dandelion, and is much esteemed by epicures. It is also known as lamb's lettuce, possibly because the height of its season coincides with lambing, possibly because sheep, especially in Europe, enjoy huge quantities of the wild plant while grazing. It can be grown for picking at any time of the year, but the best time for a first sowing is in late summer. with two or three successional sowings up to mid-

autumn. In cooler climates, sowings can begin in mid-summer. These sowings will provide a supply of corn salad where winters are mild, when other salad crops are not usually available in the garden and are expensive to buy.

Suitable site and soil

Choose soil which has been well cultivated, and preferably enriched for a previous summer vegetable crop. A sandy soil suits these plants especially well. Corn salad makes most of its growth when the amount of daylight is decreasing, so a sunny spot is vital to maintain progress.

Cultivation

Make shallow drills 15 cm [6″] apart and sow the seeds 1.5 cm [½″] deep. Thinning is not essential but for a neat look thin the plants to 15 cm [6″] apart. Although corn salad is fully hardy – it can withstand fairly severe winters – you can keep its leaves fresher during hard weather by covering the plants with a portable cold frame from late autumn onward. If the frames are not available, straw or hay drawn up over the plants will achieve somewhat the same results. Birds and slugs are the only pests, when plants are young.

Harvesting

Ideas on how to harvest corn salad differ. Some prefer to cut whole plants, as with lettuce, but it is probably wiser to pluck tender young leaves from different plants as they grow, just as you would gather spinach or kale. Make sure, however, that you do not take too many leaves from each plant – no more than two or three – otherwise, you may weaken it beyond recovery. Wash the leaves well to remove any soil or grit, and use as soon as possible after harvesting.

If you do not like the slightly bitter taste of corn salad, you can partially blanch the plants to create a milder flavor. Do this by placing boxes or plant pots over them for a few days.

Protect young plants from birds, and from slugs after rain.

Corn Salad
Valerianella locusta (fam. *Valerianaceae*) also known as lamb's lettuce.
Hardy annual.
Size: grows to 15-23 cm [6-9″] high.
Climate: cool temperate.
Sowing to harvesting time: 5-6 months.
Yield: about 20 plants per 3 m [10′] row.

Courgette

SEE ZUCCHINI

Crabapple

Crab apples produce a tart fruit, about 2.5 cm [1″] across, which make excellent jelly and preserves.

The crab apple, *Malus sylvestris* (*Rosaceae*), makes a fine ornamental tree, rivalling the ornamental cherries when covered with spring blossoms, and covered with yellow, red or orange fruit in autumn. They are longer lived than many other apple trees. Though standards are common, crab apples are available on the same dwarfing rootstocks as other apples. They are often planted in the ornamental section of the garden where they are useful as a pollinator for other apples. Not all apples are edible.

For cultivation *see* APPLE.

Cress

Common cress (left) shown with mustard (right), land cress and watercress are all peppery little plants, easily grown for use in the kitchen.

The name cress is used rather loosely for a variety of salad plants, most of which belong to the mustard group of the *Cruciferae* plant family.

The three main types of cress are similar for culinary purposes, but are grown in different conditions, so the gardener may choose the one which is best suited to the available space and situation. Common cress is often grown indoors in trays, land cress is a hardy, year-round outdoor crop, and watercress is grown in a pure natural stream, a flooded bed or a container of fresh water.

COMMON CRESS

Common cress (*Lepidium sativum*), which is also known as garden cress or pepper cress, is often grown as part of 'mustard and cress'. It is the seedling stage of a plant which is a native of Iran; the adult plant, which grows to about 45 cm [$1\frac{1}{2}$], has small white flowers. There is also Golden or Australian Cress, which is shorter, grows more slowly and is a yellowish color.

Cultivation

Common cress is best grown indoors at the times of year when other salad plants are rare.

It is essential to sow fresh seed. It is not satisfactory to grow common cress outdoors in the open ground because it is easily beaten down by rain or overhead watering, and it readily becomes spoiled. Seed which is more than a year old will germinate at different rates, and the younger seedlings will be choked by the older ones.

If you want to grow it with mustard, cress should be sown three days before to be ready for cutting at the same time. Quantities of mustard and cress required at any one time are not great; a standard seed tray $35 \times 20 \times 5$ cm [$14 \times 8 \times 2″$] will hold a crop of about 125 g [4 oz].

For a succession, sow the seed once a week, allowing 8 days to cutting in autumn and spring, 7 days in summer and 11 days in winter. 15 g [$\frac{1}{2}$ oz] of cress seed will fill a standard seed tray in autumn and spring; in winter 20 g [$\frac{3}{4}$ oz] will be needed. Half fill a 5 cm [2″] deep container with either a standard potting soil mixture watered well, or with peat soaked in a liquid fertilizer. The growing medium needs to be well watered beforehand as watering during growth can result in damping-off, or rotting.

Sow the seed evenly and thickly on the surface, press it lightly into the growing medium and cover with a black plastic sheet, or glass and brown paper. The temperature should be 10°C [50°F] at night, rising to 18°C [65°F] maximum during the day.

Germination will occur about four days after sowing, when the covering should be removed and the seedlings given a good light and kept in the same temperature as when sown. The atmosphere should be moist.

Harvesting

Cress can be cut when just over 0.5 cm [2″] high, doing the cutting 0.5 cm [$\frac{1}{4}″$] above soil level. Use quickly once it is ready.

LAND CRESS

Land cress, *Barbarea praecox*, which is also known as yellow

105

1. *Cress grown with mustard should be sown three days before. Keep the box covered until after germination.*

2. *Mustard and cress seedlings can be harvested with a pair of scissors, two to three weeks after sowing.*

1. *Thin land cress out to about 20 cm [8"] apart.*

2. *Pick only the outer leaves at first, but when these become tough, take the larger central ones instead.*

3. *Remove flowering stems to encourage new leaves.*

cress, bank cress, early winter cress and American cress, is one of the few herbs or salad plants which can be grown outdoors for eating all year round, including winter, in mild regions. It is exceptionally resistant to cold weather. Land cress used to be very popular as a winter salad and is well worth reintroducing into the herb garden. Although a perennial, it is usually treated as an annual, with a succession of sowings each year throughout spring and summer.

A compact plant, it forms a rosette of lobed leaves, several inches in diameter and about 15 cm·[6"] high. If allowed to seed, it will send up flowering stalks 30 cm [1'] or more high, bearing small white flowers.

Cultivation

Land cress is easy to grow, makes only small demands on space and has the great advantage that it thrives in the shady, damp corners most other plants will not tolerate. It should be planted in a damp border shaded from the direct rays of the summer sun. The cress is also an excellent crop to grow in tubs or boxes in a shady part of a patio. Land cress thrives in a rich, moist soil. Add generous applications of well-rotted animal manure or garden compost. A top layer of organic matter helps to retain moisture within the soil.

First sowings can be made in early spring, as soon as hard frosts are over, with a succession of sowings at three-week intervals throughout the summer. Sowings can be continued right into late summer for winter use.

Sow in drills – shallow furrows – about 0.5 cm [¼"] deep, the rows being 30 cm [1'] apart. After a few weeks, when the plants are large enough to handle, either thin to about 20 cm [8"] apart or transplant into rows with 20 cm [8"] between the plants. The thinnings are good to eat too.

Watering is as important in spring as in the height of summer for, without it, the seeds can take a long time to germinate and there is the danger of weeds taking over. Weeding is not easy as cress seedlings are very similar to those of several common weeds. Sow the seed in marked rows, so that at least the space between the rows can be kept clear of weeds in the early stages by hoeing.

Harvesting and after-care

One of the attractions of land cress is that you need only pick a few leaves at a time. Under favorable conditions, the first pickings can be made about eight weeks after sowing. At first, pick only the outer leaves, allowing the center to continue producing new ones. Later, when the outer leaves tend to toughen and discolor, pick the larger of the central ones. The leaves, at their best, will be deep

Common cress must be eaten soon after it is harvested but curly cress is more resilient which makes it good for garnishing. Both are grown in exactly the same way.

Prepare the watercress bed with peat and soil. Flood it and, when drained, broadcast but do not cover the seed.

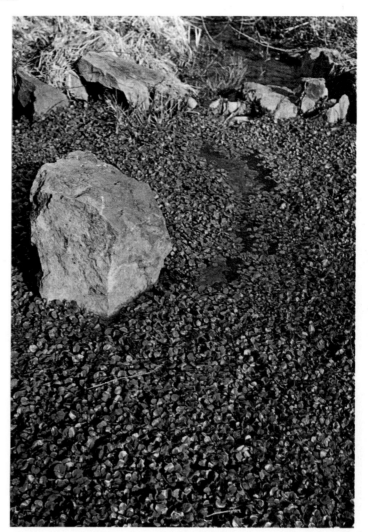

A watercress bed should be in a partly shaded place and must be kept moist. Sow in mid-spring or late summer.

green and succulent. Keep pinching back; do not allow the cress to get too lanky. Removing flowering stems will encourage the continued production of leaves. Picking can go on indefinitely if the plants are well watered and growing vigorously.

If the plot of ground is required for another crop, simply dig in what remains of the cress plants. They make excellent green manure for conditioning the soil.

Plants which are being kept through the winter where the climate permits need complete protection only in severe weather. Then the frames in which they are being protected may need to be covered with sacking during extremely severe spells of hard frost. This should, however, be removed during the day because the plants need light. A little ventilation may also be given on all but the coldest days. During winter, watering should not be necessary, but be sure the soil is moist.

When spring arrives, remove the protective coverings and fork around the plants, mulching with a little compost or rotted farmyard manure if available, and sprinkle with a general fertilizer.

Pests and diseases

The only pests likely to give trouble are snails and slugs. Scatter slug and snail bait as required.

WATERCRESS

Watercress is *Nasturtium officinale*, a hardy annual. There are two types: green cress, which is best for summer supplies, and brown, best for winter and spring.

Cultivation

You must be very careful about the water in which you grow watercress. Never plant it in a garden pool. If you have access to a natural stream you can sow along the bank about 15 cm [6″] above the water line, but you must be sure the water is free from pollution. It is best grown in a permanently moist and partially shaded position from seed sown in mid-spring or late summer.

Dig the soil deeply and incorporate moisture-holding peat or other organic material. The surface of the bed should be about 2.5 cm [1″] or so below that of the surrounding soil. Firm and rake the bed and flood it with fresh water. When the water has drained spread the seed generously. Do not cover it with soil. Seedlings will be ready to eat from about two weeks after sowing. Watercress bought from a grocer may be used as cuttings. Some have roots already but if not they will easily develop roots if you stand them in a glass of water. Watercress may also be grown in pots or clay pans stood in shallow containers of fresh water, well shaded, or in a container sunk in the ground.

Cucumber

Cucumbers are a very refreshing salad crop, because of their high water content. The small, rough-skinned varieties, called gherkins, are used for pickling.

A tropical trailing or climbing plant of Asiatic origin, the cucumber was known to the Romans. It is an important commercial crop, and one that is well worth cultivating in the garden. With a little care it is not a difficult crop to grow well.

There are two basic sorts of cucumbers; the first is the long smooth-skinned variety about 20-38 cm [12-15″] in length, known as greenhouse cucumbers in cool temperate areas, because there they need a frame or greenhouse. These are grown as climbers so that the fruit can hang down. Outdoor varieties, which are the most widely grown and which include those used as gherkins for pickling, are shorter, with a knobbly or spiny skin.

There are new Japanese outdoor varieties which are long and slim, like the greenhouse kinds, which can be trained to grow vertically.

Apple or lemon cucumbers have round fruit the size of a small apple with a pale yellowish-white skin and are of good quality. Another trailing variety, they are generally regarded as more digestible than green-fruited varieties. They can be grown in pots or boxes in a greenhouse, in a frame or outside in most parts of the country.

Wild cucumbers bear separate male and female flowers on the same plant. This is also true of the outdoor types, which must be pollinated to produce crops. Indoor

---

Cucumber
Cucumis sativus (fam. *Cucurbitacae*)
Tender plant, grown as an annual, trailing or climbing.
Size: controlled to 2.5 m [8′] in the greenhouse and 1.2 m [4′] square in a frame or the open.
Climate: warm temperate.
Sowing to harvesting time: 10-14 weeks.
Yield: greenhouse cucumbers 20 fruits per plant, outdoor cucumbers 25.

---

cucumbers, on the other hand, are parthenocarpic, that is they can bear fruit without pollination. The unfertilized fruit are superior for cropping purposes, and so care is taken to prevent pollination.

GROWING UNDER GLASS

If you raise your own plants and have more than enough, save the short stocky plants, dark green in color with three or four true leaves and their seed leaves still intact.

Sowing

The best way to raise the seedlings is in a propagator or in a warm greenhouse, at an absolute minimum night-time temperature of 15°C [60°F], but 18° to 25°C [65° to 75°F] is safer. It is vital that the seeds germinate quickly. Seeds sometimes show considerable variation: select only plump, clean ones and discard those which are flat or discolored. Sow the seeds singly in late winter or very early spring in 6-7.5 cm [2½-3″] plastic pots, containing a good seed mixture to within 1.25 cm [½″] of the top of the pot. Do not use old soil because it has not been sterilized. Place the seeds on edge, about 1.25 cm [½″] deep, and firm the whole surface. Water the soil and then cover the pot with black plastic or a sheet of glass and brown paper. The seeds should germinate within two, or at most three, days at the highest temperatures. Remove the covering and place the plants in a light position in the greenhouse. In a temperature of at least 15°C [60°F], growth should be rapid.

Making a hotbed

Until recently, it was customary to put down a layer of fresh manure 45 cm [18″] wide and 15 cm [6″] deep to produce heat for the plants. This should be spread out in the open beforehand and turned over occasionally for a few days to allow the excess nitrogen to be given off as ammonia. A more up-to-date way of producing heat is to use an electric soil heating cable with a thermostat to maintain the hotbed at the right temperature.

Planting

When the pots are full of roots and two to four leaves have expanded, nip out the growing point and plant the cucumbers in 23 cm [9″] pots or in boxes containing potting soil, or in a hotbed.

Training

Indoors, carry out cordon training of cucumbers on roughly the same principles as those used for tomatoes. Space the plants 45 cm [1½′] apart. Erect two wires, the top one about 2.1 m [7′] above ground level, the basal one running along the surface of the bed, both about 30 cm [1′] from the outside glass. Tie a string for each plant onto the wires so that it runs vertically and tie the leading shoot to this at intervals. Remove all sideshoots up to a height of 38 cm [15″] from the base of plant; beyond this, stop any sideshoots at the one- or two-leaf stage, depending on

(Right) The long smooth-skinned cucumber is grown as a climber, needing a greenhouse in cool temperate areas.

where the fruit is developing. Continue the operations of tying the plant to the string, stopping sideshoots and removing unwanted flowers beyond the second leaf, until the leading shoot has reached the top wire, when it is tied in and stopped.

Cucumbers may also be trained like melons in the greenhouse (*see* MELON).

Care and development

The cucumber must be given plenty of moisture at all times; its fruits have the highest water content of all vegetables. Never allow the soil in the pots, boxes or beds to become dry, especially in hot dry weather. The atmosphere in the greenhouse should be very humid; damp down two or three times a day in hot weather, although ventilation must also be provided. A drip or trickle irrigation system can be of considerable help.

It is difficult to lay down hard and fast rules regarding feeding. You can begin before the fruits start to swell. After formation of the fruit, apply a complete fertilizer about once every two weeks, following the directions on a brand-name compound.

Preventing pollination

Varieties are available which produce only female flowers, but these require slightly higher greenhouse temperatures. Where ordinary varieties are grown, it is usual to remove male flowers to prevent pollination. It is easy to recognize males, because they do not bear miniature cucumbers behind the petals, as do the females. Some growers fix fine gauze over ventilation openings in order to keep out insects. If they do manage to enter and pollinate the female flowers, the resulting fruit will be swollen-ended, bitter-tasting and full of seeds.

Growing cucumbers in a frame

Where a greenhouse is not available, cucumbers can be grown successfully in a cold frame which probably has a stout wooden, brick or concrete base to retain warmth. Plant the cucumbers in late spring in the center of the frame in a hotbed, made in the way described earlier. If you have no hotbed, delay planting to early summer.

Keep the frame closed, except for occasional ventilation on warm days. When the weather becomes warmer, it may be left open throughout the day.

Pinch out the growing tip of the plants in the same way as was recommended for greenhouse plants, when four or five leaves have been formed on each plant. Subsequently shoots will be produced in the axils (joints) of these leaves and you should select four and train each one towards a corner of the frame.

Carry out watering, feeding and pinching out sub-sideshoots as described earlier.

GROWING OUTDOORS

Outdoor cucumbers may be sown in the garden in most parts of the country or under Hotkaps, in a sunny sheltered position where it is cooler.

Dig a generous helping of garden compost, leaf mold or rotted farmyard manure into a trench 30 cm [1'] deep and the same width, and cover with the excavated soil, mounding it up into a low ridge. Alternatively, dig the organic matter into holes 90 cm [3'] apart and 30 cm [1'] deep by 30 cm [1'] square, again finishing off with a low mound. If organic material is not available, use a general fertilizer at the rate of 60 g per sq m [2 oz per sq yd], forked into the top of the soil two weeks or so before sowing. Sow the seed in the open late enough to avoid frost, two or three weeks earlier under Hotkaps. Sow a group of three seeds on the mounds or 90 cm [3'] apart on the long ridges, and thin to one plant in due course.

Allow the plants to grow about six leaves and then remove the growing tip. The sideshoots that are produced as a result are trained out singly and evenly, stopping those which have produced fruit at the seventh leaf, and the further shoots if needed to restrain the plant.

Pollination is by insects but, if you want to make doubly sure fruit will set, you can pollinate them by the method described in melon (*see* MELON).

In dry weather frequent watering will be necessary around the plants, being careful not to wet the stems. Liquid feeding should be started when the fruit begins to swell, and continued at two-weekly intervals.

A framework may be erected to support Japanese varieties, so that the fruit can hang down. Buy 2.2 m [7½'] poles and insert them so that they are 1.8 m [6'] above the ground and 1.8 m [6'] apart. Run wires between them and attach netting with a 20 cm [8"] mesh. Plant the cucumbers singly 30 cm [1'] apart and train them upward, pinching out the leaders when the top of the net has been reached. Stop sideshoots, as previously described.

HARVESTING AND PROTECTION

Greenhouse cucumbers will start to crop in late spring or early summer, and should be cut when about 30-35 cm [12-15"] long. They will continue cropping into winter.

Outdoor cucumbers which have been sown under Hotkaps should begin to crop in midsummer and slightly later if sown in the open soil. The first frosts will end the crop, as the plants will be killed. All cucumbers should be harvested before they reach full size and turn yellow, as this impairs the flavor. Early harvesting also helps to encourage the production of more fruit.

Pests and diseases

To prevent cucumber mosaic as far as possible use resistant varieties in troubled areas, and avoid contaminating healthy plants with knives or fingers infected from diseased plants, when trimming plants. Affected plants should be cleared and burned as soon as they appear.

Sometimes the young cucumbers wither from the tip and die when only 5 cm [2"] or so long. This is usually due to overwatering. To rectify this condition, the soil should not be watered for a few days, the plants should be sprayed overhead daily, and old stems removed. Then give a mulch and start watering again.

Cucumber leaf blotch (*Cercosporamelonis*) is a fungal disease which may be serious and require spraying and even soil sterilization. Powdery mildew may also occur. Again, select resistant varieties if the trouble is common in your area.

1. *To prepare ridge cucumber bed, dig garden compost into straight trench and cover with soil ridge.*

2. *Sow cucumbers in late spring. When first leaves have developed, thin to one seedling per group.*

3. *Train out sideshoots singly and evenly. Protect cucumbers from the soil by placing a tile under them.*

1. *To plant : dig hole the size of pot, fill with moist peat, press in empty pot and twist clear.*

2. *To remove cucumber from pot turn upside-down and, holding soil, tap out on table edge.*

3. *Put cucumber plant into hole made by empty pot and water it with warm water, 15-20° C [60-70° F].*

Gherkins grow to only 7.5 cm [3"] long and are used for pickling.

The larger yellow flowers of the outdoor cucumber are male. The smaller female ones quickly develop young cucumber fruits behind them.

Also, spray with Mildex if permitted in your locality.

Striped cucumber beetles, squash bugs and other chewing insects may be controlled with Diazinon or Sevin. Treat cutworms with snail and slug bait. Aphids, too, can be troublesome and spread disease. Spray with rotenone or pyrethreum.

Some troubles, although not common, are worth mentioning. Red spider mite is foremost among these and can result in destruction of the entire plant. When trying to control this pest be extremely careful to check out local regulations. Cucumbers are sensitive plants and could easily be damaged by insecticide.

Collar-rot is generally caused by excessive damp close to the stem and can result in a complete plant wilting and dying. There are approved mixtures that can be applied around the stem. Again, check with local authorities. A mulch of well-moistened peat applied afterwards close around the stem will induce new roots to grow above the diseased area. If the plant is too far gone, it is best destroyed.

Damson

Smaller than the plum, oval and dark-skinned with yellow flesh, damsons are usually cooked, and they produce a delicious red juice. They can be regarded as a cold weather plum.

The damson, *Prunus damascena*, is a member of the plum family and closely related to the sourer and smaller bullace, *P. insititia*. They are late-ripening, in early autumn. The fruit is 2.5 cm [1″] long, with mealy rather juiceless flesh, but develops a peculiarly rich flavor when cooked. They are excellent for jam and jelly, can be made into a stiff paste known as 'butter' or 'cheese', and into wine. When really ripe they can be eaten raw.

Grown as standards or half-standards, they make small trees, from 3.6-4.5 m [12-15′] high. Damsons are very hardy, and in the colder parts of temperate areas may be a

better choice than the early flowering plums. They crop abundantly in thin soil, provided there is excessive rainfall. In some colder areas they are grown as a hedge to provide shelter from the wind. Though they are not evergreen, they retain their foliage well into the autumn, and the branches interlock to form an effective and productive windbreak. They are cultivated in the same way as conventional plums (*see* PLUM).

Dill

A herb with a distinctive flavor, dill is chiefly used in pickles. Both seeds and leaves are used for flavoring.

Dill (*Anethum graveolens*) is a very spindly annual of the *Umbelliferae* family. It is often used in Scandinavian and Russian fish dishes and for pickling cucumbers, but it is also delicious on potatoes, tomatoes, beans and peas. The seeds are good with cooked brassicas and in salad dressings. Dill is said to have digestive properties and babies may be given dill water to relieve colic.

Its feathery green leaves grow on a single stem about 60-90 cm [2-3′] high and it produces large yellow flower heads from mid- to late summer, from which seeds are freely produced.

Cultivation

Dill will grow in ordinary soil in an open sunny spot, either grouped in a border or in a row. Prepare the site by deep digging to allow unimpeded tap root growth.

Sow the seeds outside during mid-spring not more than 0.5 cm [¼″] deep and as thinly as possible. Germination takes about 10-14 days. The seedlings emerge with a pair of narrow leaflets, often with the seed shell affixed to one, with the curled growth bud in the middle. Once the seedlings are large enough to handle, thin them to 10 cm [4″] apart. As they develop continue to thin until the plants are approximately 23 cm [9″] apart – use the thinnings fresh, or dry them. Firm the remaining plants well.

Unless the weather is very dry, watering is not necessary. The area should be kept weed-free and in windy areas the plants should be supported with twigs when they reach about 60 cm [2'].

Harvesting and growing a winter crop

Leaves should be harvested when as immature as possible, before the flower buds show about eight weeks after sowing. When seeds are desired the first flower heads should be left on, otherwise remove the flower heads to encourage further leaf growth. Allow the seeds to ripen until they are dark brown and harvest them in early autumn. Then hang them in a warm dark position, over paper, until they are dry.

During mid-autumn sow seeds in 7.5 cm [3"] pots in a warm greenhouse or indoors if you want dill for winter use. Transplant carefully into larger pots when the plants are 15 cm [6"] tall. Keep the plants away from direct sunlight and radiators, water regularly and support with sticks.

Pests and diseases

During a dry season aphids may attack dill and badly infested plants should be burned. Spray the remainder frequently with pure soapy water. Do not use insecticides, which could damage the flavor.

Eggplant

Harvested young and cooked properly eggplants provide a delicious and versatile vegetable and an important ingredient of Arab, Near East, Indian and Mediterranean dishes.

The eggplant or aubergine is native to southern and eastern Asia, where it is one of the earliest known cultivated vegetables. The fruit of the most common type of eggplant has a purple, shiny skin and creamy white flesh with a high water content. There are also varieties which bear white, red or even yellow fruit. The shape of the fruit varies according to variety, from roughly egg-shaped and squat to the more usual, elongated pear shape. One variety, the snake eggplant, has fruit which is very long, thin and curled at the end. Sizes also vary – from about 5 cm [2"] to 30 cm [1'].

The plant is too delicate to thrive under extended temperatures below about 10°C [50°F], but apart from this can succeed almost anywhere if protected.

Although eggplants need plenty of sunlight and warmth to succeed, the protection and care given the plant is rewarded by a crop which is far superior in taste to the eggplants sold in shops and markets.

Suitable site and soil

Even in Mediterranean and sub-tropical climates eggplants require a very sunny location. In cooler areas be sure to pick a sunny site.

The soil must be fertile and well drained. Dig it over and enrich it with well-rotted manure or garden compost some weeks before sowing or setting out plants.

Sowing and thinning

A minimum soil temperature of 25°C [75°F] is ideal for good, even germination – sow indoors, setting out when danger of frost is past. Otherwise, sow in the open ground. Sow seeds at stations 75 cm [30"] apart, at a depth of 2.5 cm [1"]. The seed should germinate and sprout after about 7-14 days.

Care and development

Pinch out the growing point of plants when they are about 15 cm [6"] high. This will encourage the plants to produce sideshoots bearing mauve flowers which are self-pollinating. The fruit will mature within 10-14 weeks from this stage.

Keep plants well supplied with water. Lawn mowings or straw may be spread around the plants when they are growing well to prevent moisture evaporation. Use a tomato fertilizer at the manufacturer's recommended rates if the soil is not very fertile. Use a hoe to keep down weeds around the plants. The mulch will also restrain weed growth.

If your plants are bearing heavy crops and are exposed to wind they may need staking. Set a cane close to the plant and tie it on loosely. If protectors are used, these must

---

Eggplant
Solanum melongena (fam. *Solanaceae*) also known as aubergine, eggfruit or guinea squash.
Perennial, but cultivated as **half-hardy annual.**
Size: reaches an average height of 90 cm [3'].
Climate: temperate to tropical.
Sowing to harvesting time: about 8-11 weeks, depending on warmth and intensity of sunlight.
Yield: 4 plants per 3 m [10'] row, 4-5 fruits per plant.

1. *Sow seeds in seed trays filled with potting soil. When seedlings are 5 cm [2″] tall prick off singly into 7.5 cm [3″] pots leaving no stem showing above the soil.*

2. *Move to 15 cm [6″] pots when smaller pots are full. Always put stake in first.*

3. *Move to larger pot for fruiting. Pinch growing point out at 15 cm [6″].*

4. *Remove plants from pots and set at 60 cm [2′] intervals.*

5. *Spray with warm water twice daily, especially the underside of foliage.*

(Above left) Peat-filled plastic bags have proved very successful for growing eggplants in the open. Planting should take place in early summer.
(Left) Eggplants vary greatly in size, shape and color. The largest here is 'Black Beauty', the commonest variety.

allow adequate headroom for the plants. They are removed entirely when the season is warm enough, otherwise remove them during the day to ensure good ventilation and replace them at night.

Harvesting your crop

Eggplant fruit are ready for picking when they are about 15 cm [6″] long and have stopped swelling. You can test this by pressing the fruit gently with your thumb. If an indentation remains, swelling has stopped. If the imprint disappears, the fruit is still swelling. The fruit should have a good, deep color and a bright, shiny skin. The stem is sometimes prickly, so wear gloves and use shears to cut off the fruit.

Once they are ripe, eggplant fruit must be harvested promptly, or the gloss on the skin begins to disappear and seeds develop inside the flesh, which makes the fruit less palatable. Length of harvest is about 6-8 weeks, through late summer.

Growing under glass

Seeds may be sown in a heated greenhouse from late winter to mid-spring; in an unheated greenhouse or outdoors in a glass frame from mid to late spring, after the last frost. Sow seeds 2.5 cm [1″] apart in seed trays, or in small pots filled with a seed mixture suitable for tomatoes, with two or three seeds to each 7.5 cm [3″] or 9 cm [3½″] pot at a depth of 1.5 cm [½″].

Keep trays or pots fairly moist and ensure that the temperature does not fall below 10°C [50°F]. A hotbed cable will keep the pots warm in an outdoor frame. Transfer small seedlings from the trays to one per 7.5 [3″] or 9 cm [3½″] pot and thin pot-sown seedlings. Stop the young plants at 15 cm [6″] high, by removing the growing tip.

When greenhouse-raised plants are from 15-20 cm [6-8″] high, remove plants from the pots and set out at 60 cm [2′] intervals in the greenhouse border, or in the garden frames at this stage if you prefer to start them indoors. Weed regularly and ensure ventilation is good.

Growing in pots, tubs and containers

Eggplants are excellent plants to grow in containers where space is limited. One plant should produce from four to six fruits.

Sow as directed for growing under glass. Transfer seedlings from the small pots to 15 cm [6″] pots and finally to 25 cm [10″] pots. Keep in a greenhouse or indoors in a sunny spot and stand outdoors in warm weather. They can be kept on a patio all the time if it is warm and sunny.

Plants in pots need feeding when the first fruits are swelling, and from then on until the last fruits have reached full size. Feed as directed under **Care and development.**

Pests and diseases

Avoid planting eggplants in soil where either tomatoes or potatoes, which belong to the same family, have been growing in the previous two or three years. Lack of crop rotation can lead to wilt diseases. Other pests common to the family include aphids, red spider mites (especially under glass) and Colorado potato beetles. A routine spray

should take care of this. Under glass, slugs can attack seedlings. Should this occur, scatter slug bait as necessary. Gray mold (*Botrytis cinerea*) will affect flowers and fruit if the ventilation is bad.

Endive

Endive, called chicory in both the United States and Europe, is delicious raw or cooked. There are two varieties – the curled, or staghorn types and the round-leaved, or Batavian, variety

Endive (note our use of the species, as in Great Britain, rather than the genus) is bitter if not blanched – much that is offered for sale has been insufficiently blanched by the grower or has lost most of its blanch during the journey to the market. When properly treated, however, endive is a delicious vegetable and one that is quite easy to grow.

Neither of the two types of endive is entirely hardy, though the stronger-tasting Batavian varieties will tolerate the sort of light frost that would ruin the last of the summer lettuces. Cold frame cultivation, however, will ensure survival of both sorts of endive through moderate frosts. The curly-leaved varieties can be sown in mid-spring if a crop is wanted in summer, but usually they are sown in early summer for an autumn crop. The tougher Batavian types

---

Endive (Chicory)
Cichorium endivia (fam. *Compositae*)
Half-hardy annual, resistant to light frosts.
Size: 12.5-20 cm [5-8″] tall; 30-38 cm [12-15″] wide.
Climate: cool temperate.
Sowing to harvesting time: 2-3 months in summer, longer in winter.
Yield: about 10 plants per 3 m [10′] row.

To blanch endive, place inverted pot over plant. Plug up drainage holes.

If growing endive under frames, cover them with black plastic sheeting.

The Batavian, or round-leaved, are the tougher type of endive.

Curly-leaved endives are more often sown for harvest in the autumn, but may be sown earlier for summer salads.

are sown in midsummer so that they mature in late autumn and early winter.

Suitable site and soil

Soil which is light and well-drained is ideal for endives. Of all vegetables, endive appreciates a humus-enriched soil more than any other, although it can be grown, with more effort, on heavier land. In spring, work in handfuls of peat or leaf mold on ground that was manured for a previous vegetable crop. Mix fertilizer into the soil about a week before sowing.

Sowing and transplanting

Do not sow all the seed at once, otherwise there will be a glut of seedlings and, inevitably, many will die. Draw V-shaped drills, spaced about 38 cm [15"] from each other, and sow the seed thinly, barely 1.5 cm [½"] deep. As endive thrives in firm soil, tread the drills or compact them with the back of a spade after sowing. Germination should occur about three days later; if it takes appreciably longer, it is better to resow, as the crop will otherwise be very likely to run to seed. Early thinnings can be transplanted, but it is worth noting that, like lettuces, the later that young endive plants are disturbed the greater the risk of failure when replanting. Plants need to be finally situated 30 cm [1'] apart.

Cultivation

Endive toughens rapidly if its roots are allowed to become dry. It may also bolt if transplanted without receiving plenty of water, so select a plot in partial sunlight, free from gusty winds, preferably facing north or east, and water the plants liberally, especially during hot, dry periods. On light soil, keep the plants mulched with materials such as peat or garden compost during hot weather to retain all possible moisture. About halfway toward maturity, the plants can be given a weak solution of liquid fertilizer or manure water every 7-10 days.

Blanching

Blanching can be carried out only when the plants are absolutely dry, otherwise they are likely to rot. Protection is essential for later-sown plants, once the weather starts to deteriorate in autumn. By late autumn the crinkled leaves of the staghorns will quickly suffer if not housed under a portable frame. It is pointless to begin the blanching process if the endive's foliage is coated with water. The cardinal rule is to cover first and blanch later.

Blanching itself presents no problems. If you wish to whiten only the heart or center leaves of your endive, simply place a saucer or plate over the top of each plant – this plan works well with the flatter, frilled varieties – and leave them for between two and three weeks in the frames. Winter-maturing endives will need to be kept in the dark for twice as long. The most convenient method of blanching the inner leaves of Batavian varieties requires only lengths of raffia or some rubber bands. Gather the outside leaves together and tie them at the top to exclude the light from the center of the plants. In about a month the process should be complete.

A simple method for blanching whole plants is to cover them with clay pots, remembering to plug the drainage hole at the bottom so that the plants are in total darkness. If the plants are under cover, it is possible to cover the whole frame with black plastic sheeting and blanch them this way. Another good method is to lift some plants whole, put them into a box of soil, closely packed, and place the box in a dark cellar until they are blanched. By using these methods and sowing in succession, it will be possible to have endive available to eat for most of the winter.

Whatever method you choose, always cut the plants as soon as blanching is complete. Failure to do this could lead to heart rot.

Pests and diseases

Caterpillars and slugs may cause damage to the leaves, and you should watch out for mildew. Use non-poisonous Sevin, slug bait and Mildex, if attacks are serious enough.

Fennel

The swollen, blanched basal stems are served as a vegetable, raw or braised. The feathery aniseed-flavored leaves are used for seasoning like the herb fennel.

Florence fennel is a vegetable that was almost unknown outside Italy and the south of France until recently, when it was 'discovered' by vacationers. It is a variety of the common fennel, *Foeniculum vulgare*, which was valued by the Romans as a medicinal and culinary herb, the main difference, apart from the bulbous base, is the height – it is not so tall as common fennel. The haze of feathery, thread-like, blue-green leaves, and the golden-yellow flowers make it both a decorative and useful plant.

Suitable site and soil

As Florence fennel needs plenty of warmth at all times, it should be given a sunny, sheltered position. Soil should be well drained and fertile; add well-rotted farm manure or garden compost in the winter before planting at about a 10 L [2 gal] bucket per 5 sq m [6 sq yd] and mix it in thoroughly. Add land lime as required, if a soil test shows the pH to be acid.

A light sandy soil which has been bulked up with lavish applications of organic matter will do very well, but a heavy clay is likely to give disappointing results.

Sowing and planting

It is vital that the seedbed has several inches of fine-textured soil, and if there is any doubt about this, the addition of a 7.5 [3″] layer of seed starting·mixture is advisable. Two to three weeks before sowing, put a portable frame over the seedbed to warm up the soil, and about a week before sowing, mix a general complete fertilizer into the surface at the rate of about 30 g per sq m [1 oz per sq yd]. Lightly water the seedbed the day before sowing if no rain has occurred. Sow the seed thinly in mid to late spring, 0.5 cm [¼″] deep in drills 30 cm [1′] apart, and cover with soil. Protect with frames during cold weather, especially at night, and thin the young plants to 20 cm [8″] apart.

Care and development

The plants should be kept well watered throughout the season, especially during dry weather, and a mulch of peat, garden compost or a black plastic sheet will retain soil moisture; black plastic is particularly useful as it helps to warm up the soil. Keep the weeds down as required, and feed the plants when the base starts to thicken, overlap widely and swell, with 60 g per sq m [2 oz per sq yd] of a general fertilizer, applied when the soil is moist.

Blanching

Blanching makes the bulbous base more tender and removes any bitter taste; it is started when the base is about the size of an egg. Draw up the soil around the lower part of the stem to about three-quarters of its height.

Harvesting and storing the crop

Florence fennel is harvested about one month after starting to blanch, from midsummer onward, depending on the time of sowing. The leaves can be cut and used for flavoring from the time of flowering, or just before this.

Unless it is put into a deep freezer, the bulbous base of Florence fennel cannot be stored for very long; however,

---

Florence fennel
Foeniculum vulgare dulce (fam. *Umbelliferae*) also known as Florentine fennel, finocchio, sweet fennel.
Hardy annual.
Size: grows to about 60 cm [2′] tall.
Climate: warm temperate.
Sowing to harvesting time: about 18 weeks.
Yield: 15 plants per 3 m [10′] row.

the leaves can be dried in the same way as herbs, though they are not likely to be as aromatic as the fresh foliage. If late sowings were made, crops which were intended to mature in late autumn and early winter should be protected against frost with a heavy mulch consisting of either marsh hay or straw.

Fennel

Fennel is grown for its leaf stalks and seeds which are often used to complement fish.

Black plastic sheets keep soil warm and moisture in.

To blanch, draw soil up around base when egg-sized.

Fennel (*Foeniculum vulgare*) is a very handsome, upright perennial herb with branching, hollow stems. Fresh or dried, the leaves are used as a flavoring, or in a sauce, to accompany fish. An infusion made from the leaves is soothing to inflamed or strained eyes, and fennel tea is famous for suppressing hunger in weight-watchers. The seeds may also be used with fish, or in the same ways as dill seeds.

The fine, thread-like, dark green leaves have a licorice taste. The plant grows about 1.5-1.8 m [5-6'] high and 60 cm [2'] across and from midsummer to early autumn bears yellow umbels of flowers which produce a large quantity of seeds. It will cross-pollinate easily with dill, so should never be grown near it, as plants grown from the resultant seed will not have a distinctive flavor of either.

Cultivation
Choose a sunny position at the back of a border, since the

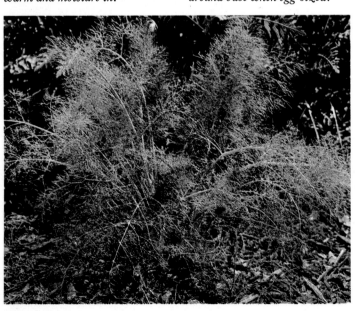

The sprays of the herb golden fennel are attractive and aromatic. They are used fresh or dried for flavoring.

plants grow so tall. Fennel will grow in any good, well drained, deep soil. Fork the growing area well to break up the subsoil, incorporating peat or well-rotted compost.
Sow the seeds outside in mid-spring 0.5 cm [¼"] deep, in rows 45 cm [1½'] apart. Germination will take 2-3 weeks. When the seedlings have produced a central, feathery leaf, thin to 45-60 cm [1½-2'] apart.

Harvesting and after-care

Water regularly and well until the plants are established and keep the rows free from weeds. In exposed areas, stake the plant. After four to six weeks the young leaves may be harvested until the flower buds show. If seeds are not required the heads should be removed to encourage leaf growth. When seeds are required leave the first flowers on. They will start to appear from midsummer. Harvest when the seeds start to turn brown. Hang the seed-heads over paper in a dry place and store them in an airtight container after they have dropped.

The top growth will die down in autumn, but unless the winter is severely cold, the plants will survive then sprout again the following spring. Otherwise, for winter use, you can remove the flower stems and divide the roots in early autumn. Put into pots and keep them indoors or under glass.

Fig

This brown or purplish, pear-shaped fruit is peeled for its delicious pink interior, and is best eaten raw straight off the tree. There are also greenish-yellow varieties with white flesh. Figs grown in the garden are almost seedless.

The family *Ficus* includes the well-known rubber plant *Ficus elastica*. The fruiting species *carica* is one of the oldest fruits known, mentioned in the Bible. Originating in western Asia, it is widely cultivated in the Mediterranean.

The fruit does not transport well, so commercial figs are usually dried and are full of seeds, but the garden varieties are relatively seedless. Figs contain 50% sugar when dried, while syrup of figs is well known as a laxative.
Botanically the fig is a curiosity because there are no visible flowers; the buds swell to develop straight into the fruit. The fruit is actually made up of a collection of many flowers within the skin and some varieties require pollination, but the Adriatic fig is self-fertilizing. The fruit is about 5 cm [2"] long, while leaves may be from 10-20 cm [4-8"] long and are hand-shaped with three or five lobes.
Figs can stand quite low temperatures – even well below freezing, if protected – when dormant, provided the temperature drops slowly. A sudden big drop will do more damage. Any frost when growth has started will cause serious damage. Frost-damaged wood may be cut to the ground but the tree will reestablish itself again by means of suckers.
If planted in good soil, growth will be rank and soft so, to get the ripe wood that bears fruit, it is necessary to restrict root growth.
In warm climates with a short period of dormancy, three crops will ripen. In sheltered parts of cool temperate areas one crop will ripen if it gets plenty of summer sun. In a greenhouse two crops will be secured, but for three extra heat, up to 27°C [80°F], will be needed in late winter. This is not advised as it may be at the expense of the following year's crop.

Suitable site and soil

In sheltered parts of cool temperate areas, trees can be trained against a wall facing the midday sun. Ideally, the wall should be 2 m [8'] high and at least 4.5 m [15'] across. If lower, it should be at least 5 m [18'] across. In a warm corner, for instance the angle of two walls, a bush will succeed. Figs like well-drained limy soil; a medium to light loam with some sand is suitable. If the soil is at all acid add enough lime so that a soil test gives a pH of 7-7.5.

Planting

To restrict the root development, dig a hole at least 1 m [3'] square and the same depth. Line the sides with brick or concrete and put a 30 cm [1'] layer of broken brick or rubble at the bottom for drainage. If you do not do this, you may have to prune the roots regularly. Then fill in with soil, putting the topsoil back last. About two weeks before

---

Fig
Ficus carica (fam. *Moraceae*)
Hardy deciduous tree growing to 9 m [30'] in a natural state, but confined as a bush to 3-3.6 m high by 2.5 m wide [10-12' × 8'] or 3 × 4.5 m [10' × 15'] as a fan. Fig trees have a very long life, up to several centuries.
Climate: warm temperate.
Yield: a 1.2 m [4'] pot-grown tree will produce 2 dozen fruits, an outdoor tree or indoor fan 6 kg [13 lb] of fruit for a first crop and half that for a second.

1m [3']

*lip prevents
water run off*

1m [3']

*30cm [1']
rubble layer*

1m [3']

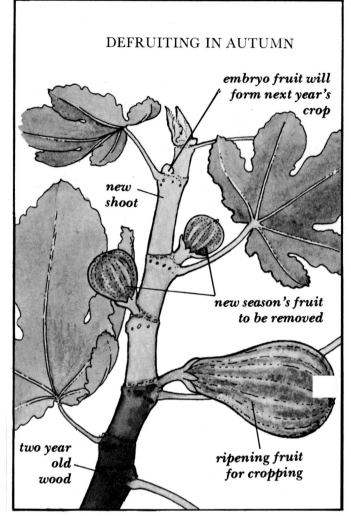

DEFRUITING IN AUTUMN

*embryo fruit will
form next year's
crop*

*new
shoot*

*new season's fruit
to be removed*

*two year
old
wood*

*ripening fruit
for cropping*

*The roots of the fig tree must be confined, otherwise it grows too
large and will not fruit. Rather than root pruning, prepare a walled
pit like this before planting.*

*In the autumn when harvesting the ripe figs on a tree outdoors, also
pick any other fruit which is already recognizable as a fig. Only the
embryo buds at the very tips of the shoots will survive and ripen
next year.*

*(Below) In cool areas fig trees can be fan-trained on a sunny wall,
where they will be protected and crop well.*

planting, add 60 g [2 oz] of bonemeal and mix in well.
Trees are best planted in early spring. Those from nurseries are usually two years old and container grown. Plant like other fruit trees (*see* APPLE), spreading out the roots and firming the soil thoroughly after replacing. Watering is particularly important against a wall. A mulch of rotted manure or moist peat will help retain moisture.

Care and development
Little watering is required until growth starts, then a good soaking every four days or so, increasing to every other day in the height of summer until the fruit is nearly ripe, will be necessary for fully grown trees. After the first year, feed with a good balanced fertilizer at the rate of 60 g per sq m [2 oz per sq yd] of the area to which the roots extend, in early spring. If the drainage is too good, a second feed will be required in early summer. Mulching in late spring, or after the second feed if needed, with rotted manure or garden compost will help to retain moisture.

A fan can be developed along the same lines as any other espalier. Train young shoots up and along the wall as they develop, pinching any out is not required. Extension growth is always from terminal buds, so as many ripe one- and two-year-old shoots with undamaged tips as possible should be tied in. Therefore, two or three of the oldest bare branches on each side of the fan can be shortened in winter to a suitably placed dormant bud at a joint, and new growth will appear from the cut-back shoot, lower down, in spring.

Disbudding the fruit
The fig bears its fruit at the tips of the shoots and simultaneously carries fruit singly or in pairs, at different stages of development on one- and two-year-old wood. Outdoors in a rather cool climate only fruit which has been started the year before has a chance of ripening.

During the summer fruit is formed in the axils of the new leaves, but those lower down the stem become too large and tender to pass undamaged through the winter; fruit which can be discerned as such in autumn is best removed. This stimulates the production of the embryo fruit at the very tip of the shoots; these will survive the winter to ripen in late summer or autumn the following year.

In the greenhouse
If the house gets plenty of sun, and artificial heat can be supplied in late winter, two crops can be obtained in the year, ripening in early summer and early to mid-autumn. The temperature should be increased to 13-15°C [55-60°F] in late winter, soil watering should be started, and the house kept humid as the new leaves start to unfold, by damping down and spraying the foliage daily.

As with outdoor figs, the root growth should be restricted and similar soil provided. The tree should be watered moderately until growth is fully underway, and then as for outdoor plants, though in really hot summer weather watering twice a day may be needed. When the first crop of fruit starts to color, give about half as much water until the crop is picked. Topdress with rotted manure or garden compost in early spring, and feed every week with a liquid fertilizer when the fruit starts to swell. Prune as for outdoor

There are many varieties of common fig: colors range from dark purple or black to a pale greenish white.

GROWING FIGS IN POTS

Fig trees are well suited to pot growing; root restriction helps crops.

Mound up earth, spread roots and use trowel to firm soil between them.

trees, but do not remove the well-developed figs as these will provide the autumn crop. In winter keep the tree moist.

Pot growing

Pot grown trees can be used outdoors or in the greenhouse. A 25-30 cm [10-12″] pot is large enough and will support a bush of about 1.5 m [5′] and with good crops. As the roots cannot spread, a richer compost can be used. Planting the tree is as shown in the diagrams, while for repotting and root pruning instructions, *see* CITRUS FRUIT. Water and feed like a greenhouse tree. In early autumn pinch out the growing tips at six to eight leaves to ensure new wood gets ripe before dormancy.

Ideally, trees should be repotted each autumn, trimming the roots to leave 2.5 cm [1″] or so between them and the pot wall, and using the same size pot. Alternatively, in the second year as much soil mix as possible can be removed from the top and replaced with a fresh supply.

Little water is required while the trees are dormant, but regular and frequent watering will be needed once they start growing.

If a crop is large or if watering has leached out fertilizer, top-dressing will be required about early summer, as well as the spring feed. You can add further soil mix around the edge of the pot, leaving a hole around the trunk, or feed with a balanced fertilizer at the rate of 30 g [1 oz] per pot, with a second application three weeks later.

Harvesting

The flavor does not develop until full ripeness, when the fruit droops and cracks slightly, usually producing a small drop of moisture at the eye. Ripe fruits are very soft and thin-skinned. Handle them by the stalk only to avoid bruising.

Propagation

Figs can be increased by cuttings of short jointed shoots about 30 cm [1′] long with three buds of wood from the previous year at the bottom. Insert half the shoot into a peat/sand mixture in early spring, preferably with bottom heat. They root readily and will be ready to put in early summer.

In early summer, strong young shoots can be layered by pegging into the soil with the tip turned up and exposed (*see* BLACKBERRY). They should have rooted enough to plant in the autumn.

Varieties

The varieties recommended for growing in the United States are limited to two: Brown Turkey and Brunswick.

Pests and diseases

In warmer climates, figs can be seriously infected with virus spotting of the leaves, but in cooler areas this is never serious. The most common pest is scale; as soon as this is seen, spray with malathion, with a second spray two weeks later. Red spider mite is another pest and, in the greenhouse, airless and humid conditions may lead to canker. Affected branches should be cut off and burned.

French Beans

These beans, also known as garden or pole beans, offer a high yield for a compact plant which demands little attention. The pods are eaten whole, when young and delicate in flavor.

Originating in South America, these beans were popularized by the French. Called kidney beans in some countries, in others this refers to a specific type.

Garden beans are an ideal crop for a small area. Most varieties are of dwarf or bush type which, when grown 23 cm [9″] apart in rows, form a dense canopy of large leaves beneath which the bean pods, 7.5-12 cm [3-5″] long, hang. There are, however, a few climbing varieties which need the support of poles. The flowers are typically leguminous or butterfly-like, and are usually white, red or pink. The pods are long, rather slender and with an almost circular cross section. They should be picked while still young and tender and cooked whole.

Of the many varieties of garden beans some of the most interesting are those which have pods of different colors from the ordinary green. One of the most popular has wax-skinned yellow pods and is known as a waxpod. There are also mottled red and white and indigo blue pod types.

Other well-known varieties belonging to the same bean species are haricots and flageolets, known in the United States as French horticultural beans. Treatment of the crops up to harvest is exactly the same as for other varieties, but flageolets are picked when the beans are fully formed

(Right) The most common varieties of these beans. Garden beans have tapering green pods; flowers are white or pink.

Garden bean
Phaseolus vulgaris (fam. *Leguminosae*; also known as snap bean and string bean.
Size: 15-20 cm [6-10″] high. 10-15 cm [4-6″] across.
Climate: warm temperate
Sowing to harvesting time: 6-7 weeks.
Yield: 1-1.3 kg [2-3 lb] per 3m [10′] row.

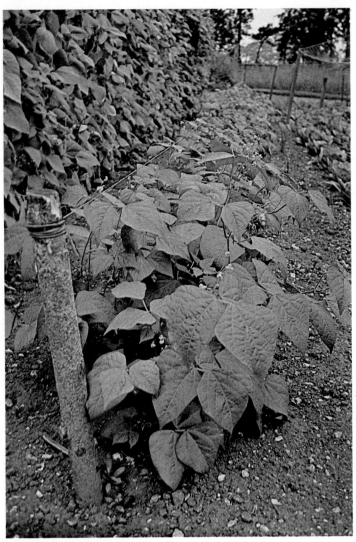

Given a sunny site and plenty of food and water, beans will produce a harvest within a few weeks of sowing.

When cooked, the tender, stringless pods of this climbing variety change from purple to green.

Among other well-known types of bean are the wax-pod varieties with yellow pods and black seeds.

in the pods, although the pods are still soft and green. Haricot beans are harvested when the seeds are fully ripe and have dried in their pods. Both flageolet and haricot beans are grown for their seeds alone, the pods being discarded. In addition to these well-known sorts there are other shell beans such as red kidney beans, navy beans, pintos and garbanzos.

Suitable site and soil

Most beans do best in a sunny situation. They will grow in almost any soil, but prefer one that is not too heavy. A heavy soil can be lightened by working in peat, garden compost or coarse sand. They like plenty of nourishment, so you should add garden compost, farmyard manure or chemical fertilizers.

Sowing

Sow outdoors in late spring, after all danger from frost is past. Most beans cannot tolerate even slight frost when young. They also need reasonable warmth – about 16°C [60°F] – in the soil to germinate.

In cool temperate climates gardeners can acquire more growing time and produce earlier crops by starting the beans under Hotkaps. There are, in fact, three alternative methods for sowing garden beans: 1. sow outdoors in rows 30 cm [1′] apart, after the last frost date, at a depth of 5 cm [2″]: 2. sow under Hotkaps about the date of the last expected frost, at a depth of about 2.5 cm [1″]: 3. sow in boxes or pots in a greenhouse, four to six weeks before the last expected frost date.

Planting

The bean plants brought on indoors should be transplanted outdoors after the last frost date. Those under Hotkaps may also be transplanted, though the more usual plan is to remove the covers when no further frosts are expected. When transplanting, keep a ball of soil around the roots and water well.

After the first sowing or transplanting, sow a succession of crops, about one per month, until about August 1st, New York and northward.

Care and development

Beans usually need to be well fed and well watered. The watering should be frequent so that the plants never experience a check to their growth. You should hoe frequently, not only to keep weeds under control but also to keep the soil broken up. In dry weather some soils, especially if watered by hose or watering-can, form a crust which, if undisturbed, will considerably decrease the yield. Small doses of liquid manure can be given but take care to keep this clear of the foliage.

The dwarf varieties of most beans do not normally require any support, except when they are grown in a position exposed to strong winds. A few short twiggy sticks can then help to prop them up. The climbing varieties need the support of tall rods or canes around which they will twine in the same way as runner beans. Erect one rod or string per plant; these should be about 2 m [6½″] high after they have been pushed well into the ground. The framework consists of a line of pairs of rods or strings straddling the

French beans

Sow seed 2.5 cm [1″] deep and firm with feet. Protect with Hotkaps.

Use short twigs to support dwarf varieties against strong winds.

Regular weeding with an onion hoe also helps keep the soil loose.

When flowers appear, spray plants to encourage pod formation.

Mulch with garden compost or peat in order to keep the soil moist.

Harvest with scissors, as pulling by hand can uproot the whole plant.

OBTAINING HARICOT BEANS

Lift plants when pods are yellow and hang up to dry in an airy room.

The beans can be shelled when the leaves are shrivelled and brittle. Store the dried beans in glass jars with loose-fitting lids.

Spread the shelled beans on trays and dry in a well-ventilated room. Pale green haricot beans fresh from the pod turn cream color when dried.

axis of the row, not less than 50 cm [1½'] apart at soil level.

Harvesting

The beans are ready for picking from 6 to 7 weeks after sowing. Once the pods have started to form, check them every day, for they mature very quickly. On no account allow them to stay on the plant too long. Test a pod by snapping it across the middle. If just right, it should break cleanly and show no stringly fibers. The beans inside the pod will not have expanded to their full size.

When picking, do so carefully, using the nails of thumb and fingers, or cut the beans from the plants with scissors or a knife. Do not pull them off forcibly or the whole plant, which is shallow-rooted, is likely to come out of the ground. Once picking has begun, continue daily.

Snap beans are best eaten fresh and cooked on the day of picking. They are also excellent for deep freezing. Apart from that, however, they do not store well.

After-care

It is possible to harvest a second smaller crop from the same plants. Apply a light dressing of a complete chemical fertilizer at an approximate rate of 60 g per sq m [2 oz per sq yd] to the soil, a hand's width away from the plants, and hoe in well. Water generously.

Late-sown crops may not produce their pods before the threat of autumn frosts, in which case protect the rows with a covering to prolong the harvesting season as long as possible. When cropping is over, cut off the dead or dying foliage but leave the roots in the ground. As with all leguminous crops, garden beans will increase the nitrogen-content of the soil as they decay, to the benefit of subsequent nitrogen-hungry plants, such as brassicas, in a crop rotation system.

Pests and diseases

Two measures should be taken as soon as the beans are sown outdoors. One is to protect them by a network of black cotton or a nylon-meshed net, to ward off birds which scratch up the seedling plants as fast as they emerge. The other is to sprinkle slug bait around the rows. Slugs attack the swelling bean seed even before the first shoot has emerged and eat the young foliage. As slugs are particularly fond of the young pods, they are most likely to eat the pods in contact with the ground, so use twigs to prevent the plants being blown over. Cutworms also cut stems.

Anthracnose of garden beans (*Colletotrichum lindemuthianum*) is a fungus disease. Characterized by blackish-brown spots on foliage and pods, it is fostered by cool, wet summers. Usually the disease is seed-borne, and seed suppliers ensure that their seed is free from it; but it can develop on un-burned vegetable debris.

Fusarium wilt, which results in bean plants wilting and decaying, is another fungus disease caused by a lack of proper crop rotation. Other diseases which may occur are gray mold (*Botrytis cinerea*) and *Rhizoctonia* – little can be done once an attack has developed, but chemicals can be worked into the soil, just before sowing or transplanting, as a precaution, if necessary.

Garlic

The garlic bulb has a powerful aroma. One of the most distinctive and popular of all flavorings, garlic is an essential ingredient in many international dishes.

Garlic, *Allium sativum*, a member of the onion family *Alliaceae*, is a perennial herb grown as an annual for the cloves contained inside the bulb. A clove or two of garlic gives an intense flavor and aroma to an enormous variety of dishes, many associated with the Mediterranean. Garlic can be crushed or finely chopped before it is added to dishes, but often it is enough to just cut the bulb in half and rub it around the inside of the cooking or serving dish. In folklore it was a charm against evil – thought to absorb and overpower anything unclean.

Garlic is thought to have come from central Asia, from where it spread to the Mediterranean. The Romans were probably the first to introduce garlic to other parts of Europe, and today it grows virtually everywhere. Because it is so simple to grow and easy to store, garlic presents welcome relief to the busy gardener and encouragement to the beginner.

The bulb is covered in several layers of papery white skin and contains up to 20 cloves concentrically arranged inside and each wrapped. Garlic bulbs average 4-7.5 cm [1½-3"] in both diameter and height though bulbs 20 cm [8"] wide are not unknown. A clove of garlic, roughly 2 cm [¾"] long, is rounded on one side, flat on the other and pointed at the top.

Culitvation

If you have a bulb of fresh garlic at hand, simply plant the cloves from that. Otherwise, order cloves from your seed supplier. Plant garlic in mid-autumn; if severe cold is unlikely, in early or mid-spring, in a sunny window box or the herb section of the garden. Garlic likes a rich, sandy loam, and it is a good idea to mix in rotted garden compost some weeks before planting and an application of 60 g per sq m [2 oz per sq yd] of bonemeal a week or so before planting.

Rake the surface down finely and place the clove about

5 cm [2"] deep, base down and tip pointing upward, so that there is 2.5 cm [1"] of soil on top of the tip. Allow 15 cm [6"] between each clove and 30 cm [1'] between the rows if you plant more than one. You will get the best results if you use the largest cloves from the outside of the bulb, particularly if you plant in autumn. If planted in autumn, give a mid-spring dressing of 15 g per sq m [½ oz per sq yd] of sulphate of ammonia and another in early summer of a potash-high fertilizer. For spring-sown bulbs, only give the potash dressing.

Hoe weeds out as they appear. Garlic is rarely prey to pests or diseases which trouble the onion family.

Harvesting and storing

Garlic produces leaves, and, like other members of the onion family, a white or red-tinted flower or a leafless stem 30 cm [1'] or more tall. When the leaves begin to wither and turn yellow, usually from late summer to early autumn, dig the bulbs out of the soil carefully with a fork; do not pull. After lifting, let the bulbs dry in the sun for a few days, covering them at night to protect them from dew. When completely dry, clean off any soil and loose skins and take the bulbs inside to a frost-free shed or room. Bunch the bulbs together by tying the stems with raffia or string and then set out in trays, or string the bulbs for hanging on the wall by braiding or plaiting them, weaving the tops with the string. They will last a year or more.

knobbly or prickly surfaces, and should be picked when young. They are pickled in boiling vinegar after being soaked in brine.

Wild gherkins, *Cucumis anguria* (fam. *Cucurbitaceae*) are weeds of the damp regions of the West Indies and of tropical and sub-tropical America. They have deeply five-lobed leaves and small fruits, 2.5-7.5 cm [1-3"] long, with prickly surfaces. The immature fruits are used for pickling, mainly in the United States.

For cultivation *see* CUCUMBER.

Good King Henry

Good King Henry is a very hardy perennial vegetable, valued in old English kitchens for its nutritious spinach-like leaves. The stems can be blanched like asparagus.

Although Good King Henry is cultivated as a vegetable, it is the medicinal herb called mercury when found growing wild. A member of the goosefoot family *Chenopodium*, it is distinguished by its name from 'Bad Henry' the weed, *Mercurialis annua*. The leaves have a characteristic triangular shape, and the green flowers have extraordinarily long stigmas. The natural habitat includes large areas of Europe,

Gherkin

Gherkins belong to the cucumber family. The small rough-skinned fruits make a very tasty pickle.

'Gherkin' is the Slavonic name for cucumber. Some small varieties of the cucumber. *Cucumis sativus* (fam. *Cucurbitaceae*) are known as gherkins when pickled. They are usually thick, small to medium-sized cucumbers, with rough

Good King Henry
Chenopodium bonus-henricus
(fam. *Chenopodiaceae*) also known as mercury,
Lincolnshire spinach, poor man's asparagus.
Hardy perennial.
Size: grows to 30-60 cm [1-2'] tall.
Climate: cool temperate.
Sowing to harvesting time: 4 months.
Yield: 2.3 kg [5 lb] per 3 m [10'] row per season.

Triangular green leaves and unusually long stigmas are the two most distinctive characteristics of this semi-wild herb.

Deservedly popular, the fruit of the red gooseberry is excellent for cooking, canning and bottling.

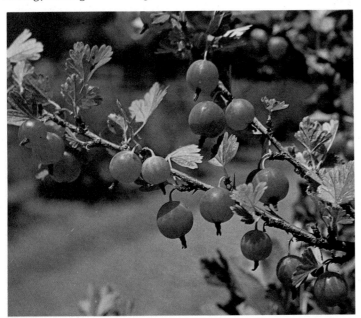

Asia and North America.

The vegetable does best in a rich, well-manured soil; although it will tolerate a poor, dry soil, the yield should not be expected to be nearly so high per plant.

Cultivation and harvesting

If propagating from seed, sow outside in mid-spring. You may also sow indoors in trays for transplanting out when the soil is more easily worked. Spring temperatures of about 15°C [60°F] give the best chances of speedy germination. Place the young plants well apart, or sprinkle the seeds and later thin to about 25 cm [10″].

Since Good King Henry is a semi-wild herb, it needs less treatment than most food crops. Nevertheless, it will benefit from feeds of diluted liquid fertilizer and frequent watering during the summer on light, well-drained soils.

Take the broad, triangular green leaves in summer, without stripping a whole plant, and use in a similar way to spinach. The firm, fleshy shoots that grow from the leaf axils can also be eaten – these bear young green leaves and end in embryo flower buds. They can be used like sprouting broccoli, or like asparagus, if they are first blanched. Cut back the stems in late autumn and cover the roots with bracken or straw. The covering provides protection and blanches the shoots for use in spring. Stop cutting shoots after early summer to allow the plant to build itself up again, as for asparagus. Once you have raised a crop of Good King Henry from seed, propagate by planting pieces of the base of the stem with roots attached.

Gooseberry

**The familiar gooseberry is hairy
and yellowish-green, although there
are creamy and reddish-pink varieties.
The flesh is juicy with many pips.**

Native to Europe, the gooseberry is closely related to currants. The bush is encouraged to grow on a single short stem like a miniature tree and is very spiny. Gooseberries are the earliest of the soft fruit to crop at the beginning of the summer. There are a number of varieties differing in size and color. All are suitable for eating raw when really ripe, for cooking and jam making, though for bottling and canning some are particularly suitable.

The Worcesterberry is thought to be a cross between a gooseberry and a blackcurrant. The bush is tall like a blackcurrant but spiny with dark gooseberry-like fruit. However it is not in the U.S. trade, although possibly in Canada.

Suitable site and soil

Shelter from frost and cold spring winds is important. The flowers appear in mid-spring and are very susceptible to frost, while wind prevents helpful pollinating insects from doing their work, and means that the fruit set is poor. Make sure you do not plant in frost pockets.

Gooseberries like a medium textured, well-drained loamy soil which retains summer moisture. They are more fussy than other bush fruits; light soils do not suit them, and only certain varieties do well on clay. They make deep 'sinker' roots in clay soil and a mass of fibrous, food-absorbing roots in the top layer.

Planting

Gooseberries can be grown as bushes, cordons and standards. Cordons may be single or double stemmed, carrying fruiting spurs, and are often trained against wires or fences. A standard is supplied on a 1.5 m [5'] high stem with the head already formed.

Autumn is the best planting time but anytime during the winter when the soil is workable is satisfactory. Bushes are usually sold as two- or three-year-old plants and are planted 1.5 m [5'] apart. Cordons are planted at about 30 cm [1'] apart if they are single and 75 cm [2½'] if they are double.

Prepare the site by eliminating all perennial weeds. Then dig garden compost into the top 23 cm [9"] at about one barrowload per 9-11 sq m [10-12 sq yd] before planting. Holes must be big enough to take the roots in comfort, and firm planting, to the same depth that the bush was in the nursery, is essential. The surface should be left slightly loose; if it is trodden, rain may lie in puddles.

Plants may arrive from the nursery already pruned to the third bud from the base of each branch. If this has not been done, you should do it immediately after planting.

Cordons must be supported by a bamboo cane driven in behind them, to which they are tied and trained, and standards will also need staking.

Gooseberry

Ribes grossularia (fam. *Grossulariaceae*)
Hardy deciduous bush with a cropping life of up to 15 years.
Size: 1 m [3'] high and 1.2-1.5 m [4-5'] wide.
Climate: cool to warm temperate.
Planting to harvesting time: 2-3 years.
Yield: 3-6 kg [6-12 lb] per bush.

Feeding and mulching

Mulch annually in spring with a wheelbarrow-load of garden compost or rotted farm manure per 9-11 sq m [10-12 sq yd]. This conserves soil moisture, provides a permanent supply of essential organic matter, and suppresses annual weeds. There is firm evidence that the root mass is greater by some 20-30% under a mulch than under bare soil, which means bigger and more productive bushes. Any perennial weeds that appear are more easily pulled out from mulched soil.

With organic cultivation little fertilizer is normally needed. Sulphate of potash at about 20 g per sq m [¾ oz per sq yd] in late summer should be all that the bushes will require, and not necessarily every year. But this dressing must be given if there are signs of potash deficiency, when leaves will have brown-gray margins and tend to curl downward.

Pruning

Bushes will consist of 10-12 main branches eventually grown from a single short stem 15-23 cm [6-9"] long. On these, fruiting spurs will be formed by routine pruning. The main branches are cut back hard in the early years, to buds on the lower surfaces if the growth is upward, or to upper surface buds if the habit is drooping. The object of this is to encourage strong branch extensions with an open center, in order to build up a sturdy framework capable of producing many sideshoots for fruit spur formation. In the second, third and possibly fourth years, the shoots chosen to form the main framework should be cut back in winter by about one-half to two-thirds, to encourage strong growth. In the third and subsequent years, the sideshoots are cut back in late summer to just above the fifth leaf, and again in winter, to the third leaf, from the base of the shoot.

The tips of the main branches are also pruned in winter, cutting back the new growth to leave about 10 cm [4"] of it. This method induces fruit spurs along the branches, and results in really large berries. Cordons and standards are spur pruned in exactly the same way. Bushes fruit on the previous season's growth.

A simpler system allows the berries to form directly on the main branches instead of on induced spurs. Branches are left to fruit for two or three years and are then cut out completely. This encourages new shoots to grow from the top of the leg, as replacements. Fewer sideshoots appear with this method; those that do are ignored if they are short, or just snipped back if long. The right sequence gives branches in fruit and new ones taking over, ensuring a steady continuity of crop. Congestion must be avoided; allow a hand's span between fruiting branches and always remove weak branches, and any which are crossing or crowding the center.

Harvesting and propagation

Varieties in general can be picked over early in the season for cooking purposes. This encourages maximum development of the main crop if it is done systematically, to leave retained berries evenly spaced.

New bushes are propagated from the new shoots in early to mid-autumn. Well-ripened lengths about 23 cm [9"]

(*Above*) Three or four
gooseberry bushes should
produce enough fruit for the
average family.

(*Left*) Standards have the
variety grafted onto the
rootstock; the wooden supports
on either side hold up the
branches.

(*Right*) To propagate, remove
all but top four buds. Put
in fine soil trench in early to
mid-autumn with all the
buds clear of the ground.

PRUNING THE GOOSEBERRY BUSH

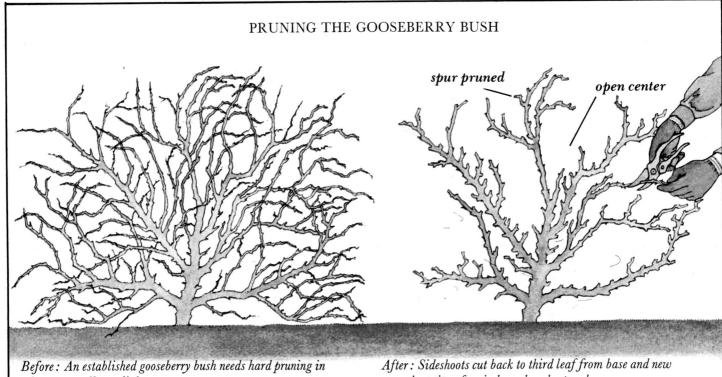

spur pruned

open center

Before: An established gooseberry bush needs hard pruning in
winter, as well as a lighter summer one.

After: Sideshoots cut back to third leaf from base and new
growth at tips of main branches shortened.

long, have all buds removed except for the top four and are inserted some 15 cm [6″] apart, with all the buds above ground, into friable soil. The following winter the young bushes should be ready to transplant into their permanent quarter. Layers can also be used, in summer, and these root very readily.

Pests and diseases

An occasional fungus disease is American gooseberry mildew. This shows as a dense, white powdery fungus on the undersurface of leaves, and on shoots in spring and later on berries. On the shoots it becomes brown and felty. Cut back to healthy growth, and spray with dinocap or a systemic fungicide. Take care to prune out felted shoots in winter, and burn.

European gooseberry mildew shows as white patches also, but on the upper surface of leaves. Treat as for American mildew, and collect fallen leaves.

For cane blight and leaf spot spray with a fungicide permitted in your state. The best cure for crown gall is to purchase plants free of it.

In many areas gooseberries are forbidden because of the danger from white pine blister rust.

Gooseberry sawfly caterpillars are easily controlled with liquid derris sprayed thoroughly all over the bushes as soon as the newly hatched caterpillars are seen. Other pests are aphids, capsids, red spider mite and birds. If birds have pecked out the winter buds, attacked branches should be cut back to the first strong bud. Occasionally die-backs of shoots will occur and this must be removed. If borers attack, cut off the damaged portions.

Grape

These luscious creamy-white, green, blue, red or black fruit may be eaten raw as dessert, pressed for their juice (and make jelly or ferment into wine) or dried to make raisins or currants.

The grape vine is one of the oldest fruit-bearing plants. Records show it was known to the Egyptians. It appears to be native to Southern Russia, near the Black Sea. Carried by conquering Greeks and Romans, it has spread to most temperate regions of the world.

Vines climb by means of coiling, forked tendrils produced opposite two out of every three leaves. The leaves grow on long stalks and are hand-shaped with toothed edges, 7.5-23 cm [3-9″] long. When the vine is kept short by pruning, it develops a stout stem. The fruit is creamy white or green (both classified as white), or dark red to blue and black with a blue bloom. Flesh is always greenish; it is the inclusion of the dark skin that gives red wine its color.

The genus includes about 60 species, most of them native to America. The fox grape, *V. labrusca*, and the muscadine, *V. rotundifolia*, both produce fruit with a musky flavour. When American vines were first introduced into Europe, they brought with them the aphid *Phylloxera vitifoliae* causing devastation. Resistant American rootstocks were then imported and in many countries, though not in Britain, *V. vinifera* is grown on *Phylloxera*-resistant roots. Happily *vinifera* was introduced into California, where it is now the main wine grape, without problems.

Vinifera grapes need cool winters and long dry summers with plenty of sun for successful ripening of the wood and to convert the acid in the fruit into sugar. The vine is hardier than the fig; it can stand moderate amounts of frost in a dormant state, down to $-12°C$ [10°F], but spring frosts occurring after growth has started will kill the shoots. Nor does it like humid summers, though the related American species *V. labrusca* and *V. rotundifolia* withstand humidity better.

Grapes are grouped by the uses to which they are put. There are about 8,000 varieties of grape and the juice of all of them can be fermented but only a few are selected for growing for wine. Dessert grapes need to have a high sugar content and low acidity. Wine grapes need a balance of acidity and sugar and, in addition, need some individuality to lend character to the resulting wine.

The grapes used for wine making can be divided into four main groups. The wines called white burgundy and champagne, named for districts in France, are both made from the same small yellowish green fruit, the Chardonnay or Pineau Blanc. Pineau Noir is a purplish black grape, and makes a rich heavy red wine called burgundy, named for the French town. This has proved popular in California. The claret grape is Cabernet, which is bluish black and produces the light red wine of Bordeaux in France; this grape is another that has been a success in America. White

---

Grape
On the West Coast most important is *Vitis vinifera*. In the East American varieties *V. labrusca*. *V. rotundifolia*, and possibly *V. vulpina* are the most important.
Deciduous vine, with a long life of several centuries.
Size: growing to 27 m [90′] in the wild, but in cultivation frequently kept to 3.5-5 m [12-16′].
Climate: warm temperate to sub-tropical.
Planting to harvesting time: 2 years.

(*Facing page*) '*Black Hamburg*' *grapes growing in a cold house.*

(*Left*) *A fine crop growing on part of a well-established vine.*

wine grapes are often grouped together as Riesling grapes. Raisins are black wine grapes frequently dried in the sun for a month, therefore varieties for this purpose must mature early. Sultanas are smaller, from white grapes, and usually seedless. Currants are the smallest of all and come from smaller, black fruited varieties. Grapes can also be made into juice, jam and jellies and a large industry is centered in western New York State.

Grapes outdoors

In this country, however, prime emphasis is placed upon the northern fox or bunch grape, *V. labrusca*, the leading variety of which is the well-known and old, reliable Concord. Fox grapes are grown throughout the Northeast, Middle West, down into the South as far as the Carolinas, the Northwest and, in smaller numbers, in other parts of the country. In the South they must compete with the muscadines which are more rampant and ripen their few-berried clusters earlier.

Fox grapes are set out in the spring or fall, the former usually being the preferred time, especially in the North, using 1- or 2-year old plants. While fairly tolerant, they do best in a good soil, only slightly acid (6.0-6.5) and well drained. They stand some shade but do better in full sun, away from competing tree roots and preferably on a slope where the cold air can drain away in spring.

Commercially they are often trained to a trunk and four arms (Kniffen System) but for home use they are customarily grown upon fences, trellises or arbors, in each case the pruning being adapted to fit the support. Generally grapes are spaced 8 feet apart each way; however, in the home garden adjustments may be made to fit the immediate situation.

The soil

Since grapes are long-lived, the soil should be prepared well, dug as deeply as convenient under the circumstances and $\frac{1}{2}$ to 1 bushel of well-rotted manure or garden compost thoroughly worked in. In most cases it is also helpful to work in lime as needed. Normally, the plants are set at the same depth they grew in the nursery but, should the soil settle a little, grapes are not as troubled by slightly deep planting.

Fertilizing

Young vines are frequently given added nitrogen in the form of a lawn fertilizer (rather than the usual vegetable or woody plant type) or $\frac{1}{2}$, 1 and 2 pounds of nitrate of soda, respectively, the first, second and third years to form good, sturdy plants. However, in order to get the best results regular balanced annual feeding is desirable. Normally 5-10-5 or a similarly balanced mixture is applied early in the spring, spread over the root area at the rate of 3 to 5 pounds per 100 square feet (10 × 10) and worked into

(*Left*) *Riesling grapes are grown for making excellent white wine.*

the soil.

Of course, where barnyard manure is available it may be applied over the soil as a mulch in place of all or part of the chemical fertilizer according to the needs of the plants. However, it is well to bear in mind that throughout the Southeast, especially, soils are likely to be low in nutrients. The East with the exception of western New York, Kentucky and some relatively small areas, is likely to be acidic. So, also, is much of the Northwest, whereas the Southwest is inclined to be neutral or alkaline.

Fruiting

No fruit should be expected the year of planting, a little the next fall and a full crop the fourth season, if conditions are favorable. It is well to bear in mind, also, that unlike apples, grapes do not need sun on them to ripen. So, leaves and stems should not be removed to admit more light. Neither is there any appreciable gain by 'tipping', cutting off the canes four or five nodes beyond the clusters. Rather, as many leaves as possible are preferred to manufacture as much sugar as possible.

The muscadines

As indicated above, these are more rampant growers, especially such varieties as Eden, Thomas and Scuppernong which are normally given 20 feet each away, if conditions permit. All are derived from *V. rotundifolia*. They will grow after a fashion in almost any soil but dislike low, wet spots and barren clay hills, in particular. Best are sandy loams and lime appears less necessary than with bunch grapes, since former hardwoods or pinelands make ideal soils for them.

Because muscadines have spreading but relatively shallow root systems, it is not necessary to have deep soils or to prepare the soil deeply. Nevertheless, planting over rock or hardpan is not recommended. Furthermore, when setting out plants (again 1- or 2-year-olds) plant more than wanted, since there is a fairly high mortality among them until they are firmly established. Because the bunches are small, they are rarely picked in the usual fashion. More likely the vines are shaken and the fruits are picked up from the ground.

European type

For the most part, the grapes grown in California are of the European type, derived from *V. vinifera*, and are divided into three groups: table grapes, raisin grapes and wine grapes. They are relatively vigorous and tend to bear large bunches of fruit the pulp of which does not slip readily out of the skin as with the others.

Since they are more cold-tender than the fox grape group, they are not grown to any extent outside of California. Neither do they like humid climates. However, considerable work has been done at the New York Experiment Station in crossing these with their hardier cousins and a number of rather reliable varieties have resulted, best known of which is Interlaken Seedless. These latter sorts are planted in the spring only.

Pruning

At planting time usually only one cane is permitted to grow on the eastern grapes. Others are removed and the remaining one is cut back to the third bud. Muscadines, being harder to transplant, should be cut back to 1 or 2 buds. All annual pruning done thereafter is done when the leaves are off. If there is danger of bud freezing, wait until all danger of freezing is past. Contrary to popular belief, bleeding does little or no harm.

The cardinal rule is: the fruit is always borne on wood of the current season which, in turn, is borne on stems produced the year before. In other words, a year-old piece of shoot produces buds in the fall. The next year it produces a shoot from each of these buds and the same year attempts to produce 1 to 4 bunches of grapes near the base of each shoot.

As indicated above, most home gardeners disregard commercial methods and prefer to grow their grapes on arbors, fences, etc., using them for ornament and shade as well as fruit. Leave one trunk per vine if possible, although any number of trunks or arms can be allowed, if their canes are shortened correspondingly to keep them within the strength of the vine. Thus, the pattern is one the gardener, himself, sets and each year all canes are cut back to within 1 to 4 four buds of where they started, varying the number of the buds with the strength of the canes. (See below.)

Where winters are more severe the fan system is sometimes used. There is no trunk. The canes are trained upwards fanwise on wires or trellis slats and the head is kept close to ground level. This allows one to release the canes and drop them to the ground so they can be covered for the winter. Each year as many canes as the vine can support are saved and several more cut back to spurs for future canes, since the canes are not permanent under this system. While muscadines are often grown on wires in a modified Kniffen System, homeowners are much more likely to grow them on arbors or other supports by an overhead system. The vine is trained to a single trunk alongside a 7-foot post. When it reaches the top it is caused to branch out like the spokes in a horizontal wheel. Thereafter, the vines are allowed to grow with relatively little pruning. Being more vigorous plants, it is not so important that vigor is revived by such severe pruning as with other grapes.

As with the other types, homeowners are likely to grow the European grapes on arbors also. However, since the trunks can suffer sun damage in the warm western climate, it is best to allow some short spurs to grow on them to shade them with their leaves. When the vines attempt to bear too heavily they are thinned by removing some of the flower clusters before they open or by thinning the clusters after the fruits have set.

If one is in doubt about how many buds to leave, he may fall back on this rule, although it applies mostly to the eastern bunch grapes. If the weight of the prunings is less than 1 pound, leave less than 30 buds; if 2 pounds, leave 40 buds; if 3, leave 50; if 4, leave 60.

Growing grapes in a greenhouse

It is also possible to grow grapes in a greenhouse and a few are still so grown on private estates, although most of us buy California-grown ones. However, properly grown, the fruits are truly choice.

PLANTING VINES OUTSIDE GREENHOUSE

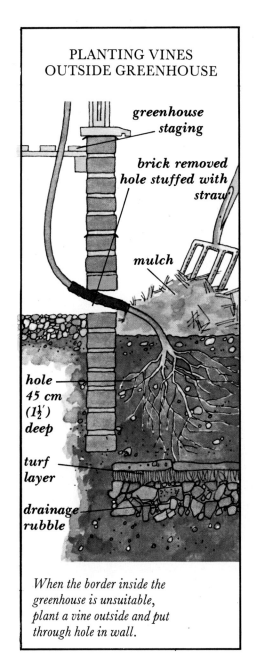

greenhouse staging

brick removed hole stuffed with straw

mulch

hole 45 cm (1½') deep

turf layer

drainage rubble

When the border inside the greenhouse is unsuitable, plant a vine outside and put through hole in wall.

TRAINING IN THE GREENHOUSE

Grapes can be grown in a greenhouse. Train the rod upright as high as the ridge and then pass horizontally along the length of the house, 45 cm [1½'] below the glass.

vine along ridge in small house

single rod

double rod

horizontal rod spur pruned

With even, three-quarter span and lean-to roofs, the vines may be grown as single or double permanent rods up the glass roof.

In a lean-to house which is also being used for other plants, the vine can be trained horizontally to allow light to enter freely.

SPUR PRUNING OF PERMANENT RODS

Pull down laterals and tie in to horizontal wires. Prune two leaves after the grape bunch and prune sideshoots to one leaf.

Prune each spur to two buds, from each of which a lateral will grow.

135

For growing in the greenhouse, the permanent rod and spur system is generally preferred. One stem is allowed to extend to the full length of the space to be filled, and gradually thickens, while pruning maintains a constant supply of fruiting spurs. For walls a variant of the permanent rod, trained to fit the available space with more horizontal wood, is best.

Suitable greenhouse sites

Grapes may be grown in a very small greenhouse. The roots may either be planted in a well-prepared border within the house, or be planted outside. In a small house, the rod is passed through the end wall, goes upright as high as the ridge and then passes horizontally along the length of the ridge of the house, some 45 cm [1½'] below the glass.

In a three-quarter span or full span house the rods are trained from the floor up under the sloping glass to within 45 cm [1½'] of the ridge. Plant two vines 1.2-1.5 m [4-5'] apart and let each one bear one rod. If each vine bears two rods, then plant 1.8-2.1 m [6-7'] apart. In a lean-to house used for other plants (but not tomatoes or cucumbers), plant one vine for each 3m [10'] and train horizontally with spur pruning.

Wire the vines horizontally at 30 cm [1'] intervals by screwing long spikes with eyes into the greenhouse framework and threading wires through them. They should be 45 cm [1½'] from the glass. These wires support the main rod and eventually take a lot of weight.

Planting in the greenhouse

Good drainage is essential to vines. In the greenhouse border you will do best to dig out the soil to 75 cm [2½'] depth and fill the bottom 15-23 cm [6-9"] with rubble. Return the soil, mixing with it two 12 L [2¼ gal] buckets of rotted manure and 125 g [4 oz] of bonemeal per plant.

Training a permanent rod

The best time to plant is late autumn. Spread the roots out

PRUNING FOR A DOUBLE GUYOT

top wire to support net at fruiting time

double wires to support fruiting laterals

pole to support young shoots

three growth buds

3 buds for young shoots

1. Double Guyot system (popular in Europe): the vine is pruned just after planting in autumn or spring

2. Next season these will produce three good shoots.

3. Second winter, prune best two to 75 cm [2½'].

4. When the sap starts rising, pull down the two shoots to the bottom wire. The third has three good buds.

5. Select six to eight laterals per vine and support between twin wires. Tie replacement shoots vertically.

buds to be removed

replacement shoots

growth nipped off

fruit bearing laterals

well, plant at the same depth as it grew, and water each vine well after planting. Stake with a 1.8 m [6'] cane to each plant.

After planting, cut the stem back hard to about 30 cm [1'] and tie to the cane. In spring, choose the strongest shoot for the main rod and set this in vertically removing any other sideshoots.

When sideshoots start to develop on the main rod, allow them to grow to 45-60 cm [18-24"] long, then stop them just above a leaf and tie them in. They should be spaced alternately on each side of the stem, with about 45 cm [1½'] between two on the same side. Remove others.

Sub-sideshoots are pinched back, just above the first leaf. The tip of the main rod is removed when it reaches the second wire from the top or if it has begun to get straggly and thin. When this has been done, all sideshoots can be allowed to grow naturally until the end of the season. Remove tendrils and the embryo flower buds constantly.

Early in the second winter, cut the main rod back one-half to one-third, and sideshoots to one or two buds, beginning the formation of the spur.

During the second spring and summer, a new shoot will grow at the end of the main rod and this is again treated as a leader, and stopped at the second wire from the top. Sideshoots are treated as before, but if the vine is growing strongly, it can be allowed to set fruit, but only two or three bunches. In the third winter, prune the new growth of the leader by about half, and sideshoots to one or two buds.

Thereafter, routine pruning of the established vine is as follows: in early winter, cut any new growth at the end of the rod, and the sideshoots, back to one or two buds. In spring: remove shoots when about 2.5 cm [1"] long so as to leave one at the tip of the rod, and one on each spur. In early summer, stop all sideshoots at just above the second leaf beyond the bunch, or at the sixth leaf if there is no bunch, and tie in. Pinch out sub-sideshoots at one leaf and remove all tendrils constantly.

Siegerrebe, reddish-brown when ripe, is an excellent grape for use both for wine and dessert.

USING CLOCHES WITH THE SINGLE GUYOT

Grow only one replacement rod. Cover fruiting rod after fruit sets. Leave cloche ends open.

THINNING GRAPE BUNCHES FOR DESSERT FRUIT

shoulders supported by raffia

Bunches should be this sparse after thinning. Be careful not to touch the fruit.

Black grapes from St. Jeannet in the south of France, grown on the popular European Guyot system. The vines must be in their fifth year before carrying a heavy crop.

VINE PROPAGATION

bud

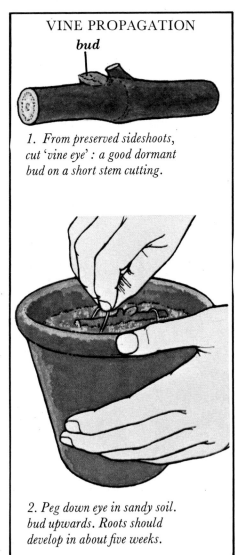

1. From preserved sideshoots, cut 'vine eye': a good dormant bud on a short stem cutting.

2. Peg down eye in sandy soil. bud upwards. Roots should develop in about five weeks.

Feeding and watering

In late winter, whether the vine is rooted inside the greenhouse or outside, rake off all the old mulch. Dress the soil surface at the rate of 0.5 kg per sq m [1 lb per sq yd] with a good general fertilizer. Fork this in lightly, then mulch if possible with half-rotted manure. If the grape is rooted inside the house or against a wall, start in early spring to soak the border with water at about 10 L per 100 sq cm [2 gal per sq ft].

On completion of thinning in early to midsummer commence regular feeding. Start with a fertilizer at 250 g per sq m [½ lb per sq yd], and follow this at two week intervals with a liquid fertilizer at the rate of 12 L [2½ gal] per vine, until colour appears in the berries.

Ventilation and spraying in the greenhouse

The vine is relatively hardy after leaf fall: for the best results if should be subjected to a few weeks' exposure to wintry weather, with the ventilators fully open.

If the house contains more tender varieties, some artificial heat to 5°C [40°F] is desirable during the winter until the end of spring, when it should rise to 15°C [60°F]. While pollination is taking place in early summer, you should try to maintain a minimum night yemperature of 10°C [50°F] for all varieties. During the growing period commence ventilation before the temperature exceeds 19°C [65°F].

Grape thinning

Vines should not be allowed to bear heavy crops till after their fifth year. Dessert grapes (but not wine grapes) are thinned to improve appearance and quality. First reduce the number of bunches. A strong rod of 4.5-4.8 m [15-16'] should be allowed to bear 10-12 bunches.

Do not touch berries as this destroys the bloom. Use a forked twig or piece of wire about 15 cm [6''] long to manipulate that portion of the bunch being thinned. Use a sharp pair of pointed scissors carefully; avoid pricking and spoiling other berries while removing those not required.

Harvesting

A dark tinge with black grapes and a slightly transparent appearance in white grapes are the signs of approaching ripening. In the greenhouse reduce humidity by ceasing to dampen the floor and surroundings, and increase ventilation by day, permitting some at night. Keep a good canopy of foliage over black grapes to improve berry color, but expose white grapes to all available light, avoiding direct sunshine. Taste for ripeness and cut with 5 cm [2''] of lateral on each side of the shank.

Pests and Diseases

The most serious disease attacking eastern grapes (muscadines are rarely troubled by diseases) is black rot which turns the fruits shrivelled and raisin-like. Spray with Ferbam or whatever fungicide is permitted. Downy and powdery mildews on eastern and California grapes may be checked by Mildex.

If leaf hoppers or aphids attack, spray with nicotine sulfate, or rotenone. Japanese beetles and grape berry moths can be controlled by non-poisonous Sevin. Root aphids

(Phylloxera) are best controlled by grafting on Phylloxera-resistant roots.

In the greenhouse, mildew (*Uncinula necatrix*) causes the most trouble of the fungus diseases, while red spider mite, aphids, scale insects, mealy bug and vine weevil are the most likely of the insect pests to attack. Vine weevil can be controlled by working an approved insecticide into soil and dusting it into hiding places. The aphid *Phylloxera vitifoliae* infests the roots, producing galls on them, and also attacks the leaves, but to a lesser extent.

When the stalks of the berries dry up before ripening, this is a condition called shanking. Another trouble is scalding, in which one side of the berry becomes sunken, dry and wrinkled. It is caused by sun shining onto moisture on the berry, and ventilation must be increased, starting earlier in the day.

Greengage

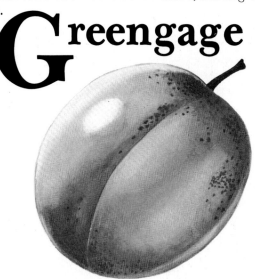

Greengage is a type of plum, with a distinctive honey flavor. The typical greengage is named for its scented green flesh, but some are gold fleshed.

The greengage, *Prunus italica*, is named after Sir Thomas Gage who reintroduced it to England in the eighteenth century. Fruit come reasonably true to seed and they have been interbred with other plums. There are two types of gage: the transparent gage which has a transparent skin when ripe, and the old English gage, with a thicker skin. Skins are green or yellow, sometimes red spotted.

They grow on sturdy bushes or small trees 3.7 m [12'] high. Like other plums, they need a lot of moisture and a climate with short springs and hot summers. Unfortunately, they are not common in the U.S.A.

For cultivation *see* PLUM.

Gumbo

SEE **OKRA**

Hamburg Parsley

A variety of the familiar herb, Hamburg parsley is grown for its thick, off-white, parsnip-like roots, which taste rather like celeriac. The leaves can also be used for flavoring.

Hamburg parsley originated in central Europe, and was introduced from Germany, hence its name. The roots can be eaten raw or cooked.

Suitable site and soil

Hamburg parsley can tolerate a good deal of shade, so it is a useful plant to grow where other crops will not thrive.

The soil should have been manured for a previous crop; failing this, work in well-rotted garden compost, or a general fertilizer at the rate of 125 g per sq m [4 oz per sq yd]. Fresh manure should not be used, because it may cause the roots to fork, as with other root vegetables. The soil must be dug thoroughly, and all stones removed.

Sowing, thinning and cultivation

Sow in early spring, putting seeds into drills 1.5 cm [½″] deep and 30 cm [1′] apart. Thin seedlings to 23 cm [9″] apart.

As long as the weather is reasonably warm and the soil is kept moist, the seeds should germinate within 10-14 days, but the process can be very slow, sometimes taking several weeks. It is a good idea to sow lettuce or radish between the parsley drills to mark their position; this also makes maximum use of the land. The salad crop will be ready to lift in early summer, leaving the root crop to mature for pulling later in the year. To have some ready for the spring,

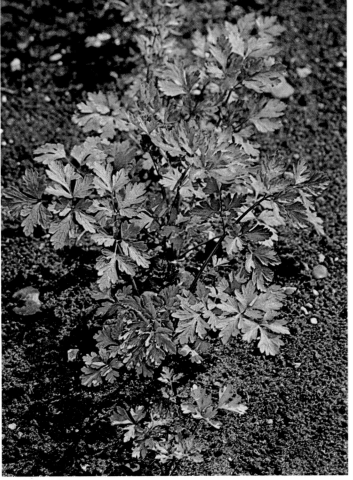

(*Above*) *The foliage of Hamburg parsley remains through the winter and can be used like parsley for flavoring.*

1. Sow Hamburg parsley during the early spring, with a lettuce or radish catch crop to avoid wasting space.

2. Harvest Hamburg parsley in late autumn or winter when the roots are fully developed. Store like parsnips.

Hamburg parsley
Petroselinum crispum tuberosum (fam.
Umbelliferae), also known as turnip-rooted parsley.
Hardy biennial, grown as an **annual.**
Size: grows to 30-60 cm [1-2′] tall; roots 17.5-20 cm [7-8″] long and 7.5 cm [3″] thick.
Climate: cool to warm temperate.
Sowing to harvesting time: 9 months.
Yield: 4.5 kg [10 lb] per 3 m [10′] row.

---

sow in the previous summer where mild climate permits. Hoe to remove weeds and water the plants generously.

Harvesting and storing the crop

Harvest spring-sown Hamburg parsley into autumn and winter when the roots are fully grown – 17.5-20 cm [7-8″] long. In contrast to those of most root vegetables, the largest roots are the best-tasting.

The roots may be left in the ground to be dug as required. The foliage remains throughout the winter and can be used, like that of the herb, for flavoring. If there is a possibility that the ground in winter may be frozen too hard to dig, cover with straw or lift some of the roots in late autumn and store as for parsnips. Reject any roots that have been damaged by pests, disease or bruising.

Horseradish

Horseradish roots have a pungent peppery flavor. The distinctive tang of horseradish sauce is a favorite accompaniment to beef and fish.

Native to Europe, the horseradish plant (*Armoracia rusticana*) is a member of the *Cruciferae* family. A perennial herb, it bears large, glossy, spoon-shaped leaves and small white flowers which appear in early summer. The plant grows up to 60 cm [2′] tall with lower leaves as long, and it is cultivated for its fleshy roots. The roots freshly grated are used in cooking.

A hardy perennial, horseradish will grow anywhere, and after dying away in winter it will take over more ground each season if it is left to itself. If the plant is allowed to run rampant it produces wispy, elongated roots.

Cultivation

Choose a small section of well-drained ground in full sun. Each plant needs 1 sq m [1 sq yd], dug to a depth of about

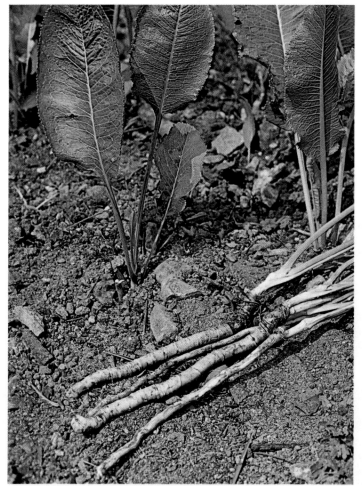

The long pungent roots of horseradish can be fitted well into a crop rotation plan, as they are lifted annually.

1. Horseradishes need a well-excavated site, to a depth of at least 60 cm [2′], as the tap root is exceptionally long.

2. Plant the roots 15 cm [6″] deep, so that the top is just below soil level, at a spacing of 45 cm [1½′] apart.

60 cm [2′] for really good roots – it produces very large tap roots. A deep, rich loam is ideal, so plenty of well rotted manure, garden compost or leaf mold should be added. It pays to be generous to the horseradish because other crops will benefit when they are moved to the site. Avoid using fresh manure.

Roots for planting should be about 20 cm [8″] long, with a bud. These should be obtained at a grocer or taken from some already established plant in late autumn or early winter. Plant the roots 45 cm [1½′] apart and 15 cm [6″] deep. Roots planted at this time will produce new shoots by spring. The only attention a horseradish bed needs is to keep it neat by removing dead leaves.

Harvesting and propagation

When the leaves are growing strongly, by late spring, there should be roots to dig near the surface which can be harvested without disturbing the whole plant.

The roots are more pungent when freshly dug and lose their essential flavor when dried, but it is usually possible to dig them throughout the year, if sufficiently mulched.

To get really plump roots and keep horseradish under control, lift the whole plant in early spring the following year. Divide for replanting in a new bed and keep the thicker roots for grating; packing them in moist sand or peat if they are not immediately required.

Kale

An exceptionally hardy plant, kale can be grown successfully even in poor soil. It makes an excellent alternative to cabbage, cooked and eaten in the same way.

There are four types of kale: the moss-leaved or Scotch kale, the most popular, grown for its parsley-like leaves; the plain-leaved type, even hardier, and grown for its

shoots, produced in winter or early spring; rape kale, one variety of which is well named Hungry Gap, as it provides shoots in late spring, when vegetables are at a premium; and fourthly, a new race of hybrid kales which are grown both for their leaves and spears, like sprouting broccoli. The name borecole refers only to the moss curled varieties. Kale is the supreme stand-in for producing winter greens and is so hardy it will stand severe frost.

Suitable site and soil

There are few places in the garden where kale will not thrive, although plants grown in the open tend to be stronger and stockier than those grown in shade, and the tall varieties may be blown over on sites exposed to the wind. Kale does best in a rich soil but will grow almost anywhere, in either acid or limy soils. Use soil that was manured for a previous crop.

Sowing, thinning and transplanting

Few gardeners want kale for harvesting at any time other than the colder months of the year. In order to obtain the main crop then, sow seed from mid to late spring.

Sowing to germination takes 7-12 days and the temperature for germination can vary between 4 and 35°C [40 and 95°F]. Sow the seed thinly in drills 1.5 cm [½″] deep and 23 cm [9″] apart, and transplant firmly when 4 or 5 leaves are present, at a spacing of 45-60 cm [1½-2′]. Put the plants in up to the lowest true leaf.

The rape kales, which are harvested from mid to late spring, are sown between late spring and midsummer, where they are to crop. Drills should be 45 cm [1½′] apart, and the young plants are thinned to the same spacing.

Harvesting and cultivation

Most varieties have loose crowns rather than the tight hearts found in cabbages. These crowns are cut first, and then, in the case of kales grown mainly for their leaves, the youngest leaves are removed, from the top downwards. This stimulates the production of sideshoots.

Little attention is required after transplanting or sowing, except to keep the plants well watered in dry weather and to control weeds with the hoe. Earth the plants up to their basal leaves in autumn.

After-care

By the end of winter, the stalks will be almost as woody as young trees. The surplus foliage may be put on the compost heap, but the stalks would take so long to rot that they

---

Kale
Brassica oleracea acephala (fam. *Cruciferae*)
Also known as borecole.
Hardy perennial, grown as an **annual.**
Size: up to 45 cm [1½′] across; height from 30 cm [1′] for dwarf varieties to 120 cm [4′] for tall varieties.
Climate: cool temperate.
Sowing to harvesting time: from 8 weeks on.
Yield: 0.5-0.75 kg [1-1½ lb] per plant.

1. Sow kale thinly in late spring or early summer in shallow drills.

2. When five leaves have developed, transplant firmly up to lowest leaf.

3. In autumn, earth up the plants to basal leaves with a draw hoe.

4. On leaf and spear varieties, harvest loose crowns in the spring.

5. Without crowns, side shoots will develop; pick these like broccoli.

6. Store kale by immersing whole head in frequently changed water.

Moss-leaved or Scotch kale variety is grown solely for its leaves.

A blue-green curly variety: kale is an excellent source of winter greens. All varieties can withstand harder frost than other brassicas.

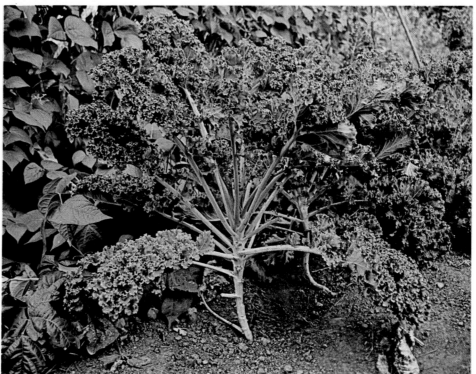

are best burned – after drying – or else put in a place where, covered with soil or debris, they can be allowed ample time to decay.

Pests and diseases

These are the same as those of cabbage, flea beetles being the chief menace, but kales have some resistance to clubroot and cabbage root fly.

Kohlrabi

Kohlrabi belongs to the cabbage family, but actually looks more like a turnip. The swollen stem is the part which is eaten and makes a delicious, nutty-flavored vegetable.

Kohlrabi is said to have been brought to western Europe by the Crusaders. Although it is usually classified as a root vegetable, the edible part is really the stem, swollen to bulbous dimensions. There are two varieties – 'white' (actually pale green in color) and 'purple'. Both have white flesh and there is little to choose between them. The quality of this vegetable depends largely on quick, unchecked

---

Kohlrabi
Brassica oleracea caulorapa (fam. *Cruciferae*), also known as turnip-rooted cabbage.
Biennial, grown as an **annual.**
Size: the swollen stem (the edible part of the plant) should be allowed to reach a diameter of not more than about 7.5 cm [3″]; the plant grows to a height of 12-20 cm [5-8″].
Climate: cool temperate.
Sowing to harvesting time: 7-8 weeks.
Yield: 20 'globes', each about 200 g [7-8 oz], per 3 m [10′] row.

1. Lime in fall or winter or before planting.

2. Sow in shallow drill outdoors, from mid spring.

3. Thin seedlings as soon as large enough to handle. Leave one at each station.

4. Lift roots of 5 cm first. Leave alternate roots to grow larger.

(Opposite) Mature kohlrabi and (below) young plants.

growth, and it is not suitable for storing, except when deep-frozen. If left in the ground it may become too large to be edible.

Suitable site and soil

The site should be sunny. Kohlrabi grows best in a fertile loam, although it can be grown in most soils. The better the soil, the quicker the growth and therefore the more succulent the vegetable, but do not grow kohlrabi in freshly manured soil; use one which has been manured for a previous year's crop. Check the soil for acidity with a pH test and apply lime if necessary.

Cultivation

Sow outdoors in mid-spring; successive sowings can be made up to early summer. For an early crop, sow under Hotkaps or in frames or greenhouses 4-6 weeks earlier. Transplant about a week after the last frost date.

Sown about 1.5 cm [½"] deep in drills 38-45 cm [15-18"] apart. Transplant to rows about the same distance apart, with 10-15 cm [4-6"] between the plants in each row. Be careful not to insert the plants too deeply in the soil when transplanting, or the 'globe' may form below the surface. Alternatively, sow the seeds thinly where they are to mature and thin them to 15 cm [6"] apart.

It is essential to keep the plants growing without a check. Keep them well-watered, and hoe frequently, not only to suppress weeds but also to loosen soil around plants.

Harvesting and after-care

Pull up the plants as soon as a moderate-sized globe has formed – 7.5 cm [3"] diameter is about the maximum; 5 cm [2"] is better. If left to grow bigger, the globe will be woody inside. When harvested young, the globes may simply be scrubbed and cooked whole; older specimens should be peeled. Cut off the roots and leaves. For deep-freezing, blanch whole if young, peel and dice if older.

Kohlrabi produces a small amount of waste material – this can be added to the compost heap. For future use of the plot, remember that kohlrabi is a brassica and avoid following with other brassicas.

Pests and diseases

The pests most likely to occur are turnip-flea beetle (*see* TURNIP), and clubroot if kohlrabi are grown in acid soil.

Lamb's Lettuce

SEE **CORN SALAD**

Leek

One of the finest of all vegetables, the leek is easy to grow. The blanched bases of the leaves make a tasty fresh vegetable in the depth of winter. The leaf tops may be used for soup.

Although some of the finest leeks are cultivated in Scotland, their connection with Wales and St. David goes back to the sixth century when the Welsh wore them as distinguishing badges in their battles with the Saxons. 'Leek' is in fact derived from the Saxon word for a plant.

Suitable site and soil

Leeks do best in moist, light soil that has been heavily manured for a previous crop, or one which was treated with garden compost or leaf mold the winter before planting. Apart from this, the choice of location in the vegetable plot may be influenced by the fact that leeks are often mulched and left in the ground to be dug up as required throughout the winter, and can occupy the site for over 12 months. If you use a strict rotation system you should bear this in mind, unless you have reserved a plot for semi-permanent crops like asparagus and artichokes, and there is some free space there for your leeks.

Sowing and thinning

Sow the seed outdoors in early spring in a well prepared nursery bed. Sow thinly (about 100 seeds to the yard) in drills about 0.5 cm [¼"] deep, and cover with fine soil. Germination should take 14-21 days, and thinning should

---

Leek
Allium ampeloprasum porrum (fam. *Lihiaceae*)
Hardy biennial.
Size: Leaves to 30 cm [1'] long; bulbs 7.5-15 cm [3-6"] long and up to 11 cm [4½'] in diameter ('pot' varieties), 15-30 cm [6-12"] long and 5 cm [2"] in diameter ('long' varieties).
Climate: temperate.
Sowing to harvesting time: about 23 weeks.
Yield: 10-12 plants per 3 m [10'] row.

1. By midsummer, leeks
should be transplanted.
Lift carefully with fork.

2. Before replanting,
trim tips of leaves to
avoid excessive drooping.

3. Also trim roots back
to within 2.5 cm [1″] of
base to improve rooting.

4. Make holes for leeks
vertical and wider at the
top; use a thick dibber.

5. After planting leeks,
fill holes with water and
leave standing upright.

6. A blanching method:
tie black plastic around
stem up to base of leaves.

7. Then draw up soil from
between rows using a draw
hoe. Repeat as necessary.

8. Harvest the leeks when
wanted; always lift with
a fork, the largest first.

9. To heel in, dig narrow
trench in cool place and
place leeks on one side.

10. Cover the leeks with
soil up to the leaves and
then firm down with feet.

ALTERNATIVE BLANCHING METHOD

1. Fix paper collar like
this soon after planting.

2. Later use 30 cm [1′]
by 10 cm [4″] drain pipe.

begin as soon as possible, when the plants are not more than thin green shoots, about 6 weeks from sowing. Thin moderately the first time, as some of the plants may die, and then thin again when all seems to be going well, to end up with plants about 10 cm [4″] apart.

Transplanting

By midsummer, when they are about as thick as pencils, the leeks will be ready for transplanting to the permanent bed. Manuring the permanent bed has already been mentioned. Water the seedbed the day before lifting if the soil is dry. You may simply plant the leeks in shallow drills, like cabbages, but it is really no more trouble to adopt the popular method of planting them in holes.

Make the holes with a thick dibber to a depth of 15 cm [6″] spaced about 23 cm [9″] apart, with 30 cm [1′] between the rows. Make sure that the holes are vertical, and move the dibber about from side to side to enlarge them at the top. Cut back the roots to within 2.5 cm [1″] of their origin, trim off the tips of the leaves to a length of about 10 cm [4″]. Then simply lower the young leeks into the holes, and gently fill the holes with water, leaving the plants standing upright. Sufficient soil will be washed in to support the plants. As you hoe the rows from time to time the holes will gradually fill up with soil.

Leeks grown in this way will not be completely blanched, but the pale green portion seems to give the best flavor to a soup. If you prefer to eat your leeks thoroughly blanched, however, this can be done quite easily, as described later.

Another way of growing leeks, used mainly by gardeners growing their plants for exhibition, is to plant them 25 cm [10″] apart in a trench. This should have been excavated to a depth of about 30 cm [1′], and if there is more than one trench, they should be about 60 cm [2′] apart. Into the bottom of each trench, dig about 7.5 cm [3″] of well-rotted manure or garden compost and cover it with about 15 cm [6″] of the topsoil. Shape the remaining topsoil into flat-topped ridges between the rows, upon which a catch-crop of lettuce, for example, can be grown before the soil is required for earthing up the growing leeks. In the now fairly shallow trench, carefully plant the leeks, perfectly upright, with a trowel.

Care and development

Water the transplanted seedlings generously until they are well established. Soon after planting give them liquid manure. If the pre-planting application of organic matter was in short supply, nitrate of soda or sulphate of ammonia may be applied at the rate of 10 g per meter [$\frac{1}{3}$ oz per yd] about 5 weeks after planting.

Blanching

Begin the process of blanching in early to mid-autumn. This is usually done by earthing up the stems. To ensure that soil does not get into the stems, 'collars' are secured

Harvesting leeks. When placing the plants remember that they may remain in the ground through the winter. Place accordingly for easier harvesting.

around them up to the base of the leaves. Various materials can be used for the collar; lengths sawn from plastic piping or, at virtually no cost at all, pieces of strong brown paper secured with string or rubber bands. The latter will need support from bamboo canes. If necessary, the collar can also be made from short lengths of clay drainpipe; this is about the right size and will remain stable, even in strong winds.

Attach the collars before carrying out the earthing up process. To do this, draw up the soil from between the rows with a draw hoe. As the plants grow, draw up more soil, fitting on another collar above the first one.

Harvesting the crop

Leeks are often harvested from late autumn to mid-spring. As mentioned earlier, they are generally left where they grow until they are wanted. The only problem likely to arise is when the soil is frozen too hard for a fork to be driven into it. Never try dragging leeks out of the ground by brute force; you will be left with a slimy handful of leaves and a ruined plant. Lift them with a fork, taking the largest leeks first, leaving the smaller ones in the ground to grow.

If the plot is needed before all the leeks are consumed, however, they may be dug up and 'heeled in'; lay them on their sides in a shallow trench in a cool place with their tops projecting above the ground, and cover them with soil, ready to dig up for cooking.

Sowing under glass

To grow early leeks, for harvesting in early autumn, sow under glass in early spring. Leek seeds, although small, are not too small to handle singly, and they should be sown about 2.5 cm [1″] apart in a seed tray containing a standard seed mixture.

About six weeks after sowing, the tray may be moved into a closed cold frame for the seedlings to be gradually hardened off. Later prick them out into another frame at about 20 cm [8″] apart. Provided that the weather is not unduly harsh for the time of year, the leeks will be ready for planting by mid-spring. In mild winter areas sow between August and mid-September.

Pests and diseases

These are generally the same as for onions, although leeks are usually free of troubles. There are, however, one or two diseases which are specific to leeks and can be a nuisance. Rust can cause trouble, especially when the autumn and winter are mild. Older leaves show orange-yellow powdery spots, and later turn yellow, dying in a severe attack. Remove badly infected plants, and possible weed hosts, and spray regularly with zineb if the attack is very bad.

White tip is a fungus disease appearing from late summer through the winter. The leaf tips die back, other parts of the leaves and stems show white patches and growth is greatly checked. Badly affected plants should be removed and destroyed, and the plants sprayed every two weeks with a fungicide approved by local authorities, until white patches disappear.

Lemon Verbena

**Lovely lilac flowers
and a delicate fragrance make verbena
a favorite in herb gardens.
Its lemony flavoring, without
the lemon's acidity, is useful
in all kinds of cookery.**

Lemon verbena (*Aloysia triphylla* also listed as *Lippia citriodoro*) is a member of the *Verbenaceae* family and is often confused with vervain (*Verbena officinalis*) which is very different and bitter tasting. The leaves of lemon verbena are dried for lemon flavoring, used to make a refreshing tea and to scent soaps and cosmetics. They can also be used fresh in salads and fruit drinks in summer. It is a deciduous, aromatic shrub, native to Chile and Peru but easily cultivated in cool temperate areas. On a sunny wall it will grow up to 1.8 m [6′] high, bearing small lilac flowers and fragrant leaves for harvesting in late summer.

Lemon verbena is also an excellent choice for container growing. Any large tub or similar container is suitable.

Cultivation
The most suitable site is by a sunny wall, but any sunny position which is reasonably sheltered is adequate. Lemon verbena prefers a light, well-drained soil. If the soil is heavy, improve it by working in coarse sand. If you are growing the plant in a tub or other container, use a standard potting mixture.

Lemon verbena is started from plants bought at the nursery. Usually one will be sufficient for domestic use. Plant in late spring. Be sure the roots are well watered while the plant establishes itself; a mulch of garden compost or leaf mold over the root area will offset the dryness common to plants grown by a wall or fence.

After young shoots begin to grow, a light pruning can be given in early summer to cut out any dead wood and shorten some of the shoots to give the shrub a good shape. Lemon verbena will survive mild winters in a sheltered position, but in frosty areas it is advisable to protect the roots and lower stem with canvas or sacking on a light frame. Do not allow the covering to become soggy – it needs to be frost-proof and dry. In areas where winters are at all

(Right) The beautiful, lilac flowers and fragrant leaves of the lemon verbena plant will thrive on a sunny wall.

severe it is better to grow lemon verbena in a tub and take it indoors or into the greenhouse in autumn.

Harvesting and propagation
Leaves may be clipped off in late summer. Tie them in bunches and hang to dry, then powder them and store the powder in an air-tight jar or container to preserve its flavor and aroma.

Once the shrub is established it can be propagated by cuttings taken from new shoots in early summer.

Lettuce

**The most popular salad green, lettuce,
is easily grown and has a high
year-round yield. Its leaves also make
a delicious soup.**

Lettuce is said to have reached Europe from the East Indies; it was introduced into England in the sixteenth century and was known in the gardens of Hampton Court in the time of Henry VIII and brought to America by the early colonists.

There are three main types: head lettuce, the taller and snappier 'cos' and the frizzy-headed loose-leaf. The latter

---

Lettuce
Lactuca sativa (fam. *Compositae*).
Half-hardy annual.
Size: between 23 and 38 cm [9 and 15″] wide.
Climate: temperate.
Sowing to harvesting time: 8-14 weeks.
Yield: 9-12 heads, each, on average, 340 g [12 oz] per 3 m [10′] row.

(Above) Butterhead lettuces being grown under cloches. Butterheads are 'head' types. They are soft and round and usually grow very quickly.

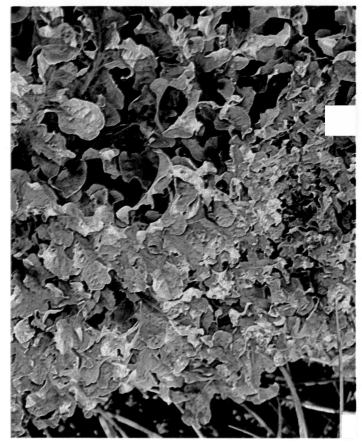

Crisp heart varieties are slower maturing and usually more heat- and bolt-resistant than butterhead types.

The 'loose-leaf' varieties are very popular in both America and Australia. This type has a high vitamin content.

is harvested by picking single leaves, not by pulling the whole plant, and can be useful for garnishing. The heading type can further be divided into 'butterheads' with tender, butter-colored hearts and 'crispheads', which are crisper and have hearts that blanch to white instead. Numerous dwarf varieties of lettuce are available.

Lettuce has been much hybridized in the last fifteen years or so, and there are all sorts of varieties available now, for growing at particular periods of the year. Catalogues will specify which varieties are suitable for which season. When growing out of season, in particular, it is important to choose the varieties which have been bred specially for that particular purpose, say, early spring cropping, or heated greenhouse winter cropping.

Suitable site and soil

Lettuce prefers a moist but well-drained soil, well dug. Well broken down clay soils produce very good plants, but so will sandy or gravelly ones, provided they are bulked well with organic matter. To ensure good water retention without sogginess, incorporate well-rotted manure or garden compost at the rate of 6 kg [13 lb] per sq m [1 sq yd]. Lettuces are 90 per cent water and there must be water in the soil in sufficient amounts for them to grow fast and form well. Poor and ill-prepared soil will produce floppy leaves and failure to heart up.

Summer lettuce

Sowing outdoors can start in early spring with the first of a succession of sowings every two weeks designed to maintain a supply of lettuce as long as possible. Suitable lettuces are the head, cos or American type.

A mechanical routine of successful sowings does not, however, guarantee an uninterrupted supply of prime lettuces. Except in a steadily favorable climate there are likely to be times when sowing is checked; alternatively, when the weather becomes hot the crop engages in a race to see which plant can bolt first. However, the new summer lettuces are somewhat less likely to bolt in hot weather, provided they never run short of water. Sowing several different kinds of seed will give varied germination and development.

Pelleted seeds are available too, but these will take longer to germinate and will not produce seedlings suitable for transplanting. However, transplanting is really only satisfactory early in the season. Later on, such plants are very liable to bolt, and lettuces are best thinned. The seeds, which are rather fine, should be sown fairly thinly in short, shallow drills about 1.5 cm [$\frac{1}{2}''$] deep and 30 cm [1'] apart. Sow about one seed per 1.5 cm [$\frac{1}{2}''$]. The seed should germinate in about 4-12 days and thinning should be carried out as soon as the first pair of true leaves have formed. Aim for a spacing of one plant at every 23-30 cm [9-12''] depending on the size of the variety. If the thinnings are required as transplants, lever them out gently with a trowel and handle only the leaves with the finger and thumb. Lower the transplants into prepared holes, then firm them down and water them well to ensure that the rootlets make good contact with the soil. When planting do not plant too high otherwise they will not heart. Too

low planting can mean infection of the lower leaves with gray mold; damp encourages fungus disease. The neck of the plant should be exactly at soil level.

Autumn and winter cropping

Besides regular lettuces which are in season from late spring into the summer, it is possible to crop them later in the year. These will be the cabbage or cos types. Seed is sown in midsummer, in succession, until the middle of late summer. The earlier sowings are thinned, the later ones transplanted towards the end of early autumn, into a frame or covered with Hotkaps or a plastic tunnel. The later ones will be slow to grow and may not be ready by early winter, but with protection should stand the winter, and will certainly be ready in early spring, if one lives in a mild climate.

Late winter and early to late spring crops

Lettuce for this (mainly heading types) are sown in early to mid-autumn outdoors under Hotkaps or in a frame or a plastic tunnel, and thinned a month later. They are kept protected all through winter, and a particularly good variety for this is Hot Weather, a very heat- and cold-resistant lettuce. It is also possible to sow in late winter, with protection, thin two or three times, and harvest in late spring; plenty of ventilation will be needed on warm days as the spring develops, if one lives far enough south.

Winter lettuce

It is also possible to obtain lettuce (heading types) from winter to spring in the North, but only with the help of a heated greenhouse. Successive sowings are made from early to late autumn in seed trays, pricking out the seedlings into boxes, and then planting in cropping positions when the first pair of true leaves is fully developed. Temperature from sowing to planting out should be 10-15°C [50-60°F], and 15°C [60°F] for three weeks after planting. Thereafter it should be kept at 10-13°C [50-55°F]. Remember that in very cold, mid-winter spells, it may be very expensive and difficult to maintain this, and it will be cheaper to purchase.

Care and development

Warmth, moisture and a weed-free environment with protection from garden pests are the main principles to bear in mind. If the soil has been well prepared it should be rich in humus to retain moisture adequately. Lettuces must be allowed as much water as their roots require, but they cannot be hurried by overwatering. In hot weather it can be difficult to keep the soil surface moist and prevent it forming a crust, but mulching will largely overcome this, especially if applied just after rain. Use either rotted organic matter, or strips of black plastic.

Hoe frequently between rows and plants, which will kill the weeds before their roots are big enough to compete with the crop.

If cos lettuces are being grown, blanching will increase their crispness. This is simply done by applying a tie of string or a rubber band around the thickest part of the lettuce as it approaches maturity. About a week later a further tie is made higher up.

1. *Start outdoors in early spring, sowing thinly in shallow drills.*

2. *Thin when two leaves are showing. Handle only leaves if transplanting.*

3. *Put the transplants in prepared holes; firm down and water well.*

4. *Sow some lettuce every two weeks until the autumn to maintain supply.*

5. *Keep soil moist; a trickle hose is ideal as water seeps out slowly.*

6. *Mulch to keep soil moist, using plastic strips with holes cut.*

7. *To blanch cos lettuce tie around middle; tie top about a week later.*

8. *Pick lettuce with a sharp knife, cutting just above lowest leaves.*

9. *To store, pull whole plant, tie plastic bag around roots and chill.*

10. *To catch crop, sow lettuce between rows of peas, running north to south to avoid any shading.*

11. *For late winter and spring crops, sow winter lettuce during the autumn under tunnels or Hotkaps.*

12. *Cold frames can also be used; sow in late winter for late spring harvest; ensure good ventilation.*

A tall, crisp, cos lettuce. Both cos and cabbage types should be cut as soon as their hearts feel quite solid.

Container growing

City dwellers can grow a few lettuces in 15 cm [6″] pots, provided they are not shaded in any way. Keep them well watered and protect them from direct sunlight at the sides, by a piece of board, or they will become baked solid.

Harvesting

Harvest lettuces as soon as they are at their best and fully-hearted, for their quality will fall off very rapidly the moment the center begins to show a point. Cut the heads with a sharp knife, just above the lowest leaves. It is better to grow a few more lettuces rather than to wait until they are as large as possible.

Varieties

Among the most popular sorts are: (Head) Buttercrunch, Dark Green Boston, Deer Tongue, Minilake, Ithaca, Great Lakes, Pennlake, Hot Weather (Cos or Romaine); Paris White, Sweet Midget, Valmaine (Loose-Leaf); Black-Seeded Simpson, Grand Rapids, Salad Bowl, Slobalt, Oak Leaf, Green Ice.

Pests and diseases

Lettuce is not particularly troubled by insects or diseases. If small green worms are present, pick them off and, if snails and slugs are troublesome, scatter a bait containing metal dehyde on the soil.

Lima Bean

Grown for their tasty ripe seeds, Lima beans need a moderate climate for successful cultivation.

The Lima bean is somewhat similar to the Garden, or snap, bean, but is less hardy. It is widely cultivated in the United States and other countries with a warm temperate climate, but the summers in cool temperate countries, such as Britain, are usually too short to grow it successfully. There are two basic types – bush and climbing (or pole) Lima beans, and several varieties of each, ranging from small-seeded Limas, also known as butter beans, to large-seeded 'potato beans'. Although the small-seeded types can be picked when young and tender and cooked whole like Garden (snap) beans, Limas are normally grown for their ripe seeds, often dried for keeping.

Suitable site and soil

Choose a sunny site, sheltered from high winds. In selecting a site for pole varieties, remember that they grow to 1.8 m [6′] high and will shade any crops planted alongside. Allow ample space, 75-90 cm [2½-3′] between rows for pole varieties, and 60-75 cm [2-2½′] for bush varieties. Lima beans need a light, warm soil that is sandy but well-manured. To ensure that the plants grow vigorously from the start, work in a compound fertilizer (with a low nitrogen content) at a rate of about 100 g per sq m [3-4 oz per sq yd] seven to ten days before sowing. A dressing of organic manure is also helpful, but dig this in well beforehand, preferably during winter.

Sowing and planting

In moderate climates, sow outdoors about four weeks after the last frost date. In cooler climates, sow under protection about two weeks after the last expected frost date, in preparation for transplanting. Protection can be under Hotkaps, in greenhouses or in frames (preferably heated, in order to make maximum use of summer weather). The temperature for germination should be 15° to 30°C [60° to 85°F]. Transplant plants grown under glass about four weeks after the last frost date, but keep coverings handy in case of unseasonal temperatures or chill winds.
Allow 7.5-15 cm [3-6″] between plants of the bush type in each row and 15-25 cm [6-10″] between plants of the pole types. The space between the rows should be 60-75 cm [2-2½′] for bush types, and 75-90 cm [2½-3′] for pole types. Alternatively, with pole types, insert the poles first, hammering them firmly into the ground to a depth of 45 cm [1½′]. Sow seeds or plant seedlings around them. The poles should be 1.8 m [6′] high above the ground. Any tall support will do, but the ideal is a stout pole with a 'T'-shaped crosspiece on top: tie strings from the end of the crosspiece to the base of the pole. Short, twiggy sticks help to prevent bush types from being blown over.
Sow the seed at a depth of 2.5-4 cm [1-1½″]. The sowing to

> **Lima bean**
> *Phaseolus lunatus* (or *limensis*) (fam. *Leguminosae*),
> also known as butter bean and Madagascar bean.
> **Size:** plants of the bush type grow to about 7.5-15 cm [3-6″] in diameter and 15-30 cm [6-12″] in height; plants of the climbing type reach a slightly greater diameter and a height of about 2 m [6½′].
> **Climate:** warm temperate to sub-tropical.
> **Sowing to harvesting time:** 12-15 weeks.
> **Yield:** 20-30 plants, each bearing about 60 g [2 oz] of beans, per 3 m [10′] row.

1. *In cool climates sow seeds in greenhouse pots.*

2. *Transplant to Hotkaps outside after three weeks.*

3. *Fertilize on moist soil avoiding plant leaves.*

4. *Shell beans by beating the pods with a stick.*

Young lima bean plants do not need too much attention, but must be hoed regularly to prevent a crust forming on the soil. Water the bed frequently but not to excess.

5. *Put the shelled beans on burlap and dry in sun.*

In tubs grow three plants. twine each up with string.

germination period is 7-12 days.

Cultivation

Little is required apart from keeping the plot well-hoed and well-watered. At all costs, avoid letting a crust form over the soil surface; frequent hoeing will take care of this. Water frequently to keep the soil moist, but do not over-water. On poorer soils, an application of the same fertilizer as used earlier in the season, at the rate of 60-90 g per sq m [2-3 oz per sq yd] will be beneficial. Apply it in strips alongside the rows, preferably when the soil is moist, about 15 cm [6″] from the plants, and hoe it in.

Harvesting

If you want the beans when they are still green for cooking whole, pick the pods when they are young and succulent. If regular mature beans are wanted, leave them on the plants for as long as possible, but pick the pods before they turn yellow, and shell them. Pick frequently to prolong the production of pods. When picking, snap the pods carefully from their stems or cut them off with scissors; careless pulling may uproot the bush plants. Finish picking about a week before the date of the earliest expected frost.

Storing and after-care

Dry the shelled beans in the sun, and then store them in sacks kept in a dry place or in sealed jars. They are good vegetables for deep freezing.

The first frost will destroy what remains of the plants after harvest. Put the debris on the compost heap, but dig in the roots at shey will increase the nitrogen content of the soil. Strip the poles of old vines and store in a dry place for use the following year.

Container growing

Lima beans are good subjects for growing in boxes, barrels and other containers, provided there is sufficient depth of soil – not less than 45 cm [1½′]. Insert a central pole and grow several Lima bean plants twining up it; you may grow flowers around the edge of the barrel, and suspend hanging baskets from the ends of the crosspieces. These beans may also be grown in plastic sacks filled with potting soil, either in the open or under glass.

Varieties

Bush sorts include: Baby Potato, Fordhook Bush, Burpee's Improved, Henderson Bush, Clark's Green Seeded, Jackson Wonder. Pole limas include: King of the Garden, Burpee's Best, Prizetaker, Sieva, Speckled Christmas.

Pests and diseases

Protect the seedlings against birds with cloches, nets or twigs laid on the ground. Support bush types with twig-like sticks to prevent them from being blown over, also to stop beans trailing on the ground and being eaten by slugs. Diseases are mostly the result of wrong treatment, such as over-watering, which gives fungus diseases their chance, while inadequate nutrition may result in poor crops and premature death.

See also FRENCH BEANS and RUNNER BEANS.

Loganberry

This long red berry resembles the raspberry in appearance, but is bigger and has a tarter flavor.

The loganberry originated in California in the 1880s, in the garden of Judge Logan. It is believed by some to be a cross between the American blackberry *R. ursinus* and a raspberry. The loganberry is a vigorous grower and, like the blackberry, it fruits on canes produced the previous year. It has proved to be the most successful and best known of reputed crosses between blackberries and raspberries. The fruit is long, up to 5 cm [2″], and remains quite acid until fully ripe. It cooks and freezes well, and can be eaten raw when really ripe.

The canes are winter hardy in the gentler climates if they are hardened off before low temperatures start. Fruiting laterals may be damaged in spring by a sudden sharp frost after a period of mild weather. Flowers are usually late enough to escape frost damage. Loganberries are self-fertile and attractive to bees. A thornless variety has now been produced which is easier to handle.

Another hybrid Californian berry is the boysenberry. Raised in the 1930s, it is reputedly a cross with loganblack and raspberries. It is now grown in many parts of the world because it will crop in dry conditions and will stand heat better than the blackberry, which is a cool climate fruit. When fuly ripe the fruit is almost black, it is almost seedless and the long berries have a good flavor. Its cultivation is like that of the loganberry.

The youngberry was raised by a Mr. Young in the United

Loganberry
Rubus loganbaccus (fam. *Rosaceae*)
Hardy perennial cane, usually prickly, with a cropping life of about 15 years.
Size: 1.75 m [5½′] high up to 4 m [13′] when trained.
Climate: cool temperate.
Planting to harvesting: 2 years.
Yield: 2-8 kg [4-16 lb] per plant.

States in the 1920s and is another berry for warm temperate conditions. It is thought to be a logan and dewberry cross. The fruit is large, round and almost black when ripe, with a raspberry flavor.

The **veitchberry** is a very useful cool climate berry, which was introduced in 1902, and should be grown more; it is a cross between an autumn-fruiting raspberry variety and a blackberry. The berries are large, red to black, and in season from the time the raspberries end until late summer.

The **wineberry**, *Rubus phoenicolasius*, originated in Japan. The berries are light orange-red and subacid in flavor and follow the raspberry in season. They grow on arching stems thickly covered with red bristles and without prickles. They can be tied in like loganberries, are trouble-free, and are sometimes grown just for their appearance.

Much hybridization was carried out in the early part of the twentieth century and other crosses between blackberries, raspberries, and loganberries are: the lowberry or King's acre berry, whose fruit are like long black loganberries, the phenomenal berry and the newberry, very like the loganberry, and the laxtonberry with berries like very large round raspberries. All these are rare in the U.S.

Suitable site and soil

The loganberry can be grown in partial shade under trees, and on walls, but it performs better in sunny sites where young canes grow and mature properly. Avoid frost pockets, and see that plants are sheltered from winds which may damage young leaves or fruiting laterals. All these are more tender than raspberries and blackberries.

The soil must be capable of holding good reserves of water. Lighty sandy loams to heavy loams are all suitable but heavy clays must have generous quantities of rotted organic matter added to them. Avoid planting in sites previously occupied by loganberries, blackberries or raspberries. Remove all perennial weeds and dig the site well two weeks before planting, adding garden compost or well rotted manure, at 12 L [2½ gal] bucket per sq m [yd].

Preparing to plant

If they are available, always buy one-year-old plants which are certified disease-free, and buy from a reputable nurseryman. Field-grown plants are normally planted in the autumn or the spring when still virtually dormant. If conditions are very wet when plants arrive, it is better to put them into containers, using a good soil or potting mixture, to await weather improvement.

Loganberries should be spaced about 3 m [10'] apart but 1 m [3'] more or less may be allowed, depending on rainfall and soil, and the vigor of the variety selected.

Erecting training wires

It is best to erect posts before planting. Posts 2.3 m [7½'] long should be driven into the ground about 45 cm [1½']. End posts need to be substantial and well supported (*see* diagrams in BLACKBERRY). For loganberries, galvanized wires are stretched tightly along the row at heights of 1 m [3'], 1.3 m [4½'] and 1.8 m [6']. You may delay erecting wires for one year by putting a post at each station, giving

Loganberries are grown in cool temperate climates. This is a thornless variety which makes handling much easier.

The youngberry, developed in the United States, is a warm temperate berry. It turns almost black when ripe.

SINGLE POLE CULTIVATION

fruiting shoots

new shoots

On one side tie four young canes and, on the other, five or six fruiting canes.

(*Above*) The boysenberry suited to warm climates, has a good flavor and is practically seedless. It crops in dry conditions.

(*Right*) To propagate, use tip layering: peg young cane down to soil with tip buried in small hole. Sever in late winter and move to permanent site.

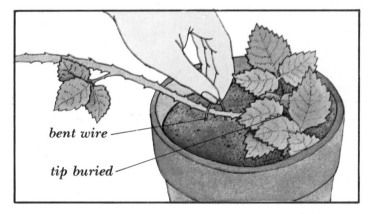

bent wire

tip buried

FAN TRAINING LOGANBERRIES

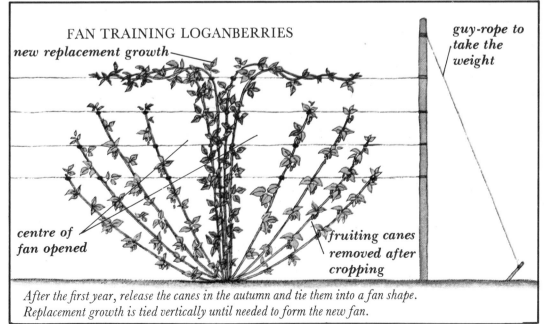

new replacement growth

guy-rope to take the weight

centre of fan opened

fruiting canes removed after cropping

After the first year, release the canes in the autumn and tie them into a fan shape. Replacement growth is tied vertically until needed to form the new fan.

support until the following winter.

Planting and training

When planting, the roots of the young loganberries should be well spread out in the planting hole and covered with selected loose friable soil. Canes should be planted at the same depth that they were in the nursery. If the canes are longer than 30 cm [1'] cut them back.

A mulch is essential and this should be applied after planting, but before growth starts in the spring and the soil begins to dry out. Almost any organic matter is suitable, lawn mowings, sawdust, garden compost or well rotted manure. Very little fertilizer is needed at this time but on the lighter sandy soils an application of sulphate of potash at 75 g per sq m [2½ oz per sq yd] is often beneficial.

The first year after planting the young canes should be tied in once they have reached manageable lengths. Initially it may be easier to bundle the canes together, giving them a post for support, and to leave the erection of posts and wires for the following spring.

The object of training is to make fruiting canes accessible and to keep the new young canes out of the way, but growing in a good light. This may be done by growing the canes straight up a pole (as has been suggested for first year plants), by bundling the canes along two bottom wires in opposite directions leaving the third top wire free for the year's new growth, or by fan training.

If young canes have been tied up to a post in their first year, release them in the autumn and, wearing a heavy pair of gloves for protection against prickles, tie them into the fan shape (*see* diagram) leaving the top wire clear, as well as the center of the fan over the roots. In the course of the year as new shoots grow, these are trained and tied in vertically and then along the top wire.

After fruiting, old canes are cut to the ground, and the young canes are released and tied into the pattern. Some selection of young canes is possible during the growing season and unwanted material should be cut out.

Care and development

To ensure the proper development of the fruit and growth of young ones, the soil should not be allowed to get too dry during the fruiting season. Once the young canes have reached the right length, no further watering is necessary as canes must be matured and hardened off before winter. A biennial application of sulphate of potash 75 g per sq m [2½ oz per sq yd] may be necessary on light soils. If the production of young canes is not sufficient, then an application of sulphate of ammonia or similar fertilizer at 75 g per sq m [2½ oz per sq yd] may stimulate new growth.

The loganberry has an unlimited life as long as it remains free from disease. But, because it stays in the same site for a long term, it is likely to become smothered with perennial weeds so control of weeds is essential from the start.

Harvesting and propagation

The fruit of the loganberry ripens over a period of weeks starting in midsummer. Constant picking over benefits the later fruit. The fruit should be picked when quite dry, otherwise it quickly becomes moldy.

The easiest way to propagate the loganberry is by tip layering. A young cane is bent down to the soil and its tip buried in a shallow hole and covered with soil. A bud or buds grow from near the end of the buried part, to lengthen into shoots, and roots are produced below ground. In late winter the new plant is severed from the parent and put in its permanent position.

Pests and diseases

The majority of pests and diseases which attack loganberries are the same as for the raspberry and blackberry. (*see* RASPBERRY and BLACKBERRY).

Lovage

This relative of the wild celery is very similar in taste and smell. Its name comes from its past popularity for use in love potions.

Lovage (*Levisticum officinale*) is a member of the *Umbelliferae* family. A handsome hardy perennial, native to the Mediterranean, it often grows up to 1.5 m [6'] high with an almost equally wide bush span. The leaves (either fresh or dried) and the stems can be used to add a celery flavor to casseroles, stews and soups made with the stronger tasting meats and fish. Lovage leaves or stems may be added to sauces, and the stems and seeds can be used in the same way as celery and its seeds.

Cultivation

Lovage thrives in a rich, moist soil. Damp peat or leaf mold forked into a dry soil will help to retain natural moisture. A certain amount of sunshine is necessary, but shade during part of the day suits lovage very well.

Sow the seed in a tray when it is just ripe in early autumn, as it is viable for only a short time. Keep it dark and in a temperature of about 4° to 10°C [40° to 50°F] when ger-

Celery-flavored lovage is a most useful cooking herb.

mination should start 14-21 days later. Prick out seedlings when large enough to handle into boxes. Transfer to permanent position 1-1.2 m [3-4'] apart, the next spring. Lovage is a thirsty plant and needs extra water at the roots when dry. In very exposed places staking may be necessary.

Harvesting and propagation
Young leaves may be clipped off the plant sparingly from late spring. Yellow-green flower heads bloom in midsummer, producing seeds for harvest in late summer. The freshly harvested seed, sown thinly in boxes under glass, will be ready for planting outdoors the following spring. Spring sowing is also possible, but germination then is less certain. Lovage can also be propagated by lifting and dividing the roots in late summer, making sure that each has a bud on it; plant 5 cm [2″] below the soil.

Mange-tout

SEE **PEA**

Marjoram

Marjoram has a sweet and unusual aroma that makes it a favorite in the traditional herb garden.

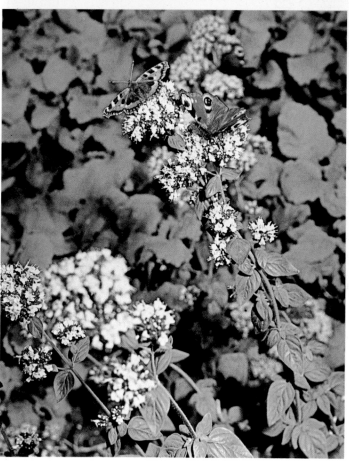

Marjoram is the name given to several species of the *Labiate* family – all of them are *Origanum. O. vulgare* is

Wild marjoram or oregano, a favorite Italian herb. The leaves are best harvested just before the plant flowers.

161

commonly called oregano or wild marjoram; it is native to Europe including the United Kingdom where it grows in the chalk downs. It is a bushy, perennial plant, growing to about 75 cm [2½'], which has light red flowers in summer and loses its leaves in winter. Its gray-green leaves are particularly pungent in flavor and aroma. There is a form with yellow leaves called 'aureum'. Oregano is a favorite Italian herb, used in pizza and other savory dishes.

O. onites is pot marjoram, also a hardy perennial, which grows to about 15 cm [6"] tall, but tends to lie on the ground, the shoots producing roots at the leaf joints. The purple flowers appear in late summer on stems 60 cm [2'] tall. It can cover a space at least 30 cm [1'] square, and is the one most often potted and grown indoors through the winter.

O. majorana is sweet or knotted marjoram, more delicate and treated as a hardy perennial in cool temperate climates, though in warmer climates it is perennial. It reaches only about 20 cm [8"] high, with rounded gray leaves, and several minute flowers coming from rounded buds or knot-like growths on the stems. Marjoram is used to flavor soups and stews and is particularly good with lamb. The leaves, either fresh or dried, are used sparingly to add a distinctive flavor, particularly in meat stuffings and omelettes.

Cultivation

A native of southern Europe, all marjoram prefers a light, well-drained soil in full sun. If the site is on clay soil this must be opened up by working in sand or wood ashes. An application of ground or land lime is also helpful if the soil is acid.

Pot marjoram and wild marjoram can be grown in the same way, from seed sown thinly outdoors in early to mid-spring, in drills 2 cm [¾"] deep, and 20 cm [8"] apart, or in seed trays with protection, with a fine covering of peat or sharp sand. Germination will take 14-21 days and the plants can be put into their permanent places when three true leaves have formed, about 30 cm [1'] apart for pot marjoram, slightly more for wild marjoram. Keep the young plants well weeded, and well supplied with water in dry weather, though older plants are not so sensitive to drying out.

Pot marjoram can be lifted in early autumn and potted up for winter use. Plants are first cut back by about two thirds before they begin to die down, then potted in a standard potting mixture when they show signs of fresh life and taken indoors to a light and not too warm position. Wild marjoram will lose its leaves in autumn and survive all but really cold weather, when it should be protected with mulches or coverings. Both can also be propagated by division in spring or autumn.

Sweet marjoram is best sown in a seed tray in mid-spring, using a seed mixture, in a temperature of about 15°C [60°F]. It will therefore be best in a propagator under glass or indoors. Germination, which will take about 8-12 days, should be followed by pricking out the seedlings 5 cm [2"] apart each way, finally planting out in late spring or early summer, with about 15 cm [6"] between plants. They are slow to grow to begin with, and need shade until well established. Hoeing and weeding are important.

Harvesting and after-care

From a spring sowing, leaves are ready for harvesting just before the plants flower in late summer. They should be dried and stored in an airtight opaque container. There may be another crop of leaves before the winter. After the best leaves have been taken from pot marjoram the plant may be left to grow for the following season. Sweet marjoram seldom survives cold weather, so the remains of the plant should be dug up and added to the compost heap.

Marrow

Best harvested before they reach their maximum size, late summer marrows make a pleasant hot vegetable dish.

One of the hardiest of the large and varied cucurbit family, also includes cucumbers and melons, the vegetable marrow is classed with squashes which have to be cooked. There is considerable confusion in the use of names. In the United States marrows are considered as one of the summer squashes; in Britain the term marrow often includes varieties which might be called squashes. The French baby marrow, 7.5-10 cm [3-4"] in size is known as courgette or zucchini (*see* ZUCCHINI) and is specially grown for eating small.

Marrows have long been popular in the cool temperate regions of Europe although they may have originated in North America. Watery in consistency and bland in flavor, they are usually served with a highly spiced addition – either with a sauce or a stuffing or with ginger. Their delicate flavor deteriorates as they grow in size.

The plant has the trailing habit, bristly stems and leaves of other cucurbits. Marrows are divided into two groups. The trailing variety will produce 2-3 m [7-10'] stems if

A marrow plant of the bush variety three or four of these will produce enough to supply the average family.

1. *In cool temperate areas, start marrows under glass in early spring. To avoid root damage while planting out, sow seeds singly in well-watered peat pots.*

2. *Having hardened the seedlings off in a cold frame, plant out at the beginning of summer in a low mound. Protect with coverings and space bushes 60 cm [2'] apart.*

3. *Make a small trough around the mound and fill it up with water.*

4. *The seedlings are very prone to slug attack, so spread slug bait on mound.*

5. *With trailing varieties of marrow, the stems should be trained as they grow. To do this, insert stakes on either side of the stems at 60 cm [2'] intervals.*

unchecked, but is usually confined by pruning to about 1.2 m [4']. The bush marrow is so-called because it has a truncated main stem: occupying about 60 cm [2'], it is more suitable for the small garden. Three or four plants of either type will be adequate for most households.

The most commonly grown form of marrow is attractive

Marrow

Cucurbita pepo ovifera (fam. *Cucurbitaceae*), one of the summer squashes, and usually referred to by this name in the United States.

Half-hardy annual.

Size: fruit at its best at about 25 cm [10"] long, but will grow to 1 m [3'], plant kept by pruning to 1.2 m [4'] square.

Climate: cool to warm temperate.

Sowing to harvesting time: 12–14 weeks.

Yield: varies according to size cut – 5–6 marrows per plant, average weight of 1.5 kg [3 lb] each.

---

pale cream sometimes with green stripes, and is long, rather than round, but there are other varieties: fruits can be the same shape but creamy white. Other shapes which may be listed in catalogues under marrow, are covered in the article on squashes (*see* SQUASH).

Suitable site and soil

Marrows were formerly grown on the rubbish heap as a suitable site, before scientific composting became widely practiced. As they took up a lot of space and needed plenty of humus, this seemed an ideal solution. Nowadays, however, marrows are normally grown in open ground. The marrow needs full sunshine and plenty of water.

At the time of sowing, prepare the eventual soil. Dig a hole to a spade's depth and 30 cm [1'] square at each station, keeping the top soil separate. Put in a bucket of well-rotted manure or garden compost. Return most of the dug-out soil, and ridge up the topsoil around the hole, so that a depression is formed in the center. When this is filled with water, it will percolate down to the spongy material

6. *If trailing stems do not grow sideshoots, tips should be pinched off.*

7. *Marrows have male (left) and female (right) flowers. Pollination can usually be left to insects, but for early crops, hand pollinate. Pick off unwanted males.*

8. *Small-fruited trailing varieties are best suited to being trained upwards.*

9. *To harvest the marrows cut them free where they lie then lift gently.*

10. *To keep marrows over the winter, hang in nets in cool but frost-free place.*

The cream and green striped marrow is one of the most common varieties. For the best flavor pick the fruits when young and tender – this also encourages new fruit.

beneath, where the roots will absorb it after planting. Alternatively, prepare a slight mound on which to plant the marrow, surrounded by a moat-like trench into which water can be poured whenever needed.

Sowing and planting
Outdoor sowing must be delayed until late spring and seeds and seedlings protected against any threat of frost by inverting flowerpots over them. Sow them two to a station, on edge, not flat, and 2.5 cm [1″] deep. Subsequently remove the weaker seedlings by cutting the stem at soil level, so as not to disturb roots of the seedling retained.

In cool temperate areas the marrow is only half-hardy and therefore it must be sown under glass in the early spring. Sow at the same depth singly in 7.5 cm [3″] pots of a standard potting mix. A temperature of 10°C [50°F] is needed for germination, which can be supplied in the greenhouse, glazed porch or cold frame. Germination takes from 5-14 days, depending on temperature. Harden off and plant out when all frost is past.

Where gardeners buy seedlings, look for springy stems and upright seedlings of good color. Space the trailing varieties 1.2 m [4′] and the bush varieties 60 cm [2′] apart.

Training marrows
The tips of the stems of the trailing varieties can be pinched out if they do not produce sideshoots. Any sideshoots should be stopped at the seventh leaf to keep them under control, if required. These trailing stems can be trained by inserting short stakes into the soil on either side of the stems at intervals of 60 cm [2′].

Another method, specially suited to the smaller varieties of marrow, whose fruit are the same size and shape as a grapefruit, is to grow them up a 'wigwam'.

Pollination
In general marrow pollination can be left to insects, but to make sure of obtaining the earliest marrows, hand pollinate. Female flowers have an embryonic marrow behind their yellow petals, and a cluster of squat yellow lobes. Male flowers have a prominent central core, bearing yellow

pollen. Pick the male flower in the evening and strip off the petals as described in melon pollination (*see* MELON). If male flowers open before the females, hold them back by cutting them and placing them in water until the females are open.

When fruit has set the petals will quickly fall off and the fruit will begin to swell.

Recently there has been some consternation about cross-fertilization between marrows, and ornamental gourds and other wild members of the cucurbit family. The fear is that the marrow will become bitter and even poisonous if this occurs. However, this cross-fertilization will only affect the seed, therefore make sure you buy your seed from a reputable source. If you grow ornamental gourds in the garden as well as marrows, do not use any seed which you may have saved from your own marrows, to avoid any cross-breeding.

Care and development

Plants increase in size rapidly, and watering must ensure that the soil never dries out, particularly in hot weather. Other care consists of giving a feed of liquid manure when watering from time to time, and hoeing to prevent encroaching weeds.

Harvesting and storing

Cutting begins in the summer. Marrows are best eaten when no more than 25 cm [10″] long, and when the thumbnail will pierce the skin easily. At one time gardeners aimed at producing marrows of enormous size, by such means as feeding them with milk, but with size the flavor deteriorates and the flesh becomes drier.

Cutting them young stimulates the production of more fruit. Since the marrow is prodigal in the quantity of fruit it bears, and the baby ones have a better flavor, you may prefer to grow them as zucchini only. For winter storage, conserves and pickling, you can let a few marrows grow to become larger. It is better to reserve a few plants specially for this purpose.

Marrows harvested at the end of the season in autumn will store much of the winter under cool, dry conditions away from frost, and with the minimum contact with the wall, floor and one another. Slatted shelves in a dry attic or cellar are ideal, or they can be hung out of the way individually in nets.

Pests and diseases

Slugs are very fond of the seedlings. Aphids may attack and spread virus diseases. Mildew and gray mold (*Botrytis cinerea*) may occur, also collar rot (*see* CUCUMBER). Fruit rotting from the tip is due to bad fertilization, or infection of the flower remnants by gray mold, in low temperatures.

Melon

Melons are one of the most refreshing warm weather fruits. The different kinds vary greatly in size with white, green, pink or orange flesh.

Both musk and watermelons are annual plants, producing tendrils, though the watermelon is a climber rather than a trailer. In a frame or outdoors in a vegetable plot melons are kept low and allowed to grow along the ground. They are warm climate plants, and generally require a temperature in excess of 19°C [65°F] rising to 32°C [90°F] or more in summer.

The watermelon, *Citrullus vulgaris*, comes from tropical and southern Africa and, because it requires even higher temperatures, the larger varieties are difficult to grow in the colder areas. It is a hairy plant with leaves often deeply toothed and lobed. The rind of the fruit is hard but not durable: the flesh is usually pink to red but may be green or yellow. Ripe fruits contain up to 97% water and have little flavor: they are chiefly eaten for refreshment. Each fruit contains numerous seeds, which are usually darkish brown or black and may be as large as up to 1.5 cm [½″] long. They are oily and highly nutritious and may be eaten salted. Really large watermelons can weigh up to 6.7 kg [15 lb] but there are also smaller varieties around 4.5 kg [10 lb], noted for their richer, more distinctive flavor.

Varieties

According to American usage of the term, the varieties

Melon
Varieties of *Cucumis melo* (fam. *Cucurbitaecea*) for sweet fleshed melons, *Citrullus vulgares* the watermelon.
Half-hardy trailing or climbing **annuals.**
Size: 30-45 cm [1′-1½′] high. 1 m [3′] across, up to 1.5 m [5′] long; up to 1.8 m [6′] high grown in the greenhouse.
Climate: warm temperate to sub-tropical.
Sowing to harvesting time: 4 months.
Yield: 6 good quality fruits, depending on variety, per 3 m [10′] row.

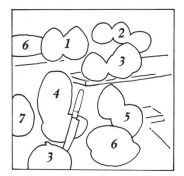

There are many different varieties of melon, which interbreed readily, so it is impossible to classify them in precise groups.

The varieties illustrated here are:

1. Crenshaw melon
2. Cantaloupe
3. and 7. Casaba melon
4. Watermelon
5. Honeydew melon
6. Christmas melon

(*Below*) Watermelons need much more heat than other types and are hard to grow even in greenhouses in cool temperate areas.

(*Below right*) Climbing melons must have their fruit supported with nets.

include: Vegetable Marrow Bush, Prolific, Zucchini F, Hybrid, Goldzini, Productive, Fordhook, Zucchini and Cocozelle (Italian Marrow).

Musk melons, *Cucumis melo*, have soft, hairy, ridged stems with leaves varying according to variety, but generally rounded with wavy, serrated edges. From Asia and Africa, the rind, size and appearance of the fruit is very variable. Slender white seeds are contained in a fibrous center.

Melons interbreed so readily that it is difficult to make precise botanical classifications. One specific group of these has hard skins and white or green flesh, without a strong aroma. Honeydew is included in this family. Skins may be yellow or dark green, smooth or slightly corrugated, but there are no ridges or suggestion of a netted pattern. These melons ripen late, can be stored for about a month, and are a warm climate melon.

Netted melons are so called for the appearance of the skin which has a raised pattern, generally lighter in color. Some also have grooved skins and some do not. The interior may be green or salmon-orange and they are also called musk melons for their aromatic flavor. In the United States it is common to refer to the orange-fleshed melons of this group as 'cantaloupes' even though botanically they are not in the cantaloupe family.

The cantaloupe group of melons is distinguished because they tolerate cooler temperatures than the other groups and can therefore be grown in colder, shorter-season areas than watermelons and honeydews. Originally a warty melon from Italy, where it acquired its name, the group now embraces a wide variety of size and color. Some of them are more like netted melons, most of them have orange flesh – the tiny Charantais melon is in this group. The small Ogen or Ha-ogen, bred in Israel, belongs to this group and has yellow skin with green stripes and green flesh.

BASIC STEPS IN MELON GROWING

Melons like a warm sheltered site in full sun. In a Mediterranean climate they may be grown outside, in cool temperate areas they do better started in cold frames (or under Hotkaps) or in the greenhouse, to provide a long enough season.

The basic steps are described below. These apply to all melons, whichever your choice of site. A fertile well-drained soil is suitable.

Soil preparation

One month before planting prepare the site by digging one spit (spade's depth) deep and add rotted organic matter at the rate of 2.5-5 kg [5-10 lb] per sq m [yd], depending on the condition of the soil. Do not use heavily nitrogenous fertilizer if manure is not available, or stem and leaf growth

1. *Tip out the plant.*

2. *Plant it on a mound. Sunken pots assist watering.*

3. *Pinch out tip to help flowers form.*

4. *Lateral shoots are trained symmetrically. Each will then bear one fruit, and all will develop evenly.*

single female flower

double male flower

will be at the expense of fruiting. If you are growing in a fixed frame, do not neglect to dig over the bottom thoroughly before fertilizing.

Sowing

Melons can be sown outdoors in late spring in warm temperate areas, protecting them with inverted pots. In cool temperate areas, seeds should be sown singly in 7.5 cm [3″] pots in mid-spring under glass. If sowing is carried out too early in cool temperate areas, the plants will have to remain too long in their pots, where they will become starved, and they may never recover from this check in growth. More seeds should be sown than are required, as not all of them may germinate. The seeds should be placed on edge in a good seed mixture which has a loam base, and about 2 cm [¾″] deep.

Germination takes place more readily in a fairly high temperature, 21°C [70°F]. To maintain this in cool areas, a greenhouse or heated propagation frame is helpful. If neither of these is available, a warm dry cupboard may be used, but germination will be longer and, as soon as it takes place, the seedlings must be moved to a light place with a fairly congenial temperature of about 15° to 18°C [60° to 65°F].

Young melon seedlings need careful watering, making sure that the soil never dries out, but also avoiding overwatering.

They must not be deprived of nutrients either—if the leaves start to look yellow add a little liquid fertilizer to the water if you cannot plant for a few days.

Planting

Before planting, the soil should be drawn up into a low mound for each plant, making the soil firm. Small flower-pots may be inserted one either side of the mound for watering. Water is subsequently poured into the pots and reaches the roots while avoiding the stem.

Water the seedling a little before moving it; the soil ball should be moist. Knock the plant out of the pot carefully, placing your hand across the top snd holding the stem between the base of two fingers, before you reverse it. Tap the bottom of the pot till the soil ball loosens.

Plant at the same level on the mound as it was formerly at in the pot. Indeed it is better to be too high than too low. This is important in order to ensure that water cannot collect around the base of the main stem and cause rotting. Make the soil firm around the roots.

Watering

Frequent watering is required as the plants grow, especially

Melons are lifted off the soil as they swell. Ripeness is indicated by smell and tiny hair cracks on the fruit.

Strip the petals off a male flower.
Insert core into female flower to transfer the pollen.

in periods of hot weather. Melons need lots of water and should on no account be allowed to dry out. In hot weather this will mean giving each plant a 12 L [2½ gal] bucket every day.

Overhead watering must be avoided during the time the plants are in flower until such time as they have set and swelling has begun.

In warmer climates a strip of black plastic 60 cm [2'] wide can be used to reduce water loss through evaporation. This is best applied at the time of planting, with a hole cut for the insertion of each young plant.

Training

Plants grown on the ground are trained by moving the young growths into the chosen direction and pegging behind a leaf with a small stick or piece of bent wire so that it holds its position. A balance of growth in each direction is desirable.

Pruning

Pruning is done in two stages. The first phase is to encourage the formation of flowers. The second phase is to remove unwanted shoots after the fruit has set (formed fruit from the flower), so that all the plant's energy goes into producing fruit of a good size.

Encouraging flowers to form: To obtain early flowers, some cutting back is necessary. Count four adult leaves from the base and then pinch out the growing point immediately above the fourth leaf. Normally this results in the production of a side growth from the axil of each leaf. Two of these should be selected – one from each side of the plant, preferably the strongest. They should then be encouraged to grow in opposite directions and each allowed to bear one fruit. The other two side growths are pinched out. If you want to grow more than two melons you can retain all four side growths and allow each to bear one fruit. This pruning should encourage the production of female flowers. If, however, none appear, it must be repeated. Again remove the growing point beyond the fourth or fifth leaf. Side growths will again appear, and normally these will bear female flowers.

Reducing plant size: When the fruit has set and you have decided which ones are to be retained, the sideshoots should also be stopped, at the first leaf beyond the fruit. Sub-sideshoots can be pinched out either after two leaves or, if growth is becoming congested, where they originate from the main sideshoot. The removal of surplus growths should be done regularly, every few days if possible, to avoid the growth checking that would occur if all of them were removed at the same time.

Pollination

The male flowers grow two or three in a group and have a prominent central core. The female flowers have a flattish center and a small round swelling just behind the flower where it joins the stalk; they grow singly. Outdoors pollination will be by insects.

To pollinate artificially remove the male flower by its stem and divest it of its petals. Then shake the powdery central core into the center of the fully open female flowers prefer-

ably just before noon.

You will do best to pollinate several flowers, if available, on either side of the plant. Outdoor melons set first by insects will swell quickly and leave behind those pollinated at a later date. When they have set and start to swell, four which are developing at the same pace on separate shoots may finally be selected. Other flowers are then pinched out. You must choose at this point whether you want two fruits of superior quality – in which case retain only two or more but smaller fruits.

Care of swelling fruit

Feeding: Applications of liquid fertilizer at the manufacturer's recommended strength should be used to help improve fruit size; an average might be 9 L [2 gal] of feed per three plants once a week.

Support of the fruit: Melons grown on the ground should be lifted off the soil by placing an inverted flowerpot, a tile, slate or piece of board underneath to prevent decay.

HALF HARDY MELONS

The cantaloupe group of melons tolerate cooler temperatures than other melons. They can be grown outdoors in cooler climates than the others. A sunny site is needed, preferably facing the midday sun and sheltered from wind.

Growing melons in a frame

A frame averaging between 125 cm × 125 cm [4' × 4'] and 150 cm × 75 cm [5' × 2½'], with an opening light, will hold one or two melons. For a small quantity of high quality fruit, a pair of melons can be planted at diagonal corners. Melons grow luxuriantly and, if you choose this method, you will have to prune back the growth continuously after the fruit sets to keep the plants in reasonable bounds.

If you would prefer to grow a larger number of smaller and less perfect fruit, one melon can be planted in the middle of the back of the frame. This allows room for the side growths to spread out naturally.

Make a low mound in the chosen spot ready for planting. After the melons have been planted the light may be closed for a few days, unless the weather is very hot when a little ventilation should be provided during the hottest part of the day. In very hot weather some shade should be given by painting the glass of the light or cover with a shading paint. This method is suitable where the season is too short to grow them with safety outdoors.

GREENHOUSE MELONS

In cool temperate climates like England the best melons are produced in the greenhouse, where the temperature can be kept above 15°C [60°F] at night, with a rise of 22°C [40°F] or more by day. It is a method which may be used by those in the coldest areas, like the mountains, Alaska and much of Canada, and where cost is secondary.

Sowing and planting

Plants are best sown and grown in 6.5-7.5 cm [2½-3"] pots. Before sowing, knock a large hole in the pot base. As the plant grows it is placed, still in its pot, in position and allowed to root through into the bed. The stem is raised up,

With a frame or cover, cantaloupes can be grown outdoors in cool climate areas. There are two alternative layouts: for a large number of small fruits, put one plant at the back of the frame; or for fewer, more perfect fruits you should plant two cantaloupes, kept heavily pruned back, in opposite corners.

Cantaloupes may also be protected by Hotkaps or plastic tunnels. Enough space must be left under these for proper plant development. Plant the melons 125 cm [4'] apart and then put the cloches over them. Train out four laterals per plant as shown in the plan, and stop them when they reach the frame limits to ensure healthy plants.

and this greatly reduces the risk of disease, as only the bed beneath is watered.

Melons require a fertile loam; the soil should be prepared as described for cucumber (*see* CUCUMBER). A hotbed of that type is also suitable. Put down a layer of fresh manure 45 cm [1½'] wide and 7.5 cm [3"] deep, to produce heat for the plants. This should be spread out in the open beforehand and turned over occasionally for a few days to allow the excess nitrogen to be given off as ammonia. Another way of producing heat is to use a 60 cm [2'] thick layer of straw, firmed down, sprinkled with sulphate of ammonia, and saturated with water. On top, put a layer 30 cm [1'] deep and 60 cm [2'] wide, of good, loamy soil. This will now be ready for melons. Remember that too much manure will encourage growth at the expense of fruit. Place the melon pots 45 cm [1½'] apart on the bed, and up to 60 cm [2'] apart for more vigorous varieties.

Erecting training wires

Melons under glass are generally trained on wires fixed to a metal or timber support, which follows the angle of the greenhouse roof, 30-35 cm [12-14"] away from the glass. In a span-roofed house the training wires should be about 23 cm [9"] apart and form an inverted V.

A more modern method is to fix 20 cm [8"] mesh wire netting to the apex of the house and again to a wire running 15 cm [6"] above the bed, with a supporting wire in the middle. A small cane is provided to support the plant until it reaches the bottom wire.

Care and development

The main shoot will grow upward, and should be stopped soon after planting when about 10-15 cm [4-6"] tall, and two sideshoots allowed to grow, one on each side of the main stem, up the netting, to which they are tied as required. They are stopped only if sub-sideshoots are not being produced. Each plant can be allowed to produce two to four fruits, two being the more usual number. Male flowers are produced about a week before the female, which can be identified by the embryo fruit behind the flower. As soon as the flowers have set, and the fruits are beginning to swell, you should stop the sideshoots at the first leaf beyond the fruit. At the same time, remove any fruits other than the chosen ones, while they are still young. The sub-sideshoots should be thinned by stopping or removing them when still young to obtain a good, even leaf cover, without swamping the fruit by excess production. This should be done little and often to avoid any check to growth.

Water the plants frequently, especially when the weather is hot and dry. Hand pollination will also be necessary if you are growing your melons in the greenhouse – or, under any sort of frame or cover. Applications of liquid fertilizer should be applied as described under Basic Steps.

Like cucumbers, melon roots may appear on the surface and should be covered with a light dressing of soil.

Ventilation

Ventilators should be opened when the temperature reaches 27°C [80°F]. Towards the end of the day they should be closed to retain heat for the night. Plants should be syringed with water in the early morning in hot weather, and the house and border damped down once or twice in the morning and early afternoon to maintain a humid atmosphere.

While the melons are in flower, more air should be admitted until the fruit has set. When ripening commences ventilation should be increased again and both syringing and watering should be reduced. The fruit flavor will improve with exposure to the sun, so tuck a few leaves aside.

Growing under Hotkaps (cloches) or plastic

A succession of barn-type cloches (a form of Hotkaps) or a 45 cm [1½'] high plastic tunnel may be used.

Plant 125 cm [4'] apart. Then erect the glass or plastic tunnel over the plants so that the first melon in the row is 60 cm [2'] from the entrance and all melons are trained equally in both directions down the tunnel. After planting, the ends of the tunnel are closed off with panes of glass or, if plastic, knotted around a stake. These may be opened up for ventilation. Shade may be given in hot weather as for frames.

Supporting the ripening fruit

Melons swell rapidly, especially in hot weather, and soon need support, otherwise their stems would break. Choose a square of about 5 cm [2"] mesh netting, large enough to encompass the expected size of your variety. Loop one string through each end and tie each to the wire above. Check from time to time that the net is not constricting the fruit and preventing its development.

HARVESTING AND PROTECTION

When a melon is approaching ripeness, hair cracks appear round the stalk where it joins the fruit. It begins to change color and soften at the blossom end – test this by pressing with a finger. Also at this time, the characteristic aroma becomes more perceptible. Reduce watering considerably and stop feeding.

It is not necessary to wait for complete ripeness before harvesting the fruit – you can do this when deep cracks around the stalk indicate that separation is near.

If placed in a warm dry place for a few days, complete ripening will take place. Melons can be stored in a refrigerator; this will delay ripening for several days or so. Most types of melon should be eaten at room temperature, as chilling tends to reduce their delicate flavor.

Varieties

Cantaloupes: Bender's Surprise, Burpee Hybrid, Mainerock Hybrid, Delicious, Iroquois, Saticoy, Burpee's Ambrosia, Fordhook Gem, Canada Gem.

Honeydew: Honeydew, Honey Mint, Tam-Dew.

Other Melons: Casaba, Crenshaw.

Watermelons: Charleston Gray, Hybrid Drive Queen, Klondyke, Black Diamond. Smalls: Market Midget, Sugar Baby, New Hampshire Midget, Yellow Baby.

Pests and diseases

Canker or collar rot may occur at the base of the main stem (*see* CUCUMBER). Red spider mite wilt, aphids and virus-carrying cucumber beetle, etc. Spray with diazinon. Gray mold (*Botrytis cinera*) and virus are also troubles which can attack melons. If plants slowly turn yellow or start to dry up, pull up and destroy.

Melons are sensitive to some chemicals, so check before you spray.

Mint is one of the oldest cultivated herbs, mentioned in the Bible and long valued for its refreshing fragrance and flavor.

Mint is the name given to several *Mentha* species of the *Labiatae* family. A hardy perennial, mint usually grows to about 30 cm [1'] high but may reach up to 60 cm [2'] depending on variety and situation. *M.* x *spicata*, (the x indicates a cross-bred species) common mint or spearmint is the most familiar type: *M.* x *villosa*. Bowles' mint or applemint, is the next best type for culinary purposes with its fuzzy leaves and rich flavor; this variety has flowers in pink spikes and is taller at 75 cm [2½']. Of the many other species, eau de cologne mint and *M* x *piperita* (from which peppermint is derived) are particularly attractive in a herb garden for their aroma and pretty purple-tinged foliage. Pineapple mint, *M.* x *suaveolens variegata*, is interesting to grow for its surprisingly genuine pineapple-like fragrance, and fuzzy leaves which are cream variegated around the margins. Pennyroyal, *M. pulegium*, used to be grown in former times; its popular name was fleabane because it was thought to drive away bugs.

Mint leaves are traditionally used in a sauce for roast lamb

Spearmint is the most popular of the mints for cooking. Best used when young and freshly picked, this is the basis of the traditional mint sauce to accompany lamb.

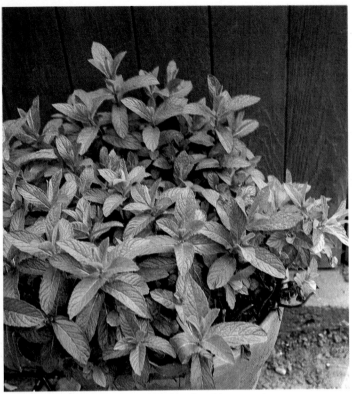

Mint can thrive in pots, provided leaf mold or peat is added to the soil and the plant is kept well watered.

To restrict spreading roots, line a 30 cm [1'] deep hole with black plastic sheeting. Plant 30 cm [1'] apart.

1. Propagating mint. Cut pieces of rooting runners.

2. Plant 7 cm [3"] long runners 5 cm [2"] deep.

or cooked with new potatoes and peas to add to their flavor. Fresh or dried, the leaves also make a delicate and invigorating tea. Fresh leaves may be used in salads, sandwiches and cool summer drinks. Eau de cologne mint is an ingredient of Chartreuse liqueur; and peppermint, *M.* x *piperita*, is widely used in candy making.

Cultivation

Mint can be erratic in habit. It usually has a tendency to send out underground runners which encroach on the territory of other plants. It can also disappear entirely from the garden or revert to a very coarse flavor. Both problems arise from leaving mint in one site for too long.

To keep plants healthy and under control they should be replanted in a different site every three years. The site may be in either full sun or partial shade, as long as the root is kept cool and damp. Rich, moist leaf mold or peat provides an excellent base, worked well into the soil.

To prevent the plants from spreading, dig a hole 30 cm [1'] deep, and line it with black plastic sheeting: then return the soil, adding leaf mold or peat, and plant your mint.

If the space is limited mint can be grown in tubs, where the roots will be restricted, but it will need to be kept well watered. Soil for tubs should be prepared as for the open ground, with the addition of rich, light loam, or a good potting mixture can be used.

All mint varieties are best started from plants obtained at a nursery and planted 30 cm [1'] apart or propagated by detaching pieces of rooting runners from an established plant and laying these in drills 5 cm [2"] deep. Either method can be done anytime from spring onward during the growing season.

Keep the plants watered until new growth appears. Any weeds that appear must be scrupulously eliminated; if they get a hold it is difficult to untangle them from the mint. Mint grows rapidly and will provide plenty of fresh leaves during summer. If the top cluster of leaves is removed first, this will encourage the stems to branch. Topdress with manure in the spring or after the first cutting.

During the summer mint can also be started from seed sown in boxes or a seedbed, but the plants will not be ready until the next season.

Harvesting

Harvesting leaves for drying is done just before the plant is ready to flower in late summer. Tie the leaves in bunches and hang up to dry, rub them to a powder and store in airtight containers.

The season for fresh mint can be extended by lifting some roots before the first frost and planting in a frame or greenhouse, where they will continue growing during winter. Plants left outdoors will die down during winter and begin a new growth in the spring. Pineapple mint is the most delicate and will not survive cold, wet conditions.

Mint can be attacked by aphids and the fungus disease rust, which shows as powdery brown slash red patches and spots on the undersurface of the leaves. The plants can be severely weakened, and such plants are best lifted and destroyed. New plants should be put in a different place.

Mulberry

Mulberries look similar to blackberries. The mulberry tree lives for several centuries and produces large quantities of fruit.

The black mulberry, *Morus nigra*, is the one most commonly planted for its fruit, although there are several species of mulberry. The white mulberry *M. alba* is chiefly used for feeding silkworms, and as a rootstock for the black; its berries are edible, light red at maturity and sweet but insipid. It is rather taller at 12-18 m [40-60']. Black mulberries are very dark red and can be eaten raw if left on the tree to get really ripe, but they have a low acid flavor and are usually picked for pies, jam, wine and for steeping in gin. The red juice stains all it touches. The fruit is a botanical curiosity, being formed from unisexual flowers, the calyx of which swells to form the berry.

The tree is comparatively small and very attractive when planted in a lawn. It can be grown as a bush with a short trunk, when it forms a spreading rounded specimen, or as a standard. The branches are crooked and when the tree becomes increasingly gnarled in old age, the limbs sometimes need to be supported on posts.

The tree is slightly tender, and needs shelter in very cold parts of the cold temperate area. Deep, rich, well-drained but moisture-retentive soil is the ideal.

If the young tree has long thick roots, the planting hole must be big enough to accommodate these; the brittle roots must not be damaged or cut, as they will bleed. Planting is as for other deciduous fruit trees, except that the best time to plant is in early spring.

No special formative pruning is needed, but only the

Mulberry
Morus nigra (fam. *Moraceae*)
Hardy deciduous tree with a useful life of several centuries.
Size: height 6-9 m [20-30'] and the same across.
Climate: temperate to sub-tropical.
Planting to harvesting time: about 8 years.
Yield: mature tree 150 kg [350 lb].

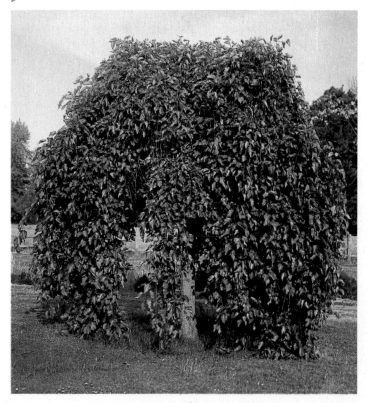

Given the right climate and soil conditions, the black mulberry tree will bear fruit for hundreds of years.

The branches are crooked and, as the tree becomes increasingly gnarled with old age, may have to be supported by posts. Lower branches are sometimes removed from very old and droopy trees.

When ripe, mulberries are very dark red. To remove any that have not dropped off, cover the ground and shake the branches with care as the brittle wood breaks easily.

routine removal of dead wood and the thinning out of crowded shoots and branches in winter. Even so, it should be kept to a minimum as the tree will bleed considerably from wounds.

Berries for dessert should be left to ripen on the tree. Spread a sheet on the ground and they will fall when ripe, mostly in late summer. Shake the tree carefully – the wood is brittle and liable to break.

Only canker attacks the mulberry and this is rarely important enough to need treatment. Protection against birds will be needed, as they are very fond of the fruit.

Mushroom

One of our most popular foods, mushrooms are different in character, shape and method of culture from other vegetables, but with a little care they are easy to grow.

Man has known of mushrooms since he first began to eat vegetables. They grow wild all over the earth wherever the conditions are right for them – from China and Japan to the Americas, and Europe. The cultivated mushroom is a close relative of the common field mushroom, *Agaricus campestris*.

Mushroom
Agaricus bisporus (fam. *Agaricaceae*)
Size: a capped fungus, 7.5 cm [3″] in height; caps vary from about 2.5 cm [1″] across for 'button' mushrooms to 10 cm [4″] for mature ones.
Climate: temperate, if grown outdoors, but most mushrooms are grown in artificial conditions.
Planting to harvesting time: 8-10 weeks; the harvest then continues for 11-12 weeks longer.
Yield: 0.5-1 kg [1-2 lb] per 900 sq cm [1 sq ft].

The entire growth above ground is edible, consisting of white, creamy or brownish caps with brown gills beneath and brownish stalks. They give a high yield and can be grown all year round in properly prepared ground.

The natural method of propagation is by spores, which correspond to the seeds of green plants. Under suitable conditions the spores develop into long, white thread-like filaments known as mycelium or spawn. Mushrooms can be used whole or chopped and eaten raw in salads or cooked by almost any method.

Suitable site and soil

The site can range from the floors of cellars and sheds to an open field, but most commercially grown mushrooms are grown in specially prepared beds in dark places. Mushrooms can also be grown in the garden. Start to prepare the site at least three weeks before planting. Stack strawy horse manure about 1.2 m [4′] high, and water it as you do this, if it is at all dry, so that it is moist but not really wet. It will then heat up and begin to ferment, when the temperature should be in the region of 65°C [150°F]. Turn it to ensure that it all rots and does not dry out, doing this four or five times, at intervals of about four days. By the end of about three weeks the manure should be brown, crumbly and moist, and it should no longer smell of ammonia. It will now have a temperature of about 27°C [80°F] and is ready for use. Commercial growers often add gypsum, at the rate of 12.6 kg [28 lb] per ton of manure – during the first turn – to prevent the finished produce from being sticky.

When horse manure is unavailable you can use as a substitute either ready-made or home-made mushroom mixture. The latter is made with the aid of an activator. A commercial brand of this chemical can be bought from your seed supplier or garden shops. Specific instructions will be provided, but the general principle is simple. Make a heap with alternate layers of straw and activator and then follow the same procedure outlined for manure. This heap must also be kept moist but not soaking.

An easier method is to grow the mushrooms in a field or lawn. Simply remove a piece of turf and place the spawn beneath it. This is a more risky method but it can sometimes produce successful results. Plant around midsummer for a crop in early autumn, keeping it moist.

Spawning and casing

The spawn, generally shaped into fibrous blocks (though now also available in granular form) is available from seed suppliers.

For the spawning of your mushrooms you need air temperatures of 12-14°C [54-58°F]. These conditions are, of course, more easily maintained within a building than outdoors.

In buildings, flat or ridge-shaped beds can be made against a wall. The mixture should be well packed to a depth of 20-30 cm [8-12″]. After being placed in position the temperature of the mixture will rise to about 58°C [100°F] and will then gradually fall. Keep it moderately well watered during this process – when squeezed the mixture should feel damp but should not drip water.

1. *Making suitable mixture. Stack manure and straw. Spray with water to promote fermentation; do not soak.*

2. *Use a fork to turn the heap four or five times every four days to ensure it all rots and stays moist.*

GROWING MUSHROOMS IN A BED

3. *Test the temperature of the mixture with a soil thermometer. Plant spawn when temperature falls to 21°C [70°F].*

4. *Break walnut-sized pieces of spawn from the cake and plant them 2.5 cm [1"] deep and 30 cm [12"] apart.*

5. *If using grain spawn, scatter it on the surface. Do not water, but cover box with black plastic to keep the mixture moist.*

6. *Prepare 'casing' by thoroughly mixing moist peat and gypsum together, in a ratio of three to one by volume.*

7. *Ten days after the white threads of mycelium appear, spread the casing lightly over the mixture at a depth of 2.5 cm [1"].*

8. *If the casing seems to by drying out, water sparingly using can with a fine rose. Always keep the box well ventilated.*

9. *Pull mushrooms from the mixture with a twist of the hand; do not cut. Fill the holes left with some of the casing.*

Plastic buckets of mixture and pre-sown spawn are available from garden centers and are easy to grow.

177

1. *To grow mushrooms in the grass outdoors, first lift a section of turf.*

2. *Using a small fork (but not a hand fork) loosen the exposed soil.*

3. *Scatter grain spawn on the surface, replace the turf and firm lightly.*

4. *Midsummer-sown seed should produce a first 'flush' in early autumn.*

The white-capped mushroom is the most popular variety, but brown-capped mushrooms resist disease much better.

After a few days the temperature will fall to 21°C [70°F]. This is the correct moment to insert the spawn.

Break the cake into fragments about the size of a walnut and insert pieces about 2.5 cm [1″] deep in the mixture, at a spacing of 25-30 cm [10-12″] in each direction.

After a few days or so, the mushroom mycelium will be seen spreading like fine, white thread through the mixture. Leave it for a further 10 days, then cover with a 'casing' of soil. This will help to retain the heat of the bed and to conserve moisture. A rich, fine, loamy soil is ideal, and if it has been sterilized, so much the better. Cover the mixture to a depth of 2.5-4 cm [1-1½″]. Alternatively the casing can consist of a mixture of moist peat and gypsum, in a ratio of three to one by volume.

Care and development

The mushrooms should appear after about two to three weeks, according to temperature. From this point until harvesting should take only a few days, again depending on temperature. During this period water sparingly and only if the casing seems to be drying out. The water so applied should not be sufficient to penetrate to the material beneath. The bed temperature should not be allowed to rise above 21°C [70°F] for more than brief periods, or the mycelium will be damaged. Keep the beds well ventilated, but avoid drafts. Moderate frosts will not harm outdoor beds.

Harvesting and after-care

When ready for picking, twist out each mushroom or break it off from a cluster. Mushrooms ripen in large numbers, in 'spates' or 'flushes'. When the first flush is over remove any dead stems and fill in the holes in the mixture. Water generously, although not to saturation. A second flush should appear in about 10 days. This pattern should continue for about three months.

When the last mushrooms have been gathered, the mixture should be cleared from the bed. On no account use it for mushrooms again, although it makes excellent manure for other crops. Give frames, boxes or other casing a thorough disinfecting to remove any trace of insects or infection. You should limewash walls and scrub floors.

Pests and diseases

The main troubles of mushrooms are the larvae of mushroom flies, mites, springtails and slugs, and such fungal diseases as bubbles and the plaster molds.

Fly maggots, mites and springtails can be dealt with by mixing Sevin dust with the mixture when bringing it in before spawning. Bubbles or mushroom disease (*Mycogone perniciosa*) results in clusters of mushrooms growing into an undifferentiated mass, smelling unpleasant and covered in white mold. Provided the manure reached a high enough temperature when breaking down, and the casing soil was sterilized, there should be no trouble with this, otherwise all affected mushrooms should be destroyed, and the bed sprayed with a copper compound between each flush.

The plaster molds make the casing look as though it has been covered in white powder, turning brown later in the case of brown plaster mold. Again, a properly produced mixture will kill this disease; otherwise take off the surface of the mixture before casing.

Mustard Greens

SEE **CHINESE CABBAGE**

Nasturtium

Nasturtiums are frequently grown for their beautiful flowers alone, but the plant is valuable in many ways as an herb.

The common nasturtium (*Tropaeolum majus*) of the *Tropaeolaceae* family is available in many hybrids, but the original garden variety has single flowers and will trail vigorously over the ground or climb to a length of about 1.8 m [6']. Although nasturtiums are hardy annuals, wherever they have grown they will appear the next year from their own scattered seed. The leaves are similar in taste to watercress. The flower petals can be added to salads and the green seed is useful for pickling as a substitute for capers.

Cultivation
Nasturtiums are native to South America and grow in dry, hot places. It is usually recommended to grow them on poor soil to encourage flowers rather than leaf growth, but the flowers are not as important if the plant is being grown as a herb. If the soil is very rich, however, the leaves will be oversized and the stems will grow long and coarse, making them less suitable for salads. If the ground you are planting them in has been well enriched for previous crops it will have to be slightly impoverished by replacing some of the soil with stonier ground.

The location should be in full sun. Seed is sown in late spring 2.5 cm [1″] deep and 30 cm [1′] apart. Germination takes about ten days. The plants grow rapidly and do not need attention, apart from keeping them within bounds. If support is provided the plants will climb by curling their leaf stems around it. Aphids are frequently troublesome.

Harvesting and after-care
Leaves may be pulled from the plants as they are required. Nasturtiums flower from early summer onwards, until the first frost, and become rampant and leafy toward the end of their life. You can start cutting back the stems from midsummer. Towards the end of summer when they have died, the sprawling trailers must be cut back quite severely and all foliage should be removed to the compost heap.

There will usually be a multitude of seeds on the ground at the end of summer. If these are gathered up and stored for sowing the following year, as well as for pickling, you will have a more orderly display of plants than if you leave them on the ground to become a forest of seedlings.

Nectarine

This delicious stone fruit is a 'fuzzless' peach, with the same flesh and taste, but the smooth skin of a plum. It is closely related to the peach.

The nectarine (*Prunus persica nectarina*) is closely related to the peach, so much so that stones from one fruit may grow into the tree of the other and sports (single deviations) may appear on trees of the other.

179

The fruit are smooth-skinned peaches somewhat smaller than the peach with a richer flavor. The plum-like skins may be red or yellow and there are both yellow- and white-fleshed varieties. More than 50 varieties are known.

Like the peach, nectarines grow into small trees, and the nectarine is even more tender than the peach, the least hardy of deciduous fruit trees. It requires a sheltered site and in mild parts of the cool temperate area is usually grown against a wall facing the midday sun. In cooler parts it should not be attempted. Like peaches, nectarines may be wintered in unheated greenhouses.

For cultivation *see* PEACH.

1. New Zealand spinach is best grown in lime-rich soil. If the soil is acid apply lime in the autumn.

2. Soak the seeds well, just before sowing. This softens the casing which speeds germination.

New Zealand Spinach

Unlike true spinach, which is a short-lived plant, New Zealand spinach continues throughout the summer, and supplies a succulent, mild-flavored green vegetable in hot weather.

Although introduced into Britain from New Zealand in the late eighteenth century, New Zealand spinach is thought to have originally come from South America or Japan. It is a trailing plant and requires ample space; if this is not supplied, it will invade the territory of other garden crops

3. Summer heat makes spinach bolt, but New Zealand spinach will continue to produce tender young leaves.

Young New Zealand spinach grows slowly and must be clear of weeds. It should also be protected from frost.

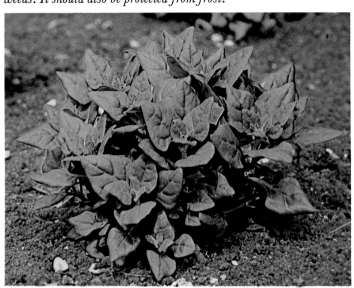

New Zealand spinach
Tetragonia expansa (fam. *Aizoaceae*)
Half-hardy annual.
Size: a low-growing trailing plant, which will spread over 1 sq m [1 sq yd] or more.
Climate: temperate to warm and sub-tropical.
Sowing to harvesting time: 7-8 weeks.
Yield: almost unlimited; the more you pick, the more you have.

and tend to smother them. It has the great advantage over ordinary spinach that it will not bolt in hot weather.

Suitable site and soil

Choose an open, sunny site. New Zealand spinach likes soil fairly rich in lime, so it does particularly well on chalk or limestone subsoils; avoid acid soils or lime them well before growing, at a rate determined by the result of a soil test. Although it appreciates a good, well-manured, deep soil it can flourish on comparatively poor ground.

Sowing and planting

The one problem with this plant, which is otherwise easy to grow, is that its seeds have a very hard casing, making germination slow. It is well worthwhile soaking them in water just before sowing – ideally three or four hours in warm water followed by 24 hours in cold water. They should then germinate quite quickly, and an outdoor sowing in late spring should start to produce a harvest of leaves within seven or eight weeks.

New Zealand spinach is much less resistant to cold than the drought, especially when young, and should not be exposed to frost. It may, therefore, be worthwhile to bring on some plants in a greenhouse or under glass. Sow two or three seeds in a 7.5-10 cm [3-4"] pot, during mid-spring, up to a month before the last frost date.

When sowing outdoors or transplanting young plants outdoors, allow 60 cm [2'] between each plant and at least 90 cm [3'] between rows: even a spacing as wide as this may not be enough. It is as well to find a border or spare plot where the plant can spread to its full extent. To allow for the proportion of seeds that may fail to germinate, sow two or three seeds together and thin out the weakest if they all happen to grow.

Care and development

During the early stages keep the hoe moving around the plants. New Zealand spinach is rather a slow starter and can quickly become crowded out by weeds. As it grows, it becomes able to take care of itself and will smother weed growth. The plants will benefit from watering, especially in the early stages, but later on they can, if necessary, survive prolonged drought and high temperatures. No feeding is necessary.

If the plants are growing in a garden with limited space, their spreading habits may be kept in check by pinching out the tips and snipping off the longer shoots.

Harvesting the crop

Pick the succulent young leaves, and keep picking them. Leave the older, coarser leaves. If the harvest begins seven or eight weeks after sowing, it can continue right through the summer until frost destroys the crop. When cooking, treat the leaves as spinach. They can also be deep-frozen.

After-care

When frost has killed the plants, dig them up and consign the remnants to the compost heap. By this time, however, they will have scattered seed over the plot, for next year's harvest. It is, therefore, a good plan to reserve a plot

permanently (or, at least, for several years) for New Zealand spinach, letting it perpetuate itself. Otherwise the young spinach plants will grow as weeds and have to be dealt with accordingly.

Container growing

New Zealand spinach is quite suitable for container growing; the plant will soon hide a tub, box or barrel with its mass of trailing green shoots and attractive leaves.

Pests and diseases

Apart from the danger of damage by slugs in the early stages, this is a trouble-free crop.

Okra

The long, finger-shaped young pods of the okra plant are among the more unusual vegetables. Although the plants need warmth and care, okra pods can be used to produce many exotic dishes.

Okra is a native of tropical Africa, but has spread to such tropical zones as the West Indies, the southern states of America and Asia, where it now is a common ingredient in many of these countries' dishes. Okra is closely related to the hibiscus cotton plants. Although tropical in origin, it

---

Okra
Hibiscus esculentus (fam. *Malvaceae*).
also known as ladies fingers, gumbo or bamya.
Tender annual.
Size: the bushy plants grow to about 1.2-1.8 m [4-6'] high. The edible pods range from 7.5-20 cm [3-8"] long, depending on variety.
Climate: warm temperate to sub-tropical.
Sowing to harvesting time: 8-16 weeks.
Yield: 5-8 plants per 3 m [10'] row.

1. In cool temperate areas, sow in peat pots in a heated greenhouse.

2. Transplant into greenhouse bed, 38 cm [15"] apart. Keep soil moist.

3. In warmer areas, plant in a sunny outdoor site under Hotkaps.

Okra pods ready for harvesting. Pick these delicately flavored pods when they are still immature, as they become too fibrous to digest when ripe.

4. If sites are not well sheltered, tie plants to canes for support.

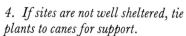

5. Use scissors to cut pods while they are still young and tender.

can be grown in our warmer climates, but it may need some protection and artificial heat since it requires temperatures of 24° to 27°C [75° to 80°F]. The plant is stout and can grow to more than 1.8 m [6'] in its native tropics. The leaves are large, often 30 cm [1'] across with three to five lobes and with toothed edges. The flowers are yellow with the same dark red spots at the base of each petal as the ornamental hibiscus. The edible parts are the long, grooved, dark green, spear-shaped pods, which range in size from 7.5-20 cm [3-8"] depending on which variety is grown.

The pods should be picked when young and tender and either steamed, fried in batter, used in casseroles, or as an ingredient in such dishes as vegetable curry and gumbo, a fine traditional Creole dish.

Cultivation

In warmer climates where okra can grow outdoors, choose an open, sunny site, sheltered from high winds. A rich, loamy soil is ideal.

In a climate with a long, warm summer, but cool winter, okra may be started under glass, either in peat pots or in greenhouse beds. Sow in spring, with a temperature of 15° to 27°C [60° to 80°F]. Transplant to a sheltered but sunny outdoor site with the protection of Hotkaps where necessary to warm the soil.

For outdoor crops in warm climates, sow 0.5-1.5 cm [¼-½"] deep in rows 90 cm [3'] apart. Thin or transplant to a spacing of about 38-60 cm [15-24"] between plants. Keep the okra moist but not overwatered. Hoe very carefully between plants to eliminate weeds, especially in the early stages of growth after planting out. In a somewhat less sheltered site, the plants may need to be supported with canes or poles.

Harvesting and after-care

Begin picking the pods when they are very young and tender and the seeds inside are soft and half-grown. If they are left too long before harvesting, the seeds will become hard and the vegetable unpalatable when cooked.

Picked regularly, a succession of new, immature pods can be harvested for several weeks. Harvest with care so that the roots of the plant are not disturbed; it is better to cut off the pods rather than pull them off.

When the plants have finished bearing new pods, pull them up and add them to the compost heap.

Varieties

With a little searching, one can find: Perkios Mammotto Long Pod, Dwarf Green Long Pod, Clemson Spineless, Emerald Spineless, Green Velvet and Red Okra.

Pests and Diseases

You should water daily and spray leaves to keep down red spider mite, if this should be a problem in your area. Okra may be attacked by the other common greenhouse pests, slugs and mildew.

Outdoors it is usually trouble-free, but may attract leaf and stem-eating caterpillars or borers. Spray with Sevin, if necessary.

In climates where cotton is grown, in the Deep South, for instance, okra may suffer the same pests and diseases, since it is a member of the same plant family.

Onion

The different kinds of onion are among the most indispensable of all vegetables; they are delicious raw, and can be cooked in many ways. A major advantage is that they can be grown on the same site year after year.

One of the oldest of all cultivated vegetables, the onion is thought to have originated in Central Asia, although it was well known in ancient Egypt. During this long period the species has split into a number of different types, some of which are now regarded as separate species or varieties. The Welsh onion, for instance, is scientifically known as

---

Onion
Allium cepa and *A. fistulosum* (fam. *Alliaceae*)
Hardy biennial, cultivated as an **annual.**
Size: average diameter of onion bulb 5-10 cm [2-4"], although much larger ones can be grown. Spring onions, 15-30 cm [6-12"] high with negligible diameter. Shallots 2-5 cm [¾-2"] in diameter.
Climate: temperate to sub-tropical.
Sowing to harvesting time: 14-23 weeks for bulb onions: 42-56 days for spring onions.
Yield: For onions, 20 bulbs, each about 125 g [4 oz], per 3 m [10'] row; for shallots, 15 plants, each bearing about 250 g [8 oz] of bulbs.

Allium fistulosum; the tree or Egyptian onion as *Allium cepa proliferum;* the shallot as *Allium cepa aggregatum.*

The gardener has to deal with seven main types of onion. They are:

a. A main crop of bulb onions, sown in spring and harvested in autumn.

b. An autumn-sown crop, grown for harvesting as bulbs in the following year where weather and climate permit, as in the South.

c. Onion 'sets' – these are small bulbs planted in the spring for quick growth.

d. Salad or spring onions, also known as scallions, which are sown either in the spring or autumn for pulling when young and green, for salads.

e. Pickling onions, which are a quick-growing type, sown in spring and harvested in summer, the small bulbs being used for pickling.

f. Shallots, planted in spring as bulbs; some sideshoots are used as spring onions while others are left to grow into bulbs which are harvested in late summer.

g. Perennial onions, such as the tree and Welsh onion.

Suitable site and soil

Onions do best in a sunny, open site. They can be grown in the same plot for years, but they are also useful for fitting into a crop rotation, as, for example, providing a break from brassicas.

Onions need a firm, loamy, fertile soil. They prefer a light soil to a heavy one, and any acidity should be corrected by applications of lime at a rate based on the result of a soil test. Any organic plant food (farmyard manure or garden compost) should be dug into the soil several months before sowing (e.g. in autumn for plots that are to bear a spring-sown crop). A complete fertilizer may also be applied, just before sowing, and worked well into the soil.

SOWING AND PLANTING

All types of onion need a firm, compact seedbed of fine soil. The sequences are sown as follows:·

The spring-sown maincrop

Sow outdoors as early in spring as soil conditions will permit, in drills, 1.5 cm [½"] deep and 30-45 cm [1-1½'] apart. Sow fairly thickly – about 10-20 seeds per 30 cm [1'] row – because the thinnings can be used as salad onions. Germination temperatures range from 2° to 35°C [36° to 95°F], and the period from sowing to germination, on average, is 14-21 days. Thin the young plants in two stages to a final distance of 15 cm [6"] apart.

As with most vegetables, an advantage can be gained in spring by sowing under glass. These sowings can be made up to 8 weeks earlier than those in the open. The extra weeks are particularly useful with onions, as they need a long growing period.

Many gardeners also achieve a flying start by planting onion 'sets'. These are small onion bulbs which have had their growth arrested in the previous autumn. Most are imported from warmer zones for planting in temperate climates in spring. Plant them in rows 30 cm [1'] apart with the bulbs 15 cm [6"] apart in each row. Set them in the soil

with the 'neck' at the top of each bulb just visible above the surface.

Onion sets and onions sown under glass have two main advantages over later-sown crops. In the first place, they grow quickly and make much of their growth while the soil is still moist from the winter rains, thus avoiding a severe check at a critical stage during a summer drought. The other is that they are also sufficiently well grown to resist the attacks of the onion fly, which is active in late spring and summer.

Autumn sowing

Sowing in autumn (in the South) gives the same results as sowing under glass or planting sets. The bulbs from this sowing should be ready for harvesting earlier than those from a spring sowing. The seed should be sown in early autumn, to give the plants time to attain a reasonable size – about 15 cm [6"] in height – before the onset of winter cold. The seed should be sown a bit more quickly than in spring, to allow for casualties. Onions are hardy but not completely so, and a severe winter will cause damage. It is important to select the correct varieties, bred for autumn sowing. Onion plants bought from nurserymen for transplanting in spring should also be of the autumn varieties.

In recent years a new range of Japanese onions has been introduced. These are sown in late summer and will continue growing right through a mild or moderately mild winter, to produce bulbs by midsummer of the following year. When grown successfully, they should fill the gap between the using of the last stored onions from the previous year and the availability of the new crop. So far they have not been fully tested in all climatic zones.

Sowing salad onions

For salad onions, both autumn and spring sowing are feasible, the onions from the autumn sowings filling the gap until those from the spring sowings are available. For spring-sown salad crops, use a quick-growing variety. A succession of sowings may be made throughout the summer. Alternatively, the thinnings of any variety may be used in salads, and pickling varieties are generally sown with this dual purpose in mind.

CARE AND DEVELOPMENT

The manner of their growth – with tall, thin, hollow leaves – makes onions a crop particularly susceptible to weed competition. Hoe the soil frequently but shallowly to avoid loosening the compact soil around the onion roots. Hand-weeding will almost certainly be necessary. Water well throughout the growing season to avoid any check in growth, which can result in bulges in the bulbs, or in thick necks and thin bulbs.

Examine onion sets a week or two after planting, as they tend to rise out of the soil and may travel several centimeters [inches] from the place where they were planted. If this has happened, press the sets back into the soil. They may also have been pulled out of the soil by birds.

During the growing period the plants may be fed with either liquid manure at regular intervals until midsummer, or applications of a nitrogenous fertilizer such as nitrate of

1. *Before planting onion sets, cut off any leaves that may be present.*

2. *Plant sets in shallow drills by mid-spring, with 'necks' facing up.*

3. *Check sets after a week or two and press back sets that have moved.*

1. *For seed, rake bed to light tilth; tread down when soil is not sticky.*

2. *Sow seed fairly thickly in drill. Then just cover seed and firm down.*

3. *The tips feed from the seed. Do not disturb; they straighten later.*

4. *Thin the onion rows twice; second thinnings can be used for salads.*

5. *Weed regularly; hand-weed close to onions to avoid loosening soil.*

6. *In late summer, bend leaves over to expose bulbs to light and air.*

7. *To harvest, lift bulbs carefully; dry above ground in dry, sunny spot.*

8. *In wet weather, bulbs can be dried on the floor of a cold frame.*

9. *When thoroughly dry the onion bulbs can be kept in slatted bottoms.*

soda, at the rate of about 60 g per sq m [2 oz per sq yd] in late spring and early summer, the latter being hoed in.

When the bulbs are ripening, as indicated by the yellowing and dying back of the leaves, discontinue any watering or feeding and bend over the tops, if they have not already bent over naturally, to expose the neck of each bulb to the sun and so hasten its ripening. The ripening process may last for four or five weeks with large bulbs.

Harvesting the crop

Salad onions may be pulled at any time when large enough, but if the thinnings of crops intended for bulbs are being used for salad, be careful to firm the soil around the remaining plants.

But onions will be ready for harvesting throughout the summer and autumn, according to the time sown. The earliest are the new Japanese varieties which should be mature around midsummer. Japanese onions are for immediate use; most other varieties can be used at once or can be stored. In stormy weather it is as well to discourage a second growth period after ripening has started, as the onions will not store well. Lift them gently with a fork and allow the bulbs to lie flat on the ground. Turn them now and again, to ensure even ripening, but in a wet season lift them onto a platform raised above ground level, allowing the circulation of air beneath it. A tray of small-mesh wire-netting is ideal. This can be moved into a shed to complete ripening, if rain persists.

Storing the crop

Bulb onions are normally grown for storing and use throughout autumn and winter. Being biennial plants, they will start to produce green shoots and, if allowed to, flower heads in the following spring.

Bulbs for storing should be perfectly healthy and quite dry. Discard any that are not. The conventional and probably the best method of storing is to tie each bulb to a length of rope suspended from the roof of a shed or cellar, arranging them spirally around the rope. They can, alternatively, be stored on trays of wire netting, or suspended in rope or nylon nets or placed on wooden shelves, though it is best to have air circulating all around them. The shed or cellar in which they spend the winter should be dry, airy, and frost-proof. If conditions in the kitchen are suitable for storage, a rope of onion can look attractive.

After-care

The onion is among the most economical of plants in its production of foliage. By the time the bulb has ripened there is very little left of other parts of the plant. Consign any dead leaves to the compost heap, if they are free from pests and disease; otherwise, burn them.

OTHER TYPES OF ONION

There are a number of other types of onion, the best known of which is the shallot.

Shallots

These are grown primarily in the South and produce a cluster of small bulbs instead of expanding to form a single

(*Above*) *Only hang onions outside in warm, dry weather.*
(*Left*) *Three stages in onion cultivation, plus shallots.*

STORING ONIONS ON A STRING

Tie string in loop and hang; knot loop end around bottom onion shoot; twist on subsequent shoots.

Egyptian tree onions in fact come from Canada. Plant in summer or fall for a crop the following year. The bulbs form at the ends of the stalks instead of flowers.

Spring or salad onions may be sown in autumn, spring and in succession through the summer. Those planted in autumn will fill in till the spring crop comes through.

large one. These too are sometimes called scallions, like spring or salad onions. The shallot used to be regarded as a distinct species but is now considered to be merely an aberrant form of the ordinary onion. Shallot bulbs are planted in spring (or fall), about 20 cm [8"] apart in rows 38 cm [15"] wide, with the tips protruding just above the surface. Planting should be as early in the spring as possible, preferably several weeks before the last frost date. Soil and site are as for onions; avoid a heavy, acid or wet soil.

The shallot plants will soon start to produce sideshoots. Some of these can be pulled for use as salad onions (their flavor is rather mild), while the rest are left to form bulbs about the size of the one originally planted – about 2.5 cm [1'] wide. During the growth period, keep the bed free from weeds by using the hoe and provide just enough water to keep the plants growing; be careful not to over-water. The bulbs will start to ripen soon after midsummer. Scrape back the soil to allow the sun to shine on them. The foliage will soon yellow and die. Lift the bulbs carefully and dry them as for onions. Store on a shelf or tray in a dry, airy place. Shallots should keep right through the winter, and their culinary uses are similar to those of onions, although shallots have a more subtle flavor.

Welsh onions

These are a perennial type of onion, with the botanical name of *Allium fistulosum*. They grow in clusters or clumps and produce masses of thickened stems, like those of large salad onions, rather than bulbs. They are used primarily for salads, though they can play a role as a flavoring agent in cooked dishes. In the second year they run to flower and seed and so can be regarded as a biennial. They can best be propagated by dividing the clumps and transplanting individual plants, rather than by seed. Welsh onions are also known as stone-leeks, onion leeks, and Japanese bunching onions, since they originally came to Europe from the Orient many centuries ago – although they differ somewhat from the Japanese varieties of autumn-sown onions already referred to.

Ever-ready onions

Further confusion may be caused by the fact that there is a sub-species of the common onion (with the botanical name of *Allium cepa perutile*) which is also known as the Welsh onion, though more properly as the ever-ready onion. This, too, grows in clumps, from which small bulbs may be split off for propagation. Each individual bulb will, if planted in spring, form a clump within a year. It is very

Ever-ready onions are hardy perennials, standing up to frost very well. They grow in clumps and a single bulb will produce a clump within a year if planted in spring.

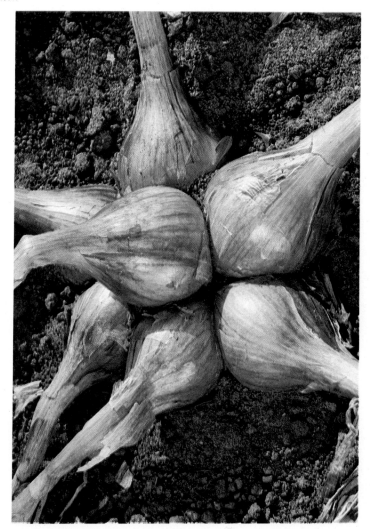

Shallots are an aberrant form of ordinary onions. They produce a clump of small bulbs rather than a single big one. Stored like onions they should keep through winter.

hardy and will produce green shoots for salad or flavoring right through a moderately mild winter. Though grown primarily for salad, it can also be used in cooked dishes. However, it is seldom seen in the U.S.

Potato onions

The potato onion, seldom seen nowadays, is a less hardy plant and growing it in cool temperate climates is a risky proposition. From bulbs planted in mid-winter in mild climates it should produce a bunch of small bulbs, about 2.5 cm [1″] in diameter, soon after midsummer. It is grown primarily for the sake of these bulbs, which have a mild flavor. When growing, it responds to occasional feeding with liquid manure and should never be kept short of water. They are cooked like maincrop onions.

Tree onions

In spite of its name, the tree or Egyptian onion originated in Canada. From a planting in summer or autumn it will produce a crop of small bulbs, or 'bulbils', in the following summer and thereafter each year, as the plant is a perennial. The bulbils are produced, however, not on or under the soil but in the flower-head cluster, instead of flowers. As the stalks may grow to a height of 90-120 cm [3-4′] or even

more, it is usually necessary to support them by canes. Unlike several of the less common types of onion, tree onions have a very strong flavor and should be used sparingly. They can also be used for pickling.

Pickling onions

Onions sown specifically for pickling belong to a group of varieties that produce small, silvery skinned bulbs. They grow quickly, producing a crop ready for harvest soon after midsummer from a mid-spring sowing. Sow in a light, thin soil. Small bulbs of other varieties of onion are, however, also suitable for pickling.

Container growing

There is no difficulty about growing onions of any variety in containers, and they have the advantage that they require a smaller depth of soil than many other vegetables. The unusual varieties are often of most interest for container growing, particularly the tree onion, which is quite an imposing plant.

Container-grown onions need plenty of sunshine, so position them on a sunny patio or similar place. Make sure that the plants are well watered, but also that they have adequate drainage to prevent waterlogging.

Varieties

Among the varieties available the following are the ones most likely to be found widely offered: (Bunching) Evergreen Long White, Beltsville Bunching, Hardy White-Bunching; (Sold as Sets) Stuttgarter, Golden Mosque, Yellow Ebenezer, White Ebenezer, White Portugal; (Pickling) Barletta, Silver Queen; (for spring seeding) Southport Red Globe, Autumn Spice, Storage Key, Sweet Spanish Hybrid, Yellow Utah, Northern Oak, Super Elite; (for Fall planting in mild areas) Bermuda (yellow, red, white) Early Harvest No. 5 Hybrid, Granex, Grano, Torpedo.

Pests and diseases

The most troublesome pest is the onion fly, the larvae of which tunnel into the plant tissues from late spring onwards. Control them by diazinon granules in late spring or early summer. Successive generations will emerge during the summer if the first is not dealt with, resulting in intermittent attacks. Young onions are particularly susceptible and, if onion fly is prevalent, it may be as well to stop pulling young plants for salad. Very early sowing will ensure that thinning is done before the onion fly is about to attack.

Stem and bulb eelworms may also affect onions. If the leaves are distorted, and their bases swollen, suspect eelworm. There is no really effective chemical control, and an attack is normally a sign of neglect of a proper rotation and a lack of garden hygiene, allowing the pest to build up to dangerous levels. Destroy any infected plants and make sure that you grow onions in a different place in the garden in future or interplant rows with marigolds.

White rot sometimes builds up in crops of salad onions in hot, dry summers. The leaves become yellow and the bases of the bulbs are covered with a white or gray fungus. It can be combated by dusting the soil at sowing time with an approved dust, but the best control is to keep onions away from any affected plot for at least eight years. Welsh onions are not affected, and some varieties of common onions are more resistant than others.

Other common troubles may be the fungal diseases, mildew, neck rot and smut, the bacterial soft rot, and the virus yellow dwarf. Neck rot is a storage rot occurring when bulbs have been insufficiently ripened or are stored in damp stuffy conditions. Smut shows as sooty spots and patches on the leaves, and can kill seedlings. There is no simple chemical control: rest the soil as long as possible, destroy the affected plants as soon as you spot them, and be extremely careful not to spread the contaminated soil about the garden to ensure against any further attack.

Yellow dwarf results in stunted stems, and yellow-streaked leaves. Onion thrips, too, can be troublesome. The safest material with which to spray in the vegetable garden is Sevin.

Oregano

SEE **MARJORAM**

Parsley

Parsley is the most familiar of herbs, widely popular as a garnish for many dishes and a rich source of vitamin C.

Parsley (*Petroselinum crispum*) is a member of the *Umbelliferae* family, grown extensively for its curled clusters of leaves. Finely chopped, the fresh leaves feature in many recipes, particularly parsley sauce, casseroles and stews. Sprigs of leaves are used to garnish fish, strong meat dishes and boiled vegetables. The plant is biennial and, if left to grow for a second year, the thin tap roots can be cooked as well. There is a moss-curled variety, more suitable for garnishing, and a French variety, which has more flavor for use in cooking. The plant grows about 30 cm [1′] high and 15 cm [6″] wide and produces small yellow-green flower heads in early to midsummer of the second year.

Cultivation

Parsley prefers a position in full sun, but a partially shaded site is acceptable. For garden cultivation it should be grown in soil enriched with well-rotted garden compost. This will help to retain moisture, which is very necessary, for parsley bolts when the roots become dry. For this reason, it will do well in a well-broken down clay soil, in which water is retained.

Sift the topsoil to make a fine, firm surface. Sow the seed thinly 0.5 cm [¼″] deep in rows 30 cm [1′] apart and barely cover it by pressing a thin layer of peat or sharp sand over it, then water using a fine rose on the watering can. Parsley has a reputation for slow germination. Delay sowing until the soil is beginning to warm up in mid to late spring and there would be no difficulty in obtaining seedlings within two weeks, otherwise they make take as long as five weeks. Keep the seedbed watered and watch for signs of germination after two weeks. If there are no seedlings in eight weeks, make another sowing. Once the seedlings have appeared keep the seedbed weeded. When the plants have produced two true leaves, you may thin them to 15 cm [6″] apart and transplant the thinnings to 30 cm [1′] apart.

Parsley sown in spring will supply leaves for cutting from midsummer and the following early spring, when it will

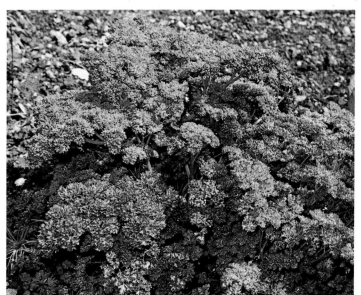

For a good crop, thin parsley well, as it is intolerant of overcrowding. Prevent bolting by regular watering.

start to produce flower stems instead of leaves. However, if a fresh supply is sown in midsummer, this will supply leaves from early autumn until the following summer under cover, so a continuous supply is possible. The midsummer sowing will germinate in a few days, due to the increased warmth of the soil and air. Hotkaps placed over the plants in winter will keep them clean and enable picking during cold weather, in the milder areas.

Parsley may be attacked while young by aphids and carrot-fly (*see* CARROT).

1. *Cover seed with a very thin layer of peat and water with a fine spray.*

2. *Cover thinnings' roots with soil to avoid drying out during transplanting.*

3. *Sheets of glass placed at the ends of a covering will protect from winds.*

Parsley sown or planted in a special 'parsley pot' can be very attractive.

Parsnip

Parsnips are one of the easiest vegetables to grow and need only the minimum of attention to produce excellent results.

The wild form of the parsnip occurs commonly throughout northern Europe, and in its taste and smell it is still recognizably the ancestor of the root now cultivated. Breeding and selection have enlarged the root and eliminated its tendency towards woodiness. There are three types of cultivated parsnip: short rooted and conical shaped; medium length and blunt-ended, or tapered; and long,

---

Parsnip
Pastinaca sativa (fam. *Umbelliferae*)
Hardy biennial.
Size: root to 45 cm [1½′].
Climate: cool temperate.
Sowing to harvesting time: 28 weeks.
Yield: about 14 parsnips, each weighing on average 450 g [1 lb], per 3 m [10′] row.

Parsnip

1. Work the iron rod back and forth in the soil to make a conical hole 75 cm deep and 15 cm wide at the top.

2. Almost fill holes with sifted soil, space 3 or 4 seeds in each and cover to a depth of 2 cm [¾″]

3. Thin out when the seedlings have two seed leaves and one true leaf.

One of the hardiest vegetables, parsnips require a minimum of attention. Their sweet-tasting roots can be roasted, boiled or made into wine.

If growing in rows, choose a site manured for a previous crop; dig a trench to a depth of 50 cm [20″].

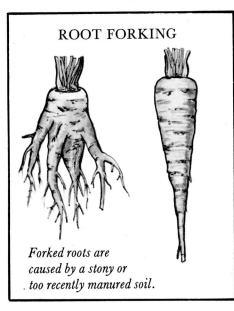

ROOT FORKING

Forked roots are caused by a stony or too recently manured soil.

with tapering ends, grown mainly for exhibition.

Freshly dug, this hardy root vegetable has a slightly sweet flavor and is excellent roasted or braised.

Suitable site and soil

An open, sunny site is preferred, but parsnips will grow in a lightly shaded plot. Growing the long variety involves quite a lot of soil preparation and it may present problems with certain soils, such as those where a poor subsoil that must not be disturbed comes too close to the surface. In this case shortened varieties are available.

All parsnips like rich soil, but if this has been recently manured the roots will be over productive and inclined to fork. It is best to grow them on a site that was manured for a previous crop. Stones in the soil are another cause of forking and these should be removed.

A family of 4-5 will need a 9-10 m [30-33'] row, or its equivalent in several rows, which will produce up to 40 roots in a year. If there is more than one row, they should be 30-38 cm [12-15"] apart. Each row must be trenched to a depth of about 50 cm [20"] for the long type, and if there are many stones to be removed from the ground it may be best to resort to a method used for producing exhibition parsnips. Drive a 1 m [3'] long iron rod into the ground to about three-quarters of its length to make holes 23 cm [9"] apart. Work the iron rod back and forth to produce a deep, conical hole about 10-15 cm [4-6"] wide at the top. Fill the hole with sifted soil in readiness for sowing. The parsnip will grow straight down.

If the soil is markedly acid it should have lime added in autumn or winter to make it almost neutral (pH 6.5); use a soil-testing kit. Ten days before sowing, it is advisable to apply a mixture of 4 parts superphosphate, and 1 each of sulphate of ammonia and sulphate of potash at the rate of 100 g per sq m [3½ oz per sq yd].

Sowing and planting

Parsnip seed does not keep well, so sow really fresh seed as early in spring as conditions will allow. Long, steady growth is the rule with parsnips, but there is no point in sowing in hard frost or sodden soil, only to have the seeds rot. Assume that germination will be poor and sow 3 or 4 seeds at every station. If the trench method is used this will be in a drill, and seeds should be sown 23 cm [9"] apart and covered with soil to a depth of 2 cm [¾"]. With the proposed crowbar holes, nearly full of sifted soil, space 3 or 4 seeds in each and cover them to a depth of 2 cm [¾"].

Germination will take 21-28 days and maturity should be attained in 28 weeks, though the short-rooted kinds may be ready in less time. During this time weeds will get well ahead of the parsnips, so weed carefully. You may also sow a quick-growing crop of lettuce or radish between the rows or stations; it will help mark the position of parsnip seeds.

Cultivation

Thin the seedlings so that only the strongest remains at each station. Keep the rows clear of weeds by hoeing regularly, taking good care not to damage the crowns of the roots. Some watering may be necessary, especially in the early stages, before the roots have gone deep.

Harvesting and after-care

Parsnips sown in early spring should start to be available in mid-autumn. They will still be improving, however, and will improve still further when the frosts come. By the following spring, the flavour will begin to fall off. It is usual to leave them in the ground and dig them up as they are needed. Obviously this is not possible in ground that is rock-hard with frost, so take the precaution of lifting some of the crop in late autumn, cutting the tops off to the shoulder, and storing them like carrots, in layers covered with a little dry sand, soil, or ashes in an airy, frost-proof store. The discarded leaves make good compost heap material. Mulching will also make digging possible much later into the winter.

Pests and diseases

The main insect pests of parsnips are carrot fly and celery fly. For treatment *see* CARROT and CELERY. The cause of the reddish-brown patches of canker, so often found on parsnips, especially the shoulders, has not yet been discovered, but dark brown, or black cankers are caused sometimes by disease, and sometimes by growing conditions. Cracking as a result of rain after dry weather allows fungal infections to take hold – so do injuries caused by the carrot fly. Cold wet weather and badly-drained soil encourage rotting. In such conditions, spray the soil with zineb regularly from late summer to lifting. On the whole, however, parsnips are singularly trouble-free in the U.S.

Pea

One of the earliest summer crops, fresh, tender peas are among the most delicious garden vegetables. They are only suitable for a cool temperate climate.

Peas may well be the oldest cultivated vegetable crop in the world; even before they were cultivated, they were gathered from the wild. They probably originated in Asia, the Near East and southern Europe.

As is only natural after such a long history as a garden crop, very many varieties of peas have been evolved. There are early, maincrop and late varieties; peas that climb fully as high as a man and dwarf peas that need no support and may be grown under frames; the small-seeded and succulent petit pois; mangetout or sugar peas, with edible pods; asparagus peas (*see* ASPARAGUS PEA) and purple-podded peas. All peas are, however, a cool-temperate crop. Trying to grow them in warm-temperate zones invites problems, as most of them will stop producing pods when the temperature rises above about 20°C [70°F].

Suitable site and soil

Choose an open, sunny site, but one sheltered from high winds. Allow plenty of space and remember that the taller varieties will shade other crops grown alongside them.

Peas have specific soil requirements. Acid soil is unsuitable, the ideal being at a pH of 7.0; carry out a soil test and correct by an application of lime in the winter before sowing if necessary.

Peas also like a rich soil, but not one recently enriched by applications of manure; it is better to sow them in soils well manured for a previous crop. Poor soils can benefit from chemical fertilizers containing superphosphate and potash, but use nitrogenous fertilizers very cautiously, because the pea plant can extract nitrogen from the air for itself, and excess of nitrogen leads to lush leaf growth at the expense of the pods. Peas need plenty of water and thrive in a reasonably heavy soil which retains moisture, although it must not become waterlogged.

Sowing

Peas are sown where they are to remain for their entire lives because they are deep-rooted and do not usually transplant satisfactorily.

The normal time for sowing maincrop peas is as early as it is possible to dig the soil, for harvesting early summer, but by using different varieties and giving the plants protection from frost you can extend the season considerably. They can also be sown in many areas in mid to late autumn for harvesting the following spring.

Prepare a shallow drill 15-23 cm [6-9″] wide, and sow the seed 7.5 cm [3″] deep in two rows with 7.5 cm [3″] between them. Sow at the rate of 6-10 seeds per 30 cm [1′]. Allow a space of 45-60 cm [1½-2′] between each drill. The temperature range for germination is 4° to 29°C [39° to 84°F] and the peas should take between 6 and 15 days to germinate.

Two types of seed

There are two types of pea seed, round and wrinkled. The wrinkled-seeded, or 'marrowfat', varieties are splendid succulent peas but hold too much moisture for autumn sowing. Peas sown in autumn must be of round-seeded varieties, several of which are very hardy. In districts where winters are moderate, they can be sown in the open; or where the snow cover is usually good all winter. It is as well to sow autumn peas rather more thickly than with spring-sown crops, scattering them along the flat drill rather than planting each seed separately; this allows for some mortality. After a mild winter, autumn-sown peas will produce a crop weeks earlier than those sown in early spring.

Spring-sown peas

Spring-sown peas are divided into three main groups: first early varieties, second earlies (also called early maincrop or mid-season varieties) and maincrops. The division is made according to the time the varieties take to grow. From sowings in early spring, first early varieties will produce peas fit to gather in 7 or 8 weeks. Second earlies sown at the same time will need 8 or 9 weeks, while maincrop varieties will require 10 weeks. It would be possible, therefore, to provide a succession of pickings by sowing varieties of the three groups in the same week. Alternatively, you can follow the usual practice and make a succession of sowings, starting with the earlies and proceeding to the second earlies and maincrop. You can also gain time by protecting the first sowing of earlies from frosts by means of Hotkaps or glass.

Peas do not transplant satisfactorily, but they can be grown in peat pots or in seed-trays with slide-out bottoms, as the important point is not to disturb the roots when transplanting. Nevertheless, the operation is unnecessary, as a rule, and may end in failure; it is wiser to sow peas in their permanent quarters.

Late peas

In general, although there are a few exceptions, early varieties of peas tend to be dwarf and the maincrop ones taller and bushier. For the latest crops of all, use early dwarf varieties, for two reasons. One is that they will mature more quickly and so be ready for harvesting before the summer; the other is that, if necessary, they can be protected in their late stages by shading.

Cultivation

One of the main hazards in growing peas is that pests attack the plants in their early stages. Many inexperienced gardeners who sow good seed in well-prepared soil finish up with half a crop, or less. Mice are the chief culprits. They eat the germinating peas and will quickly clear a row. A sensible precaution is to dress the pea seeds with a repellent or poisonous substance before sowing. Where this is necessary, use brand-name repellents or mousetraps; if

---

Pea
Pisum sativum (fam. *Leguminosae*)
Hardy annual.
Size: height varies according to variety, ranging from 30 cm [1′] to 1.8 m [6′]; pods range from 7.5 cm [3″] to 15 cm [6″] long.
Climate: cool temperate.
Sowing to harvesting time: 9-13 weeks.
Yield: 40 plants per 3 m [10′] row, each bearing up to ⅛ kg [¼ lb] of peas.

Choose early dwarf varieties of pea for the latest crop of all, as they should mature before the summer.

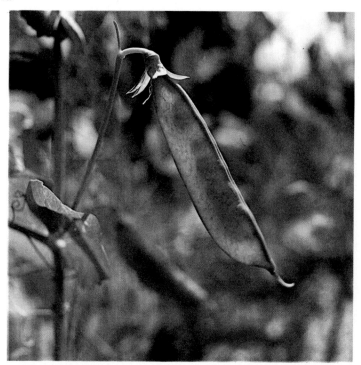

Succulent garden peas, ready for harvesting. Pick about 3 weeks after flowering, when the pods have filled out.

The pods of the snow pea or sugar pea have a crisp and crunchy texture and sweet flavor. Cook them whole.

1. *To dress seeds against pests, use a recommended poisonous or repellent substance.*

2. *Sow first early varieties under tall covers, in double rows 7 cm [3″] apart and 5 cm [2″] deep. Allow 10 seeds per 30 cm [1′]. Protect at either end with a mousetrap.*

3. *Sow maincrop peas without protection, following the method for early types.*

4. *Protect young plants from birds with pea-guards of fine mesh netting, 12 cm [5″] high and 20 cm [8″] wide.*

5. *Remove weeds by hand to avoid damaging roots.*

6. *Support growing dwarf peas with twigs.*

using the latter take precautions against pets, birds, or other creatures being injured.

The other prime pests at the early stages are birds. Protect the plants with pea-guards, which are half-cylinders of small-mesh wire netting for placing over the peas. You can easily make these. An alternative is to construct entanglements of black cotton; even twigs placed flat on the ground will act as a deterrent. Protection is necessary for only a week or so for, once they have emerged, the plants grow quickly.

Peas require frequent attention throughout their lives. Remove weeds by regular hoeing. Be careful, however, when pulling out weeds growing very close to the peas; the pea-roots may come out as well or be damaged.

Peas need ample moisture and require frequent watering during droughts. A mulch will help, consisting of garden compost, lawn trimmings, peat (unless the soil is acid) or well-rotted strawy manure. Apply this as near as possible to the base of the plants, where it will not only supply nutrients and help to retain moisture but will also smother some of the weeds.

Unlike beans, which climb by twining themselves around a support, peas grasp the support with their tendrils. They therefore need twigs or netting, both of which give them plenty of tendril-holds. With dwarf varieties, the sticks need be only small twigs, 45 cm [1½′] or so high. Even with taller varieties it is useful to help the young plants with short twigs in the early stages, or with fencing.

If the peas are sown in well-prepared, well-manured soil, little additional feeding should be necessary during the growth period. In poorer soils they will benefit from an application of a complete fertilizer that is low on nitrogen and high on phosphates and potash. Apply this at a rate of 90-125 g per sq m [3-4 oz per sq yd].

Harvesting and after-care

Garden peas are usually grown for eating when they are fresh and green. If allowed to become ripe and hard, they lose much of their flavor. Usually, they are ready for harvesting about 3 weeks after flowering. Harvest when the pods have filled out and are firm to the touch although, during a drought, some pods will fail to fill completely, and it is better to pick too early than too late. Cut the pods from the plants rather than picking them, or you may pull up the whole plant.

Two harvests per plant may be expected. The first is the

Taller varieties can be supported on a trellis 125 cm [4'] high, made of chicken wire with a 5 cm [2"] mesh. Support trellis with nails hammered into wooden stakes.

Use scissors to harvest ripe pods, as picking by hand can pull the entire plant out of the ground.

After harvest, clear the site. Remove bits of pea haulm from netting and store it for future use.

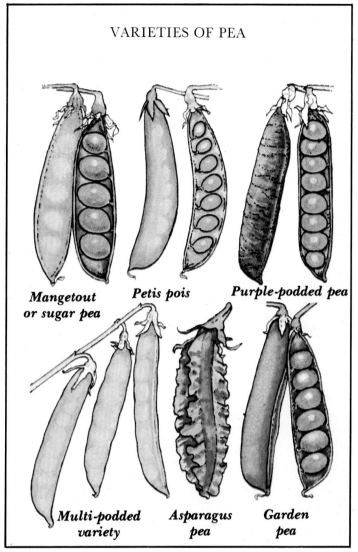

VARIETIES OF PEA

Mangetout or sugar pea   **Petis pois**   **Purple-podded pea**

Multi-podded variety   **Asparagus pea**   **Garden pea**

main one; the second consists of pods which are later to mature and are usually not of the same quality as the first. With early varieties it is sometimes possible to pick a few early pods a few days in advance of the main picking. Before cooking or deep-freezing, shell the peas.

There are, however, a number of varieties in which the pods are eaten with the peas in them. The best known of these is the **mange-tout** or **snow pea** of which there are two main types – a dwarf sugar pea and a tall one, up to 1.5 m [5'] high, grown largely in France, where it is known as the mange-tout. Both are more heat-tolerant, producing an abundance of pods in early summer. The pods are stringless and are best steamed, having been gathered when they are young.

Petits pois produce an abundance of very small, sweet-tasting peas. Pick as soon as the pods have filled and steam them whole. After cooking, the peas will fall out of the pods, which are then discarded. The **purple-podded pea** also has small pods but the peas are shelled in the normal way and the deep purple pods discarded. This is a tall pea, growing to a height of 1.5 m [5'], and it continues to

bear pods for an unusually long period, allowing a succession of pickings. Peas of many varieties can be dried and stored for winter use. They are also one of the most successful vegetables for the freezer.

There is no point in trying to retain the plants after the pods have been removed. Clear the site and use it for another crop immediately; brassicas are a good choice.

The pea plants should be incorporated in the compost heap, unless there was a bad attack of some pest, but the roots, which are rich in nitrogen, can be left in the ground to benefit the following brassicas.

Freezing and storing

Peas are a vegetable that freezes particularly well. Certain varieties are better than most for this purpose, Freezonian and Wando, for example.

You should make sure to harvest them before the pods become really tight and there is still some give in them. Try to cook or freeze them as soon as possible after picking as their flavor deteriorates rapidly.

To prepare, shell peas; mange-tout or snow peas should be washed and left whole. Blanch one minute, then open freeze and place in plastic bags.

Peas stored this way will have a freezer life of approximately 12 months and may be cooked straight from the freezer in boiling water.

Pests and diseases

Peas are subject to few pests and diseases. Clearly the most troublesome pests are aphids and pea weevils.

Pea weevil (*Sitona Lineatus*) may attack the plants by eating regularly notched holes in the edges of the leaves. The larvae feed on the roots. Adults are white, brown or black beetles 0.5 cm [$\frac{1}{4}$"] long, and are controlled by spraying with malathion or diazinon.

Another one of the pests of later crops may be the larvae of the pea moth (*Laspeyresia nigricana*). These have white bodies and black heads and look like maggots. Their prevalence is one reason for gardeners concentrating on the early crops, which are seldom attacked. Treatment consists of spraying with a nicotine spray about 7-10 days after flowering to catch the maggots just after they hatch, but before they get into the pod. The plants should be thoroughly saturated.

Pea thrips (*Kakothrips robustus*) are sometimes numerous enough to cause damage, especially in dry seasons. Symptoms are silvery mottled patches on the pods and leaves, which later turn brown. Treat the plants with a locally-approved spray, applied just after the flowers have set.

Other pests may be pea and bean seed beetles, and birds attacking the pods to get at the peas.

Occasionally such diseases as mildew, gray mold and root rot may occur. For the last named remove the entire plant, and also any leguminous weeds.

Peach

This delectable white or yellow-fleshed fruit has a felt-like skin. It grows on small trees and is therefore well suited to the small garden.

Despite its name, *Prunus persica*, the peach originated in China. It was probably brought to Persia along the trade routes and was introduced from there to Europe by the conquering Greeks and Romans. It reached a high standard of cultivation in France in the seventeenth and

Peaches growing on a sunny wall. This variety Peregrine has white flesh and is a heavy and reliable cropper.

eighteenth centuries. It is a member of the *Prunus* genus which also includes plums, cherries, nectarines, almonds and apricots.

Widely grown in areas with a Mediterranean climate, it does not stand extended temperatures below zero. Also, the delicate blossoms are quite liable to be damaged by frost or sudden temperature drop.

Like other deciduous trees, they need a dormant period and their cultivation is only possible where there is winter cold. The ideal condition is a moderately cold winter so the tree remains dormant, followed by a warm, frost-free spring.

Peaches may be divided into groups by the color of their flesh. White has the best flavor and the tree is hardier in a cold climate. The yellow-fleshed peach needs a warm climate, but is popular for canning.

Nectarines are a sport (naturally occurring variant) of peaches, with the smooth red or yellow skin of plums. The trees are less hardy. The same is true of apricots and almonds.

CULTIVATION

The peach can be grown in the open in favorable areas (roughly to the New Hampshire border). Shelter for blossoms is particularly important. The peach can be grown outdoors as a half standard, or standard, but a two- to three-year-old bush is generally most satisfactory. Against a wall or under glass it is grown as a fan. In cooler areas plant early fruiting varieties. If a peach stone is planted, a tree will result, but it will not come true to variety and is slow to reach bearing.

Soil preparation and planting the tree

The ideal soil is a medium to heavy well-drained limy loam, not less than 60 m [2'] deep, though the peach is tolerant of a wide range of soils.

Dig thoroughly and deeply several weeks before planting an area of 2 sq m [yd] and add one wheelbarrow-load of garden compost or manure. Then about a week before, fork into the top 23 cm [9"], 125 g [4 oz] of a balanced fertilizer, and the same amount of dried blood.

Do not plant if the soil is frozen, but keep the tree in a cool, frost-free place until conditions improve.

Early spring – or late autumn in warm climates – is the best planting time. Do not plant if the soil is frozen, but keep the tree in a cool, frost-free place until conditions improve. The root system must not be allowed to dry out or be exposed to frost.

> **Peach**
> *Prunus persica* (fam. *Rosaceae*).
> **Hardy** deciduous tree, often short-lived.
> **Size:** 4.5 to 5.5 m (15 to 18').
> **Climate:** temperate.
> **Planting to harvesting time:** 1-3 years, depending on whether the tree is 2 or 3 years old when planted.

Feeding, watering and pollination

Generous feeding is necessary. Each spring topdress with a balanced complete fertilizer at 90 g per sq m [3 oz per sq yd]. Mulch with manure, or other bulky organic material. Once the fruit have started to swell use a commercial liquid feed every 7 to 10 days, but stop when the fruit begins to color.

The soil can become very dry under certain weather conditions, which will cause poor fruit set and excessive fruitlet drop. Water thoroughly and deeply whenever there is drought, at blossom time and when the stone is developing.

The peach is self-fertilizing but flowers very early in the spring when few pollinating insects are around, especially in cool temperatures. A light fruit set can result in some years.

Training and pruning a bush

Peach trees begin to droop under the weight of fruit and in later years more upright branches from near the center will be trained to replace those which have become too low. Alternatively, cut drooping branches back to suitably placed vertical shoots.

Very little pruning is needed. In the North in early spring cut out any winter die-back to a healthy bud. As far as possible avoid making large pruning cuts because of the disease risk. After cropping encourage new fruiting shoots evenly over the tree by cutting back to a stub about a quarter of the fruited sideshoots.

TRAINING A FAN

A wall (or a wire fence) is needed with wires spaced 15 cm [6"] or two brick courses apart, and held 10 cm [4"] away from the wall by lead wall eyes. The bottom wire is erected 30 cm [1'] above the soil level.

Training a fan tree from a maiden

If you wish to train a fan yourself, buy one of the genetic dwarfs, and in early spring cut it down to 60 cm [2'] from the ground to a good bud, checking that there are at least two good buds below this.

In the first summer, several shoots will result. Choose two good ones, one on each side to make your left and right branches. These should be 23-30 cm [9-12"] above the ground. Rub out all other growth on the main stem. When the sideshoots are about 45 cm [1½'] long, tie them to two long bamboo canes with soft string, and tie the canes to the wires at an angle of 45° to the ground, so that they are at an angle of 90° to each other. If one shoot grows more strongly, it should be temporarily lowered, which slows growth, until the other has caught up with it. The main stem should be carefully cut out immediately above the higher of the two branches, and the wound made smooth. In early spring the two side branches are then shortened to a bud 30-45 cm [1-1½'] from the main stem. During the following summer an extension shoot will grow from each of these buds and will eventually be tied in. Growth will be made along the length of the branches. Select two on the upper side of each branch and one on the bottom and tie them to the wires to help build a framework. Prune out all other shoots.

In early spring, the third the tree has spent in your garden, cut back these eight branches to a triple bud (consisting of flower and growth buds) so as to leave 30-45 cm [1-1½'] of ripened wood. If the wall is large and you plan to have a large framework, you can continue this summer and winter schedule for another year, otherwise pruning is adjusted to stimulating fruit production.

Formative pruning

Prune in early spring, at bud break, and shorten the previous summer's growth on all the shoots by a quarter to an upward-pointing bud. This will stimulate the topmost bud and those behind to produce more shoots, some of which can be tied in during the late spring to fruit next year.

Train on each leading shoot and select others growing parallel with the wall and tie them in. Rub out any shoots growing directly towards or away from the wall.

Pruning an established fan

The peach flowers only on the wood made in the previous summer and therefore is pruned on a replacement system. After sideshoots have cropped, they are cut out and new growth is tied in. But since the peach can produce one or two fruit buds and one shoot bud from a single point, a good deal of thinning has to be done.

Rubbing out in spring: At blossom time or just after the flowers fade, deal with the newly produced shoots, which will be about 1.5 cm [½"] in length. Rub out altogether those in the wrong direction. Those growing directly away from the support should be pinched back to one leaf.

Now turn to the blossom-bearing sideshoots which grew last year. There will nearly always be a new shoot growing near the base on such a shoot, or nearby, and this new shoot is left to grow as a replacement. The end bud on the fruiting shoot is also allowed to produce a shoot. The remaining new shoots are rubbed out, except any produced at the same point as the fruit. These are stopped at one leaf. Do this in three stages at intervals of about ten days. At this stage you should also cut out any winter die-back to a healthy bud, and protect the cut with tree paint if it is very large.

Pinching back and tying in: Tie in the young shoots in spring and summer while they are still flexible. They must not overlap but should radiate out like the spokes of a wheel. Check that the shoots carrying fruit are securely tied. Pinch back the replacement shoots to six leaves, and stop the new shoot at the end of the fruit-bearing shoot in the same way. At the center of the framework, where the branches converge, young shoots will need to be pinched back fairly short to about six leaves.

Pruning after cropping

As soon as the winter is over cut out the fruit-bearing laterals back to the replacement shoots. Tie in the new growths and renew any ties where constriction is taking place. The fan should present a neat, flat appearance well secured against winter.

When the tree has filled its space, prune the leaders like a

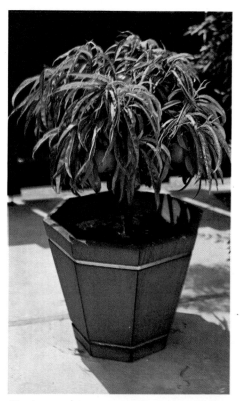

Tender nectarines are excellent pot-growing plants. Their small, smooth-skinned shiny fruits are either red or yellow with a blush, and very richly flavored and juicy.

(*Right*) A fan-trained peach showing a good crop of ripe fruit. The plastic net will catch any fruit that falls.

Nectarines produce beautiful pink blossoms. They do best in warm areas.

PRUNING A FREE-STANDING BUSH

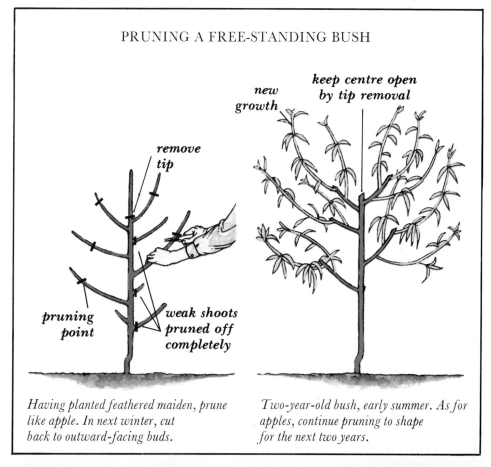

Having planted feathered maiden, prune like apple. In next winter, cut back to outward-facing buds.

Two-year-old bush, early summer. As for apples, continue pruning to shape for the next two years.

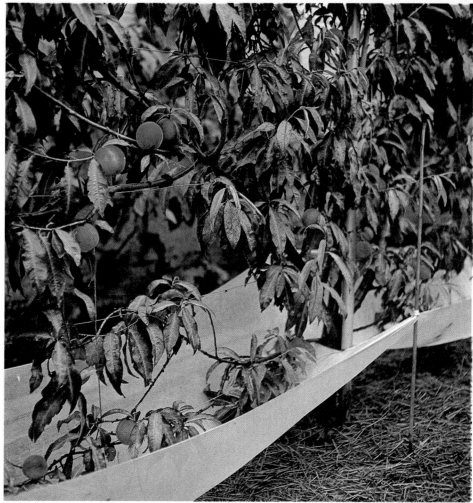

sideshoot, back to the replacement shoot. It is safer, but more difficult, to prune in late summer. In an area where disease in not prevalent, it will be easier to prune in early spring, when the leaves are off.

Peaches and nectarines under glass

In cool climates peaches and in particular nectarines are successful under glass, away from frost. If heat is available the season is extended by forcing, and by growing the late varieties.

Heated or unheated, a greenhouse should be 3.7 m [12′] long and 2.2 m [7½′] to the ridge. A lean-to should be the same length and ideally slightly higher at 2.5 m [8½′], with a wall facing the midday sun. The fan follows the sloping roof line in a span greenhouse supported by horizontal wires erected 38 cm [15″] away from the glass. In a lean-to the fan is grown on the back wall.

Take care over feeding, watering, ventilation and pollination. More rigorous control of tree size is necessary by rubbing out and pinching back. A daily spraying from mid-spring until the fruit begins to ripen keeps down the risk of red spider mites.

At the end of the season, the fan should be untied, and subsequently retied, with the lower shoots about 7.5 cm [3″] apart. The glass should be cleaned and the tree sprayed with a winter dormant spray to clean up any scale insects and the eggs of aphids. The border soil is lightly pricked over and the top 2.5 cm [1″] renewed afterwards. Fertilize and mulch as before.

CARE OF THE FRUIT

Overcropping will result in small fruit and will reduce the

TRAINING A FAN TREE FROM A MAIDEN: FIRST YEAR

attach wire to nails every 60 cm [2′]

15 cm [6″]

60 cm [2′]

30 cm [1′]

In early spring of first year, when buds on cleared maidens are starting to break, prune to good bud, leaving two other buds for left and right branches.

pruning point

new growth

prune off flush with stem

Young peach in summer of first year, just before it is pruned to remove the leader. The sideshoots have been tied to long bamboo canes placed at 45°.

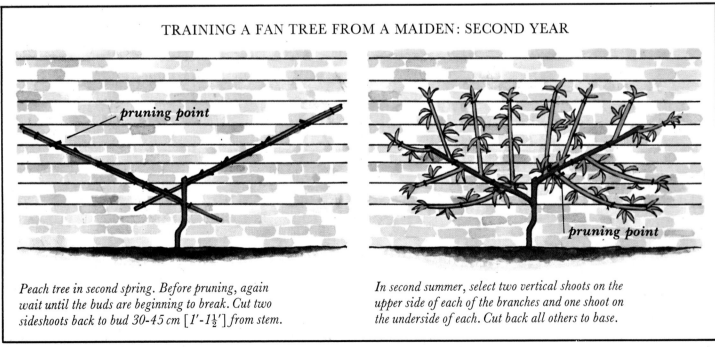

TRAINING A FAN TREE FROM A MAIDEN: SECOND YEAR

pruning point

Peach tree in second spring. Before pruning, again wait until the buds are beginning to break. Cut two sideshoots back to bud 30-45 cm [1′-1½′] from stem.

pruning point

In second summer, select two vertical shoots on the upper side of each of the branches and one shoot on the underside of each. Cut back all others to base.

following year's crop. Start thinning when the peaches are the size of peas, but wait until after the natural fruitlet drop is over befor completing the task. First remove under-sized fruit and then thin out peaches to 23 cm [9″] and nectarines to 15 cm [6″] apart.

Drape a 2 cm [¾″] mesh net over ripening fruit to protect it against birds. If wasps are troublesome, each fruit can be enclosed in a bag or an old nylon stocking as a simple form of protection.

Early varieties start to ripen in midsummer and cropping can continue for two months. Fruit is ripe when the flesh feels soft to finger pressure at the stalk end. In an unusually rainy season the flavor and color can be improved by tying back some of the foliage a little before this for peaches, but not nectarines as they are much more delicate than peaches and will burn in the sun.

Varieties

Belle of George Champion, Earlihale, Hale Haven, Red Oso Gem, Stark Hal-berta, Triogem. Genetic dwarf: Bonanza. Genetic dwarf nectarine: Nectarine.

Methods of preservation

Freezing is the most successful way of preserving peaches – a highly prized fruit of short season which one would especially like to have available year round. First prepare a sugar syrup in the ratio of 250 g [1 cup] sugar to ½ l [2½ cups] water and add ascorbic acid to it. Peel, halve and pit the fruit under cold running water and add immediately to the syrup. Then pack in rigid containers. Expect a freezer life of 12 months. Thaw in the refrigerator for about 4 hours and either serve while frosty or make into jam or jelly or fruit sauce.

TRAINING A PEACH FAN: THIRD YEAR

In the early spring of third year, prune back the eight branches to a triple bud (flower and growth buds), leaving 30-45 cm [1′-1½′] of ripened wood.

TRAINING A PEACH FAN: FOURTH YEAR

Unless wall to be covered is very big, after the third year pruning should aim to stimulate the fruit with branches tied in and evenly spaced.

PRUNING ESTABLISHED FANS

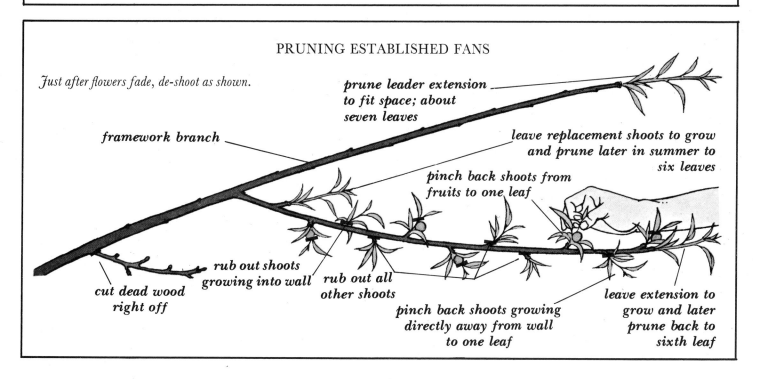

Just after flowers fade, de-shoot as shown.

prune leader extension to fit space; about seven leaves

framework branch

leave replacement shoots to grow and prune later in summer to six leaves

pinch back shoots from fruits to one leaf

rub out shoots growing into wall

rub out all other shoots

cut dead wood right off

pinch back shoots growing directly away from wall to one leaf

leave extension to grow and later prune back to sixth leaf

Pests and diseases

One common and often serious trouble of peach trees is the fungus disease, peach leaf curl, *Taphrina deformans*. The leaves become puckered and curled downward in early spring, and are pale green or yellowish. The discolored areas later become reddish and thickened, and develop white bloom as the sporing stage is reached. Defoliation occurs early, and new growth is severely stunted, though new leaves are often produced late in the season. Affected leaves should be destroyed as soon as seen and the tree sprayed with a spray recommended by your state authorities following their timing.

Other pests and diseases of peaches are Crown gall, brown rot, San Jose scale and peach tree borers.

Pear

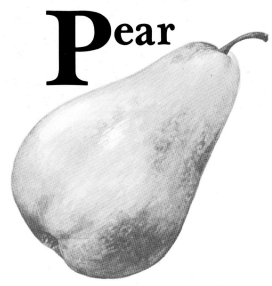

One of the most delectable tree fruits, dessert pears are best home grown, because of the short period when they are in perfect eating condition.

Native to Europe and western Asia, pears have been cultivated since early times. They need a warm temperature climate, moist conditions and a rich soil to reach perfection. The trees are longer-lived than apples and retain their fruit-bearing powers longer.

Pear
Pyrus communis (fam. *Rosaceae*)
Hardy deciduous tree with a rather long life.
Size: dwarf on quince rootstock 3.7 m [12'] high, 2.7 m [9'] wide. Standard 12 to 15 m [40 to 50'].
Climate: cool to warm temperate.
Planting to harvesting time: 3 to 5 years.

Many pears need a pollinator nearby, flowering at the same time, to set fruit. White pear flowers appear in early to mid-spring before the apple. The fruit has a gritty texture until ripe. Both shape and color vary according to variety, from long to round and from green to yellow, red-flushed or russet-coated.

Pears can be divided into three groups. Cooking pears are not acid, but lack flavor; slow cooking with sugar enhances this. They are, however, prolific and store well. Often hardier than dessert pears, in colder parts of the cool temperate area they are likely to be more successful. Dessert pears are softer in texture with a strong scent. Pears can also be pressed for juice which is fermented to make perry. Except for those living in the coldest part of the temperate zones, home gardeners will do best to plant dessert varieties, as these will cook and bottle equally well when picked before complete ripeness.

Pears grown abroad are mostly open-centered bushes, and this is one easy method for the amateur and gives a good yield in suitable conditions. However, pears train very readily. The dwarf pyramid or central leader tree follows the natural shape and is space-saving and convenient to pick. In cool areas where shelter is required, it is worthwhile training an espalier.

Suitable site and soil

In colder parts of cool temperate areas growing only the hardier types of cooking pears should be attempted.

Also strong winds at spring flowering prevent insects from pollinating, and strip tender young leaves from the tree, as well as severely browning the older leaves during the growing season. In autumn, winds may cause premature fall of leaves and, in particular, large well-grown fruit.

The best soil is deep, well drained, rather heavy and slightly acid. It should have enough clay to ensure plenty of moisture during the growing season and enough sand and grit to allow for good drainage.

Buying your tree

Unless you choose a self-fertilizing pear you must plant two trees to ensure pollination. Some popular varieties such as Bartlett do not unite readily with quince when grafted. They must therefore be double grafted by the nursery before purchase with an intervening compatible variety to prevent a future break at the union.

Buy two- or three-year-old trees, certified disease-free if possible and train any way you wish.

Planting the tree

Prepare the soil in advance by breaking up the subsoil and incorporating well rotted manure. Correct the pH level if it is below 6 by liming, and work in a general complete fertilizer about two weeks before planting. Autumn-planted trees establish the best. Heel in the tree if necessary. Plant, stake and mulch as for apple (*see* APPLE).

Take care to keep the union of the scion with the rootstock at least 7.5 cm [3"] above soil level. If the scion roots, the

Bartlett, a popular variety of pear which must be double grafted to quince A stock.

Louise Bonne pears are a very old variety; they ripen in late autumn and are heavy croppers in warmer areas.

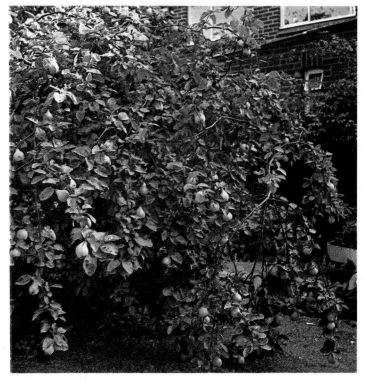

Pears are an ideal bush for the small garden; grafted onto quince A rootstock, they never grow too big.

Pyramid pruning enhances the natural shape of the tree. Branches are tied down here to encourage wide angles.

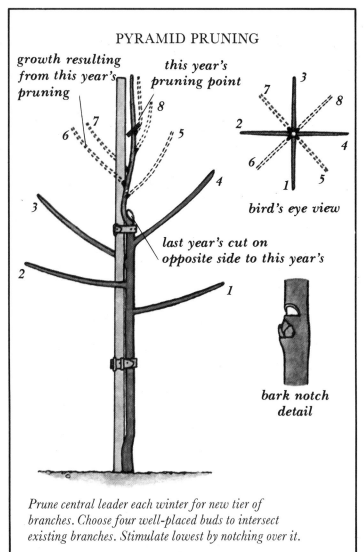

PYRAMID PRUNING

growth resulting from this year's pruning

this year's pruning point

bird's eye view

last year's cut on opposite side to this year's

bark notch detail

Prune central leader each winter for new tier of branches. Choose four well-placed buds to intersect existing branches. Stimulate lowest by notching over it.

pear will quickly dominate the quince roots and a vigorous, standard tree will result.

A pear that is to be espaliered on a wall or fence should be allowed 2 m [8′] height and 3.7 m [12′] width. Take care to spread out the roots so that they occupy the maximum amount of soil from which to draw water and nutrients. If soil texture is poor, perhaps after building operations, it is wise to use old potting compost as the immediate covering for roots to ensure a good start.

Fertilizers and care

The pear responds more than any other fruit to bulky organic matter. It needs plenty of summer moisture and high levels of nitrogen. This should be supplemented by an application in early spring each year of general complete fertilizer at the rate of 60 g per sq m [2 oz per sq yd]. This helps to maintain full cropping.

In extreme cases of poor growth, spray the foliage with urea-based commercial feeds; this might be at three intervals of two weeks, from petal fall in late spring.

If the tree is excessively vigorous then both pruning and manuring should be reduced. The growth of a mature tree may further be modified by growing grass under it.

Trees planted against walls are particularly susceptible to lack of moisture, so pay attention to watering.

Pruning

Also note, pears, if correctly pruned, carry their fruit on spurs close to the main branches and therefore more main branches can be allowed for each tree, than on apples. Secondly pear branches in the young tree are naturally slender and the result can be a drooping tree. To counteract this, continue to prune the leading shoots on the main branches back by one third or a half, according to vigor, while young.

There are four good reasons for pruning back the leaders: to strengthen the branch, to encourage more side growth, to remove deformed or diseased wood and to remove a branch growing in an undesirable direction. If none of these apply, then leader pruning should cease.

Pears bear fruit on short spurs, which are freely produced on two-year and older wood, though some are tipbearers, including many weeping pears. These should be pruned little and then to an upward pointing bud.

Training and pruning a pyramid

Pyramids grow with a strong central leader. From this the cropping branches grow away at wide angles with one tier occupying up to 30 cm [1′] of trunk. The resulting tree is compact and very efficient at fruit bearing.

Training and planting an espalier

The espalier is usually trained on a wall, fence or specially erected wires with horizontal branches in pairs on either side of the central stem. Nurseries usually sell two- and three-tier espaliers but if you train your own you can fill your own space.

Wire your wall with the lowest wire 30 cm [1′] from the ground and additional wires for each tier at intervals of about 30 cm [1′]. A horizontal space 4.2 m [14′] is best. To train your own espalier, buy a maiden and, immediately after planting, cut the single stem down to a strong-looking bud about 5 cm [2″] higher than the lowest wire. This will produce vertical growth. Below this top bud choose two more buds, on opposite sides of the stem which will produce shoots growing in the direction of the support wire. Rub out any other buds and if, in spring, growth starts from any buds further down, rub this out. The top and second buds are likely to grow strongly. To stimulate the third bud, cut a notch of bark from just above it.

As growth develops, tie the shoot from the top bud to the vertical cane with soft string, fastening the cane in turn to the horizontal wires. As they become long enough, tie the shoots from the next two buds to canes fastened to the wires at an angle of 45°. Thus, the two lower shoots will be at an angle of 90° to each other. Try to keep the two growing equally strongly so that they are the same length; slightly lower one cane to slow down growth and raise the other a little to increase growth.

In autumn unfasten the two side canes and bring them down to the horizontal and secure to the bottom wire. In winter prune the vertical shoot to a good bud about 5 cm [2″] above the second wire (this will make your new vertical) and proceed as in the first winter choosing two more buds to fill the second wire. Continue in this way until the required number of ties has been formed but with the last tier allow only two shoots to grow, one one either side. Prune the branches of the espalier just as if they were cordons: in summer cut the side growths as they mature to the third leaf beyond the basal cluster, and cut shoots from laterals that were pruned previously to one leaf beyond the cluster at the twig base as shown in the **diagram overleaf.**

Spur and fruit thinning

Pears make spurs more easily than apples and as the tree gets older the spurs become overcrowded, therefore spur thinning is beneficial.

The tree that is not growing sufficiently needs stimulation, provided by a harder winter prune and better manuring. The more frequent case is the tree growing too vigorously – all shoots and little fruit. Therefore prune lightly or not at all in winter and prune assiduously in summer. You can tie down the most vigorous sideshoots instead of cutting them out, so that they incline to the horizontal, which encourages them to produce fruit buds. This is particularly true of espaliers which incline to produce strong vertical growths from the horizontal arms.

In cool temperate areas all the fruit that sets may be cropped. In warmer areas oversetting may occur, and then the fruit should be thinned out to about 15 cm [6″] apart.

Standard trees

Perhaps we have given undue attention to espaliers and other dwarf forms of pear trees but we have done this intentionally, since pear trees grown as standards eventually reach a large size and may not be as suitable in small home gardens. However, for the benefit of those who will be growing full-sized trees we are including a few words on their training.

As with dwarfs, standard pear trees are grafted on other

roots but, instead of planting high so that the scion or top cannot grow its own roots and lose its dwarfness, it is preferable to plant deeply enough so that the top can also strike its own roots, if it wishes. (This tends to reduce suckering). Preferably one or two two-year plants are set out, allowing about 6 m (20′) each way, and the tree cut back to a single whip. Thereafter, the emphasis should be upon building a tree with a leader and well-spaced structural branches. The crotches should be as near 90° as possible and no branches should rub, shade or interfere with one another. Varieties like Bosc produce few smaller branches and many fruiting spurs, Bartlett the opposite. Prune the first group harder by heading back branches to maintain the fruiting spurs in a vigorous condition.

With all pears, if blight is present in your area, disinfect your shears after any cut where there is the least suspicion of its presence. When pruning, do not cut back severely to force excessive and weak growth and do not overfeed with nitrogen.

Harvesting and storing

Picking starts in late midsummer and can last for several months. The early varieties can be picked and eaten as soon as they are ripe on the tree. This will be when the fruit parts readily from the spur when gently lifted to the horizontal. Such varieties have a very short season and deteriorate rapidly if allowed to become overripe, to the extent of rotting the center. Mid-season and late varieties can be picked before ripe for storing. Pick before the stalk end changes to yellow. If a sharp tug is needed to get the

TRAINING AN ESPALIER FROM A MAIDEN

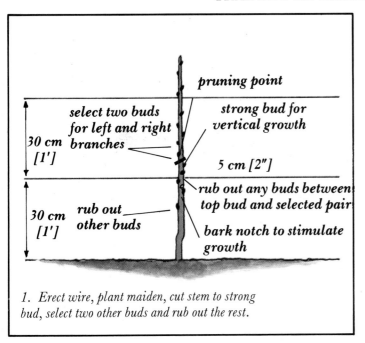

1. Erect wire, plant maiden, cut stem to strong bud, select two other buds and rub out the rest.

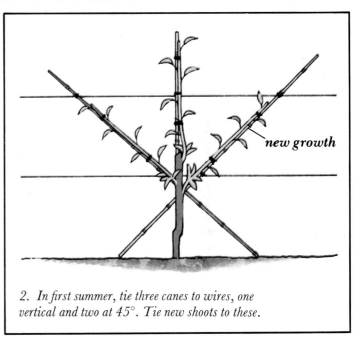

2. In first summer, tie three canes to wires, one vertical and two at 45°. Tie new shoots to these.

3. In autumn undo the two side canes, lower them to the horizontal and fasten to bottom wire, one on each side. In second winter same procedure is followed to produce second tier: cut back stem to a bud just above the second wire, choose two more buds for second tier, fix their shoots to 45° canes in second summer moving down in autumn. Repeat this procedure up to the last tier but then stop the stem and leave only the pair of buds for the top tier.

fruit off, it is not ready for storing. Too early harvesting results in 'sleepy' pears, which shrivel and become soft in the outer flesh before they become sweet. Leave later varieties until frost is expected.

Pears bruise easily: only store if sound and disease-free. Lay in slatted trays in single layers in cool 7°C [45°F] but moist conditions. Stored fruit may be lightly sprayed with water to maintain a moist atmosphere; too much warmth and dryness also produces sleepy pears. Watch carefully for signs of ripening indicated (in all but russets) by a yellowing skin and a softening of the flesh at the stalk end. Bring into room temperature before eating.

Methods of preservation

To dry: peel, core and cut into halves or quarters depending on the size of the fruit. To prevent discoloration, place into a bowl of cold, salted water (2 tablespoons salt to a gallon of water) for a few minutes. Lift out with a slotted spoon, pat dry with paper towels and place in single layers on the drying tray which should be covered. Place in a low oven (120°-150°). When completely dry (two or three pieces pressed together should feel rubbery and spring back when pressure is released) remove the tray from the heat and, after about 12 hours, place into airtight jars or containers and store in a cool, dry place.

To freeze: Peel, core and cut into quarters or slices. Immediately sprinkle with lemon juice to avoid discoloration. Then cook for about five minutes in light sugar syrup. Drain the fruit, cool and pack in containers in medium sugar syrup with ascorbic acid leaving headspace. Freeze and store either in pieces or as a puree. They should have a freezer life of 6 to 9 months.

Jam made from pears with ginger is an excellent way to make use of this delicate, hard-to-store fruit and enhance

PRUNING ESPALIER LATERALS

pruning point one leaf above basal cluster on sub-sideshoot

pruning point three leaves above basal cluster on sub-sideshoot

basal cluster of leaves

Pear espaliers must be pruned in midsummer. Cut mature laterals growing from horizontal branches back to three leaves above the basal cluster and sideshoots growing from these to one leaf above.

An espalier pear in blossom. Pears flower in early spring and so risk damage from late frost. On cold nights, hang strips of plastic over the blossom.

SPUR PRUNING ON OLD TREES

Pear spurs will become overcrowded in time. Prune oldest and least fruitful ones back to their base.

its flavor even more.

Peel, quarter and core 1 lb. pears. Tie the peel, cores, thinly pared lemon peel of three lemons and a 2.5 cm [1"] piece of ginger crushed into a large piece of cheesecloth. Place all in a preserving pan and after bringing to a boil, simmer for 30 minutes or until fruit is soft. Add 10 cups of sugar and stir until dissolved. Stir in juice of three lemons. Bring to a boil for 15 to 20 minutes. Then remove pan from heat, skim off foam and let stand for 5 minutes before placing into jars. Fill, cover and label. Store in a cool, dry place.

Varieties
Bartlett, Beurr Bosc, Clapp's Favorite, Doyenne du Comice, Kieffer, Kyle's Sugar, Red Anjou, Seckel, Starking.

Pests and diseases
Pears suffer from the same troubles as apples, but to a lesser degree. Scab, mildew, canker and brown rot and fireblight (the most serious) are the chief fungus diseases. Aphids, psylla, leaf-eating caterpillars, red spider mite and scale insects are common pests. Birds may attack buds or ripening fruit.

Peas are also attacked by fireblight, which first causes the flowers to blacken and the twigs to die and then begins to affect the branches. Cure by cutting off the wood beyond the affected area and destroying it.

Milder than chillies, but still very 'hot', the fruit of the long red pepper is powdered and used as a spice.

Peppers

Native to tropical America, peppers are now increasingly used both as a vegetable in stews and casseroles and as an ingredient in salads.

The two most common types of pepper are *Capsicum annuum*, which includes the large red and green sweet peppers and *C. frutescens*, which embraces chilies and hot red peppers. *C. annuum* is a narrow, roughly oblong vegetable with a mild, peppery flavor.

Capsicums at different stages of maturity. Do not leave overripe fruit on the plant as this will reduce yields.

(Right) Rich in vitamin C, sweet peppers are delicious stuffed and baked or shredded and eaten raw in salads.

210

1. Put the tray on a windowsill to give seedlings plenty of sunlight.

2. At the three-leaf stage, prick seedlings out into 7.5 cm [3″] pots.

3. Pot on to 12 cm [5″] pots with a richer mixture for fruiting outside.

4. Harden off in a cold frame prior to moving plants to the open garden.

5. Prepare homemade liquid manure; dilute it before feeding the plants.

6. Alternatively, buy liquid feed. Always feed when fruits are forming.

7. Pinch out the first few flowers by hand to encourage the formation of larger fruit. Keep well watered.

8. Prevent infestation by the pest red spider mite by a daily spray of water on undersides of the leaves.

9. Sweet red and green peppers can be stored: thread a string through the stalks and hang in a dry place.

The small tapering fruits, about 2.5-5 cm [1-2"] long of the *C. frutescens* types are renowned for their strong 'hot' flavor, and the paprika made from one of these is much used in Hungarian cooking, especially goulash. Because of their pungency, these peppers are mostly used for flavoring only, often being ground to powder or shredded. Natives of warm climates, peppers are grown as half-hardy annuals in cool climates. The fruits of chili peppers have to ripen completely before being picked and are more likely to be grown in the warmer parts of the country.

Suitable site and soil

Peppers will thrive in any rich, well-worked soil. Thus outdoors, a well-drained and fertile loam is preferable. Choose a sunny place.

Sowing and planting

Sow seeds during early spring in a warm greenhouse or propagator, or a warm room if the climate is cool. They can be sown outdoors (either in the ground or in peat pots) after the last frost, in warm areas.

If being sown indoors, sow seeds in trays, spacing them about 2.5 cm [1"] apart and pushing them just beneath the surface of the mixture. A soil temperature of 18°C [65°F] is ideal, but seeds will germinate if it drops a few degrees below this for a short period of time. The first leaves should be showing within 10-24 days of sowing, depending on the temperature.

When the seedlings reach the three-leaf stage, prick each out into a 7.5 cm [3"] pot. Do not allow the plants to become root-bound; as they grow, pot them in larger pots and into richer soils to encourage the development of good growth.

Maintain the temperature at between 10° and 16°C [50° and 60°F] during this period. Never move these half hardy plants straight from a warm greenhouse or kitchen window-sill into the open garden. If the peppers are to be placed outside when the danger of the last frost has passed, get them accustomed to a lower temperature gradually, preferably by transferring them to a cold frame for a short one or two weeks the plants can safely be left out permanently.

Where only a small number of plants are being raised and no cold frame is available, an easier method is to stand the pots outdoors rather than transplanting from pots into the ground. The pots can be left outside during the day, and

returned to the greenhouse or a warm room at night. After one or two weeks the plants can safely be left out permanently.

Young plants which are to be dug into open ground should be set out in the warmth of late spring at 38-60 cm [15-24"] apart, depending on the size of the variety. Always water the soil well before planting, unless it is already fairly moist.

Care and development

The quantity of water which you should give peppers depends on the type of soil in which they are growing, the temperature of the environment and the age of the individual seedlings or plants. If a light soil becomes too dry, even for a very short time, especially at midday, the plants will droop.

Peppers respond well to liquid feeding once the fruit begins to form and this can be done at ordinary watering times. If soil is very dry, however, soak the ground before using the liquid feed solution according to the manufacturer's instruction. Alternatively, make liquid manure by steeping a bag of rotted manure in a tub of water; use this after diluting it to the color of straw.

Peppers should not be planted in areas where perennial weeds are persistent. Bindweed and similar weeds must be eliminated and annual weeds can be kept down with a hoe worked between the rows before the roots get a hold on the soil, ensuring the minimum disturbance to the roots.

Canes for support may be necessary for tall varieties, but the dwarf kinds stand up well and do not need sticks.

Artificial pollination is not really necessary as the greenish-white flowers set fruit readily, and may indeed need thinning to get the best-sized peppers. However, a daily light spray of water from a garden syringe may help, at the same time benefiting the leaves which, being thin, tend to dry up more quickly than most. It will also help to ward off attacks of red spider mite.

Harvesting and after-care

The fruit should be in season from late summer until early autumn, or late autumn in warm areas, coming to an end as the weather becomes colder. The length of the harvesting season depends on the local climate, and can also vary from summer to summer. The fruits should be picked as soon as they are of sufficient size, and the flesh is firm and well filled out. A good quality pepper has a smooth, pleasing shape and an even color. Green peppers that have been left on the plant will ripen to a rich scarlet, yellowish green or golden yellow color, depending on the variety. The ripe fruit should be cut from the parent plant with a sharp knife, leaving the other peppers, which develop at different rates, undisturbed. The peppers taste delicious at all stages, but for those who prefer it, the mature red or yellow fruit are somewhat sweeter. Handle peppers carefully, for they bruise easily. The yield from each plant can be as high as 30 fruit in a good season, and three to five plants should provide a steady supply of sweet peppers during summer and early autumn.

To store the fruit, thread a string through the stalks and hang them up in a dry place. Late picked peppers can last until early winter. If picked green, they will gradually

---

Peppers

Capsicum annuum, C. frutescens (fam. *Solanaceae*).
Also known as capsicum, bell or bullnose pepper, sweet pepper and pimiento; chili and red pepper.
Perennial, but most culinary capsicums are grown as **half-hardy annuals.**
Size: plants vary in height from 30-90 cm [12-36"]. Fruit of dwarf varieties about 2.5 cm [1"] across; large varieties from 7.5-12.5 cm [3-5"].
Climate: warm temperate to tropical.
Sowing to harvesting time: 8-11 weeks.
Yield: 0.75-1 kg [1½-2 lb] per plant.

change color until they are red. You should not leave over-ripe peppers on the plants, because this may reduce yields by draining food reserves.

The plants should not be left in the soil after the last pepper has been picked. For the sake of pest and disease control, it is better to pull up and burn or compost old plants as soon as the days start becoming shorter and colder and the fruiting process has stopped or frost has killed them.

Methods of preservation

There are, at present, several varieties of pepper being developed which will withstand the cold weather.

In the meantime, however, you should note they can be stored in several ways, preserving their texture and flavor: they may be put up in jars, frozen (for up to 12 months) or pickled.

Varieties

Stokes Early Hybrid, Bell Bay, Golden Bell, Vinette, California Wonder, Pennbell, Sweet Hungarian, Canada-Cheese, Sunnybrook Pimento, Crimson Hot, Long Red Cayenne.

Pest and diseases

Greenfly and red spider mite may be troublesome, both indoors and out. If virus mosaic stunts the plants, destroy them.

Plum

Plums are generally popular stone fruits, and the hardiest in cool areas. Red, blue-black or yellow-skinned, they are delicious raw or cooked.

Plums are related to peaches and cherries but are hardier than both. *Prunus* is the Latin name for plum. Among hardy fruit trees, the European plum, *Prunus domestica,* is second in

some ways only to the apple. It probably originated in Southeast Asia and is widely grown throughout Europe, North America and Australia. It is thought to be a hybrid from a wild blackthorn or sloe (*P. spinosa*) with very acid dark purple fruit, and myrobalan or cherry plum (*P. cerasifera*), now widely grown as an ornamental. The latter is chiefly grown for hedging, but it bears a reasonable crop, excellent for jam.

Cooking plums are mainly dark-colored with rather less flesh and a tart flavor. The trees are larger, more vigorous hardier and heavier and more reliable croppers. Dessert plums have a richer flavor, high sugar content and may be yellow, red, black or purple. Blue plums, described as prunes, may be dried or eaten fresh.

Most places the Japanese plum, *P. salicina,* is also successful; this was originally native to China. It blooms very early; fruit have thick skins but may lack flavor. *P. americana* is most important of the native American plums.

Damsons, *P. damascena,* produce a smaller and richer fruit on a smaller tree. The old fashioned bullace, *P. insittia,* has soft dark fruit with a sharp flavor; used for cooking they are left on the tree till into autumn for maximum ripeness. Greengages, *P. italica,* have green-toned flesh and having been interbred with the European plums are usually classed with them.

Suitable site and soil

There is no really dwarfing rootstock. But they readily fit into most gardens. Plums generally bloom early in mid-spring when blossoms may be damaged by frost, so avoid low-lying spots. Shelter is needed from strong winds. Shallow or sandy soils, and ill-drained soils and heavy clays should be avoided.

Buying the trees

A few plums are self-fertilizing, but most require a compatible pollinator flowering at the same time.

Some varieties of tree are upright, others have a weeping habit. Droopers are best as standard trees, otherwise the branches will trail on the ground.

Planting

With a heavy soil, work in coarse sand before planting, at 3 kg [7 lb] per sq m [yd]. Make well-drained soil more water retentive by mixing in rotted organic matter, half a 12 L [2½ gal] bucket per sq m [yd] four weeks before planting. No lime is needed unless soil gives pH of less than 6.0. Space less vigorous varieties as closely together as 5.5 m [18'] for those on Myrobolan B stock. Plant the tree as for

---

Plum
Prunus domestica (fam. *Rosaceae*).
Hardy deciduous tree with a useful life of many years.
Size: 6-9 m [20-30'].
Climate: cool to warm temperate.
Planting to harvesting time: 3-4 years.
Yield: mature standard up to 45-52 kg [100-120 lb], less for trained trees. Greengages yield half this.

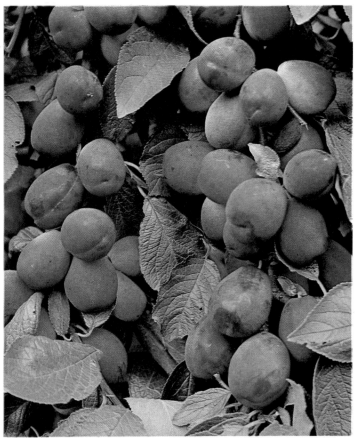

Cooking plums are much hardier than dessert varieties. The tart fruit is used for pies, preserves and desserts.

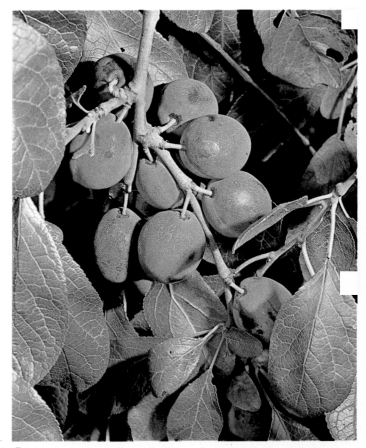

Best grown as a small standard tree, damsons bear sweet oval-shaped fruit which is excellent for homemade jam.

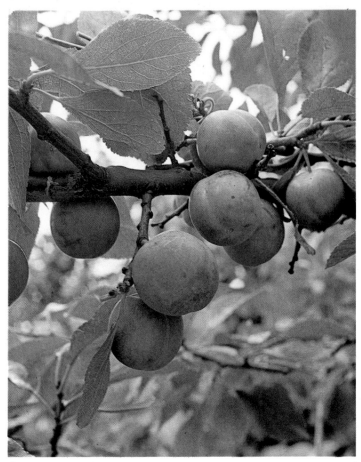

Greengages are highly prized for their flavor. Grown like plums, they yield only half the quantity.

To produce high yields, prune plums need a cold winter followed by a hot, dry summer. Their fruits are dried.

215

WINTER PRUNING FROM THE SECOND YEAR ON

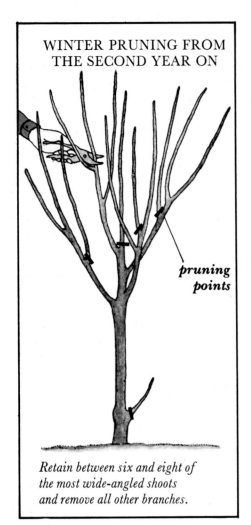

pruning points

Retain between six and eight of the most wide-angled shoots and remove all other branches.

TRAINING A PYRAMID

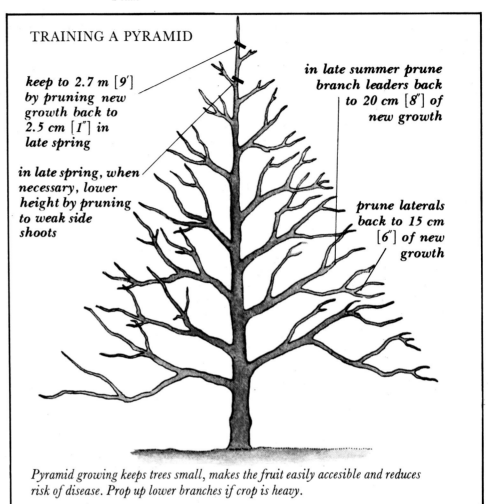

keep to 2.7 m [9'] by pruning new growth back to 2.5 cm [1"] in late spring

in late spring, when necessary, lower height by pruning to weak side shoots

in late summer prune branch leaders back to 20 cm [8'] of new growth

prune laterals back to 15 cm [6'] of new growth

Pyramid growing keeps trees small, makes the fruit easily accesible and reduces risk of disease. Prop up lower branches if crop is heavy.

THINNING THE FRUIT

With a heavy crop, thin to avoid small juiceless fruit. Allow 7.5 cm [3"] or more between fruits depending on variety.

SUPPORTING LEADER BRANCHES

Put stake close to the trunk and support the branches with strings attached to its top.

apple (*see* APPLE). Be careful not to injure bark while planting, otherwise bacterial canker may get a hold.

Fertilizing and care

Plums need plenty of nitrogen, and should never run short of potash. A good mulch of rotted farmyard manure or garden compost is especially helpful to young trees, applied in late spring every year. In addition in early spring give 15 g per sq m [½ oz per sq yd]. If organic matter is not available, double this dressing of nitrogen and add 15 g per sq m [½ oz per sq yd] sulphate of potash. Dress an area of soil slightly in excess of that covered by the branches. Water well in very dry weather.

Pruning

For the first two or three years the head of the tree will be pruned to form the main framework. A maiden tree consists of a single straight stem, possibly with a few wispy branches called feathers. After planting the main stem is cut to 15 cm [6″] above the desired height of the lowest branch. Several branches will then grow below this cut. In the following winter choose three or four well-spaced, wide-angled shoots tending to horizontal and remove everything else flush with the stem. Selected shoots are then cut back halfway to an outward facing bud.

In the next summer two or more shoots will grow from each of these cut back branches and in the winter after this six to eight well-spaced shoots should be retained and all vigorous and more upright branches removed.

No tipping is required. Future pruning is only to cut out shoots too close together and diseased and broken branches. The best time to prune established trees to avoid infection is early spring before growth starts.

Plums tend to produce suckers and these should be removed by pulling out by hand rather than cutting.

Training a plum pyramid

Plum pyramids are smaller and can be grown in a restricted space. Only large-growing varieties are unsuitable. Pyramids are easier to pick and disease is less likely as large wounds and branch breakages are much reduced.

Buy a maiden tree with some feathered growth (side branches). When planting, support the tree with a stout bamboo cane or post standing 1.8-2 m [6-7′] out of the ground. In mid-spring cut the main leader to 1.2-1.5 m [4-5′] from ground level. Remove all feather growth up to a height of 30 cm [1′] above the soil, and shorten the remaining feathers to half their length. Tie the leader loosely to the stake to allow growth.

In late summer of the same year, the leading shoot growing from each of the shortened feathers is cut back to 20 cm [8″] and lateral shoots to 15 cm [6″]. The main central leader is gently tied to the stake and is not cut.

In subsequent years the main central leader is cut back in early spring, to within 2.5 cm [1″] of the previous year's growth, and branch leaders and laterals are pruned as they were in the first year. Cut main leader back harder if growing too tall. If very upright shoots grow from the main trunk they should be removed completely as only wide-angled laterals will be fruitful.

Thinning fruit and supporting branches

Plums tend to crop too heavily one year and lightly the next. In a heavy crop the fruit can be small with little flesh. Thin out the fruit to maintain quality and prevent possible branch breakage. Remove diseased, badly shaped and injured fruitlets first. Thin when fruit are swelling and are about one third of their final size after those which have not set have dropped off. Allow 7.5 cm [3″] between any two plums, 10 cm [4″] for larger fruits. Even after thinning weighty branches may need support with a prop (*see* MULBERRY) or drive in an upright stake next to the trunk; branches are then supported by strings attached to the top of the stake.

Harvesting

Trees bear in three to five years and cropping is from late midsummer to early autumn. Dessert fruit should be left on the tree until thoroughly ripe. For canning or bottling plums can be picked when fully colored, for jam when firm and almost ripe. Go over the tree several times picking fruit as it ripens. If they have a bloom pick carefully with finger and thumb – plums bruise easily. Some are easily parted from their stalks, but others need careful picking to avoid removing spur. Plums can be kept a few days if laid out not touching, in a cool place, such as a cellar or storage shed.

Methods of use and preservation

Both methods of use and preservation of plums are incredibly varied.

This delicate fruit that has such a short life once it has been picked may be made into jam (possibly combined with apples for a subtle blending of flavors) or, when dried, into a luscious Plumb Cobbler – a tempting form of a traditional dessert. Plums may also be candied, becoming both delicious and decorative; and they may be made into a liqueur.

Plums may be dried, put up in jars, candied or frozen.

Varieties

Burbank Elephant Heart, Fellemberg, Abundance, Santa Rosa, Superior, Tecumseh, Yellow Egg, Idaho Prime, Green Gate, Damson.

Pests and diseases

The fungus disease silver leaf (*Stereum purpureum*) is a common complaint of plums in some areas and especially affecting certain varieties. This disease is extremely difficult to control. The leaves on one shoot, and then on all shoots, on a branch will become silver on the top surface, and if the branch is cut through, the wood will be irregularly stained purplish brown on one side, if not both. The disease can spread all over a tree and kill it, when purplish leathery sheets or projecting brackets of tissue are produced in layers from the bark, usually in autumn. Disease enters through wounds, such as pruning cuts. When trees are badly silvered all over or have reached this spore-producing stage, they should be destroyed. However, trees can recover, grow and crop if the disease is mild. There is no known cure but you should cut the branches 15 cm [6″]

The beautiful bloom of a healthy crop. Unlike dessert plums, cookers should be picked before fully ripening.

beyond the affected area, paint and destroy the wood. Remove gall growths.

Although not widespread, especially in the United States, another potential pest which can attack fruit from early summer onwards is the small red caterpillars of the plum fruit moth; spray with a locally-approved spray in early summer, to control the larvae as they hatch out before they enter the fruit. The creamy white caterpillar of the plum sawfly may also cause problems and feeds on the fruit, but much earlier, from the time when they first set. Again, spray with a locally-approved spray, but wait until evening when pollinating insects are not around.

Gumming of fruit can be because of injury by capsids or sawfly larvae, or because water supplies have been irregular.

In many districts, birds are the worst enemies, both when the fruit is on the tree, and in winter when they peck out the blossom buds. Either net the tree, if possible (*see* CHERRY) or spray in winter with bird repellant.

Brown rot, black knot, caterpillars, curculio, scale insects and various aphids are also likely troubles.

Potato

The potato is a versatile and staple food, high in carbohydrates but also containing vitamins and minerals. Though widely grown as a farm crop, garden produce tastes best.

Although most potatoes are grown on farms, it is still a important garden crop. Some high-quality varieties a

unsuitable for large-scale commercial cultivation; they may not be able to stand shipping without injury, they may give a low yield, or serve too specialized a purpose. Early, or 'new' potatoes are also at their best shortly after being dug, and maincrop potatoes grown in the garden usually give a higher yield than with field cultivation.

Suitable site and soil

In a rotation system, potatoes are generally grown to follow roots and to precede the cabbage family, which appreciates the clean, well-turned condition in which this crop leaves the soil. Potatoes are a good choice for a first crop on old pasture that is being taken into cultivation. As a precaution against disease, they must not be grown in the same soil two years in succession. Remember that tomatoes and nightshade weeds are also members of the family *Solanaceae* and can transmit infection. Potatoes are not particular about soil, but on heavy clay soils choose your varieties carefully. Early varieties prefer light land.

The ground should be well dug and treated with rotted manure or garden compost, but not limed. Lime will encourage attacks of scab, while too much nitrogen will produce growth of the 'haulm', or stem, at the expense of tubers. An excess of chloride will give 'soapy' potatoes.

Seaweed, dug into the soil the previous autumn, is an excellent manure. If organic matter is not available, a fertilizer of 2 parts each by weight of superphosphate and sulphate of ammonia with 1 part of sulphate of potash may be applied during preparation at the rate of 40 g per sq m [1⅓ oz per sq yd] of the mixture. The site should be open and not overshadowed by trees, walls or buildings.

Planting the crop

The tubers from which potatoes are grown are dormant ones known as 'seeds'. These are obtained from vigorous plants before they are fully mature and exposed for a few days until they have greened. Potato crops are grown from tubers produced on government certified farms. (After the Irish potato famine in the 1840s, breeders worked to develop blight-resistant strains.) Certified stock is often bought every year, but it is considered safe to grow from tubers of your own (undiseased) crop every other year. 'Seeds' should be about the size of a hen's egg and look plump and healthy, but a delivery usually contains some larger ones. These may be divided as described later.

If you wish to have potatoes all year round, you will need three varieties: an early, a second early, and a maincrop variety. The earlier the variety, the faster the growth and

---

Potato
Solanum tuberosum (fam. *Solanaceae*), known as white or Irish potato where sweet potatoes are also grown.
Half-hardy annual.
Size: tubers average 7 × 6 cm [2¾″ × 2¼″]; height of haulms (stems) about 60 cm [2′].
Climate: cool temperate to sub-tropical.
Planting to harvesting time: 13-17 weeks.
Yield: 13.5 to 22.5 kg [30 to 50 lb.] per 75 m [25′] of row.

the lower the yield. Order 2 kg [4½ lb], 5 kg [11 lb] and 2.5 kg [5½ lb] respectively, of each kind per person, if a supply is to be maintained through the winter and spring, in time to begin sprouting at the end of winter (slightly earlier for early varieties). Allow 20 sq m [24 sq yd] of land for this amount. If you can only grow a more limited number, it is best to sacrifice the maincrop and grow the earlies, which are harvested when potatoes are dearest in the shops.

Put the seeds in trays or empty egg-boxes in a light, well-ventilated frost-proof place. This enables growth to begin before it would be wise to plant outside. The wooden fruit trays that have a short leg sticking upwards at each corner for stacking are ideal. Look for the end of the tuber where the 'eyes' or dormant buds are crowded together – this is the top. Stand them upwards in the trays or egg-boxes and, if there is any risk of frost, spread newspaper over. This process takes about six weeks and is done, not only to get crops earlier, but to get heavier ones.

Plant when the sprouts are 3 cm [1¼″] long, which is usually in early or mid-spring. Rub off all except two or three of them with the thumb, removing first the one at the extreme top, then any that are white (if most of them are purplish), and lastly the least promising of any surplus remaining. Large tubers can be cut into pieces, each having at least two strong sprouts. Dust the cut faces with flowers of sulphur or plaster of Paris to check loss of moisture; alternatively, bring the exposed surfaces together and cover with a damp cloth until planting. Take great care not to knock off the sprouts.

Potato rows should run north and south so that the plants receive the maximum amount of sunshine and do not shade other crops. The rows should be 50 cm [20″] apart for earlies and 75 cm [30″] apart for the bulkier maincrop plants. This allows room for earthing up later on.

Take out V-shaped furrows from 8 cm [3¼″] deep for a heavy soil to 15 cm [6″] deep for a light one. Never use a dibber for planting because it is liable to leave an air-space underneath the tuber. For improved yield spread a forkful of manure where each piece is to go and throw 3 cm [1¼″] of soil over it, so that manure and set will not be in direct contact. Place lawn mowings in and around the drills before filling them in; this will help prevent attacks of the potato scab fungus, which is less likely to bother the potatoes when other organic matter is available. Use small amounts of grass only.

Place each piece in position in the drill, top uppermost, 30 cm [1′] apart for earlies and 40 cm [16″] for maincrops, covering each with soil by hand to protect the sprouts from damage when refilling the furrow. Rake the soil level and scatter fertilizer along the row. The earlies should go into sheltered ground in early spring, with second earlies and maincrops at monthly intervals.

Care and cultivation

Protection is necessary for all potatoes when there is any risk of frost, as there nearly always is with the earlies. Once the shoots are above the surface, ground or wind-frost can burn them black, causing a 3-week setback. When they are only a few centimeters [1-2″] high cover them gently with powdery soil, but when they are 7.5-10 cm [3-4″] tall they must be covered with straw or newspapers if danger exists.

Wait until the shoots can be clearly seen before doing any hoeing, and then do not work the hoe too close to them. Start earthing up when the shoots are about 20 cm [8″] high. The haulms of potato plants are jointed, and the tubers arise from underground joints in the haulm. Therefore the more of these there are the more tubers can be formed, hence the practice of earthing up.

Earthing up also keeps the tubers well buried so that they will not turn green through exposure to light – green tubers contain a poisonous substance and are dangerous to eat. Loosen up the soil between the rows and push some up with a draw-hoe on both sides of the haulms several times during the growing period, leaving the top 15 cm [6″] uncovered.

Spray against the fungus disease blight once in mid-summer and again in late summer with a state-recommended spray. These can protect against blight but not cure it. Any flowers that appear during growth should be nipped off. When growth slows and the haulms turn yellow the tubers mature. If isolated plants show these signs you must suspect disease; cut their tops down and burn them, although the tubers of these plants may be left in the soil until they are of usable size and are harvested.

Harvesting and storing the crop

Early or 'new' potatoes are eaten immature in early summer, when they are no larger than a pullet's egg. Carefully lift one or two to see if they are ready for eating; they can be covered up again if they are not. Some people unearth them by hand, pick the tubers they want, and return the soil to let the rest grow on. In the South this is called 'grabbing'. Dig up the earlies as you need them day by day, because after they are lifted they quickly lose flavor. A potato fork is a great asset: its flat, blunt tines miss more tubers and damage fewer than any other tool. Whole potatoes or pieces of tuber remaining in the ground over winter are not only lost, but will be a nuisance growing up among the brassicas the next year, and negate the principle of not growing potatoes in the same soil two years running.

The earlies can go straight into the kitchen as required, but the later crops must be stored. After lifting, let them dry-off on the ground for an hour or two, but no longer before being taken in. Clean off adhering soil by hand, discard any diseased or damaged tubers, and take the opportunity to do any grading required if, for instance, any are required for seed. Store them in the dark or under-cover from light in a dry frost- and draft-free storeroom. Bags or boxes will do for storing, but put straw under the bags and take precautions against vermin. The potatoes should be inspected once a month, when rotten ones should be discarded and any sprouts rubbed off.

If supplies are large and accommodation small, one solution is a ridge raised in a dry, open location out of doors on a thick bed of straw. Heap the potatoes on this into a ridge and cover them thickly with more straw, then put some soil on to keep it in place. After 24 hours' drying cover the straw with 15 cm [6″] of soil, obtained by digging

Encourage the tubers to sprout by placing seed potatoes in cardboard egg boxes, with the 'rose' end up.

Long and spindly shoots, unfit for planting, are caused by keeping the sets in too much warmth or darkness.

Rub off any white shoots and at the extreme top, using your thumb; retain the two most sturdy shoots.

When large tubers are cut, be sure each piece has two shoots. Protect cut surfaces from loss of moisture.

Plant by hand in V-shaped furrows. Use small amounts of lawn mowings to discourage potato scab fungus.

Protect sprouts by crumbling soil over them before raking level. Then scatter fertilizer along the row.

When haulms reach 7.5 cm [3"], they must be covered with straw to give protection against damage by frost.

Begin earthing up when haulms reach 17 cm [7"], to stop exposed tubers going green and protect from blight.

Yellowish leaves indicate the crop is ready. Lift with a potato fork to reduce risk of damage to tubers.

A high quality second early variety, this one prefers a heavy soil.

One of the most popular maincrop varieties.

The traditional method of earthing up potato rows encourages more tubers to form and protects them from light, as well as helping keep down weeds.

Leave the crop on the soil for one or two hours to dry before storing.

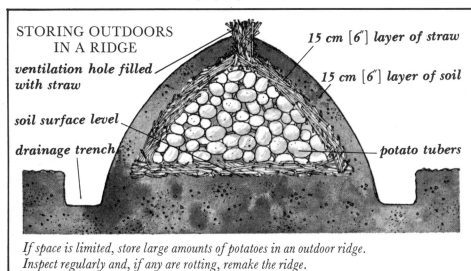

STORING OUTDOORS IN A RIDGE

ventilation hole filled with straw

soil surface level

drainage trench

15 cm [6"] layer of straw

15 cm [6"] layer of soil

potato tubers

If space is limited, store large amounts of potatoes in an outdoor ridge. Inspect regularly and, if any are rotting, remake the ridge.

a drainage trench all around the ridge. This is then beaten flat with the spade so as to shed rain. Leave ventilation holes at 1 m [1 yd] intervals along the top, pulling up tufts of straw from below to keep them open. When removing potatoes, inspect those exposed to view before closing the breach. If many are rotten, you must remake the ridge. Take the haulms away and burn them; do not add to the compost heap.

Alternative methods of cultivation

It is not essential to earth up potatoes but the traditional method described is still widely favored. Cultivation time may be cut by planting the tubers individually along the rows with a trowel (without making a trench) and covering the rows with lengths of black plastic sheeting tucked into slits made in the soil, at both its sides and ends, so as to anchor them. When the shoots start to grow and make bumps in the plastic make openings with scissors in the form of plus signs to release them. The opaque sheeting conserves moisture, inhibits weeds, and shields the shallow-grown tubers from light. Harvest the potatoes, after cutting or rolling back the plastic, by lifting them up with a hand fork or potato fork.

Other gardeners grow them under heavy mulches of straw, etc. This works fairly well in dry seasons but the same gardeners never mention the rot in an unusually wet season. Spring supplies of 'new potatoes' can be produced by planting them in warm frames in mid winter, either directly in the soil or in pots, but few gardeners have this much frame accommodation. Half-bury upright sets each in a 20 cm [8″] pot about a third full, and earth them up as they grow. Patio-gardeners sometimes grow three or four earlies in half-wine barrels. Some earlies may be given a good start with plastic tunnels, but keep the end of the tunnel closed.

Storage methods

Although varieties of potato are available the year round, it is worthwhile knowing they can be stored frozen so that they will be conveniently ready for use in any of a number of forms.

First, note that only new potatoes should be frozen uncooked. Simply wash and scrape or peel. Pack in plastic bags or preferably in boiling bags with a large lump of butter. Cook direct from the freezer.

For boiled potatoes, use new potatoes only which have been parboiled, drained and tossed in butter. Cool and pack in plastic bags or boiling bags with a lump of butter. Thaw loose potatoes and reheat in melted butter or, if in boiling bags, reheat in boiling water.

For French fries, fry about 2 minutes in clean oil until soft but not colored. Drain thoroughly on towel paper. Open freeze and pack in plastic bags. Deep fry direct from the freezer to deep golden brown, but beware, they will spit a lot.

For baked potatoes, remove from shell, mash with butter and return to their shells. Wrap each potato individually in foil. Reheat in oven for 30 minutes at 400° while still in foil.

Uncooked will last 12 months; French fries, 6 months; all others, 3 months.

GROWING POTATOES IN CONTAINERS

Plant one seed potato in each 30 cm [1′] container. Use a hand fork to harvest crop.

GROWING UNDER PLASTIC SHEETS

1. *Use a trowel to plant tubers in holes along row.*

2. *Secure plastic sheet in slits dug in the soil.*

3. *Free emerging haulms by cutting holes in sheet.*

4. *Lift with a hand fork after rolling back sheet.*

Varieties

Anoko, Chippewa, Iris Cobbler, Early Gem, Green Mountain, Katahdin, Redskin, Shoshoni, Teton, White Rose, Kennebec, Norland.

Pests and diseases

Potato blight (*Phytophthora infestans*) is probably the best known; it is a fungus disease which occurs in consistently wet weather and which produces dark brown-black patches on the leaves and stems; infected tubers have sunken areas on the outside which will be found to be brown in the flesh underneath. The disease spreads quickly in warm wet weather and can destroy the top growth completely in midsummer. Protect plants by spraying with a locally-recommended fungicide in early midsummer, if the weather warrants it, and repeat as the makers instruct. If the disease persists, and the spotting on the leaves becomes black instead of brown, then cut down and burn the foliage and lift the rest of the crop.

Common scab is a superficial fungus disease, affecting the skins of the tubers only, but it makes peeling difficult; line the drills at planting time with small amounts of lawn mowings. Peelings should be destroyed.

Wireworms can cause some trouble by boring into the tubers. Follow your local state recommendations.

Colorado potato beetle is dark red and black larvae feed voraciously on the leaves; the adult beetle is striped black and yellow. Handpick the larvae or spray with Sevin. Green potatoes are mildly poisonous and should not be eaten.

squashes, and the Cushaw pumpkin *C. mixta* from Mexico. Both are members of the *Cucurbitaceae* family.

Though they are half-hardy, they are more tolerant of cool conditions than melons and cucumbers in the same family. They need summer heat to ripen.

Cooked with cinnamon and brown sugar in pumpkin pie, they are one of America's traditional dishes for Thanksgiving and Christmas dinners.

Pumpkins grow into large hairy plants, and unless trained they can extend as much as 3.7 m [12']. They are best limited to an average of about four fruits to a plant.

The only real pests to be wary of are slugs, for which you can scatter slug pellets.

Pumpkins must ripen fully on the plant, though frost will spoil them. After cutting, they are left for a week for the skin to harden before storing in a cool place. They should not be eaten overripe. For cultivation *see* SQUASH.

Pumpkin

Associated with Thanksgiving and Halloween, the golden round pumpkin can grow to great size, up to 45 kg [100 lb].

There are two sorts of pumpkins: those from *Cucurbita pepo*, which is the same species as marrows and many

Quince

This unusual fruit is pear-shaped and has an astringent flavor. With the addition of sugar in cooking, it makes delicious pies, preserves and jellies.

The quince is probably a native of western Asia and belongs to a genus closely related to *Pyrus*, best known for the

---

Quince
Cydonia vulgaris (fam. *Rosaceae*)
Hardy deciduous tree with a life of many years.
Size: 4.5-6 m [15-20'] tall by about 3.7 m [12'] wide.
Climate: cool to warm temperate.
Planting to harvesting time: at times, 5 or more years per tree.
Yield: 18 kg [40 lb] per tree.

The quince bears golden fruit having a strong aroma when ripe.

pear, and has been reclassified several times.

Quinces make attractive small trees and are self-fertilizing. In old age they form spreading trees which become contorted. Quince provides the main rootstock for pears.

Cultivation

Quince is propagated by cuttings, suckers or by stooling and is grown on its roots. It only grows really well in warm sheltered sites and moist conditions; a position near a pond is ideal.

Quinces can be grown as half standard trees on a stem of 1.4 m [4½'] but in cool temperate areas they are better grown as bushes on a short leg.

Planting is in autumn or early spring and is like that of other fruit trees (*see* APPLE). 3 m [10'] should be allowed between bushes, and twice that distance for standards. On moist fertile soils the quince requires little manuring but, like pears, responds well to surface mulches of rotted manure or garden compost. Weed regularly.

Pruning can be minimal and is confined to the cutting out of overcrowded, unproductive or damaged branches. Long sideshoots should be cut back to encourage growth of fruit-bearing shoots.

Leave fruit on tree until ripe and pick when dry. If stored in cool conditions, fruit will yellow and mature at intervals over three months, when it will still be quite hard. The ripening fruit gives off a pronounced aroma which can adversely affect apples and pears, so store separately.

Radish

An excellent catch crop, the crisp, tender roots of the summer radish are usually eaten raw in salads. Winter or giant radishes can also be cooked like turnips.

Quick growth and frequent small sowings in a rich, moist soil are the essential requirements for succulent radish roots.

The shape and color of the roots varies according to type. Those of the salad radish can be red, white or red-and-white, small and round or longer and tapering. The more solid roots of the winter radish can be dark brown or bright red and sometimes weigh up to ½ kg [1 lb].

Suitable site and soil

Sow in a sunny patch of soil which has been well-manured in recent years. A heavy clay soil can be lightened by the addition of peat. If necessary, work this in at sowing time. But in cool countries add the peat early in the winter when digging and allow the frost to break down the clay. In warm countries choose a cooler site.

Sowing and planting out

Seed can be sown directly outdoors from mid-spring until autumn. Seed may be sown under glass frames which can be covered with newspaper or sacks if a frost is expected. In any case make sowings at two-week intervals for a continuous supply. Winter radishes should be sown in midsummer. Sprinkle the seeds thinly to a 0.5 cm [¼"] depth in neat rows, later thinning to 2.5 cm [1"] spacing for the smaller salad varieties and 15 cm [16"] for winter varieties. With both, allow 15 cm [6"] between rows. Radishes are often intercropped with other vegetables. Their distinctive heart-shaped seed-leaves mark the rows and the roots are soon ready to be pulled for eating, leaving space for the other crop to spread.

Care and development

Moisture is essential. Water regularly in warm areas and during the summer months everywhere. Weeding should not be a problem if the seed is sown in ground which has been well prepared; radishes grow quickly and are ready to pull before any weeds can become established.

Harvesting the crop

The summer radishes are harvested about three to four weeks from sowing, while they are still young. They should be pulled as soon as the root is large enough to use and the plant has a few leaves. When the flowering stem develops the roots become stringy and have a hot, unpalatable flavor. Large winter radishes can be harvested in autumn and stored in damp sand or they may be left outside and pulled when needed.

Pests and diseases

Radishes are generally trouble-free, especially early spring-

---

Radish
Raphanus sativus (fam. *Cruciferae*)
Biennial, usually grown as an **annual.**
Size: varies according to type, from thumbnail to forearm length.
Climate: cool to warm temperate.
Sowing to harvesting time: 3-4 weeks for summer varieties; several months for winter varieties.
Yield: 2 kg [4 lb] of summer radishes and 4.5 kg [10 lb] of winter radishes, per 3 m [10'] row.

Sow seed under glass from autumn to late winter. Sprinkle the seed thinly to a depth of 0.5 cm [¼"].

If you expect frost, cover the frame lightly with sacking or newspapers to protect the seedlings.

Thin the seedlings as soon as they are large enough to handle. Thin to about 2.5 cm [1"] apart.

To protect seedlings from birds put wire hoops in ground and cover with fine-mesh netting. Water frequently.

Radishes growing intercropped. The roots are soon ready to harvest, leaving space for the other crop.

Large winter radishes can be pulled in autumn and then stored in a wooden box full of damp sand.

Radishes grown under Hotkaps will receive protection and run-off rain.

Newly harvested summer, or salad, radishes. These varieties are ready to pull three or four weeks after sowing, when the root is big enough to use and the plant has a few leaves. Left longer, they are stringy and hot.

sown crops. However, if slugs are a nuisance, place half an orange cut-side down to collect slugs or use slug pellets for large crops. Wire worms and root maggots can be troublesome. Sprinkle the furrows at planting with diazinon.

Raspberry

These delicious juicy berries do not travel well, so they are a very worthwhile fruit to grow in the garden, as you will enjoy quality you can never purchase.

The raspberry, *R. idaeus*, grows wild throughout Europe and parts of Asia, and has been cultivated since the sixteenth century. Though red berries predominate, both yellow (a form of red) and white berries are known.

The cane is a cool climate plant, but can be killed off by exposure to very low temperatures. Snow acts as a good protection. Spring frosts can damage fruiting sideshoots and wind may break canes.

Raspberries are self-fertilizing and grow from a perennial stool. The root system can spread over a considerable area. The fruit is round or oblong depending on variety, and up

---

Raspberry
European species derived from *Rubus idaeus* (fam. *Rosaceae*) and in North America in addition from *R. strigosus*.
Hardy perennial prickly cane with a useful life of 12 years.
Size: up to 2.5 m [8'] high untrimmed, kept to about 1.2-1.5 m [4-5'] when fruiting.
Climate: cool temperate.
Yield: up to 3 kg [7 lb] per plant or 15-22 kg [35-49 lb] per 3 m [10'] row.

---

to 3 cm [1¼"] long.

There are a number of autumn fruiting or everbearing raspberries, which produce fruit on the tips of current season shoots. Fruit quantity may be smaller than that of summer fruiting canes.

Suitable site and soil
Raspberries prefer good light, though they will tolerate a little shade, and a sheltered position in deep, moisture-holding soil. The best soils are deep and well drained, as the roots of the plant are likely to be killed off in very wet soils in winter. Heavy clay soils are not suitable without careful preparation and maintenance. Raspberries will accept more acid conditions than most fruit, though they will suffer from the unavailability of iron in too alkaline a soil, like many other fruits. Avoid planting in sites previously occupied by berries of the same genus and plant as far away as possible from old fruiting canes.

A heavy soil should be prepared well in advance and left open to the weather. If the subsoil is hard and impervious to water, it should be broken up with a fork. Fork in well-rotted manure at the rate of a 12 L [2½ gal] bucket per plant. Raspberries will occupy the site for a long time so be particularly careful to remove perennial weeds.

Erecting training wires
The simplest system suited to gardens with limited space is to drive a 2.25 m [7½'] pole 45 cm [1½'] into the ground at each end of the row. In the second autumn erect horizontal wires at 45 cm [1½'], 105 cm [3½'] and 1.2 or 1.5 m [4 or 4½'], depending on vigor of variety, and tie on the new canes singly. For the first year string will be adequate.

Planting
Buy one-year-old canes and plant in early spring or in suitable weather conditions. If very wet or cold, either plant the canes temporarily when they arrive, or wrap the roots in plastic and store them in a cool place.

Spacing is 40 cm [16"] for less vigorous varieties to 60 cm [2'] for the more vigorous.

Care and development
If dry weather occurs when the plants are flowering, watering is essential. Otherwise the new canes, which are growing at the same time, will be small and sparse and the next crop will be poor.

Weeds, which compete for moisture, must be controlled. Under good conditions raspberries will not require extra fertilizer, but if cane production is inadequate, scatter a nitrogenous fertilizer such as sulphate of ammonia at 75 g per sq m [2½ oz per sq yd]. Alternatively, mulch in mid-spring, just before the new shoots start to come through the ground.

Training and pruning
Young canes will grow from below ground; when they reach 25 cm [10"] cut out the old stumps entirely. Apart from provisional support on either side with string or wire, they need not be tied in until the autumn.

Select six canes per stool on the basis of length, removing

TRAINING RASPBERRY CANES

1.4 m [54″]

45 cm [18″]

45 cm [18″]

In autumn cut out old canes and tie in new ones : continuous stringing (below) keeps canes separate.

string

wire

CUTTING BACK IN SPRING

If the canes grow very long, they can be cut back to just above top wire at the beginning of spring.

A good crop ripening. A picking season lasts 4-6 weeks.

NETTING RASPBERRIES

To protect fruit from birds, use a homemade cage of netting draped over 'T bars' joined with wires.

PROPAGATION

Usually remove suckers in summer but to propagate leave until autumn, sever and dig up with spade.

others. Tie them to the wire by continuous stringing (*see* diagram) to keep them separated and firm. If the canes are very long, the top 30 or 60 cm [1' or 2'] are usually cut back in early spring of the next year.

Raspberries produce suckers, so all canes not emerging from the stool should be hoed off. Retain only six new canes on each stool, as they must not compete with fruiting canes. After harvesting, remove and burn the old fruiting canes and tie in the young canes for next year.

Growing black raspberries

Newly planted canes of black raspberry varieties are best cut off at ground level after planting. Young canes produced during the first growing year are cut back 50-75 cm [20-30"] high to stimulate side growth. The following spring this is cut back to leave 2-6 buds, depending on the strength of the cane: the stronger shoots can support more buds. Fruiting branches are produced from these buds. It is not necessary to provide support for black raspberries, but they can be tied in for convenience. In the second and subsequent years, the primary canes should be limited to four per stool, preferably by early selection or during the post-harvest clean up. Tipping and spurring of laterals continues each year. Treat purple ones the same.

Protection, harvesting and propagation

The raspberry is a favorite target for birds and netting is the only satisfactory solution. For traditional raspberry rows, fix a T-piece to each end post so that the horizontal is about 1 m [3'] wide and above the canes. Stretch two wires between the crosspieces and drop net over to cover the canes. This is simpler than constructing a soft fruit cage. The first varieties to crop can be harvested in early midsummer; the season lasts for about 4-6 weeks. Autumn fruiting varieties are cropped in early autumn. Pick the fruit over several days, without the center plug. Constant picking helps the later fruit, and reduces the risk of overripe fruit going rotten and spreading disease.

Red raspberries are normally propagated by rooted suckers removed from cane beds. Autumn fruiters are propagated in the same way, but the American black raspberry is propagated by tip layering (*see* LOGANBERRY).

Varieties

Red: Canby, Durham, Earlibird, Tallred, Latham, Newburgh, Taylor. Black: Blackhawk, Bristol, Logan, Morrison, Cumberland. Purple: Amethyst, Clyde, Sodus. Yellow: Amber, Fallgold, Golden Queen.

Pests and diseases

Raspberries have pests and diseases in common with the other *Rubus* fruits, loganberry and blackberry. Most serious is the raspberry beetle, *Byturus tomentosus*, the white maggots of which feed on the fruits as they hatch from eggs laid on the blossom. Spray with derris at the start of early summer. Anthracrose causes circular gray spots on canes. Cane blight or wilt causes canes to suddenly wilt and die.

Canes infected with the first two diseases should be cut completely out as soon as seen. The rest of the growth should be thinned, as they often cause trouble in crowded

Black raspberries are unusual and taste rather like mulberries when fully ripe. Delicious for tarts and jam.

PRUNING BLACK RASPBERRIES

Black raspberry plant shown before and after spring pruning. Having stopped the main canes during the first year, prune the laterals to 2-6 buds, depending on strength of each cane.

plantings, and the remainder sprayed in early spring and once or twice more at intervals of three weeks with the systemic fungicide benomyl. If gray mold has been very troublesome, benomyl can be used when the flowers open and again three weeks later, spraying in the evening only. Aphids can carry the virus disease mosaic. Control aphids with rotenone and destroy infected plants at once.

Red and White Currants

An excellent bush fruit in a cool temperate climate, with a high yield of smooth-skinned fruit, the red currant is useful for jams and jellies because of its high pectin content, and makes delicious pies and tarts.

Red currants belong to the same family as the gooseberry and blackcurrant. Most are derived from three principal wild species – *Ribes petraeum*, a native of the mountains of Europe, North Africa and Siberia, *R. rubrum* (the northern red currant) which grows wild across northern Europe and Asia, and *R. sativum*, which is found in Britain and Western Europe.

The white currant can be regarded as a pale-fruited

Red and white currants
Ribes sativum (fam. *Grossulariaceae*).
Hardy deciduous bush with a cropping life of at least 15 years.
Size: bushes grow 1.5 m [5′] high and 1.2 m [4′] wide.
Climate: cool and warm temperate.
Planting to harvesting time: 2 years.
Yield: 3 kg [7 lb] per bush each year.

PRUNING AFTER PLANTING

Just after planting, cut strong shoots to half their length and any spindly ones to two-thirds.

WINTER PRUNING A BUSH

A mature bush before pruning in winter with the sideshoots already summer pruned to five leaves.

Cut back the tips of the leading shoots in winter and prune the sideshoots further back to two buds.

Laxton's No 1 growing as a U-cordon; a good cropper with firm berries.

Fruit cages are very
important for growing
all soft fruits. The
crop will be ruined by
the birds if left free
of protection. Cages
are commercially made
and come in a variety
of sizes. Most are long-
lasting – made of steel
frames and plastic-coated
wire. They are quick to
erect and more spacious to
work in than a homemade
cage. Group soft fruit
together to use the cage.

PRUNING RED CURRANTS TRAINED AS CORDONS

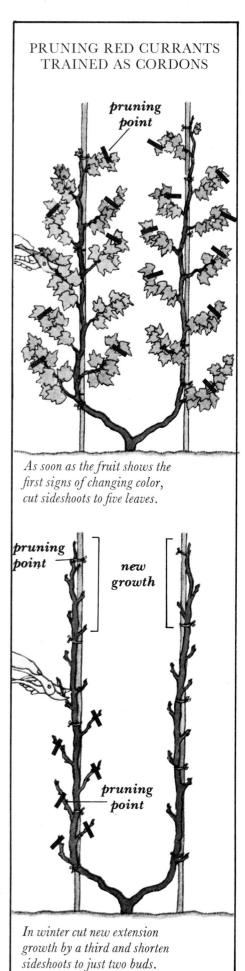

As soon as the fruit shows the first signs of changing color, cut sideshoots to five leaves.

In winter cut new extension growth by a third and shorten sideshoots to just two buds.

variety of the red. Slightly less vigorous, but with a sweeter fruit, they require the same treatment as red currants. Unfortunately, currants are not grown as often as they otherwise would be because of their reputed transmittal or hosting of the white pine blister rust.

Suitable site and soil

Red currants prefer a sunny position, but will tolerate light partial shade. They should be sheltered from cold winds, both because of pollination, and because the shoots of red currants are easily blown out. The bushes do best on a fairly deep, light, slightly acid soil, which contains sufficient vegetable matter to retain moisture in summer. If this is lacking, dig in a 9 L [2 gal] bucketful of suitably rotted organic material about a month before planting for each plant. Make sure that the site is completely weed-free.

Planting

Red currants are usually grown as bushes on a short leg, like miniature trees, but they are extremely amenable to training and may easily be grown as single cordons, U-shaped cordons or double U-shaped cordons. Cordons may be grown against walls or fences where they are easily covered with netting to protect the fruit or buds from birds, or with some thicker material to guard the blossom from late frosts in spring.

Plant as early as possible in the dormant period when the soil works freely. Set the bushes at the same depth as they were in the nursery, as indicated by the soil mark on the stem. Rub off any suckers on the roots, or buds on the 'leg'. Bushes should be spaced 1.5 m [5'] apart each way.

Feeding and mulching

Immediately after planting spread a 5 cm [2"] deep mulch of well-rotted farmyard manure, garden compost or moist peat over the root area to prevent evaporation from the soil if spring and early summer prove to be dry. During the summer water when the soil is dry and weed well.

Dress annually in late spring with rotted farmyard manure. In very light or other soils deficient in potash, give an additional early spring dose of sulphate of potash at the rate of 15 g per sq m [$\frac{1}{2}$ oz per sq yd]. Where farmyard manure is unobtainable you can give a commercial general garden fertilizer according to the maker's directions but remember that red currants do not need much nitrogen and they do need potash.

Pruning

A red currant bush is trained with a leg tall enough to keep the lowest branches well clear of the ground and with branches well spread out so as to expose the center of the bush to air and sunshine.

Begin immediately after planting by cutting back all the main branches to half their length, making each cut just beyond a bud pointing away from the center of the bush. Repeat this each winter for two or three years until a framework of sturdy branches has been built up. After that only tip the branch leaders unless harder pruning is necessary to stimulate growth.

Cut back sideshoots along the main branches to just above

their fifth leaf during the midsummer weeks and then further cut these back during the winter to the second bud. In summer just as the fruit shows the first sign of changing color, shorten sideshoots to five leaves and then in winter cut these back further, each to its second bud.

Harvesting and propagation

The first small crop can be taken in the second summer after planting, but it is better to wait another year, and let the bush strengthen. Picking can start in early summer and continue, with the right varieties, until late summer.

Do not be in a hurry to pick your crop; red currants are slower to ripen than their rapid coloration suggests. Pick the fruits in complete little bunches or 'strings', not individually, preferably using scissors. The currants are easily stripped off their stalks after picking, but will keep for a few days longer, where they are still in strings.

It is very easy to raise new red and white currant bushes from cuttings. Take well-ripened, straight and strong shoots of the current year's growth from healthy bushes in mid-autumn. The shoots should be 30-38 cm [12-15"] long after the unripened wood towards the tip has been cut off. Rub off all the growth buds from these shoots except the four uppermost on each cutting. This is to ensure that the new bush will start life with a good, clean leg, free of sideshoots and suckers from below ground.

To make doubly sure of success, press the ends of the cuttings (the cut surface only) onto some hormone rooting powder and then immediately plant in a 15 cm [6"] deep slit trench, spacing the cuttings 20 cm [8"] apart. Unless the soil itself is sandy it helps rapid rooting if you first sprinkle a little river sand along the bottom of the planting trench. Return the soil to the trench and press firmly around the cuttings with foot pressure.

See that the cuttings never lack water during the following spring and summer, and that weeds have no chance to choke them. By the winter of the next year the cuttings should have rooted and should be ready for transference to their fruiting quarters.

If the plants are to be grown as bushes, prune all the year-old's branches back by half.

Varieties

Red: Red Lake, Cherry, Red Duchess. White: White Dutch, White Grape, White Pearl.

Pests and diseases

The worst pests in many gardens are birds which peck out the buds in winter and take off the fruit in summer. Bushes in the open garden will require some kind of netting cage.

Besides the white pine blister rust, of which currants are labelled as alternative hosts, watch for cane blight. If present, destroy such canes and prevent spread of the disease by eliminating aphids with rotenone. Also destroy stems attacked by currant borers and stemgirdlers. Spray with Sevin for currant worm larvae.

It is good to be aware of other pests that may cause trouble, although they are far from widespread. Capsids and aphids may be troublesome. The red currant blister aphid causes the leaves to pucker and produce reddish blisters, and gooseberry sawfly sometimes causes trouble.

A die-back fungus disease known as coral spot sometimes gives trouble. It derives its name from the tiny coral red pustules which appear on dead wood. Cut off all dead wood and cut back several inches into healthy tissue. Paint the larger wounds with protective tree paint.

Rhubarb

No garden should be without rhubarb. In a small space, it produces large quantities of stalks, which are used for desserts in a similar way to fruit.

Rhubarb, *Rheum rhaponticum*, is a native of Siberia, the Himalayas and Eastern Asia. Used as a food, it is less than two centuries old, though *Rheum officinale* was formerly used for its medicinal properties. Of hybrid origin, garden rhubarb's reddish stems are used cooked for dessert. The leaves are wide and spade-like and are poisonous. The plant is tolerant of frost and will continually reproduce.

Suitable site and soil

Choose a sheltered, sunny site where it can be undisturbed, since the plant is a perennial. It will not do well in competition with tree or hedge roots or too near other cultivation.

Rhubarb

Rheum rhaponticum (fam. *Polygonaceae*)

Hardy perennial with a useful life of 20 years.

Size: about 45 cm [1½′] high, 1 m [3′] wide.

Climate: cool to warm temperate.

Planting to harvest time: 18 months.

Yield: 2.8 kg [6 lb] per plant per year, 3 plants per 3 m [10′] row.

The ideal soil is deep, rich and slightly acid.

As the plant is to stand for a number of years, careful preparation of the site is required. Do this several weeks in advance of planting. Dig deeply to a depth of 45 cm [1½′] eradicating all weeds. The plant is very greedy and manure or garden compost should be worked into the bottom of the hole as well as into the returning soil at the rate of five barrowloads per four sq m [yd]. Two weeks before planting scatter a general-purpose compound fertilizer over the surface – 90 g per sq m [3 oz per sq yd].

Planting

Buy planting crowns early in the spring. A total of six plants should supply most families for many years. Dig the holes large enough to take the roots comfortably spaced 1 m [3′] apart. Set the plants sufficiently deep for the woody rootstock to be covered, but not the pink growth buds from the center of the crown. After planting, pull up 5 cm [2″] of soil over the crowns. Make the plants firm and water if the soil is on the dry side.

Rhubarb can also be grown from seed. The initial cost is less but the plants can be variable, and from sowing to harvesting takes longer. Seeds should be sown in mid-spring in drills 2.5 cm [1″] deep and 15 cm [6″] apart under a cold frame, or may be sown a month earlier in the heated greenhouse. Prick out when the seedlings have four leaves, into 10 cm [4″] pots for greenhouse-sown seeds, or to a prepared bed in a frame or the open ground with Hotkaps at 15 cm [6″] apart. The following spring discard the weaker plants and transfer the best to permanent beds.

Care and development

In temperate regions rhubarb requires little extra watering, but do not allow the soil to become dry during the summer months. Should any flowering shoots appear, they must be removed before the buds open, otherwise the plants exhaust themselves. Hoe regularly around the stems.

Forcing

Forced rhubarb is desirable early in the season when fruit is scarce. By forcing out-of-doors, pulling dates can be advanced several weeks. After strongly established plants have been exposed to the first frosts of winter, water them well and cover them in early winter. Plants may be covered individually with any large earthenware pots or some old barrels, boxes, buckets or oil drums. This pushes growth ahead by keeping off winds and cold, and excludes light. The container should be 60 cm [2′] tall, be completely clean, and have a detachable lid so that you can inspect the crop occasionally. The whole may then be heaped up on the outside with lawn clippings, straw, dead leaves or garden compost.

If rhubarb is brought indoors, the first sticks may be pulled after midwinter. Lift the roots in late autumn and expose them to the weather for a few days, even to frost. Place them on a bed of good soil in the greenhouse or other warm place. The plants may be quite close together and the roots just covered with soil and kept moist. Drape them with black plastic to cut off the light. Screen them from direct heat (such as greenhouse hot pipes) with a

1. *Plant rhubarb crowns with roots well covered and buds at soil level.*

2. *Pull up soil over buds and firm down with feet; water if necessary.*

3. *Remove any flowering shoots to encourage stem growth next spring.*

4. *Pull few stems in second spring; grip the stem as low as possible, then twist and pull simultaneously.*

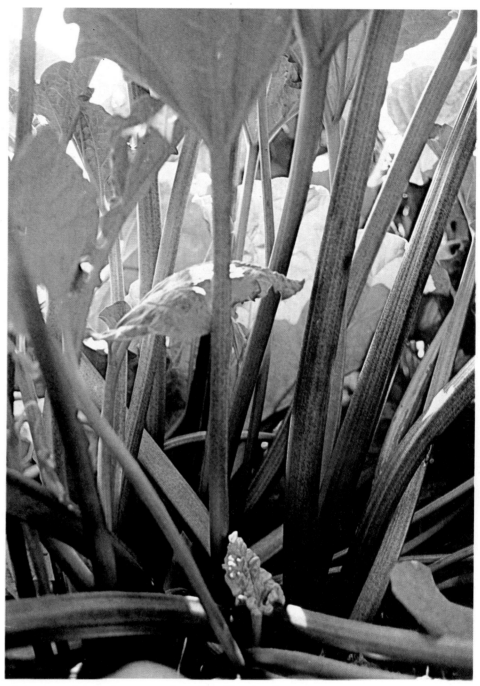

A fine crop of rhubarb stems; a clump like this takes three years to grow.

ALTERNATIVE METHODS OF FORCING RHUBARB

1. *Cover with a lidded barrel after first frost and pile manure on top.*

2. *Under heated greenhouse staging, draped with black plastic or sacks.*

board. A steady temperature of 4° to 10°C [40° to 50°F] is needed until growth is well under way. Then raise to 16°-18°C [60°-65°F], but no higher.

Harvesting, after-care and propagation
Do not pull any sticks in the first year and only a few in the second. By the third you should have good-sized clumps. Unless you are forcing, pulling begins in mid-spring and continues for about two months, but not more, as the plant must be allowed to renew itself. Pull by gripping the leaf stems as low as possible and then twisting and pulling simultaneously. Only take stems whose leaves have fully unfolded. When the season's pulling has finished, topdress the plants heavily with rotted organic matter, making sure that the soil is moist first. Roots from forced plants should be burned.

When the quality of the sticks begins to deteriorate or to replace rhubarb used for forcing, propagate by division. Lift the clump and divide it with a sharp spade so that each division has one good growth bud. These should then be replanted in their permanent positions.

Pests and diseases
The disease called crown rot, though infrequent, can be quite serious if it occurs. The leaves become a dull gray-green, the stems thin and weak except for the bases, which become swollen. The internal flesh of the crown turns brown, and the crown is easily broken off. There is no remedy and plants should be lifted and destroyed.

Rosemary

A hardy shrub, rosemary is grown mainly for its pleasantly pungent leaves. A favorite herb with lamb, it is equally popular for cosmetic uses.

Rosemary (*Rosmarinus officinalis*) is a member of the *Labiatae* family, a long-lived, evergreen shrub, native of the Mediterranean and often grown for its significance as

(Right) Sweet-scented rosemary is an attractive plant for the shrubbery as well as being a popular flavoring.

the 'herb of remembrance'. Under favorable conditions it will live 20 years or more and may reach up to 1.8 m [6'] in height, although half this is more usual.

For culinary purposes the distinctive flavor of rosemary enhances roast lamb or duck, whether the leaves are chopped and used for stuffing, or whole sprigs are cooked with the joint. The narrow, fragrant gray-green leaves and blue flowers are popular as a purely decorative shrub.

Cultivation
Rosemary thrives in a sunny, sheltered position. It may be grown either as an individual bush or planted to form a continued hedge, which is very attractive.

Rosemary does not do well in water-retaining clay soil, so if clay is present it must be broken down to a more open texture by working sandy loam in well. The best soils for it are the lighty sandy ones, containing a little lime.

Rosemary can be bought as plants from a nursery or easily raised from cuttings. These are taken from young shoots of an established plant in late spring or early summer. They should be about 7.5 cm [3"] long, either cut below a leaf joint or torn off with a 'heel'. Set 3 or 4 in a 7.5 cm [3"] pot of sandy potting mixture, well watered and covered with a clear plastic bag until they root, when they are ready to be planted out. Keep them in a temperature of at least 15°C [60°F] while rooting. Rosemary does not transplant well, so new plants should be placed directly in their permanent positions.

For hedging (where winters are mild), space plants 38 cm [15"] apart and keep well trimmed by clipping each year, after the plants have flowered. This clipping is also important with individually grown bushes. Left to grow unchecked they will develop a bare, woody stem with new growth occurring only at the top of the plant. This is why mature rosemary bushes often have a top-heavy appearance, since they are unable to produce new stems from anything older than one-year-old wood. If you have a rosemary bush which has already become unwieldy, it is more satisfactory to take fresh cuttings from it in late spring or early summer and start again, afterwards clipping annually and allowing only one year's growth to remain. In cool temperate areas it is a good idea to keep one or two pots of rosemary in a greenhouse or on a sunny windowsill indoors, in case winter cold kills your outdoor plant. Apart from regular shaping, rosemary does not need any attention once it is growing well. Water when young; when established, it will survive moderate drought.

Harvesting
Fresh sprigs can be gathered throughout the year. If dried rosemary is desired, the shoots removed by the annual clippings can be dried carefully by tying them tightly into bunches and hanging them in a warm, dry place. Rub the leaves off the stems and store in an airtight container.

Burning the boughs from old bushes gives a pleasant aroma, so if you have a fireplace you may like to get rid of the waste wood by burning it indoors.

Runner Bean

**Reliable and easy to grow, the
'amateur's vegetable', as the runner bean
is sometimes called, is ornamental as
well as good to eat.**

A vigorous climber, the runner bean is a native of South America. Introduced to England as an ornamental, it did not become popular as a vegetable until the 19th century. Runners are perennials in their sub-tropical homelands, but in cool temperate zones they are tender and susceptible to frost, so they are always grown annually from seed. The gardener can control when the plants appear by the sowing time. In cool climates runner beans may be lost if they break the surface too early, although they can be protected by Hotkaps.

As part of a good rotation plan, runner beans are moved from site to site to follow cabbages or potatoes. Runner beans, like other members of the family *Leguminosae*, possess root bacteria which convert nitrogen gas from the air into nitrogen compounds that can be used by plants, thus enriching the soil for the following crop.

Both climbing and bush runner beans are grown; until the introduction of the natural dwarf in 1961, bushes were produced by pinching out the shoot tops of climbers. The pods of modern bean varieties can attain enormous lengths and will snap clean and tender unless deprived of water as they ripen. The bean pods vary in length and color, depending upon the variety. One variety has purple leaves, stems, flowers and pods; the pods change to green when cooked. The flowers are usually red. (Some abroad have

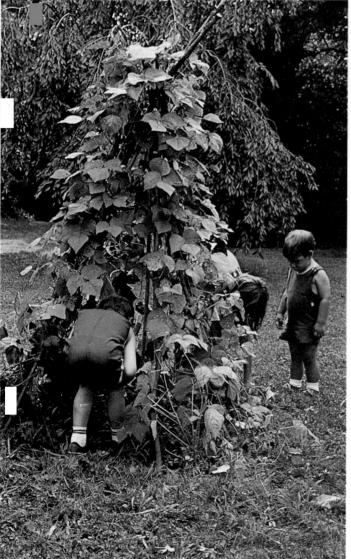

Runner bean
Phaseolus coccineus (fam. *Leguminosae*)
Perennial, grown as a **half-hardy annual.**
Size: grows 2-3 m [6½-10′] high, dwarf varieties
30-38 cm [12-15″].
Climate: cool temperate to sub-tropical.
Sowing to harvesting time: 10 weeks from sowing.
Yield: 0.75-1 kg [1½-2 lb] per plant.

---

*Growing runners on a wigwam frame is amusing and saves
space. Make the frame with a few poles and garden twine.*

(Right) Dwarf runner beans which grow like French beans do not need support and are ideal for use with Hotkaps.

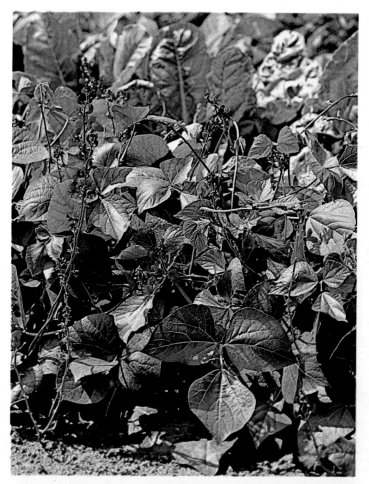

white, pink or red and white flowers.)

Suitable site and soil

Beans like an open site but it should be as sheltered as possible; in windy or cold conditions pollinating insects do not visit the flowers. Gaps in fences and hedges through which frost is liable to enter should be avoided or blocked off. A row of climbing beans will form a dense wall of foliage at least 2 m [6½′] high. This will shade neighboring rows of shorter plants on either side for several hours a day, even if the row runs from north to south, so the beans must be placed accordingly, perhaps at the end of the plot, or even against a wall.

The ideal soil is lighter than that for broad beans, but not so light that it will dry out. On such land drainage is likely to be good, so that digging need not be deep. Garden compost or old manure must be incorporated to make the soil moisture-retentive. On clay soil deep digging to a depth of 45 cm [1½′] may be necessary to provide better drainage, and compost and manure should be added to keep the soil open. The deeper the soil the better, as the plants produce a great deal of top growth and crop very heavily in a comparatively short time.

Soil in town or industrial districts is often prone to acidity due to pollutants, the use of unripe manure or too much chemical fertilizer. Test the pH of the soil and, if it is moderately acid, add 1 kg [2 lb] carbonate of lime per 3 sq m [yd] but do not add too much lime.

In the late autumn or winter before sowing, dig a trench 45 cm [1½′] wide and the same depth, and fork well-rotted manure or garden compost into the bottom at the rate of a 9 L [2 gal] bucketful to every 60 cm [2′] length. Then return the topsoil and leave the soil to settle over the winter. About two weeks before sowing, rake superphosphate and sulphate of potash into the top few inches at the rate of 60 g [2 oz] and 30 g [1 oz] per sq m [yd] respectively.

Sowing and planting

Allow about 10 plants per person if you want to deep freeze some of the crop; otherwise less. This means 1.5 m [5′] of double row for each person.

Seed is generally sown outdoors in late spring, to provide a crop from midsummer to mid-autumn. Earlier sowings may be made in early spring, if the locality is mild, to give a crop starting in early summer. Confine early sowings to a few seeds at one end of the row as they may rot if the soil fails to warm up sufficiently. Hotkaps put over the soil two or three weeks before sowing will warm it, so that germination is helped and, left there, will protect young plants from damage until all danger of frost has passed.

Draw out a 5 cm [2″] deep drill, water it and sow two seeds every 30 cm [12″] in two lines 25 cm [10″] apart, staggered

(Right) 'Fry', a stringless variety. These types have been developed to make preparation for cooking easier.
(Facing page) Runners produce beautiful scarlet flowers which brighten up the vegetable garden in early summer.

Runner bean

1. On heavy soil, double dig trench using a fork to incorporate manure.

2. Two weeks before sowing, rake in superphosphate and potash.

3. Wind twine loosely up canes; sow in deep drills, two seeds per cane.

4. As seedlings start growing, cut or pull out the weaker of the two.

5. Wind beans up an inverted V framework held firm by crosspiece.

6. Look out for large yellow pods in thick foliage and pick them off.

ALTERNATIVE METHODS OF SUPPORTING RUNNER BEANS

Growing on a pole: save space by training one shoot vertically and a second diagonally, four per pole.

Growing on netting: fix the net to sturdy posts at intervals of 3 m [10'] sunk 1 m [3'] into the ground.

Growing on vertical canes: place stout poles at end of each row with guy ropes and a wire linking canes.

240

or not, depending on the method of support used (*see* following). When they begin to develop remove or cut off the top of the weaker seedling.

Method of support

The simplest method is to give each plant one cane or pole pushing it 45 cm [1½'] into the ground, and allowing a height above ground of 2 m [6½']. A space of 38-45 cm [15-18"] should be left between the double lines of supports. Each cane is linked to the next by thin wire or strong twine, and at each end of the row, two much sturdier posts are inserted, linked by crosspieces. These posts require additional support from guy ropes (*see* diagram in BLACKBERRY). If the row is very long, stronger posts and struts may also be required halfway along it.

One very common method of support is to plant in pairs across a row, with each pole at an angle so that the tops cross at a height of about 1.6 m [5½']. They are tied together at the crotch, and then more poles are laid horizontally along the crotches, overlapping, and bound to one another and to the crotches. This keeps the whole framework rigid. If bamboo canes are used, it is a good idea to twine string up the length of the slippery cane to give the climbing bean stems a better hold.

A third method is to grow the beans up netting, supported between strong posts. These should be 2.5 m [8'] long, hammered 45 cm [1½'] into the soil at each end of the row, and at a spacing of 1.8 m [6'] along it. Two internal struts will be required for each post to take the weight, reaching about 90 cm [3'] up each and being well buried (see diagram in BLACKBERRY).

Remember that one cropping plant can weigh anything up to 2 kg [4 lb], and a 3 m [10'] row will be tremendously heavy. A row of beans of this length will present an area of dense foliage of about 6 sq m [7 sq yd] to a summer gale, so it is very important that the supporting framework be soundly constructed. Once a row of beans collapses, it cannot be re-erected. It will smother rows of neighboring vegetables and must be removed immediately after gleaning what proportion, if any, of the crop has ripened and was not damaged in the fall.

If a very small number of beans are to be grown, wigwams of six or seven poles planted in a circle and tied together at the top will be adequate. The beans will do very well, although there will be some crowding when they reach the top. Beans can be also grown in large tubs with strings tied to the top of a central pole, and radiating out to hooks on the perimeter of the tub. A tripod of three canes can also be used in a tub.

There are one or two dwarf runner bean varieties, which have the same habit of growth as the bush Garden beans. For cultivation *see* GARDEN BEAN.

Care and development

The crop will never be of good quality if the plants are allowed to get dry at all. As their roots penetrate deeply, early preparation of the trench is important. In dry conditions mulching in the early stages will be helpful. Later the shade cast between a double row of beans will conserve the moisture. Always apply mulches to moist soil.

Under normal conditions runners should require no further feeding. But it is important to be careful about weeds while the seedlings are developing. Hoe the weeds out while they are still tiny, but with care, as the roots and stems of the young beans are very tender. Once the beans have started to climb and are making plenty of leaf few weeds can compete with them and the plot can be hand-weeded when necessary.

When the first vines start to search for something to climb, tie them loosely with raffia to their own poles. This is important, otherwise the ensuing chaos will be impossible to disentangle and the beans will grow up one another, fighting for light. Once they have been shown their own pole they will stick to it. When they reach the top, pinch them out. Sometimes in dry weather flowers fall off, leaving no tiny beanlet behind. These have failed to set, usually because of lack of moisture deep down in the soil. There may be other reasons for the flowers not setting. In windy or cold conditions, pollinating insects do not visit the flowers. In very hot, dry weather, on the other hand, the flowers droop and close up so that insects cannot enter. Spraying to encourage setting is harmless but ineffective.

Harvesting the crop

Runner beans will be ready for picking in late mid-summer. The golden rule is to keep picking. Do not let any beans get too large; 15-20 cm [6-8"] is right for most varieties, though some modern varieties have been known to produce beans 25-30 cm [10-12"] long. Beans that are too old have coarse-textured, unhealthy colored pods, and the beans inside stand out like swollen finger joints. Such beans are fit only for the compost heap or to use for seeds next year. Care should be taken to remove coarse beans which may have been overlooked amid the dense foliage, as they are a drain on further production.

Pests and diseases

Runner beans generally give little trouble, although halo blight is encouraged by the quite unnecessary practice of soaking the beans before sowing. The disease is bacterial and takes the form of small transparent spots surrounded by a yellow ring. The spots coalesce and dry up and the whole leaf withers. Seedlings may be killed, and older plants wilt completely. Diseased plants should be destroyed as soon as seen. Some varieties are resistant. Blackfly, capsid bugs, slugs attacking the seedlings, and pea and bean seed beetle are also possible, though not of much concern.

Rutabaga

SEE **SWEDE**

Sage

One of the essential herbs, sage used to be a medicinal cure-all. Even today its popularity with rich foods is due as much to its digestive properties as its spicy taste.

Sage (*Salvia officinalis*) is a member of the *Labiatae* family, a hardy, evergreen shrub grown for its gray-green leaves, which are used fresh and dried. One bush is adequate for the average family. The common violet blue-flowered sage usually grows to about 60 cm [2'] high, with the same diameter. Of the several varieties, common sage is best for cooking – red sage for herbal cures.

Although it is a hardy perennial, even the more robust types of sage will not always survive the winter, so it must be in a dry, sunny, sheltered position or taken indoors.

Cultivation

The soil for sage should be light and well drained but rich in organic matter. On ground that has not been recently cultivated, add good quality garden compost and a handful of bonemeal to each planting site, some weeks before planting. With the exception of broad-leved, non-flowering sage, most types can be raised from seed in shallow drills in the spring. However, sage is slow to germinate and you will have no herb to cut for over a year. It is more practical to buy a rooted cutting. If a bush is available, and for your own replacements, take cuttings from established plants in late spring or at the end of the growing season, from shoots about 5 cm [2"] long. Each cutting must have a heel or piece of the main stem at its base. Insert the cuttings in moist sand putting 3 to a 8.5 cm [3½"] pot, and keep them moist, covering them with clear plastic sheeting until rooting takes place. Warmth of about 18-21°C [65-70°F] is also required. Then transplant to the prepared site, giving the plant at least 60 cm [2'] of room all around.

Pinch out the growing tip of the plant when it is growing strongly. Put a light, firm stake in the center of the bush when planting for support. The main stem is brittle and, even with support, it may split under the weight of foliage. If this does happen during summer it is often impossble to save the bush by laying the broken stem on the ground and

Common sage has the greatest value in the kitchen, and a bush of this size will supply all the leaves needed.

covering it with soil. Kept moist, it will have a chance to produce fresh roots and resume growth. Take cuttings and keep plants in reserve to replace your bush after 3-4 years.

Harvesting

Fresh leaves can be used whenever they are available. Harvesting is done from midsummer onwards, when the leaves should be dried for about a week until they are crisp, and stored in an airtight container.

SCORZONERA AND Salsify

Salsify (above) and scorzonera (below), often called black salsify, are two roots of different genus but they are grown and used in the same way. Their flavor has earned them the name 'vegetable oyster'.

Of these two plants of the family *Compositae*, salsify is the more frequently grown. It has a white, tapering root and

---

Salsify
Tragopogon porrifolius (fam. *Compositae*)
Hardy biennial.
Size: grown primarily for the long narrow tap root, which is up to 30-45 cm [1-1½'] long with a maximum diameter of 5 cm [2"] at the top; also for the young shoots in spring, which are cut when about 15 cm [6"] long. Mature plant grows 1-1.2 m [3-4'] high.
Climate: temperate.
Sowing to harvesting time: 16-17 weeks if roots are left in the ground; young shoot harvested next spring.
Yield: up to 450 g [1 lb] per root.

---

a delicate unusual flavor, traditionally supposed to resemble that of oysters. Its leaves are narrow and grass-like. A native of northern Europe, it is not difficult to grow and deserves wider attention.

Native to Spain, scorzonera is similar to salsify in cultivation, appearance and taste. Though introduced in most European countries centuries ago, it is not popular; it must be purchased in the U.S. from British dealers or those who deal with them. It gives a much lower yield than salsify but the flavor is superior. It can also be used as a coffee substitute, like chicory.

The leaves of the scorzonera plant are oblong and end in a point. The thin black roots are the edible part. They are slightly difficult to prepare because they have to be boiled and skinned while still hot; rubbing off the skin rather than peeling is easier. The roots contain inulin, which is found in many other plants of the family *Compositae* (such as the Jerusalem artichoke), a sugar substitute which is used in making bread for diabetics.

Suitable site and soil

Both plants require a deep soil, free from stones. A good, rich loam is ideal, but it should not have been freshly treated with farmyard manure. Both salsify and scorzonera have long roots which should grow straight, and obstacles such as stones, unrotted manure and an impervious subsoil cause them to fork. The crowbar method of making planting holes is ideal (*see* PARSNIP). An open, sunny site is best.

Sowing

Sow salsify in mid-spring, 1.75-2.5 cm [$\frac{1}{2}$-1″] deep, in drills 30 cm [1′] apart. Temperature required for germination is from 4-21°C [38-69°F]. Germination takes place in 7-21 days according to temperature. When the plants are large enough to handle thin to about 25 cm [10″] apart.

To ensure straight roots, make a hole 60-90 cm [2-3′] deep with a crowbar and fill to within about 10 cm [4″] of the top with well-rotted garden compost. Add a layer of fine soil to complete the filling of the hole. Plant three or four seeds, thinning to one later.

Alternatively, salsify can be sown in late spring following the usual method to have a crop of roots ready for harvesting from late autumn onwards.

Procedure with scorzonera is almost exactly the same,

Scorzonera
Scorzonera hispanica (fam. *Compositae*), also called black salsify.
Perennial, grown as a **biennial.**
Size: grown primarily for the cylindrical black-skinned root, which is up to 20-45 cm [8-18″] long with a diameter of about 2.5 cm [1″]. The mature plant grows to a height of 1-1.2 m [3-4′].
Climate: temperate.
Sowing to harvesting time: 18 or more weeks. Possible secondary harvest of young shoots.
Yield: about 125 g [4 oz] per root.

Salsify has long, tapering roots with grass-like leaves. The flavor of the roots is said to resemble oysters.

For making planting holes use the crowbar method to ensure deep enough holes.

Fill holes to about 10 cm [4"] below top with well-rotted compost, then soil.

Sow 3 or 4 seeds in each hole. The holes should be about 23 cm [9"] apart.

When the seedlings are large enough, thin them to one at each station.

When lifting roots, great care must be taken not to damage them in any way.

Use a sharp knife to trim all the side roots from the main tap roots.

After lifting, store the roots, laying them flat in box of sand. Store the box in a well ventilated, dry place. Alternatively, leave roots in the ground until needed.

PRODUCING BLANCHED SHOOTS OF SALSIFY

In early winter, cut down any remains of foliage to leave about 2.5 cm [1"] of stem above the soil.

To blanch shoots, heap soil around cut stems. Cover the shoots with 18 cm [7"] pots, blocking up the pot drainage holes to prevent light from entering the top of the pot. Make sure the soil is light and powdery.

In early spring, when tips appear through soil, draw soil aside to expose shoots. Cut as required.

except that the sowing date should be about a month later. Scorzonera is more susceptible than salsify to late frosts and, if checked by them tends to run to seed.

Cultivation
Keep well hoed and well watered. Both plants are reasonably drought-resistant but are liable to bolt in prolonged dry weather. Also, rain after a long drought may cause salsify roots to grow so quickly that they split open. Otherwise, neither crop needs any attention during the growth period.

Harvesting
Both plants are ready for harvesting by mid-autumn, although the roots may be left in the ground until needed. If left in the soil the roots will survive a normal winter, but frost will not improve their flavor. To obtain maximum flavor lift them as required for use, taking them straight to the kitchen and using them all before the onset of winter.

Alternatively you can lift and store the roots, laying them flat in boxes of sand and storing these in a dry, well-ventilated place. The hazard in storing is that both roots 'bleed' very easily which loses much of their flavor. For this reason they should be lifted with great care, and even then it may be impossible to avoid some damage.

If you choose a late spring sowing for salsify, the crop will be ready from late autumn onwards.

Most gardeners will want to retain part of their salsify crop for producing a green vegetable in spring. No special treatment is required. For spring greens, cut the shoots when they are about 12-15 cm [5-6"] high. They are then known as chards. They are cooked like asparagus, to which they are at least equal in flavor.

Blanched shoots may be either cooked or used as a salad in late winter or early spring. To produce these, cut down what remains of the foliage in early winter, leaving about 2.5 cm [1"] of stem above the root, and earth up until the top of the plant is covered by about 15 cm [6"] of soil. To keep the soil dry, cover the earthed-up plants with pots of 17.5 cm [7"] diameter, making sure you close up the drainage holes. Cut the resultant blanched shoots in early spring, just as the tips appear at the soil surface, or a little before, drawing aside the soil to search for them. Any blanched shoots not used can be left to grow as greens.

After-care
Both the dying foliage and the discarded roots make excellent compost material. There should be no difficulty in clearing the ground of the crop, although broken pieces of root occasionally live and send up shoots in the following year.

The seeds of both species are sometimes difficult to obtain, so it is worthwhile to leave a few plants to flower and go to seed. Both are quite attractive in the garden – salsify bears reddish-purple flowers and scorzonera bright yellow.

Pests and diseases
Like most plants in the family *Compositae*, salsify and scorzonera are virtually free from both pests and diseases. Occasionally both may be infested with a fungus disease,

white blister (*Albugo* species), which forms unsightly white patches on the leaves. Treatment consists of cutting off and burning the affected leaves.

Savory

Savory has a strong aromatic scent and a definite digestive effect. It has been most popular in Europe for hundreds of years as a flavoring for all kinds of beans.

There are two species of savory commonly grown: summer savory (*Satureia hortensis*) and winter savory, *S. montana*. Both are members of the *Labiatae* family and they are among the oldest of herbs, grown for their small, powerfully scented leaves. Summer savory is annual, grows about 30 cm [1'] high and bears pale lilac flowers, from late summer to autumn. It is tender. Winter savory (*Satureia montana*), is a perennial sub-shrubby form which tastes much the same but is more strongly aromatic and grows to about 38 cm [15"].

Low-growing and compact, savory is ideal grown as a border plant. It is also good for ambitious knot-garden patterns in herb gardens, since it can be clipped to shape and controlled easily. Otherwise, because the scent seems to deter aphids, it may be planted between rows of broad beans, which are particularly prone to their attack.

The leaves are almost always dried for use in all kinds of recipes including stuffings, stews and as a flavoring for beans. A sprig hung among clothes will keep moths away. and savory leaves ease the sting of insect bites when crushed and rubbed on the skin.

Cultivation
A situation in full sun is best for savory, and there is no need to enrich the soil for it. If, however, the ground is

Both summer and winter savory will grow from seed. They need an open, sunny site. Plants can also be propagated by lifting and dividing the roots for replanting.

heavy clay, it should be broken up with lighter material such as coarse sand or burned earth from the garden bonfire worked in.

Both summer and winter savory can be raised from seed sown outdoors from mid to late spring, and thinned to a spacing of 15 cm [6″] between plants. Rows should be 60 cm [2′] apart. Seeds should be only just covered, and will germinate in about 10-14 days. Water regularly until the plants are well established, when they can do quite well in dry conditions.

Although winter savory is a perennial it may, like all small herbs, die a natural death, or be killed by severe cold. To start new plants for a reserve supply, take cuttings from small shoots in spring or late summer and root them in sand. Plants can also be propagated by lifting and dividing the roots for replanting, again in spring or late summer. Seed of winter savory can be sown in late summer as well as spring, but it is slow to grow, even if the seed is left uncovered, and cuttings or division will give quicker and much more reliable results.

Harvesting

The annual summer savory will be ready to use within three months from the spring sowing. Harvesting is done just as flowering is about to start and again in mid-autumn. Hang up stems with several sprigs on them in bunches in a warm, dark, well-ventilated place until the leaves are sufficiently dry. Then store the leaves in an airtight container.

Leaves may be taken from winter savory from late spring onwards in the second year but the dried leaves are rather hard, so it is best to keep a pot indoors in winter and use the fresh leaves.

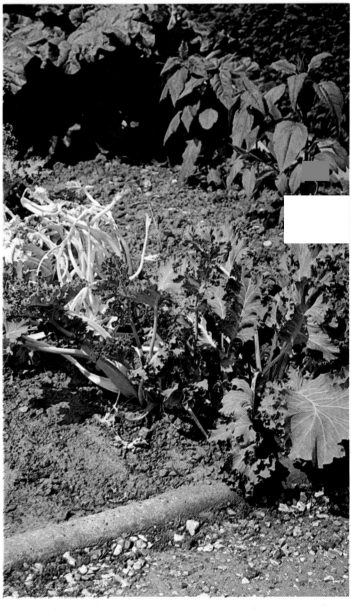

Scallions

SEE **ONION**

Scorzonera

SEE **SALSIFY**

Seakale

The blanched shoots of this unusual vegetable, available in early spring, are a welcome crop at a time when fresh vegetables are scarce.

A native of the coasts of western Europe, seakale still grows wild on British seashores, but is seldom cultivated in gardens today. Its disadvantages are that it takes a long time to mature from seed and needs blanching. The time factor can be reduced, however, by planting 'crowns' (root cuttings bearing buds). The blanched shoots can be used as a second vegetable, separately like asparagus, as a basis for cheese dishes or eaten as a salad. In the U.S., seakale is available only through British seed houses.

Suitable site and soil

Seakale, being a seashore plant in its native state, requires a sandy and fertile soil, well supplied with lime. Heavy soil should be lightened by the addition of sand and given a dressing of limestone if a soil test shows it to be acid. In winter, dig in farm manure or garden compost at the rate of 9 L [2 gal] bucketfuls per sq m [per sq yd]. Composted or fresh, wet seaweed is ideal manure. As the seakale bed is a relatively permanent one, choose a plot where it will not need to be disturbed for several years. An open, sunny site is best.

Sowing and planting

The main difference between sowing and planting is that

> **Seakale**
> *Crambe maritima* (fam. *Cruciferae*)
> **Hardy perennial.**
> **Size:** plants grow to a height of about 45 cm [1½′].
> Blanched shoots are cut when they have reached 20-23 cm [8-9″].
> **Climate:** cool temperate.
> **Sowing to harvesting time:** 2 years from sowing seed; 10 months or more when grown from root crowns.
> **Yield:** about 450 g [1 lb] per plant.

A row of seakale, one section unblanched. Unblanched the flavor is bitter – always blanch for a delicate taste.

sowing will not produce a harvest for two years, whereas planted crowns should yield one the following fall.

Using bought crowns and taking root cuttings from these to maintain a stock is the easiest method, as well as being the quickest. Crowns are planted in early spring, with a dibber 30 cm [1′] apart, with 38 cm [15″] between the rows, covering them with a 5 cm [2″] depth of soil. All the buds should be removed to prevent flowering. If the seakale is to be 'forced', a slightly wider spacing of plants and rows is advisable, to obtain stronger plants.

If you are growing from seed, it should be sown in the permanent site, and thinned. Sow seed in early to mid-spring 1.5 cm [½″] deep, in drills 38 cm [15″] apart. Germination takes about 6-12 days. Thin the young plants when large enough to handle to about 30 cm [1′] apart.

Care and development

Never allow the plants to lack water; water heavily in hot, dry weather, and mulch liberally with organic matter in late spring, when the soil is moist. Keep the weeds under control, and topdress in midsummer with rock salt at 30 g per sq m [1 oz per sq yd]. Remove all flowering stems as soon as they are seen.

Blanching

To blanch outdoors, wait until the foliage has died down in late autumn, clear it all away, and break up the soil around the plants lightly with a fork. Cover the required plants with large flowerpots, boxes or buckets, weigh the covering down with stones or bricks, and surround each with a cylinder of wire netting to about 7.5 cm [3″] above the containers, filling in the space with leaves. This protects the plants from much of the cold, and ensures white stems, ready for cutting the following early spring.

'Forced' seakale is blanched by lifting successively in mid to late autumn and planting in deep boxes in a dark cellar or shed. Lift the plants, cut the main root back to about 15 cm [6″], cut off all the side roots, and put them upright in the containers, 10 cm [4″] apart. Pack them with leaf mold, moist peat, a potting soil or similar material, which should be about 23 cm [9″] deep. The crowns should be just above the surface. Keep the light out completely – any which gets through will make the shoots bitter – and keep the soil moist. The temperature to start with should be about 7°C [45°F], later rising to 13°C [55°F], but no higher. Shoots will be ready for harvesting in about 7 weeks, if lifted early, and in about 5 for those forced later.

Harvesting the crop

The blanched shoots are ready to be cut when they are 17.5-23 cm [7-9″] long. Scoop the soil away and, using a sharp knife, cut cleanly where the shoots emerge from the roots. Cut with about 2.5 cm [1″] of stem attached. The largest shoots can be removed first and the others taken when they have grown bigger.

After-care and propagation

Do not expect a second crop of shoots. Throw away the roots that have been used for indoor forcing. Remove protection from roots that have been outdoors, fork around

Before planting dig fresh
seaweed into the soil, at
about 45 cm [18"] depth.

Rub off pointed buds from
crowns before planting to
prevent them flowering.

Use a metal-tipped dibber to make holes for planting seakale crowns.
Crumble soil into hole around crown covering it with 5 cm
[2"] of soil. Pat soil into a small mound.

In midsummer topdress the
seakale bed by sprinkling
with agricultural salt.

To blanch outdoors, cover
emerging plant with a
bucket and top with brick.

Invert a bucket over the plant and surround it with wire
netting, secured to a post driven into the ground.
Fill the intervening space with leaf mold.

FORCING SEAKALE INDOORS

Cut the main roots from the plant, then remove the side root or thong,
from main root. The top end of the thong is cut straight
and the bottom end slatted, so that you can tell which
is which. Bundle and store in moist sand.

To force the crowns, pack
them in a wooden box full
of moist peat so that top
is just showing. Cover.

When seakale is ready for
harvesting remove the top
growth, cutting off a little
of woody crown as well.

the plants and topdress with rotted organic matter. Then leave them to grow on naturally.

The seakale bed is a comparatively permanent one. In time, the crowns in the center will die away and new ones will form around the perimeter. Keep the bed free from weeds, or a vigorous weed-patch will develop, and keep it well fed with mulches of garden compost or manure. When abandoning an old bed, be careful to dig out the roots thoroughly, as every bit left in the soil will grow.

The side roots discarded when lifting the plants for forcing can be used for propagation. Take those of pencil thickness, cut to about 15 cm [6″] long, with the bottom end cut slantwise as a guide to planting the right way up. Store in damp sand or soil until early spring, and then plant about 2.5 cm [1″] deep at the normal spacings.

Growing in containers

Seakale can be grown in deep containers and it is possible to transfer them to a cellar or dark shed in autumn for forcing without disturbing the plants.

Pests and diseases

These are unlikely, but clubroot, violet rot, and black rot may occur. Symptoms of the latter are yellowing of the leaves, and blackening of the internal tissue of the roots. Such plants should be destroyed.

Seakale Beet

SEE **SWISS CHARD**

Shallot

SEE **ONION**

Snap Bean

SEE **FRENCH BEANS**

Snow Pea

SEE **PEA**

Sorrel

Sorrel's slightly bitter leaves are best used to make a very good soup. The leaves can be added to salad, but should be used sparingly because of their acid content.

Sorrel (*Rumex scutatus*) belongs to the *Polygonaceae* family and is related to rhubarb. The cultivated type is grown for its leaves which are always used fresh, as a substitute for spinach or in small quantities in salad. This is called French sorrel to distinguish it from the wild or common sorrel of Britain, *R. acetosa*. A hardy perennial, French sorrel grows to about 30 cm [1′] high.

Cultivation

Native to the open fields of Britain, wild sorrel prefers sandy soil in full sun. However, lush and rapid supply of leaves should be encouraged for culinary uses, and for this the soil must be moderately rich, especially in nitrates. Well rotted animal manure, particularly poultry manure, will provide nitrogenous material. A good site for sorrel is one where peas or beans have recently been grown, since these leguminous plants leave nitrogen behind in the soil. Sun or shade are equally suitable.

Sorrel can be raised by sowing the seed thinly in shallow drills or by division of established plants. Either method should be done in late spring to provide a good crop of sorrel throughout the summer.

Like spinach, sorrel reduces considerably with cooking; since the quantities of leaves required for soup are usually quoted in kg [lb], it is advisable to allow sufficient room for about 40 plants, unless you wish to use the leaves for flavoring or additions only.

Seedlings must be kept well watered, and when they are large enough to handle they should be thinned to 38 cm [15″] apart. The plants will need further watering if the weather is dry, and if growth is slow, an application of liquid manure will stimulate the formation of leaves. (Liquid manure is made by immersing a bag of animal or poultry manure in a bucket of water and diluting the solution with more water until it is a pale amber colour.) Soak the roots with this once a week, after watering them well beforehand.

Harvesting and after-care

Leaves should be gathered regularly once the plant is established to promote further growth. Sorrel grown in the garden must be kept strictly to its own quarters; it will become a nuisance if flower heads are allowed to develop and disperse seed. Pinch off flower buds as they appear in summer to prevent this, and to encourage leaf production. The plant will die down in autumn and resume growth the following spring.

Soya Bean

Grow this Oriental vegetable for its green beans which contain a higher proportion of protein than any other vegetable.

There are over a thousand varieties of soy bean producing brown, black, green or yellow pea-like beans or seeds. The plants are generally grown for the high vitamin and protein content of the beans, although oil is also pressed out and used for cooking, salads and making margarine. Soy sauce, used so much in Chinese cooking, is also made from the bean. The world's most grown commercial bean, soy is less often grown in gardens.

In appearance the growing plant is dense and hairy all over, with a trifoliate leaf pattern and short pods; the purple or white flowers are inconspicuous. The species is thought

to have originated in south-west Asia, and has long been an important food-plant in China and Japan. In Britain where success depends largely on the weather, late summer needs to be hot for the crop to ripen.

Unlike other beans, the soy bean gets its signal for flowering from the day-length. Most varieties have only a narrow range of day-length in which they will mature properly and produce a satisfactory crop. Each group of varieties is adapted to a different narrow range of latitude.

Suitable site and soil

Choose a sunny patch of soil, preferably sandy and well-drained, which has been manured in early winter. Make sure that every perennial weed has been removed, and the ground raked to a fine tilth before sowing.

Sowing and thinning

In sub-tropical and warm temperate climates sow in spring, 4 cm [1½″] deep at 15-30 cm [6-12″] intervals in rows of 23-60 cm [9-24″] apart.

Germination is straightforward at temperatures between 18° and 21°C [65° and 70°F], the first shoots emerging in 5-10 days. There is no need to thin seedlings as the seeds are large enough to space out at sowing time.

In cool temperate climates sow in late spring or early summer and sow singly indoors in 7.5 cm [3″] pots one week before the last frost is expected, then plant out as above. Seed may also be sown in a warm greenhouse in mid spring for planting out later. Protect with cloches if cold after the young plants have been put out.

In cool temperate climates the main problem in sowing outdoors is germination: a minimum soil temperature of 10°C [50°F] is necessary. Cloches can help here. A high night temperature in midsummer when the plants are flowering is also needed for a successful crop.

Cultivation

Do not hoe too close to plants or you will damage the root system. Mulch with peat after sowing, avoiding line of seeds, to help keep down weeds and retain moisture.

Moisture is essential, since soy beans grow quickly only when there is adequate water around the roots. Provide extra water during an unusually dry season. No staking is necessary for plants up to 50 cm [20″] tall.

Harvesting and storing

A spring-sown crop should be ready for gathering by the

Soy Bean
Glycine max (fam. *Leguminosae*), also known as soybean.
Half-hardy annual.
Size: 40-50 cm [18-20″] tall in warm temperate zones; up to 1.8 m [6′] in sub-tropical zones. Pods 5-7.5 cm [2-3″].
Climate: warm temperate to sub-tropical.
Sowing to harvesting time: 12-16 weeks.
Yield: depends on climate, but 50 pods per plant possible; 3-4 beans per pod.

Sow seed singly in 7.5 cm [3″] pots indoors, one week before last frost.

Seedlings do not need any thinning. After planting, protect from any cold.

Make sure there is plenty of water around the roots to ensure quick growth.

Harvest by pulling up the whole plant, removing all the pods at one time.

A hardy and vigorous soy bean plant – both bushy and compact.

end of summer. The pods turn from green to dark yellow and should appear swollen with the ripening beans. The best way to harvest is to pull up the whole plant, taking off all the pods at one time. Remove the beans from the pods by soaking the latter in boiling water for five minutes before cracking them in half and squeezing out the contents. The harvesting period can be lengthened by several weeks if a second crop is sown two weeks after the first spring sowing. Store and dry soy beans just as you would shell beans (*see* GARDEN BEANS).

Pests and diseases

Pests and diseases vary with the area but, ordinarily, few troubles can be expected.

In some areas of the world the fungus *Fusarium* causes wilting by infecting the roots. This may be avoided by not growing the beans on the same patch two years running. Aphids may also be troublesome.

Spinach

Spinach is much richer in protein than other leaf vegetables and has a high vitamin A content. It is easy to grow, but take care not to let summer varieties run to seed.

Spinach grows wild in parts of the East, and it was once cultivated by the Chinese. The Arabs may have brought it to Europe in the tenth century during the occupation of Spain, and it reached England about the middle of the sixteenth century, thence to America.

There is some confusion over the name spinach, the word often being haphazardly employed for any plant whose leaves are eaten like those of true spinach. 'Perpetual spinach' is the same as 'spinach beet'. 'Seakale spinach', 'Swiss chard', 'silver beet' and 'seakale beet' are one and the same plant; both these plants are beets. 'New Zealand spinach' is neither spinach nor beet; it belongs to the ice-plant family. 'Seakale' is a member of the brassica family, found growing close to the sea. These vegetables are dealt with elsewhere in the book.

True spinach is winter spinach; summer spinach is a variety and there are long-standing types of both. Cultivation is described for summer spinach, with any modifications for winter spinach following. Both make an excellent green vegetable (cooked with little or no water), while the summer variety is the main ingredient of an exquisite summer soup, and with cream cheese makes a superb filling for a *quiche*.

Suitable site and soil

To grow year-round supplies of spinach, you must make up to seven successional sowings in a season, since the rule is to grow enough for a few pickings little and often. The conditions needed for successful growing will change throughout the growing season, with shelter and warmth required for winter spinach and some shade needed for summer spinach during hotter periods. This complicates a rotational cropping plan, so catch-cropping of this fast growing vegetable should be borne in mind. As they need only a few weeks from sowing to gathering, the summer crop can be grown in spaces between other vegetables without interfering with their neighbors. Summer spinach is notorious for bolting, but this can be prevented by using suitable varieties and the right cultivation.

It is a waste of time to sow on dry, poorly-worked soil. The ground should be well dug over and watered, using as much as 10 kg per sq m [22 lb per sq yd] of well-rotted manure if the soil is sandy. At the same time a dressing of a fertilizer containing 12% nitrogen and 6% each of phosphate and potassium should be worked in at a rate of 30 g per sq m [1 oz per sq yd]. No further feeding should then be needed. Similar amounts of garden compost may replace the manure, the idea being not merely to feed the plants but also to keep the moisture content of the soil steady and as high as possible.

Sowing, planting and thinning

The bolt-resistant varieties are best for spring sowings. Allow about five plants per person per sowing: that is, a row of about 75 cm [30"]. Make the first sowing under Hotkaps in early spring and make successional sowings once every two weeks until the end of summer. Make the drills about 5 cm [2"] deep and 30 cm [12"] apart. The germination rate can be less than 50% so it is advisable to sow one

---

Spinach, summer and winter.
Spinacea oleracea (fam. *Chenopodiaceae*), winter, or the summer or round-seeded spinach.
Hardy annual.
Size: height of 18 cm [7"]; width to 40 cm [16"].
Climate: cool temperate.
Sowing to harvesting time: 6-8 weeks.
Yield: 140 g [5 oz] per plant before it bolts for summer type; 225 g [8 oz] per plant for winter type, 20 plants per 3 m [10'] row.

---

capsule, which contains several seeds, every 7.5 cm [3"] and then thin. Cover the capsules with 2.5 cm [1"] of soil only and firm lightly. The drills can be flooded with water during hot, dry weather, so that the growing plants will not bolt. Germination will take 1-2 weeks, and maturity is attained in 6-10 weeks. Since the seed germinates best at 4.5°C [40°F], it can be started in the refrigerator and planted out when far enough along where summers are warm.

The rows will need thinning to leave the best seedlings at a spacing of 15 cm [6"]. As a rule, thinning should be done as early as possible because any delay slows down the development of the favored plants, resulting in ones which quickly run to seed. The thinnings are often cropped for use in cooking.

Cultivation and harvesting

Keep the soil moist, watering whenever necesary, and always bear in mind that spinach hates sudden change but that the object is to keep the moisture contents as even as possible. Drills drawn as suggested will contain the water, but use a rose on the can to prevent washing the soil away. Applied mulches are best avoided, but the regular shallow hoeing that should keep the rows clear of weeds will also prevent the soil from caking in hot weather and provide a dust-mulch.

Start to gather the larger leaves as soon as they are big enough to use, taking several from each plant at each picking. Twist the midribs and pull them off outwards, or cut them with scissors to avoid tearing the main stem. Do not strip the plants of leaves, or they will die.

Winter spinach

This variety has prickly seeds instead of the smooth ones of summer spinach. It forms a more spreading plant with more broadly triangular leaves. Make two or three sowings in a fairly sheltered site at the end of summer on soil that is not so rich as that recommended for the summer variety. The sowing procedure is the same, but moisture is not so critical for winter spinach. Fill the drill completely and indeed, if there is any possibility of the soil becoming soggy, it is an advantage to ridge the bed up a little.

Supplies of winter spinach should last through winter until spring provided enough is sown, as this kind does not share the tendency of summer spinach to bolt. Pick only the larger leaves. This is for milder areas. Where winters are cold fall-sown spinach is harvested in spring.

Though it was thought to be hardier than the summer varieties this has been disproved and the latter are now preferred even for winter use. After harvesting the leaves, the remaining plants of both spinach types should be chopped up well with a spade, and then dug back thoroughly into the soil.

Pests and diseases

Spinach is almost trouble-free, although aphids and slugs may occasionally occur. Mildew is the commoner disease but the virus spinach blight is more serious. It produces small puckered yellow leaves and is spread by aphids. Destroy affected plants.

1. Sow seed in the bottom of 5 cm [2"] deep drills, 30 cm [12"] apart.

2. Thin rows to leave the best of the seedlings spaced at 15 cm [6"].

3. When watering use a rose on can to prevent soil being washed away.

4. Spinach takes only a few weeks to grow, ideal for intercropping

5. To harvest leaves, twist midrib, pull outwards or cut with scissors.

6. When harvest has ended, chop up plants and dig into soil.

Sow winter spinach in ridged bed to prevent soil from waterlogging.

To protect winter spinach from the frost, pile straw over the plants.

Spinach makes an excellent and very nutritious green vegetable.

Spinach Beet

Although it resembles spinach in taste, spinach beet is no relation. It produces larger, fleshier leaves, which make excellent winter greens.

Spinach beet is simply a variety of beet that has been bred for leafiness instead of for its root. The whole leaf can be eaten, including the long green stalk. Beet is thought to have been first used as food on the Mediterranean coast, where it grows well on chalky soils. It is rare in America. The cultivated spinach beet is much hardier than spinach, more stable, has larger, fleshier leaves, and will, unlike spinach, withstand hot weather without bolting. It can be picked for months, even through winter in mild parts of the country, and will bridge a seasonal gap when there are few greens.

Cultivation

Spinach beet prefers a rich but loamy soil and an open, moist location; shade is not needed. It is a good crop to follow celery, gaining from the manure incorporated in the soil.

The frequent successional sowings associated with spinach are unnecessary for spinach beet because it continues to produce leaves for a long time. For continuous supplies throughout the year it is enough to sow once in early spring and once in summer.

Sow several rows. Allow 40 cm [16″] between rows, and sow the seeds 2.5 cm [1″] deep, at a spacing of 20-30 cm [8-12″] apart. Germination (which takes 7-14 days) cannot be expected to be much over 50%, so it is usual to sow 3 or 4 seeds at each station and remove all except the best when the seedlings appear. Keep the rows well weeded, and

Spinach beet does well on a soil enriched by rotted manure or garden compost dug into the top spit.

Sow seed 2.5 cm [1″] deep with 40 cm [16″] between each row to allow for future growth.

When thinning, remove all but the best seedlings. Water the remaining plants in dry weather.

Spinach beet will produce plenty of leaves if the larger ones are picked at fairly regular intervals.

Spinach beet has large, fleshy leaves and will not bolt in heat. It harvests when other vegetables are scarce.

Spinach beet
Beta vulgaris cicla (fam. *Chenopodiaceae*)
Also known as perpetual spinach.
Hardy biennial.
Size: edible leaves attain a length of 30 cm [1′].
Climate: cool temperate to sub-tropical.
Sowing to harvesting time: 7-10 weeks.
Yield: 4.5 kg [10 lb] per 3 m [10′] row.

water in dry weather.

The leaves will be ready 7-10 weeks from sowing. Pick a few of the largest from each plant ar regular intervals – partly to have them at their best before they become coarse and tough, and partly because this will stimulate the production of new leaves. The spring-sown beets should overlap the summer-sown ones with the latter carrying on until the following spring.

Pests and diseases

The fungus disease rust will occasionally appear, towards the end of summer. The leaves wilt and develop tiny bumps covered with rust-colored powder. The treatment is removal of the worst affected leaves.

Spring Onion

SEE ONION

Sprouting Broccoli

Sprouting broccoli is grown for its flowering shoots, which are harvested over a period of time. It is hardier than heading broccoli and cauliflowers.

Sprouting broccoli is a brassica of ancient origin, its home being southern Europe. Broccoli spears are usually obtained from the Calabrese variety, which takes its name from Calabria, the region of southern Italy where it was once extensively grown. The shoots or heads of Calabrese are green; those of the northern sprouting varieties are purple or white.

Sprouting broccoli is closely related to the cauliflower and heading broccoli, or winter cauliflower (*see* BROCCOLI), but instead of forming one large flower head, it produces a number of smaller ones. Each is formed like a miniature cauliflower, with a 'curd' (composed of a tight mass of flower buds) surrounded by small leaves. It seems likely that sprouting broccoli is the older type from which cauliflower and heading broccoli have been developed.

Suitable site and soil

Like all brassicas, sprouting broccoli thrives in a rich, fertile soil though it will grow in one manured for a previous crop or even one that has not been treated at all. Preferably, however, work plenty of well-rotted manure into it, in late autumn or early winter. This must be done early in order to ensure that the soil has time to settle and become really firm before planting. Soil should be one that does not become sodden in winter.

Sowing and planting

Sowing in general resembles that of other brassicas (such as broccoli, cabbage and Brussels sprouts), except that sprouting broccoli is so hardy that there is little point in striving for early crops by the use of Hotkaps and frames. Sow in the open from early to late spring, depending on variety. The seed can be sown either where the plants are to grow or for transplanting later. The latter is probably better, as transplanted plants generally have their roots more deeply set in the soil.

Sow the seed thinly 1.5 cm [$\frac{1}{2}$"] deep. If the plants are not to be transplanted, allow 60-76 cm [2-2$\frac{1}{2}$'] between the rows. In the rows either thin as soon as large enough to handle, or transplant, so that there is a space of 60 cm [2'] between plants. The temperature for germination is from 4° to 29°C [40° to 84°F], and the period for germination, from date of sowing, is from 7 to 12 days.

Transplant firmly with care, as described for CABBAGE and other brassicas, retaining a ball of moist soil around the roots of each plant if possible. In dry weather, dig a hole for each plant and flood with water first.

Sprouting broccoli
Brassica oleracea botrytis cymosa (fam. *Cruciferae*)
Includes Calabrese (green sprouting broccoli)
Hardy annual, biennial or perennial.
Size: grows to a height of about 90 cm [3'] although there is great variation in size. Maximum diameter of plant with mature heads about 45 cm [1$\frac{1}{2}$'].
Climate: cool to warm temperate.
Sowing to harvesting time: 10 to 14 weeks.
Yield: about 9 plants, each yielding up to 1 kg [2 lb] for Calabrese, and about 0.5 kg [$\frac{1}{2}$ lb] for other varieties.

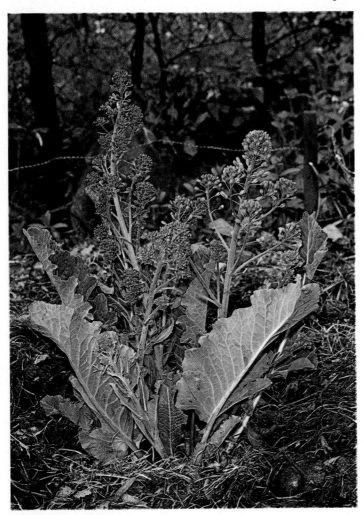

Closely related to cauliflower, the northern varieties of sprouting broccoli are either purple or white.

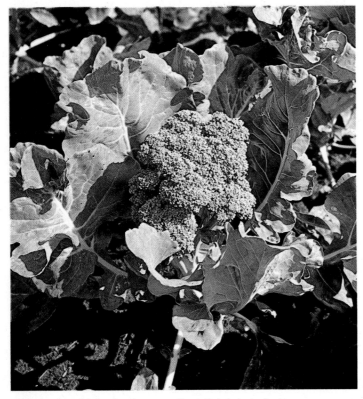

Calabrese, which takes its name from Calabria in Italy, is green, most broccoli varieties originated from this.

Cultivation

Keep well hoed. A mulch of garden compost or rotted farmyard manure around the plants will aid weed control as well as feeding them and preventing the soil from drying out. At intervals of about a month, starting a month after transplanting, a top-dressing of nitrogenous fertilizer at the rate of 30 g per sq m [1 oz per sq yd] will be beneficial. Varieties to stand winter (in the South) are sometimes earthed up in autumn, the soil being drawn up to a ridge of about 15 cm [6"] around the stem to give these tall plants better anchorage against winds.

Harvesting the crop

From a sowing in early spring Calabrese will produce a crop of green heads in midsummer and early to mid-autumn, with a large, almost cauliflower-like one in the center. Cut this large one first when 15-23 cm [6-9"] long, and the plant will continue to produce smaller green heads for several weeks.

The flowering shoots of the other varieties of sprouting broccoli are harvested individually, when about 23 cm [9"] long, removing the top 15 cm [6"] of each shoot by snapping it off. The top few shoots are removed first and this will stimulate the plants to provide more in succession lower down. Always pick while the flower buds are still closed.

In the kitchen the large heads of Calabrese and the shoots of the others are treated like broccoli or cauliflower. The smaller side-heads of Calabrese, however, may be tied in bundles and cooked like asparagus.

Storing the crop

As all these types of sprouting broccoli, are somewhat frost-hardy, they may be left in the garden until needed. For deep-freezing sprouting broccoli, other than Calabrese, trim off the outer leaves and any woody parts and split into small sections or sprigs. Calabrese is ideal for freezing (see below) as it is less woody (though stems may need peeling).

Care after harvesting

Consign all debris to the compost heap. The stalks of the wintering varieties will be very woody and should be placed where they can rot for some time, or they can be destroyed by burning.

After taking a crop of heads from perennial broccoli, feed the plant well with compost or farmyard manure, mulched or worked in around it.

Freezing as a method of preservation

As already pointed out, sprouting broccoli freezes quite well. Premium Crop and Green Comet are two other varieties in addition to Calabrese that adapt to this method of preservation.

After waiting until the shoots are about 30 cm [12"], cut out the center spears first (to encourage lateral growth in those remaining).

Trim off outer leaves and any stems more than 3 cm [1"] thick. Wash very thoroughly and cut into stems of even lengths. Blanch thin stems for approximately 3 minutes and thick stems for 4 minutes.

1. *Keep a ball of moist soil around the roots and transplant with care, allowing 60 cm [2'] between plants.*

2. *Mulch with garden compost to aid weed control, to prevent the soil drying out and to feed the plants.*

3. *When topdressing, sprinkle around plant in a circle the size of the top growth.*

4. *In autumn earth up the varieties that have to withstand winter to a height of 15 cm [6"] around the stem.*

5. *When harvesting Calabrese, cut the main head first, to encourage the growth of smaller, green heads.*

6. *The sideshoots are removed next, to stimulate further growth. Always pick while flower buds are closed.*

7. *Harvest the flowering shoots of other varieties individually. Begin with the top shoots, snapping off the first 15 cm [6"] of each one.*

8. *After harvesting a crop of heads from perennial broccoli, feed the plant well with a mulch of either garden compost or farmyard manure.*

9. *After harvest, the tough, woody stems of wintering varieties can be burned or put on the compost heap and left to rot for some time.*

Open-freeze and pack in rigid containers. You may expect a freezer life of about 12 months. To use, simply cook direct from the freezer in boiling water.

Varieties
Premium Crop Hybrid, De Cicco, Calabrese, Green Comet Hybrid, Neptune, Waltham 29, Spartan Early.

Pests and diseases
These are the same as for other brassicas (*see* CABBAGE). Sprouting broccoli is among the hardiest of the group and is likely to experience little trouble once well established, though flea beetles may ravage the seedlings.
Protect against cabbage root maggot and club root by dipping the roots in a thin paste of diazinon, used according to instructions, and water when transplanting.

Squashes

These sun-loving fruits of varied size and color and shape contain bland, watery flesh and seeds inside a skin that may be hard or soft.

Squashes
The summer squashes are varieties of *Cucurbita pepo*; *Cucurbita maxima* are winter squashes; *Cucurbita moschata* is also a type of squash (fam. *Cucurbitaceae*)
Half-hardy annuals.
Size: sprawling plants, smaller varieties are pruned to 1 m [3'] square, larger ones to 1.8 m [6'] square.
Climate: temperate to sub-tropical.
Sowing to harvesting time: 7-9 weeks for summer squashes, 11-17 weeks for winter squashes.
Yield: extremely variable, 4 or 5 plants of one variety should be ample for a family of 4, according to variety.

Pumpkins belong to the same family as summer squashes. They are used when mature for making sweet spiced pies.

An attractive variety of bush-type summer squash which has a yellow, scallop-edged fruit and milk-white flesh.

(Right) A popular variety, crookneck squash has brightly colored fruits which are best eaten young and tender.

Cover female flowers with muslin bags to avoid the risk of cross-pollination

Summer squash: cut before skin hardens. Fingernail should puncture it easily.

Store winter squash on slatted shelves in a frost-free, dry place. Handle the fruit with care to avoid bruising.

Trailing varieties can be grown on the ground or on a trellis. In either case, they require plenty of room.

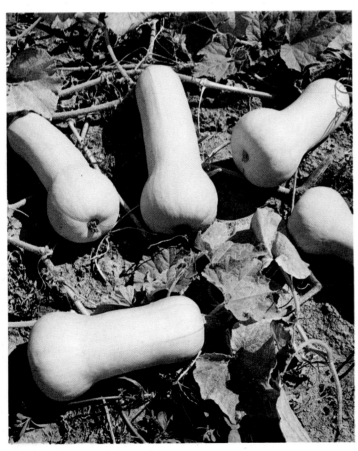

Squash is an American term covering a wide range of vegetables of the *Cucurbitaceae* family. All of them like a warm climate but they may be grown as half-hardy annuals in cool temperate areas.

Squashes are divided into two main groups. Summer squashes, varieties of *C. pepo*, are believed of North American origin and are so called because they do not store. When young they can be eaten with both skin and seeds. Marrows cocozelles and young marrows called zucchini (*see* MARROW and ZUCCHINI) belong to this group. There are some exceptions to this rule, as pumpkins, which belong here, have hard skins like winter squashes. This group includes a variety of colors and shapes, including the orange or yellow hookshaped crookneck, the flattish, white, scalloped custard marrow or cymling and straightnecks.

Winter squashes, *C. maxima*, originated in South America, require a longer ripening period. The skin is hard (except for the butternut) and unless the squash is baked whole it is removed, together with seeds and stringy portion, before cooking. This group stores successfully, which gives them their name. Included here are the gray-green or orange Hubbard, acorn, turban and smooth yellow butternut.

Most squashes are bland in flavor and require spicing before eating. There are two types, trailing and bushy.

Suitable site and soil

Squashes like a very rich soil; farmyard dungheaps, compost heaps or well manured soil (*see* CUCUMBER) are all suitable. Choose an open, sunny site.

Sowing and planting

To protect early crops from frost in cool temperate areas, wait until mid to late spring; then plant. Germination temperature for pumpkins (which may be taken as representative) is 21-32°C [69-90°F], and seed should germinate in 5 to 14 days. When transplanting, remember that these trailing plants can cover a lot of space. A pumpkin plant, well rooted in a compost heap, will send out stems 3.6-4.5 m [12-15'] long, though these can be trained to go in the desired direction and surplus growth pruned away. On the other hand, zucchini are bushy plants and do not require so much space. Plant trailing types 1.8 m [6'] apart and bushy types 1 m [3'] apart.

Care and development

All squashes must be kept generously supplied with both water and food. Plants embedded in a compost or manure heap are well provided with nutrients, but require an abundance of water, and this will also keep down aphids in young plants. Those planted in garden soil, though with an underlying layer of compost or manure, will benefit from a summer mulch. With trailing plants, such as the pumpkin, after one or two fruits have formed, it may be advisable to pinch out the tips of the vines, so that the plant can concentrate on the existing fruits.

Squashes do not require hand pollination.

Harvesting

With summer squashes, cut before they are ripe and use immediately. Your fingernail should easily penetrate the thin skin; if it does not, it is too late. Such plants will then produce a succession of fruits over a period of several weeks. Winter squashes should be allowed to ripen on the plant though with these, as with pumpkins and summer squashes, it is common practice to cut the first fruits early for immediate use, then to allow later ones to ripen.

Storing and after-care

Winter squashes should be allowed to ripen and develop hard, horny shells before cutting. If harvested when the weather is dry, they can be stored in a dry place which has an even temperature and is frost-free, for several months. Store on slatted shelves in a small shed or hang them out of the way individually in nets. After midwinter watch for watery spots indicating decay; if this occurs, use up the rest of the store quickly.

The first frost will kill all foliage and remaining fruit. Clear away and add to the compost heap.

Pests and diseases

Squashes may be subject to the same pests and diseases as melons, but are usually untroubled.

Varieties

(Summer) Baby Crooknecks, Straightneck, Patty Pan, Aristocrat, Cocozelle, White Bush Scallop, Zucchini.
(Winter) Table Queen, Butternut, Acorn, Turban, Blue Hubbard. Pumpkins: Small Sugar, Connecticut, Field Jack O'Lantern.

Strawberry

With its mouth-watering red berries and distinctive aroma, the delicious strawberry is the best loved of all summer fruit.

Unlike most fruits, strawberries are produced on a low-growing, herbaceous plant. The cropping life of the plants is short but most of them readily reproduce themselves by means of runners. Botanically the fruit are a curiosity; each consists of a large fleshy receptacle with the seeds (pips) embedded in the surface. They are the quickest cropping of all fruit.

Large modern hybrids derive from a cross in France between two modern American species, *F. chiloensis*, from the Pacific coast, and *F. virginiana* from the east.

Modern strawberries can be divided into three groups – summer-fruiting varieties, everbearers and alpines. Summer-fruiters are by far the most popular although they generally only crop once in the season. A few varieties may bear a second crop in the autumn if conditions are favorable, or if the first crop has been brought on with cloches or plastic tunnels. All produce runners. Some of the new varieties produce exceptionally large fruit, weighing up to 90 g [3 oz] each.

Everbearing strawberries (or remontants) produce fruit all summer, beginning in midsummer and continuing into autumn. Removing the first trusses of blossom from the plants prevents overlapping with summer-fruiting varieties and ensures a heavier yield from the later flushes. The berries are not as large as those of the summer fruiters. Everbearers mostly produce only a few runners or none at all, although there is one variety, known as the climbing strawberry, that does bear runners. Botanically speaking, however, this is not a climbing plant, despite its name.

Alpine strawberries are small (thimble-sized) but rich in flavor. They can be raised from seed and fruit sometime between early summer and autumn, depending on the age of the plants. Their main disadvantages are their tiny size and the time taken to pick them; they also have few or no runners depending on variety. They freeze well.

Strawberries are susceptible to a number of serious virus diseases. However, stocks have been improved greatly by the introduction of government certification schemes. Buy disease-free certified stock if this is available.

NORMAL OUTDOOR CULTIVATION

Summer-fruiting and everbearing varieties have similar site and soil requirements. Despite their woodland origins, they do best in full sun, ideally on a site that slopes slightly to the south, but need to be in a sheltered position to prevent cold spring winds checking their growth. Choose a site which will not be required for another crop for possibly three years. The soil should be well-drained and slightly acid. Soils with a very high lime content are not suitable.

Preparing the bed

Start at least three weeks before planting. Where the

Strawberry
Hybrids of *Fragaria* (fam. *Rosaceae*), derived from *F. chiloensis* and *F. virginiana*.
Hardy perennial herbaceous plant with a cropping life of about 3 years.
Size: 15-30 cm [½-1'] by 15-20 cm [6-8"] high.
Climate: temperate.
Planting to harvesting time: 6-10 months.
Yield: from 115-450 g [¼-1 lb] per plant.

ground has previously been used for vegetables, single digging will be enough. Otherwise, double dig down to the second spit to encourage a good root-run but always keep the topsoil uppermost. Dig in rotted manure or garden compost at about half a garden barrowload per sq m [sq yd]. This opens up a heavy soil and improves the moisture-retaining capacity of a light one. If neither are available, work in peat or leaf mold at the same rate and then scatter and rake in an equal-parts (by weight) mixture containing superphosphate, sterilized bonemeal and sulphate of potash at 190 g per sq m [6 oz per sq yd]. After digging, lightly roll or tread down, and then rake level.

Planting

Plant summer-fruiting strawberries in early spring or late summer. Plant everbearers in late summer, only when soil conditions are first class; otherwise wait until spring. You will not lose a crop by waiting.

Plant in crumbly, friable soil; wait if excessive rain has made the bed sticky, or if the soil is dry. Planting straw-berries close together increases the yield from the plot as a whole but reduces the yield per plant. However, growing more plants also increases the initial cost. A sensible com-promise is to leave 30-45 cm [12-18″] between plants and 75 cm [2½′] between rows, for the hill system and 45 cm-1 m [18-36″] when grown under the matted row system. (Under this method the runners are permitted to make a solid mat 1-1½ m [3-4½′] wide.)

If you plant them too deep, the crown rots; if too shallow, the roots may dry out and the plant die. The crown of the plant should be just level with the soil surface.

If the plants come from pots or have been lifted from open ground, make a shallow hole with a little 5 cm [2″] mound in the center and set each plant on top of the mound, spreading the roots out over and down it to their full extent. If the plants come in peat pots, do not remove them but soak the pots in water for 10 minutes and then plant at once with the rim of the pot (and the crown of the plant) just level with the soil surface. Always plant firmly, then water. Preferably, plant in the evening, but if this is not possible shade plants temporarily from strong sunshine.

Care and development

Water frequently, possibly even every day in the early weeks, if the weather is dry. Once the plants are established, they will probably not need further watering until the berries begin to swell the following summer. In late spring the plants will develop runners: long stems with a plantlet at each joint, which should be cut off at their point of origin as they appear unless they are wanted for propagating if grown under the hill system.

No feeding is needed as plants come quickly into bearing, but competing weeds should be kept down by light hoeing. Remember that roots are fine and close to the surface.

Cutting off all the blossoms on summer-fruiting varieties in their first spring gives more than two seasons' crop the following year, but few gardeners have the patience to wait this long. If planting was later in the season, however, it may be helpful to cut off the first season's blossom. Ever-bearers should always have the first blossoms removed to allow them to build up strength for fruiting.

Care of the fruit

To keep the ripening berries off the ground and free from soil splashes, strawberry beds are traditionally covered with hay straw. Wheat straw is harder to obtain and oat straw more likely to carry pests. Try to obtain straw which has been properly thrashed, otherwise any grains left in it will sprout. Do not spread the straw until the weight of the developing berries is pulling them down to the ground, as premature strawing cuts them off from ground warmth, increasing the risk of damage from late spring frosts: frosted flowers which do not set fruit are recognizable by their black 'eyes' in the center. Spread the straw thickly around each plant, tucking it under the fruit. If straw is unobtainable, a substitute material or black plastic strips can be used.

Keep the plastic in place with a few stones and make sure that it slopes evenly away from the plants so that pools of water cannot collect around them. If slugs are likely to be a problem, scatter a few slug pellets around the plant before putting down the fruit protector. The plants may be sur-rounded with wire collars to hold the fruit trusses clear of the ground.

Protect the crop from birds with lightweight plastic netting spread over the beds. Drive in short posts and run taut wires between them. These can remain in place for the life of the bed. Invert glass jars over the tops of the posts so that the netting will slide without catching, and throw the netting over the plants as the berries develop; mice and squirrels will take them while still small and green. Make sure the netting clears the tops of the plant and can be removed easily for picking.

Harvesting and after-care

Outdoors, the first strawberries are likely to be ripe between four and six weeks after the blossom opens – sometime in early summer for the main crop. To start with, only a few berries will ripen at a time. These will be the biggest but not the tastiest. The pickings then increase quickly and the plants should be looked over at least every two days. Summer-fruiting varieties usually fruit for three or four weeks, but hot, dry weather will shorten the season. Pick the fruit when it is dry, particularly if it is to be used for making jam. Do not touch the berries when picking: simply break off the stem about 2 cm [¾″] behind the fruit and put it carefully into a container or basket. Always remove damaged fruit and burn it to minimize the risk of infection. Summer fruiters will produce a first-year crop.

After cropping, cut back the top growth of the plants of both ordinary and everbearing varieties with shears to about 7.5 cm [3″] above the crown and burn the cuttings to destroy any pests or disease spores. Remove straw and weeds and then water the bed if the soil is dry. Hoe the soil lightly and scatter general garden fertilizer as recom-mended for tomatoes around the plants, following the maker's instructions, or mulch with garden compost.

Summer fruiters should be grown on a 3-year rotation, with the bed divided into four strips. Remove 3-year-old plants after cropping, leave the site fallow for a year, and *correctly planted*   **planted too high**   **planted too deep**

1. The crown must be just level with the surface of the soil. If planted too high, the roots may dry out; too deep, the crown may rot.

2. If planting after autumn, always cut off the first season's blossom.

3. Protect the ripening fruit with a layer of thrashed hay straw.

4. Make a frame for the netting by stretching wires between the posts.

5. Jars inverted over posts support the netting and stop it catching.

6. Pick ripe berries when dry. Snap off stems; avoid bruising fruit.

Forcing under covers; make sure insects can fly in to pollinate.

Choose strong, healthy runners for propagation; pot them in individual pots, peg them down and keep moist.

A few weeks later sever the rooted runner from its parent plant, using a sharp knife to cut off the stolon.

If space is limited, an excellent alternative method is to grow this fruit in special 'strawberry pots'.

plant maiden runners in the fourth strip, which has had a year's fallowing, so that you always have one, two and three year-old plants cropping in your garden.

Propagation

Strawberry runners are very easy to root but should only be used if they are definitely healthy and the parent plants are free from any sign of disease. Reserve some plants for propagation and cut the berries off before they start swelling, so that the plants' energy goes into the runners.

For rooting runners, sink small pots containing seed mixture or a mixture of equal parts loam, peat and sharp sand at convenient points around the parent plants. Peg each runner down with a piece of bent wire, one per pot, so that the tip with leaves on it is held in close contact with the soil. Keep the pegged-down runners moist and they will root rapidly and in a few weeks can be cut from the parent plant, though not dug up. Transfer the rooted runners to their fruiting quarters a week after cutting.

EARLY CROPPING

An extra early crop can be grown under glass or plastic tunnels or in a greenhouse. An unheated greenhouse has no advantage over glass, although a heated one can advance cropping by several more weeks.

Forcing under glass or plastic

Outdoors, crops can be pushed up by three or four weeks using glass covers, or by two or three weeks with plastic covers or tunnels. Many varieties crop earlier than usual in their first year, so do protect your new plants.

The plants are smaller in their first year, so they should be planted 23 cm [9″] apart, allowing 90 cm [3′] between rows – the wider spacing makes the placing of covers and tunnels easier. After the maiden crop has been picked, pull out alternate plants and leave the rest uncovered.

There is no point in using covers or tunnels too early; early to mid-spring is usually quite soon enough. Before covering, weed the bed and scatter slug pellets around the plants. There is no need to 'straw' the bed but the plants must be protected from birds with netting when the covers or tunnels are opened during the ripening period.

Using tunnels will lead to poor berry development unless insects are allowed to fly in to pollinate the blossom. Open the tunnels wide in the middle part of the day when the flowers are out.

In the heated greenhouse

Use very early rooted runners (*see* Propagation) for greenhouse forcing. By the end of midsummer these should be planted singly in 15 cm [6″] pots filled with rich potting mixture. Keep the pots outdoors until the early winter, making sure that the plants always have enough water and the pots are not cracked by frost. Once inside the greenhouse, keep the plants quite cool with no artificial heat until signs of growth can be seen, usually ten days or two weeks later. Now raise the temperature very gradually, reaching a maximum of 10°C [50°F] by the end of midwinter, and increase humidity by damping.

Once the flowers have set and the berries begun to swell,

allow the temperature to rise, ideally to 18°C [65°F], and maintain moister conditions until the fruit starts to color, when the air should again be drier. Feed the plants occasionally with diluted liquid manure or fertilizer as the berries swell. Forked sticks or bent galvanized wire can be used to hold the fruit trusses up and keep the berries clean. Plants cannot be used again once forced.

CONTAINER GROWING

Summer-fruiting and everbearing varieties can be grown in barrels with drilled holes, patio pots or tubs and other containers. (*See* diagram.) By growing in such a barrel or pot, a large crop is obtained in a small space. Smaller containers can be moved under cover for earlier cropping. Use a rich potting mixture and work upwards, inserting the roots of the plants from the outside as each planting hole is reached. Make sure the strawberries are not planted too deeply or too shallowly and firm the soil mix layer by layer to minimize soil settlement after planting.

ALPINE STRAWBERRIES

Alpine strawberries are raised from seed. Sow in a greenhouse between midwinter and early spring at 10 to 16°C [50 to 60°F], or in a cold frame or beneath Hotkaps in mid-spring, or in the open in late spring. However, the later the sowing, the less certain is the first season's crop. In the greenhouse fill a seed tray or pan with fine seed mixture, scatter the seed as thinly as possible and just cover with a sifting of the same. Germination may be rather erratic and is slow without heat. Prick off separately into another box, placing them 5 cm [2″] apart each way, using potting mixtures.

Alpine strawberries need a partially shaded site with soil rich in organic matter. Glass-raised seedlings should be set outdoors at the end of spring, while those sown in the open should be transferred to their final quarters in early summer or midsummer. Transplant Alpine strawberries as early as possible in their development.

Set the Alpines 30 cm [1′] apart in both directions and make sure that they are never checked by drought.

Varieties

(Spring-bearing) Albritton, Armore, Blakemore, Catskill, Florida Ninety, Midway, Pocahontas, Shasta, Sparkle, Tennessee Beauty, Trumpeter; (Everbearing) Ozark Beauty, Streamliner, Ogallala, Superfection, Giant Gem.

PESTS AND DISEASES

Red stele is a serious soil-borne fungus disease invading the roots. Plants wilt during summer, and roots are dark brown with a red center. There is no control. Plants should be destroyed and disease-free ones set out in fresh soil. Some varieties are partially resistant. Viruses can also be troublesome, distorting the leaves and weakening the plants. Set out virus-free plants of resistant varieties.

Leaf spot weakens the plants, sometimes browning and drying the leaves. Spray when the leaves appear and when the blossoms open with a locally-approved fungicide, such as Captan, if permitted. You may also use it to prevent fruit rots, if permitted.

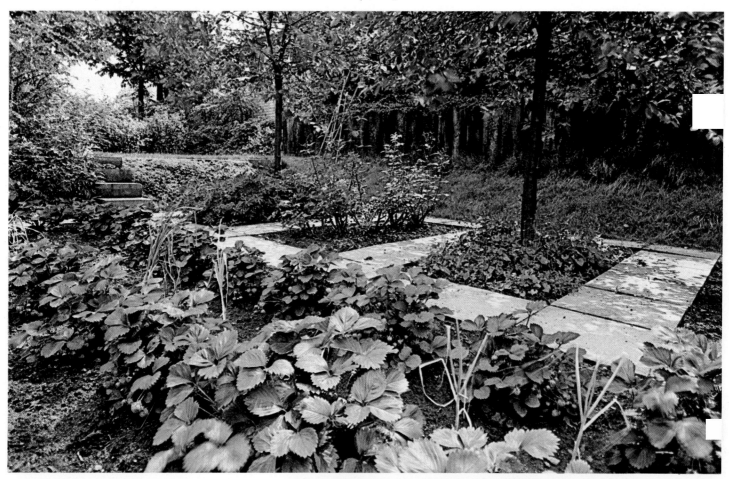

A south-facing, open but sheltered site is the ideal place for strawberry beds.

(Right) Decorative containers provide a feast for the eye as well as the table.

GROWING IN A BARREL

wire netting tube

column of shingle or pebbles

holes 7 cm [3"] wide

drainage layer in base

drainage holes underneath

Take care to leave a layer of soil between central drainage core and base drainage or water will run out.

265

Plump, juicy berries ripe for picking. This luxurious summer fruit is only at its best fresh from the garden.

Spray with a product specifically for mildew before it gets started. To deter nematodes buy clean plants from reliable nurserymen and rotate the plantings. In some cases planting marigolds (preferably dwarfs because of size) between the plants appears to discourage or reduce nematode infestations.

If Japanese beetles and other grubs attack the roots, curb the adults with sprayings of non-poisonous Sevin (most soil-treatment materials are either banned or under question in many states). This should also control weevils, leaf rollers and other insects.

For red spider and cyclamen mites spray with a locally-approved miticide.

String Bean
SEE FRENCH BEAN

Swede

Among the hardiest of all vegetables, they can withstand the rigors of the worst winters. This hybrid cousin of the turnip is ideal for stews.

Swedish turnip, or Swede as this vegetable is known in Great Britain and the Continent, was developed from the turnip for use in Sweden and other northern countries around 1780, possibly earlier. One of its chief qualities is extra hardiness – it can be left in the soil throughout winter and will be perfectly wholesome and edible after being frozen solid for weeks.

In some areas the rutabaga has almost completely superseded the turnip – when someone talks about 'turnips' he will almost certainly be referring to them. This applies to other countries as well as to the United States.

Although the crop is grown primarily for its roots, any roots left in the ground till spring will produce a mass of pale green leaves which can be cooked as greens.

Cultivation

Although rutabagas will grow almost anywhere, a fertile soil is needed for a good crop, and in this respect they are rather more exacting than turnips. One which was manured for a previous crop is the best, but if this is not available give a light dressing of a complete fertilizer about 10 days before sowing. They do well in a heavy soil, provided it is not acid, though acidity can be corrected by an application of lime.

Rutabagas can be sown at almost any time from early spring to autumn but early crops, except in localities with a cool summer, will almost certainly be attacked by leaf mildew. While in the cool areas sowings can be made in late spring, in warmer (though still only moderately temperate) regions sowing should be delayed until about early summer. After that, a succession of sowings can be made, but those varieties which are sown too late (after midsummer) may have insufficient time to produce good-sized roots and may have to be used solely for greens.

Scatter the seed 1.5 cm [½″] deep in drills 45 cm [18″] apart. Germination temperature is 4-40°C [40-100°F]; time from sowing to germination varies according to weather conditions but is about 7-12 days. Their seedlings, having short stems, sit closer on the ground than those of most other brassicas. They are not transplanted but are usually thinned at intervals, the final spacing being about 30 cm [12″] between plants.

Once the plants have become well established, little cultivation is necessary beyond hoeing to control weeds. Water well in dry weather.

Harvesting, storing and after-care

Though rutabagas may be of sufficient size for harvesting in early autumn, they are usually left undisturbed until all

---

Swedish Turnip or Rutabaga
Brassica napus napobrassica (fam. *Cruciferae*), also known as Swede.
Hardy biennial.
Size: at its best for eating when 7.5-12.5 cm [3-5″] in diameter and 12.5-17.5 cm [5-7″] long, though it will grow much larger.
Climate: cool temperate.
Sowing to harvesting time: 12-14 weeks.
Yield: 0.5-1kg [2-4 lb] per root, but can be much heavier.

1. Scatter seed at depth of 1.25 cm [½"] in drills spaced 45 cm [18"] apart.

2. Thin at intervals with a draw hoe to leave final spacing of 30 cm [12"].

3. Water often and well, especially in dry weather.

4. Pull as needed throughout the winter, or store.

HOW TO PRODUCE BLANCHED SHOOTS

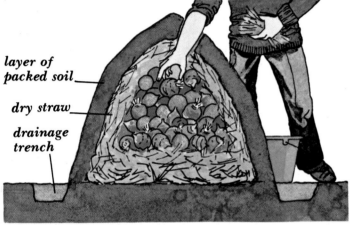

layer of packed soil

dry straw

drainage trench

5. Storing in a pit. To take a few rutabagas, just remove a plug of straw. To take more, break open a soil layer.

1. Put roots in moist soil; keep dark and quite warm.

2. Cut blanched shoots when 20 cm [8"] long.

A purple-skinned variety showing the usual ridged neck.

A white-skinned variety. Both have sweet, yellow flesh.

the summer vegetables have been harvested and frost has set in. They can then be pulled if mulched throughout the winter whenever the ground is not too hard to dig. Those leftover till spring will produce a head of greens which may be welcome in a time of scarcity.

Gardeners with an adequate stock of these and sufficient storage space often take the precaution of storing a few in boxes or in an outdoor pit, simply to ensure that a supply will be available when the rest of the crop is frozen hard into the soil. An outdoor heap covered with straw and encased in a layer of soil makes an adequate place. It is feasible to persuade their roots to produce 'chicons', after the manner of chicory, for winter salad. Dig the roots up, cut off any top growth and place them in moist soil or peat in a box or barrel. Keep dark and moderately warm as for chicory when forced. Cut the blanched shoots when about 20 cm [8″] long. (*See* CHICORY.)

Any residue left by the crop makes good compost. Clear as soon as crop is finished to avoid flea-beetle.

Pests and diseases

The flea-beetle (*Phyllotreta* species), a common scourge of brassicas, is almost always active when the seedlings are emerging and can cause trouble (*see* CABBAGE).

Rutabagas are also vulnerable to other brassica pests and diseases, though some of these do not thrive in the high northern latitudes which the crop finds congenial. Soft rot and mildew may be troublesome, as well as dry rot (*Phoma lingam*) caused by using manure containing rotten roots.

Sweet corn

The plump kernels of the sweet corn cob, one of the most delicious of vegetables, must be eaten freshly harvested.

Sweet corn is a refined variety of Indian corn, or maize, and notable for its higher sugar content. Originally an American crop, corn was widely cultivated in Central America at the time of the Spanish Conquest and was introduced to Europe by Columbus. Today corn is grown as a crop, for both human and animal consumption, over vast areas of the tropics and has extended its range into the temperate zones. However, it does prefer a longer, hotter and sunnier summer than is usual in cooler temperate zones, even with the newest varieties.

Suitable site and soil

Sweet corn thrives in sun, so an open, sunny site is best, but it is a tall plant with a shallow root system, so it also needs some shelter from high winds. It will grow in almost any kind of soil but prefers a light, sandy and reasonably fertile one. Prepare the ground in advance by digging in plenty of well-decayed farmyard manure, compost or other organic matter, as well as bonemeal or wood ashes. Correct an acid soil by the use of lime and, just before sowing or planting, work in a complete fertilizer at about 125 g per sq m [4 oz per sq yd]. Sweet corn is botanically a grass, and grasses like to be well fed, so give a further application of a quick-acting nitrogenous fertilizer about six weeks after sowing or planting at the rate of 30 g per sq m [1 oz per sq yd].

Sowing and planting

The germination temperature for sweet corn is from 10-35°C [50-95°F], preferably above 16°C [50°F]. If kept watered and at a satisfactory temperature, seed should germinate within six to twelve days of sowing. Except for the coldest areas, successional sowings may be made outdoors from late May at intervals of two or three weeks until July 1st or thereabouts, protecting the earlier sowings if cold threatens. Alternatively, early, mid and late season varieties may be sown at the same time and, by reason of their varying times of coming to maturity, will provide a succession of harvests. In the coldest areas sowing outdoors is limited to late spring, so that there is little scope for a succession, although crops can be obtained earlier than normal by sowing in 7.5 cm [3″] peat pots under glass in mid-spring.

Draw out a drill 5 cm [2″] deep and sow in the bottom at the rate of 5 or 6 seeds per 30 cm [1′]. The drills should be 75-90 cm [30-36″] apart. (This allows for the normal germination rate of about 75%.) Start thinning when the plants reach a height of about 20-25 cm [8-10″] so that they are eventually spaced 25-35 cm [10-14″] apart. Take care when thinning to avoid disturbing the roots of the remaining plants.

Sweet Corn
Zea mays (fam. *Gramineae*).
Half-hardy annual.
Size: plant grows to about 1.2-2.4 m [4-8′] or more; cobs are 15-25 cm [6-10″] long.
Climate: temperate to sub-tropical.
Sowing to harvesting time: 9-14 weeks.
Yield: 2-6 ears (or cobs) per plant; 2 the maximum in cool temperate areas.

1. *Immerse peat pots in water so that they expand, then sow 2 seeds in each.*

2. *As seedlings grow, remove the weaker ones and leave the strong ones to develop.*

3. *If dry when transplanting dig hole and flood before planting pot and plant.*

4. *As plants grow, put heavy mulch of straw around the plants to retain moisture.*

5. *To hand pollinate, shake tassel (male) onto the 'silks' (female flower).*

6. *Just-ripe, green ear with green to brown silk, and overripe, faded ear.*

7. *To test for ripeness, use thumbnail and press seeds. 'Milk' spurts out if ripe.*

8. *To pick, grasp ear then split it from the stalk, pulling downwards.*

Very preferable, however, to growing in single rows is block planting. This involves sowing or planting in a rectangular block, allowing 25-35 cm [10-14″] between the plants in each direction. The advantage of block planting is that it gives the silks (the female flowers) a better chance of being pollinated – pollen from the male flower, on the top of the plant (the tassel), must fall onto the silky stigmas of the female flowers on the stems below. If wind blows strongly across a single row when the pollen is falling, most of the pollen will be wasted. On very still days, an occasional shake will ensure pollination.

In a cold climate Hotkaps give sweet corn an earlier start. Place them over the soil about ten days before sowing to warm it up. Alternatively, many gardeners bring on their earliest crops in a heated greenhouse, in frames or even in pots in the home. Peat pots filled with potting mixture serve the purpose well, as transplanting can take place with the least possible interference to the root system. Sow two seeds per pot and eliminate the weaker plant.

Transplant outdoors when the likelihood of frost is past. If dry, dig a hole for each plant and flood with water before setting the plant. Avoid disturbing the roots. Plant 25-45 cm [10-18″] apart if grown in rows or blocks. Alternatively, two rows can be set fairly close together without access between them.

Care and development

Sweet corn is well able to smother most weeds when growing vigorously and approaching maturity, but in the early stages it often grows slowly, especially during dry weather, and is then very vulnerable to weed competition. Keep the plants well watered and hoe frequently, but take care not to disturb or sever the shallow, spreading roots.

Some gardeners carefully earth up their sweet corn plants, as with potatoes, to a height of a few centimeters (inches). This encourages the production of more roots and so a

A sweet corn bed in flower. Mature plants will smother most weeds. If they grow tall they may need staking.

stronger plant. Others aim to retain moisture around the roots by means of a strawy mulch.

Liquid feeding is beneficial, at regular intervals from pollination time to harvest.

Harvesting and after-care

A common mistake is to leave the ears too long before harvesting. In general, ears will be ready for harvesting about three weeks after the silks have first appeared on each plant. To determine when the ears are ripe, watch the silken tassels on them. While the grains are growing they are moist and pale green. When ripe they turn dark brown but still remain damp. If they become completely dry they have been left too long. The sheath of the ear should be dark green and should on no account be left to turn yellow or faded brown. You can test one of the grains, or kernels, by piercing it with a thumbnail. If 'milk' spurts out, the corn is ready. If ears are left too long on the stalk, the sugars they contain will start turning to starch. Because the conversion from

sugar to starch takes place, in most varieties, as soon as the ear is parted from its parent plant, it is important to leave picking the ear until just before it is needed in the kitchen. However, certain varieties of sweet corn have been developed which improve rather than deteriorate for a few hours after picking. These extra-sweet varieties should not be grown near other types, as cross-pollination will affect their flavor. To pluck the ear, grasp it firmly, and split it downwards from the stalk. It should break off easily. Ears on the same plant will ripen at intervals of a few days.

Unlike field corn (or maize), which can be stored in a dry place for indefinite periods, sweet corn is harvested while succulent and is best used almost immediately (or prepared for the deep-freeze) although it will keep for up to two days if stored in a cool, moist place. Do not remove the husks until you are ready to cook the ears.

The dry stalks of sweet corn after harvesting form a kind of straw which can be used as litter for domestic animals, or added to the compost heap; it makes excellent compost.

Varieties

Popular ones include: Earlibee, Golden Miniature,

Sweet corn was first grown in Central America but today it is successfully cultivated in many temperate areas.

Seneca, Sugar King, Improved Carmelcross, Golden Grass Bantam, Honey and Cream.

Pests and diseases
Gardeners in temperate climates may have trouble with the seedlings, which may be attacked by rabbits and birds. Once the plant is established, two pests which may then cause trouble are the corn ear worm and the European cornborer. For both of these, as well as fall army worms and most pests attacking corn, spray with Sevin as directed by the manufacturer.

Mulch between rows, using manure or peat. This prevents weeds and preserves moisture.

In a dry summer, watering plants will make a lot of difference to leaf size.

Harvest when leaves reach a large enough size. Pull from the base carefully.

In winter put dry marsh hay over plants to protect them from frost damage.

Swiss Chard

Rarely grown commercially, Swiss chard is an easy vegetable to raise in the garden. It thrives in a partly shaded site – usually the most difficult part of the vegetable patch to fill.

Swiss chard was derived from a wild species that grows in some coastal areas of Europe. Closely related to the beet and sugar beet, Swiss chard is grown for its foliage rather than its roots. The stalks and midribs of the leaves are

Ruby chard is a variety with showy scarlet stems.

Swiss Chard
Beta vulgaris cicla (fam. *Chenopodiaceae*)
Also called seakale beet, silver beet, seakale spinach.
Hardy biennial, useful for year-round cropping.
Size: 38 cm [15″] high, 30 cm [12″] across.
Climate: cool temperate to sub-tropical.
Sowing to harvesting time: 8-9 weeks.
Yield: about 10 plants per 3 m [10′] row, each giving 250-375 g [$\frac{1}{2}$-$\frac{3}{4}$ lb] leaves.

unusually wide, and these are tasty and tender to eat when cooked like asparagus or seakale. The green part of each leaf, high in vitamin content, is torn off and served separately. When boiled quickly the greens resemble spinach in texture but have a much milder flavor.

Suitable site and soil
Chard is ideal for the partly shaded area of the vegetable garden, which is the most difficult spot to fill. Any well-drained garden soil will be suitable. Unless it is well-broken-down clay, dig the chosen patch over twice in autumn or early winter, working in plenty of manure and, if available, a fishmeal may be applied as a top-dressing.

Sowing and thinning
A mid-spring sowing will provide plants for summer and autumn eating, and some leaves for winter, and a late-summer sowing will give good winter and spring crops. Seed is usually sown 30 cm [12″] apart in 2.5 cm [1″] drills which are made 38 cm [15″] apart, and later the seedlings are thinned to one good one at each station. Germination occurs readily in open ground during normal spring weather, and seedlings appear in 12 to 21 days.

Cultivation
Weeding is best carried out by regular hoeing along the rows. Another method is to place black plastic between the rows of plants, keeping it on the soil with stones. If the ground has been well-prepared before planting, additional feeding will not be necessary. In a dry summer, however, watering with a can or hose will make a noticeable difference to the size of the leaves.

Harvesting and after-care
Remove a few leaves from each plant at regular intervals when they are large enough, but pull them up carefully from the base. Do not strip it or pull it up.

A succession of pickings may be made throughout the late summer and autumn from the spring sowing. In the following spring in mild climates, remove any old leaves from the overwintered plants and hoe in a top-dressing of nitrogenous fertilizer. Within a few weeks a new harvest of leaves can be gathered. In autumn it is advisable to put some straw or marsh hay over the plants so that the new leaves which are growing are protected in winter. In early summer, the plants will start to produce flower stems and should be dug out and placed on the compost heap.

Growing in containers
A few plants can be grown in a large tub or trough if there is between a 30-60 cm [1-2′] depth of soil for the deep roots. Mix well-decayed manure into the potting mixture; if obtainable, rabbit manure is ideal. Water regularly. Plants in tubs may need soaking twice a day during the height of summer. Containers can be put in a cold frame or greenhouse for winter protection.

Pests and diseases
Swiss chard is virtually trouble-free; slugs may attack and seedlings occasionally dampen off.

Tarragon

Tarragon leaves are used to flavor wine vinegar and, either fresh or dried, they are excellent with chicken, in egg recipes and in Hollandaise sauce.

Tarragon (*Artemisia dracunculus*) is a member of the family *Compositae*. The name tarragon is derived from a French word meaning 'little dragon', because the herb was thought to cure poisonous bites. French tarragon, an aromatic, shrubby, hardy perennial, 1 m [3′] high and wide, is best for kitchen use. It is a native of southern Europe. Russian tarragon may grow twice as tall, but lacks the tang of the French type and is decidedly inferior as a culinary herb.

Cultivation
Tarragon must be grown where there is sun for most of the day and shelter from cold winds. Good drainage is essential as persistent damp causes root rot and the plant dies quickly. Add plenty of organic material before planting.

Do not try to grow tarragon from seed; in any case in cool climates the seed will not be fertile, and the flavor is always inferior to plants propagated vegetatively. The best means of propagation is division of the roots from a mature plant in late spring. Any small piece of root with a shoot on it will grow. Otherwise, cuttings may be taken in spring or late summer.

Plant bought roots or cuttings outdoors in late spring or early autumn 60 cm [2′] apart. In extremely dry weather water the plants well from time to time. In moderate or severe winters protect the plants with a mulch; also protect them in winter if planted in autumn.

After four years, transplant tarragon to a new location so that the soil is not impoverished and the flavor of the leaves does not diminish.

Harvesting
Fresh leaves may be taken anytime during the growing season, from spring to autumn. If dried tarragon is required, shoots should be taken in late summer just before the plant produces its greenish-white flowers. An alternative in cool temperate areas is to lift the plants and store during winter

Tarragon will grow prolifically in a sunny, sheltered spot. Always transplant to a new site every four years.

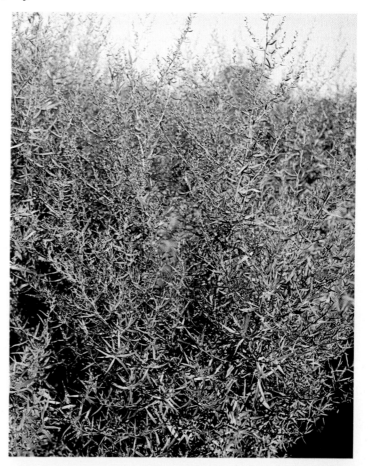

in a cool greenhouse or a frame where they will provide fresh leaves throughout the year.

Thyme

Common thyme (left) and lemon thyme (right) are strongly aromatic herbs. Common thyme is an essential ingredient of 'mixed herbs' and bouquet garni.

Common or garden thyme (*Thymus vulgaris*), a member of the family *Labiatae*, is one of many species grown for its leaves. One of the standard herbs, it is well known as a flavoring for lamb, pork and fish. It is an ornamental plant often grown in the rock graden, between paving stones or in a border. Most species are low-growing, reasonably hardy perennials. Common thyme grows up to 20 cm [8″] high, with a spread of about 30 cm [1′], and it bears small lilac flowers from mid- to late-summer. Lemon thyme (*Thymus x citriodorus*) is a slightly higher, looser bush with deeper pink flowers in late summer and broader, lemon-scented leaves.

Cultivation

Thyme grows best in a sunny and sheltered position. All types grow well on gravel or loam but a clay soil should be avoided. Work over a heavy soil to improve drainage and add fibrous garden compost. Do not give it an over-rich supply of organic material, however, because this promotes sappy growth that will not endure the winter.

Common thyme (but not lemon thyme) can be grown from seed, although cuttings from a nursery are more reliable. Sowing must be done carefully because the seed is extremely fine and needs the barest covering of fine soil. Sow in moist

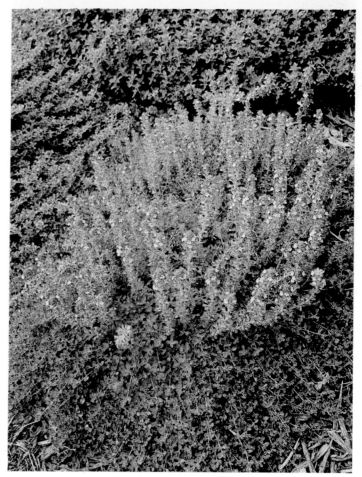

The typical small lilac flowers of common thyme. Thyme is a pretty plant to grow in a rockery or in a border.

seed mixture in trays in late spring and keep warm, about 16°C [60°F], until germination takes place. Pot into deeper trays or singly into 5 cm [2″] pots until the plants are growing strongly. Plant these (or bought plants) at a spacing of 30 cm [1′].

Thyme seldom needs watering. Because it is small, watch it to ensure it is not choked by weeds. For more vigorous leaf growth in young plants, sprinkle nitrate of soda around them but only in damp weather. Remove any flowers.

Cuttings of young shoots, about 5 cm [2″] long, can be taken from established plants in early summer. Put three cuttings into a 7.5 cm [3″] pot and, when rooted, plant them out in early autumn. A quicker method of propagation is to lift and divide the roots of a mature plant during spring. These will produce plenty of leaf growth in the first season, while seedlings and cuttings will not do so until the following spring.

Under good conditions, thyme will usually grow in the open for many years. However, lemon thyme will need protection in the winter and so will common thyme in severe winters. Protect lifted plants during winter indoors.

Harvesting

Fresh sprigs of thyme can be harvested throughout the summer as long as the weather is dry, until the plant flowers. Dried thyme keeps its flavor well. Cut the leaves off in sprigs and put them in a dark, warm, dry and airy place. After a few days crush and store.

Tomato

Perhaps the most delicious and versatile of the vegetable fruits, tomatoes are well worth the care they require.

The tomato is one of the most intensively bred vegetables grown, and there is a wealth of varieties and types from which to choose. It flourishes in hot climates, but often needs artificial heat and light to induce growth in the cold, short days of early spring in cool climates. Yet even in quite inhospitable areas you can raise a successful tomato crop outdoors provided you choose the newer, hardier F_1 hybrids. Tomatoes can either be raised from seed, or plants can be bought when they are between 6-8 weeks old. The latter method has the advantage of saving the cost of the heat needed to raise the seed and eliminates the risk of failure, but it means you are limited to the nursery's choice of varieties. The best course for a novice tomato grower would be to buy plants the first year and, if they do well, attempt to raise them himself the following year.

GROWING OUTDOORS

Growing tomatoes outdoors will produce excellent crops provided care is taken in the choice of site, as heat and light are essential.

Suitable site and soil

It is unwise to grow tomatoes on land previously used for potatoes because of the risk of the microscopic potato eelworm (*Heterodera rostochiensis*), which attacks the roots of tomatoes, too.

Enrich the soil with rotted manure or garden compost in the autumn or winter before planting. The soil should be slightly acid (pH 6.5). If too acid, add lime at the rate of 125 g per sq m (4 oz per sq yd] two weeks before planting. Very alkaline soils are not suitable.

Sowing and planting

Sow from mid-February onwards, depending on the climate and season in your area. Seed can be sown in a greenhouse, in a thermostatically controlled propagator, inside a slightly cooler greenhouse or in a heated frame. The temperature must remain steady at 18°C [65°F] until the seeds germinate, which takes about eight days, and can then be reduced at night to 13-15°C [55-50°F].

Either sow seeds singly in a seed mixture compost in a tray, covering with 0.5 cm [¼″] soil, and prick out the seedlings into 7.5 cm [3″] pots filled with a potting mixture, or sow individually in peat pots filled with the mix. In this case the plants do not have to be transplanted until they are moved to the garden. Whichever method is followed, the growing plants must never be allowed to dry out.

The plants should be at least 15 cm [6″] tall, compact, and dark green, not leggy and pale, preferably with the first flower truss well formed at the planting out stage. This can only take place once all reasonable danger of frost is past.

Tomato
Lycopersicon esculentum (fam. *Solanaceae*)
Perennial, grown as an **annual.**
Size: plants from 45 cm -2 m [1½-6′] tall, depending on variety.
Climate: cool temperate to sub-tropical.
Planting to harvesting time: from 7-12 weeks, depending on variety.
Yield: 27-40 kg (6-9 lb) outdoors.

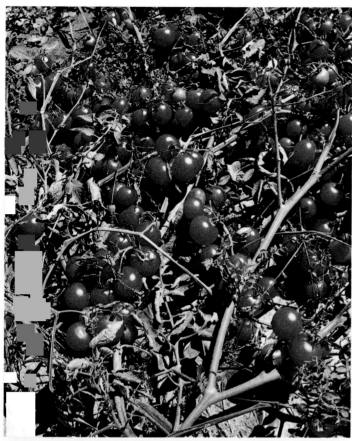

Outdoor bush varieties need no staking and very little pruning. Fruit should be kept off the soil with straw.

This bush variety bears straight-sided fruit. Bush tomatoes are ideally suited to Hotkaps cultivation.

F_1 hybrid greenhouse variety. This ripens early and is resistant to the diseases greenback and leaf mold.

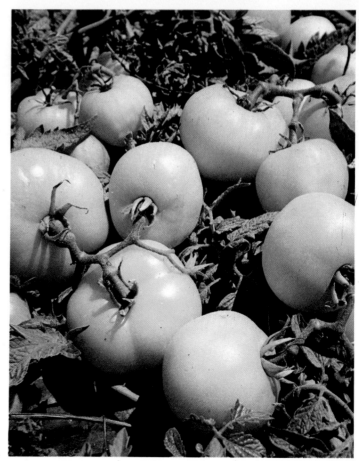

The many tomato varieties bear fruits of different shapes, sizes and colors. This one has round, yellow fruit.

GROWING OUTDOORS

1. Sow seeds 1.5 cm [½"] apart in a propagator from late winter onward.

2. Prick off seedlings into 7.5 cm [3"] pots of potting mixture.

3. Plant in moist warmed soil and tie to stakes with soft string.

4. Remove sideshoots of single-stem types using a clean knife.

5. Give liquid fertilizer every two weeks from start of fruit swelling.

6. Put dry straw under bush types to keep them from soil and slugs.

7. When four trusses are ripe, cut main stem one leaf above top truss.

8. Harvest tomatoes as they ripen, leaving the calyx on the fruit.

9. Pick by severing the stalk at the knuckle just below the calyx.

10. Lay plants on straw and cover with Hotkaps to ripen green fruit.

The plants can go straight into the garden if they have the protection of Hotkaps which have been in position for two or three weeks beforehand to give the soil a chance to warm up. If no covers are available, harden off the plants in a frame two weeks before planting out.

Water the soil ball the day before planting, and make sure that the soil into which the plants are going is also moist. Take care to disturb the roots as little as possible if planted from pots. Plant in holes 75 cm [2½'] apart in rows 75 cm [2½'] apart. Firm the soil around the plant by hand, and replace Hotkaps, if used, for two or three weeks. Do not water in immediately after planting, but water the soil ball only, as required, until plant begins to grow well.

Care and development

Make sure that the plants are adequately supported by tying them gently to canes or poles with some soft but strong twine. Remove all sideshoots as soon as they appear, to encourage the formation of fruit rather than foliage. Feed with liquid fertilizer every two weeks from the time the fruits begin to swell, using one with a high proportion of potassium which is vital for good quality fruit. Keep the plants regularly and adequately watered, otherwise they will suffer from dry set and blossom end rot (*see* **Pests and Diseases**). Remove any yellowing or rotting basal leaves and keep the weeds under control.

The above applies to plants grown as single stems, but some varieties, called 'bush' types, have a main stem which ends in a flower truss at about 1 m [3'] tall, so that it stops growing upward. All the sideshoots which then grow carry the rest of the crop but, as a plant can become a very leafy tangle, it is advisable to thin them out a little. Those kinds can also be laid on the ground, but will need straw or wire netting to keep them off the soil and away from slugs.

Pollination

In dry weather, spray the flower trusses with water, early in the day, to encourage the flowers to set fruit. When the required number of trusses has been produced the main stem is cut (pinched out) at one leaf above the final truss, so that the plant's energies can concentrate on fruiting, not growing.

Harvesting the crop

Pick tomatoes as they ripen, removing them from the plant with the calyx still attached. Towards the end of the season, before there is any danger of frost, take any still green tomatoes indoors to ripen or, preferably, cover the plants with plastic to hasten natural ripening. Cut the tie supports and lay the plants along the ground on straw to keep them off the damp soil and then cover with glass or plastic tunnels.

GROWING IN A HEATED GREENHOUSE

Tomatoes are at times grown in greenhouse borders in soil that has been properly prepared: sterilized each winter, well watered, properly drained and periodically renewed. Prepare the soil by digging in well-rotted horse manure, garden compost or rotted seaweed in the autumn or early winter at the rate of 5 kg per sq m [11 lb per sq yd]. Rectify

any lime deficiency known. The pH of the soil should be about 6.5. Flood with water about one to two months before planting, to ensure the subsoil will be sufficiently moist. Rake in a commercial tomato-type fertilizer according to the manufacturer's instructions, shortly before planting. If it has been necessary to sterilize the soil with formaldehyde, flooding, manuring and any liming should follow, in that order.

Sowing and planting

Sow seed as described for outdoor tomatoes, the time of sowing being late autumn to early winter. The main crop is usually planted during winter and early spring. Heat the greenhouse for about 14 days before planting to achieve a soil temperature of 15°C [57°F]; cold soil checks growth and encourages root decay. Plant as for outdoor tomatoes, and when the plants are at the same stage. Allow 30-45 cm [12-18"] between plants, depending on the variety, and 45 cm [18"] between rows. Do not plant too close to the edge of the border or the heating pipes.

Supporting

Greenhouse plants can reach approximately 2 m [6'] in height and, when in full cropping, are very heavy. It is most important that the house is structurally sound and firmly based if it is to be filled with tomatoes. One method of support is to run a horizontal wire along a row, 5 cm [2"] above the soil, and another directly above it, 15 cm [6"] from the glass of the roof. A length of soft twine or string is then knotted to the lower wire and to the top wire, by each plant, and twisted around the plants as they grow. The string should be loose to start with – the plant will take up the slack as the stem is twisted around the string. An alternative method is to replace the lower wire with a stout 30 cm [12"] wire stake, placed by each plant and hooked at the top end. It should project by about 5 cm [2"], and the string is then attached to the hook and taken up to the roof as before.

Care and development

Tomatoes require a warm but well-ventilated atmosphere. The air temperature should average 15-16°C [60-62°F] during the day, but must be regulated to outside conditions; in dry but dull winter weather raise to 18°C [65°F], higher when sunny. Night temperatures should be 13-14°C [55-57°F] until the end of winter, rising to 16°C [61°F] in early spring and 18°C [65°F] from then on. Maintain a soil temperature of 13-15°C [55-60°F] and avoid drafts.

Remove the leaves below the bottom truss, in stages during the first three weeks, to provide a clear space below the crop and to allow the air to circulate freely above the soil.

Remove all sideshoots as soon as they appear. Smokers should use a sharp knife which is cleaned before touching each plant, as tomatoes are related to the tobacco plant and nicotine-contaminated fingers can transmit disease.

Water lightly until the plants have set about 1½ trusses. Too much water in the early stages leads to soft, sappy growth. But take care not to let the roots get dry; lack of water is one of the greatest causes of failure. When the plants need water they must be thoroughly soaked. A peat

GROWING IN A GREENHOUSE

1. Support plants by twining with soft string tied to horizontal wires at top and bottom of greenhouse. Tie string to top wire as in inset for easy removal later.

2. Remove leaves below bottom truss in stages during first three weeks for free air circulation.

3. If dry and sunny, spray plants with water in mornings to encourage pollination of flowers.

4. Mulch plants with peat to conserve moisture, and keep well-watered. Shade from hot sun with blinds.

5. Remove growing tip at top wire at least three leaves beyond last truss, to ensure truss sets.

mulch helps conserve moisture. Protect the plants from fierce summer sun with shading blinds.

Tomato flowers do not set well in a dry atmosphere so spray the plants with water in the mornings if it is sunny. This overhead damping should begin when the first flower opens and continue until the last flower has set. Although this will also help dislodge pollen, a further insurance is to either tap the trusses sharply, or use the tip of a small clean paintbrush or a small cotton ball to transfer the pollen from one flower to another. Spraying with a blossom-setting hormone is a big help.

Liquid feed the plants regularly according to manufacturer's instructions; it is usually advisable to start feeding when the fruits are the size of a marble, but if they are growing very well, feeding can be delayed for a little while. In general, tomatoes require high potash feeds for the first half of the season, and high nitrogen towards the end of it. Greenhouse tomatoes can develop up to ten trusses, though it is usual to stop the growing tip when it reaches the top wire. When pinching out the tip, do so at least three leaves beyond the last truss, to ensure that it sets. If top growth is spindly and there is a heavy set of fruit on the first four trusses, it is wise to cut out the spindly growth to just above one leaf.

Harvesting and after-care

Pick tomatoes as they ripen, breaking the stalk off at the knuckle. Yellow or green tomatoes will ripen if picked and put in single layers in trays in a warm place. The tomato stem will make good compost-heap material; remove the roots completely and destroy, in case they are infected with soil-inhabiting fungus diseases.

CONTAINER CULTIVATION

Best are bottomless containers made of various materials, 23 or 25 cm [9 or 10″] in diameter and 23 cm [9″] deep. Place the rings 38 cm [15″] apart in rows 45 cm [18″] apart on a bed of aggregate (coarse sand, pebbles or gravel) at least 15 cm [6″] deep. Fill the rings to within 1.5 cm [½″] of the top with a good potting mixture two weeks before planting, to give the medium time to warm up. Water the mixture and the aggregate two days before planting, which takes place at the same time as border-grown tomatoes.

The roots will draw their nutrients from the medium, but take up most of the liquid they need from the aggregate. Once the plants are in the rings give each about 1 L [2 pt] of water but do not water them again unless they wilt on a hot day. The roots should reach the aggregate, which should be kept watered, in 10 days; after this, only the aggregate should be watered. In hot dry weather each plant will need about 2 L [3¾ pt] of water each day; less in cool, dull weather. Feeding is always given through the rings. Begin the regular weekly feed of a commercial liquid feed high in potash when the fruit is forming on the first truss, at the rate of 1 L [2 pt] per plant. Make sure that the plants are adequately supported, with stakes put in about a week after planting, if growing outdoors, or with wire and

This single-stemmed variety is an extremely heavy cropper that can be grown outdoors or in a greenhouse.

METHODS OF TOMATO GROWING

Sow plants in potting mixture in bottomless rings on a bed of aggregate, such as gravel. Once established, plants are watered via aggregate and fed via the rings.

Plant bush tomatoes near back of slightly shaded, sun-facing frame and train them forwards.

Grow single-stem tomatoes on stakes in a trench and protect them as long as it is necessary.

Single-stem plants can be grown in a peat bag against a sun-facing wall. Water as manufacturer instructs. Loop the fillis string around base of each plant stem and tie other end to a horizontal wire held on wall with nails.

fillis as for border plants. Topdress the plants with fresh potting compost or granulated peat halfway through the season, about 2.5 cm [1″] deep.

COLD GLASS AND CLOCHES

Germinate seed in late winter by one of the methods described in GROWING OUTDOORS, or buy in young plants. For a frame, choose a slightly shaded, south-facing site, or up against a south-facing wall. Prepare the soil during winter as for outdoor plants then, two weeks before planting, water generously, put the lights on and let the soil warm up. Just before planting in mid-spring, give a top-dressing of garden compost mixed with a quarter part of granulated peat and a sprinkling of bonemeal. Set the plants towards the back of the frame, with 45 cm [18″] between them if bush types and train forwards; otherwise plant 45 cm [18″] apart each way and support with a stake. Keep the bush types off the soil with a layer of straw or wire netting. Thereafter treat all types as for outdoor varieties. Cloches can be used in two ways: they can be left on to protect bush types throughout the season, or they can be put over single-stem plants from planting time until early summer, and then taken off or up-ended along the row for the rest of the season. Prepare the soil for both methods as for outdoor cultivation; then, for the second method, dig a V-shaped trench 15 cm [6″] deep, 30 cm [12″] wide at the top and 15 cm [6″] at the bottom, a week before planting, and mix the same top-dressing into the bottom of the trench as was used for frame growing. In warm districts, planting can take place from mid-spring, a little later in cooler areas. Plant bush varieties 90 cm [3′] apart, and single-stemmed kinds 45 cm [18″]. The cloches can be raised even more by putting them on bricks, and tall barn cloches will give greater height still. Remove them when the growing tip of the single-stemmed kinds is about to touch the top, and then treat as for outdoor tomatoes.

CONTAINER GROWING

Even without a garden a small quantity of tomatoes can be raised in containers such as pots, peat bags or troughs on patios and balconies. Tomatoes grown out of doors in containers require the same treatment as those grown in the open garden. They can be grown by ring culture outdoors. If grown in any container except a peat bag, they must have 17.5 cm [7″] minimum depth of compost. Supply a reliable growing compost and feed regularly with a commercial liquid fertilizer. Take care that tomatoes grown in peat bags do not become waterlogged or dry out, by watering exactly as the manufacturers instruct.

Varieties
Big Boy, Better Boy, Early Girl, Tiny Tim, Yellow Plum.

PESTS AND DISEASES
Tomatoes, especially those grown in greenhouses, are vulnerable to a host of pests and diseases, the most serious and common of which are: leaf mold, *Verticillium* wilt, sundry viruses and whitefly.
Leaf mold (*Cladosporium fulvum*) is a fungus disease producing pale yellow spots on the upper surface of the leaves, with

a brown fur on the undersurface in these areas. The leaves die completely and plants can be destroyed. A stagnant, moist atmosphere is often responsible, especially if this occurs at night. Remove the most badly affected leaves and spray the plants with benomyl.

Verticillium wilt, or sleepy disease, is a soil-borne fungus disease which invades the roots. The plant wilts at the top during the daytime, but recovers at night, then the bottom leaves do the same and start to turn yellow; finally the whole plant wilts permanently and dies. The stem is stained brown internally from the base upwards. Badly affected plants should be removed complete and destroyed; others may be helped by spraying overhead during the day, shading the greenhouse, and mulching close against the stem to induce new roots. The soil should be sterilized before planting tomatoes again.

Virus diseases are numerous, for instance fern leaf, in which the leaves are reduced to thread-like growths; spotted wilt, which produces brown leaves at the tip, a stunted plant and brown spots on the fruit; mosaic, which turns the leaves mottled yellow and green; and streak, resulting in plants spotted and streaked with brown. Destroy all infected plants completely. Where verticillium or virus diseases are troublesome select only V7N (resistant) varieties.

Whitefly can be very troublesome, feeding on the under-surface of the young leaves as the plant grows, so that growth is stunted, leaves curled, gray-green and sticky, with black patches; in a bad infestation the plants die. Spray with pyrethrum or rotenone or, better, put up bright yellow cards coated with the sticky Tack Trap. For tomato horn worms spray with Sevin, and for aphids use rotenone.

Fruits with green shoulders which do not turn red are afflicted with greenback, due to lack of potash, or too much or too strong sun. Blotchy ripening, in which fruit is yellow and red, can be due to lack of potash also, and too great a contrast between day and night temperatures. Blossom-end rot of fruit shows as sunken black patches at the blossom end, due to irregular supplies of water; cracking of nearly ripe fruit is for the same reason. Leaves bright yellow between veins, gradually yellowing all over and withering is due to magnesium deficiency, and often occurs where too much potash has been given, which the plant takes up in preference to magnesium. Spray the plants with a solution of 60 g [2 oz] Epsom Salts (magnesium sulphate) in 4.5 L [1 gal] of water, using a fine mist spray, as soon as the first yellowing is seen. The condition known as dry set results in flowers falling or fruits remaining the size of a pinhead; this is due to a dry atmosphere at pollination; spray with water in the morning.

There are some regional problems, which may or may not affect you, but it is best to be aware of them. Canker (*Didymella lycopersici*) affects the stems, first at the base and higher up later in the season, as brown sunken streaks, and the plant dies. You should use a locally-approved tree paint. The green-brown caterpillars of the tomato moth can do great damage to the leaves; two sorts of eelworm can infest the roots and potato blight the top growth (*see* POTATO). Gray mold may present problems as may red spider mite. For either of these, check with your local authorities for proper methods of control.

Turnip

The hardy turnip can be grown most of the year. The swollen root stores fairly well, while the leafy tops are a useful spring green, rich in iron and vitamin C.

Cultivated in Europe since the earliest times, the turnip root consists of about 90% water, but has the same vitamin C content as potatoes. The leaves have a significant iron content and are rich in vitamin C.

Turnips were formerly regarded as autumn and winter crops, but with good cultivation and the correct choice of varieties they can be harvested much of the year. In the gardening cycle they can be regarded as three distinct crops and different varieties are selected for each. Early turnips are those which, as quite small roots, are ready to harvest from late spring to early summer. They may be grown in a hot bed in a frame, or started in greenhouses or outdoors under Hotkaps. Maincrop turnips are sown in late spring to produce roots 7.5-10 cm [3-4"] in diameter in the autumn. These can be used straight from the garden or stored for winter use. Finally, there are turnips grown, either in spring or autumn, for their leaves, which are cooked like cabbage. Roots left in the ground through the winter will produce leaves in early spring unless the weather is severe.

Suitable site and soil.

Turnips require an open, sunny position. If grown in the shade of trees they will produce foliage rather than roots.

Turnip
Brassica rapa (fam. *Cruciferae*)
Hardy biennial.
Size: roots harvested when 7.5-10cm [3-4"] across, but can grow much larger; leaves to 30 cm [12"].
Climate: temperate.
Sowing to harvesting time: maincrop 8-9 weeks; early crops 4-6 weeks.
Yield: average root weighs 250-450 g [½-1 lb], but can be much heavier.

---

1. *Prepare a hotbed in a frame for growing early turnips, covering the 15 cm [6"] layer of manure with good soil.*

2. *Sow 3 seeds in each hole, spaced 12.5 cm [5"] apart.*

3. *Thin seedlings to one per hole. Give plenty of air.*

For early spring sowing, choose an early, quick-growing variety. Sow thinly.

Maincrop turnips are sown in drills and thinned to 22-30 cm [9-12"] apart.

Hardy varieties can be left in the ground until needed, but pull less hardy.

Pull green 'turnip-tops' when they are 15 cm [6"].

This early turnip variety has purple-topped roots.

Many of the early varieties of turnip, which mature quickly, have white roots.

Though they will grown in most types of soil, turnips do best in a rich loam. They like calcium, and are grown extensively on chalk and limestone soils; they also need a soil well supplied with phosphates. Supply any enrichment that the soil may need in autumn or early winter, in the form of rotted organic matter, well before sowing time, and avoid the use of unrotted farmyard manure. If lime is needed, allow six weeks to elapse before an application which follows farm manure. If the maincrop follows early potatoes or any other crop for which the land was manured, there is no need to give further dressings.

Sowing and care

In theory the gardener can grow a succession of crops from early spring to late autumn. Two crops are more practical, an early one harvested in spring or early summer, and a maincrop harvested in autumn and stored through the winter. An intermediate crop would coincide with the main summer vegetables.

For early spring sowing choose an early, quick-growing variety and start under glass or cloches. For the maincrop, sow in mid- to late summer, again selecting a suitable variety. A further sowing in early autumn will provide green turnip-tops in spring, with a cutting if required in late autumn, within a few weeks of sowing.

The early early varieties generally have white roots. A succession is provided by more white varieties, by white turnips with red or purple tops, and by golden ones. Certain white varieties with green tops are among the hardiest and the best for lasting the winter to supply early spring greens.

Sow seeds thinly 1.5 cm [½"] deep in drills 30-40 cm [12-16"] apart, thinning plants to a spacing of 23-30 cm [9-12"] for the maincrop. Early crops and turnips for greens can be grown with a narrower spacing of 15 cm [6"] between plants and rows. The germination temperature is 4-40°C [40-104°F]. The sowing to germination period varies according to temperature, but in reasonably warm weather germination is rapid and can be less than a week, otherwise it may take up to 12 days. Turnips should not be transplanted.

Turnips are susceptible to drought and should be kept well watered, especially in the early stages. Good, well-flavored, tender turnips will only be obtained if they are kept growing fast and continuously. Hoe frequently to aerate the soil and control weeds.

Growing in frames

A quick crop of early turnips can be grown in a garden frame, using compost from which some previous crop has been removed. Alternatively, you can put a 15 cm [6"] layer of warm, decaying farmyard manure in the frame and cover it with good soil. Insert seeds, two or three together, in holes about 12.5 cm [5"] apart in late winter. Thin to one per hole when the plants are large enough to handle. The bed can be covered by sacks or mats to help retain the heat and promote quick germination, but these should be removed after seedlings have appeared. Allow plenty of air after this and water moderately every day. It should be possible to harvest a crop within four to eight weeks.

Harvesting and after-care

Turnips should grow quickly and be harvested while still young and tender. If they are allowed to remain in the soil too long, or if growth is checked (by drought, for example) the interior of the roots will become fibrous and tasteless. Turnips are pulled from the ground, and the leaves cut off. When harvesting for storing, leave about 2.5 cm [1"] of green attached to the root. The less hardy types of turnips should be out of the ground before the onset of hard frosts, but the hardier varieties can withstand a moderately mild winter and may be pulled as required. The spring crop of leaves may be picked or cut any time after they are about 10-15 cm [4-6"] high.

For winter use, grow hardy varieties which can remain in the ground until needed. Alternatively, store in layers in boxes of dry sand or peat, or in heaps or ridges covered with a layer of soil and straw. The tops should be first taken off, but not too closely.

It is possible to leave a few small plants in the ground, and harvest the leaves which they produce next spring. As soon as they form flower heads, however, scrap them.

To avoid pests and diseases, clear away all surplus plants and the remains of vegetation after harvesting and take them to the compost heap.

Pests and diseases

Turnips are subject to all the pests and diseases of brassicas; the most troublesome is the turnip flea-bug (*Phyllotreta* species). For their treatment *see* CABBAGE. Soft rot may attack roots in storage.

Zucchini

Appreciated for their delicate flavor, zucchini are marrows which are picked while still very young and tender.

The popularity of zucchini as a vegetable delicacy has increased enormously in recent years. In addition to the

The yellow zucchini flower. Keep picking young fruits regularly and more female flowers and fruits develop.

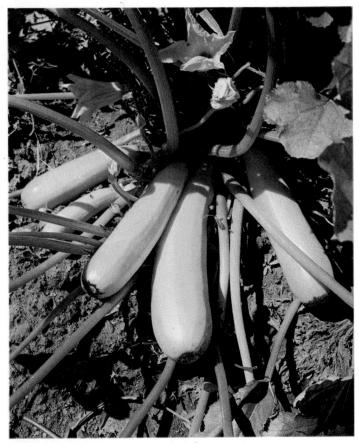

The golden zucchini is a less familiar variety, but its butter-yellow fruits are just as tender and delicious.

traditional dark green variety there is a less well-known type which bears gold-colored fruits. Both are equally delicious lightly steamed or fried, used in vegetable or meat dishes or raw in salads. Zucchini may also be stuffed, like marrows, with a savory meat or cheese mixture.

Suitable site and soil
Since zucchini are baby bush marrows, the plants from which they come require the same growing conditions as those which provide adult marrows. For preparation of the site *see* MARROW. Remember that an open, sunny position and a rich soil are essential.

Sowing and planting
Follow directions for MARROW. Take care to harden off the young plants gradually as a sudden drop in temperature can be fatal. A cold frame is valuable for this process, which usually takes place in late spring. Remove the top of the frame during the daytime only, then gradually expose the plants to the night air.

If no frame is available, expose the plants to outdoor temperatures for an hour or so during the day, increasing the length of time slowly. The plants should be ready for planting out in early summer, when the risk of frost is minimal. Space them 60 cm [2′] apart.

Care and development
Remember that plants providing zucchini should be grown without check to their growth – generous watering is vital if the embryo fruits are to swell; otherwise they are shed prematurely and the plants themselves take time to recover from the lack of water.

Keep the soil moist but not sodden and water regularly, particularly during dry weather. Take care not to splash the young stems with water because of the danger of collar rot (*see* CUCUMBER). Pollination by hand is unnecessary. Weed when necessary, taking care not to damage the young fruits. Give regular doses of liquid manure as soon as fruiting begins.

Harvesting the crop
Pick zucchini as soon as they are 5-20 cm [2-8″] long. Fruit can be left on the plants to grow into mature marrows, to a maximum length of 25 cm [10″], but this practice is not desirable as it discourages further fruit production.

Pests and diseases
Plants providing zucchini are vulnerable to cucumber mosaic virus (*see* CUCUMBER) and mildew (*see* MARROW). Red spider mites and slugs may also be a problem.

Zucchini
Cucurbita pepo ovifera (fam. *Cucurbitaceae*), also known as courgette and baby marrow.
Half-hardy annual.
Size: Fruits at their best when 5-20 cm [2-8″] long; plant kept by pruning to 1.2 m [4′] square.
Sowing to harvesting time: about 7 weeks.
Yield: About 20-30 fruits per plant.

BASIC GARDENING GUIDE

Planning your garden

Start by listing the crops you want to grow. For planning, it helps to divide them into four basic categories:
1. Quick-return, seasonal crops: greens, root crops and salads.
2. Quick-return, permanent crops: herbs, cane fruit and strawberries.
3. Long-term, permanent crops: apples, pears, plums, rhubarb.
4. Luxury crops: e.g. asparagus, globe artichokes and cardoons.

DRAWING UP A PLAN

KEY TO PLAN

1. Measure extent of main roots of trees and allow for this.
2. Gap in hedge at bottom of sloping garden to both allow frost to escape and prevent frost pockets from developing.
3. Incinerator sited far enough from crops for heat to do no damage.
4. Wet area of garden avoided.
5. Rhubarb will tolerate shade from trees and damp ground.
6. Garden shed and water barrel accessible via path.
7. Cold frame sited against sun-facing wall for maximum warmth.
8. Loganberry grown on trellis to hide compost heap and incinerator from view.
9. Work out which areas receive the most sun.
10. Vegetable patch sited in sunny part of garden, protected from prevailing winds by hedges and trees, well drained.
11. Seedbed sited next to vegetable patch, protected from strong sunlight (kills seedlings), well drained.
12. Soft fruit grown within protection of fruit cage.
13. Hedge grown to screen view of vegetable patch from house.
14. Paths laid down (and use made of existing ones) to link important areas of garden and to link garden to kitchen: paths should be wide enough to take wheelbarrow, etc.
15. Alpine strawberries will tolerate partial shade from fruit tree.
16. Fruit trees planted in frost-free positions; allow for future spread of trees.
17. Measure shade cast by trees and allow for it when planning.
18. Locate house drainage system and avoid it when cultivating.
19. Locate house drainage inspection chamber and do not cover it (or cover it with a movable container).
20. Herb garden sited in dry, sunny part of garden near kitchen for convenience.
21. Fruit or vegetables growing in containers. Fit these with castors to make them movable.

Positioning the plot

Once you have decided which crops you would like to grow, you must gather facts about your garden. Where you would like to have the plot is not necessarily the best place for suitable growing conditions. There are several factors to consider in determining the position of vegetables.

Good light is essential; most vegetables and fruits will not grow in shade.

Soil drainage is important; water-logged soil will cause crops to rot and encourages many diseases.

Frost pockets tend to form at the base of sloping sites against solid fences, walls and hedges, and it is safer to avoid such pockets when planning the garden. Frost damage in spring is associated with fruit crops, but it can be just as destructive to any newly-emerged vegetables.

DRAWING UP A PLAN

1. Find out the overall dimensions, the exact shape of the garden and the position of the house.

2. Note where house drains are. If in doubt, try to obtain the plans of your house. The vegetable garden will have to be placed to avoid these drains.

3. Note the position of trees, and especially the area of shade they cast on the ground. Try to estimate the spread of their roots; extensive root systems of trees will compete with vegetables for water and nutrients.

4. Mark in areas that receive most sun.

5. Note any wet areas where drainage may be needed.

6. Find out the direction of prevailing winds. This is important if screening is desired for the protection of crops on very exposed sites.

7. Mark the position of existing paving borders, shed and any other structures if you do not intend to move them. From all this information you can make an accurate drawing of the garden to assess which parts are most suitable for vegetable and fruit growing and how large a plot can be planned. Graph paper, marked out in squares, will make the job much easier. Use a simple scale and keep the plan big.

Having decided on the size, the next step is to find out how to make the best use of the space. Look up in the A-Z section the amount of space to allow between individual plants and between the rows of specified crops, their sowing time and their harvesting time. In addition, the expected yield of each crop given here helps you plan on a row-by-row basis in relation to your eating requirements.

Understanding crop rotation

The purpose of crop rotation is twofold: to gain the best possible return from the soil and to keep certain devastating pests and diseases in check. Growing the same crop on the same patch of soil year after year is inefficient, because the crop will gradualy use up the nutrients it needs most, while the other nutrients will be very little depleted. Also the roots of different crops grow to different depths, so that growing only one crop will exhaust the nutrients at one level.

Crop rotation makes more economic use of garden compost and manure because some crops respond best to fresh application of rotted organic material, while others do well on land that has been prepared for previous crops.

Crop rotation can also solve the problem of disease. For example, club root, a fungus disease which attacks brassica crops, is highly infectious. Control is very difficult because the disease can linger in the soil for years, even when brassicas are no longer grown there. Severe attacks are brought on by continuous cropping of the same piece of ground, causing a slight infestation to increase rapidly. Crop rotation prevents the disease from building up.

Always move vegetables around every year, even if the garden is too small to group crops into separate, neat beds. A rotation system can extend over as many years as you want, but the simplest method is to divide a vegetable garden into three plots, of roughly the same size, excluding any perennial beds. (Perennials such as globe artichokes and asparagus have to stay in one place and so do not enter a rotation system.)

The cycle of one of the plots over three years follows this outline:

First year: Everything except roots and brassicas. Manure or garden compost is applied during the winter and the ground is dug over well. On this plot grow crops that need the richest soil conditions – peas, beans, celery, leeks, lettuces, onions, beets and spinach.

Second year: Roots. Now the plot will be used for raising root crops – beets, carrots, parsnips and potatoes, but not rutabagas and turnips because they are brassicas. All these do well on soil that has been manured the previous year.

BASIC CROP ROTATION

	Bed 1	Bed 2	Bed 3
First year	Other Crops	Brassicas	Roots
Second year	Roots	Other Crops	Brassicas
Third year	Brassicas	Roots	Other Crops

The breaking up of the lower layers of soil by deep-rooting crops helps improve its structure for subsequent crops of shallow-rooting vegetables.

Third year: Brassicas. In the last year of the cycle the plot is used for shallow-rooting brassicas – cabbages, cauliflowers, broccoli, Brussels sprouts, kale, rutabagas and turnips. All brassicas like a firm soil to encourage stable root systems. Since the soil has been cultivated in the first two years, it is only necessary to fork it over lightly for most brassicas. Cauliflowers, Brussels sprouts, rutabagas and turnips, however, like deeply-dug, well-manured ground. Cauliflowers also do best in freshly-manured soil.

Intercropping and catch-cropping

Quickly-maturing crops, such as lettuce and radishes, may be 'intercropped' between rows of maincrops. They will be ready for harvesting when the maincrop is still growing. Such quick growing vegetables can also be 'catch-cropped' on a bed left vacant between maincrops.

A flexible system

You may choose to start with all three beds at once, starting each one at a different 'year'. Alternatively you may begin with one first year bed, turn it over to roots in the second year and start another first year bed, gradually building up a three-bed rotation system. If you have room for only one plot, simply follow the cycle through, starting with the First Year crops.

While some potatoes can be grown in a Second Year bed, to grow a year's supply for the average family requires as much as 9 sq m [11 sq yd]. Those with large enough gardens can work to a four-bed rotation system with potatoes grown alone as the second of four crops. The potatoes leave behind a clean, enriched and finely broken-up soil that is ideal for the root crop to follow.

Successional sowing

If you sow all the seed of a particular vegetable variety on the same day, you will be faced with a glut of the crop during the few weeks of harvesting time, and nothing at all during the rest of the year.

Instead, by making several smaller 'successional' sowings of the crop at intervals during the growing season, you will be able to harvest the crop over a longer period; also the plants have more chance of surviving pests, diseases, drought or other troubles if the sowing is spread out in this way.

Another method of achieving the same result is by sowing different varieties which need different lengths of time to mature. The first sowing is of an early variety, the next of a maincrop type and the final one of a late variety.

Choosing your fruit

Both fruits and vegetables have their proper place in the kitchen garden. Fruit trees give a very high return in relation to the area of ground occupied, and fruit requires less continual attention and number of hours' work than vegetables. Although the initial outlay for fruit is greater than with vegetables, and there is usually a couple of years' delay before the first crop, soft fruit continues to crop for 10 to 15 years once established, and tree fruits will continue for 20 to 50 years.

Where to grow

When planning your garden think, if possible, in terms of grouping all your fruits together in one plot. This makes protection against birds easier; it facilitates spraying and reduces the risk of spray damage to adjacent crops. It also makes manuring easier.

Do not be deterred, however, if you have no orchard space. In an average garden there are many suitable spaces that are impractical for vegetables but useful for fruit. Fans, espaliers and cordons can be trained against the shed or garage and boundary walls. Fruit can be made an ornamental feature. Cordon apples and pears, and in suitable climates Chinese gooseberries and grapes, can be trained over pergolas. Both tree and cane fruit can be trained on wire fences separating one part of the garden from the other, and low one-tier espaliers make an attractive edging to the kitchen garden.

Fruit in general requires full sun. Raspberries, blackcurrants, blackberries and loganberries are the most tolerant of partial shade. Shaded walls may be used for training gooseberries and red and white currants as cordons, and for blackberries, loganberries and Morello cherries. Remember that your trees – and fruit grown on fences – will themselves cast a shadow, so plan their positioning to avoid your vegetable garden's losing much-needed sun.

Planning your requirements

Think very carefully about your planning; it may be some years before mistakes are revealed, and then you have lost both time and money. Check the yield of the mature tree, bush or cane before buying it, and plan to spread out your harvest over the maximum period without a glut. If you have a home freezer or plan to bottle fruit, use your space intelligently; your family will tire of a single crop.

Many species crop over a couple of months at least. Choose varieties that will spread your harvest, and spread out the season to the utmost for favorite fruits. In a very small space, it may be better to rely on shop produce at the height of the season, and grow your own for the early and late seasons, when the bought price is higher.

Take care with tree fruit, however. With apples, pears and many of the best plums, you will have to select varieties that flower at the same time (and therefore crop near together) in order to get cross-pollination. Even self-fertilizing varieties of these trees crop better when cross-pollinated.

Types of tree

When buying, choose two-year-old fruit trees and two-year-old soft fruit. Do not imagine that by buying an older tree you will shorten the waiting time before mature cropping. Young trees transplant better, and if you buy those on dwarfing rootstock they will quickly come to bearing. Maiden trees, that is unformed one-year whips, are cheaper and you can train them to your chosen shape, but cropping is more delayed.

Dwarfing rootstocks are available for apples and pears. These induce early cropping and ensure that the tree will never become too large for its garden surroundings. A standard, half-standard or even a full-size bush on a vigorous rootstock is too large for the average garden; it would require a ladder for picking and pruning, and many of the branches would be out of the reach of ordinary garden sprays.

Rootstocks are carefully classified and are bred vegetatively, so that they are always true to type. They influence the growth and behavior of the tree, while having little effect on the flavor, size or appearance of the fruit.

The top part of the tree (known as the scion) is worked onto the rootstock by budding or grafting. To bud a tree, the nursery will make a slit in the bark or the stem of the rootstock soon after midsummer and bind into it a growth bud from the chosen variety with a little shield of bark.

Rootstocks conform to nationwide standards and offer protection against disease. Scions are also taken from virus-tested mother trees where available. Rootstocks can also be chosen to suit a particular climatic area, to make the variety chosen more suitable to local conditions.

CROPPING SEASONS FOR FRUIT

Late winter:	Forced rhubarb.
Mid-spring:	Strawberries forced in heated greenhouse, early forced rhubarb.
Late spring:	Early strawberries under Hotkaps or tunnels, the first thinning of gooseberries for cooking, rhubarb.
Early summer:	Gooseberry thinnings for cooking, strawberries in the open, early sweet cherries, black, red and white currants, raspberries.
Midsummer:	Early apples and pears, sweet cherries and cherry plums (Myrobalan), early plums, early peaches, nectarines and apricots. Loganberries and other hybrid berries, black currants, red and white currants, gooseberries, raspberries, strawberries, blueberries.
Late summer:	Early apples and pears, mid-season peaches and nectarines, plums and gages, apricots, later sweet cherries and cooking cherries, blackberries and later hybrid berries, black currants, figs, gooseberries, late summer raspberries, everbearing strawberries, blueberries, mulberries, grapes.
Early autumn:	Apples, pears, plums, damsons and grapes, late peaches and nectarines, blackberries, figs, autumn raspberries, perpetual strawberries, last of the blueberries and grapes.
Mid-autumn:	Apples and pears, quinces, strawberries, grapes, the last outdoor figs.
Late autumn:	Apples, everbearing strawberries under cover, late grapes.
Winter:	Stored apples, pears, grapes with stalks in water.

Garden hygiene

Cleanliness in the garden leads to healthy, heavily cropping plants, just as much as hygiene in the home ensures freedom from human and animal disease. Key points to remember are:

1. Keep the garden clear of various kinds of debris – bricks, stones, wood, logs, glass, old machinery and rotting weeds and leaves that are not made into a proper compost heap. Otherwise they will harbor slugs, insects and particularly mice.

2. Tools and machinery should be kept scrupulously clean.

3. Be on the alert for the first pest or rotting leaf on a plant. Destroy virus-infected plants as soon as seen; also badly diseased vegetation. Do not put them on the compost heap.

4. Roots of vegetables should be dug up when the tops have been harvested, die-back shoots on fruit pruned off and bonfire material burned frequently instead of leaving it for months at a time.

5. Constant vigilance and control of weeds – deal with them before they set seed. Out-of-the-way and unused areas of ground should be kept clear and free from weeds, too.

Sterilization of the soil will free it from soil-borne pests and diseases. Wash down the interiors of greenhouses, frames and hotbeds and all greenhouse equipment with sterilizing solution.

DEALING WITH WEEDS

There are three groups of weeds: annuals, biennials and perennials.

The annuals have shallow roots and abundant seed. Annual weeds can usually be fairly easily controlled by regular hoeing off and digging up before the flowers develop and set seed, as they die when their tops are removed.

Biennial weeds tend to develop a swollen root or stem below the ground which stores food for flower and seed development in the second year. Few of these are troublesome; they should be destroyed in the first year.

Perennial weeds are difficult to deal with, as they mostly have tenacious and spreading root-systems, and will spread rapidly by means of these if not treated. Sporadic digging, hoeing and hand removal are ineffective, although regular removal of the top growth by cutting or mowing will eventually eradicate them. This prevents food being stored in the roots of rhizomes, which therefore die of starvation. Mulching the top growth heavily is a long term method of control.

Using weedkillers

Modern weedkillers fall into three groups also. Firstly the **non-selective** or total kinds; they kill all plant growth, weeds or not, and in general are applied to the soil, to be absorbed through the plants' roots. The use of these is limited to uncultivated areas such as paths, or ground which needs to be cleared for future use, and they include sodium chlorate, dichlobenil and simazine. One or two, however, are suitable for use around crops, at much less concentrated rates. Secondly, there are the **selective** or hormone types, which are applied in solution to the top growth through which they are absorbed and then circulate around the plant's system in the sap. These mostly deal with broad-leaved plants. If painted or sponged carefully onto the weeds growing amongst crops, there should be no harm to the crop, as its top growth will not have been treated. Such weedkillers include those known as 2,4-D, 2,4,5-T, MCPA, mecoprop and so on. Finally there are the **residuals,** formulated to control and kill weed seeds in the soil as they germinate. These are applied in solution to the soil, and can be put on before or, with care, after planting. They can be effective for up to ten weeks. The residual herbicides include chloroxuron, chlorpropham and propachlor. With all these it is extremely important to follow the manufacturers' directions exactly and ascertain if they are locally permitted.

STERILIZATION

Soil used for potting, propagation and greenhouse growing does not have the normal benefit of crop rotation. The soil becomes 'unhealthy' and pests and diseases associated with a particular plant can accumulate. These must be destroyed by sterilization if good growth is to continue. The alternative is to change the soil every three years – a costly and laborious job.

Soil can be sterilized by heat or by chemicals. Although heat sterilization is more thorough and heat-treated soil is ready for immediate use, chemicals are more convenient and less expensive for the home gardener.

Chemical sterilization

The main chemical sterilants are formaldehyde and cresylic acid, which are diluted according to the maker's instructions and watered into the soil where they change into gases. Another chemical sterilant is dazomet, which is applied in solid form. These are all selective in their action – formaldehyde is more effective against diseases than pests, while cresylic acid destroys pests more thoroughly than fungi. Remember that all chemical sterilants can irritate the skin, eyes, nose and mouth, so use them with care.

Method

1. Sterilants cannot spread properly through soil that is too wet. It should be just wet enough to retain its shape when pressed in the hand.

2. The temperature of the soil should be between 16-26°C [60-80°F].

3. If dealing with the soil of the greenhouse floor, dig it 15-20 cm [6-8"] deep before sterilizing it. Make sure the soil is free from clods and lumps.

4. Sterilization is perfectly safe in the open air, but in the confined space of the greenhouse it should not be done near growing plants. Add 5 L [1 gal] dilute solution of formaldehyde to 0.03 cu m [1 cu ft] soil, and mix thoroughly with a spade. The best results are obtained from sandy soils; soils high in clay and humus may need a higher dosage. Cover the heap with a plastic sheet or burlap for 48 hours.

5. Remove the cover and spread the soil out to dry. Turn the soil over several times during the next few weeks to clear the fumes. The soil must not be used for planting for at least six weeks.

6. As pests and diseases can be harbored in cracks, apply the chemical thoroughly around walls and any supporting posts. Remember to spray or wash the inside of the greenhouse before starting on the soil.

Heat sterilization

Soil treated with heat can be used immediately. There are a number of different methods. A **steam sterilizer** consists of a galvanized water tank enclosing a metal soil container which fits tightly over a water trough, heated electrically from below. Follow the maker's instructions. **Boiling** is an alternative. Trays of potting soil mix can be sterilized by thoroughly drenching with boiling water. To sterilize very small quantities of soil, bring 0.3 L [½ pt] of water to the boil in a 3.4 L [6 pt] saucepan, then fill to within 1.5 cm [½"] of the top with very dry soil, cover tightly and boil for 7 minutes. Remove from heat. Be sure to follow quantity and timing instructions exactly. Cool for another 7 minutes before removing the lid. **Electrode sterilizers,** made from metal, consist of a box containing electrical plates. Soil is packed around these, and a current is passed through it, warming it up. Follow the manufacturer's instructions.

Tools

A gardener's tools will be in constant use, so buy the best tools you can possibly afford – they do a better job and last much longer. The basic tools are the spade, fork, hoe, trowel and rake. Apart from the tools described below, there are a few other items which are very useful. For hoses and watering cans, *see* WATERING. A pair of gardening gloves is helpful for pruning and can be worn for almost any gardening job to protect the hands. A wheelbarrow is usually indispensable. Choose a galvanized barrow and not a painted steel one. There are many different makes available; balance is the most important factor to bear in mind, so try out the barrow with something in it before buying. If you have a small garden and no room for a barrow, a sturdy plastic container will do instead. A sieve or screen, of 1.5 cm [½″] mesh will enable you to refine your own soil, compost or leaf mold, thus saving you money. A ladder or step-ladder is very useful for pruning or harvesting large fruit trees; this should be either hardwood or rustproof aluminum. When you finish using any tools, always clean them. Rinse off all dirt, dry and then wipe with a little oil. After cleaning, tools should be put away somewhere reasonably dry and clean. The best method of storage is to hang them on sturdy nails or hooks in a shed or on a protected wall. Smaller implements can fit on a shelf. Never leave tools lying on the ground or floor – they can cause accidents.

1. Watering can
This is the most useful shape. Metal cans are more serviceable than plastic. *See* WATERING section.

2. The spade
The spade, the most basic of all garden tools, is used for heavy digging. A full-sized standard spade with a blade 30 cm [1′] long and 20 cm [8″] wide is ideal. Make sure the joint between the shaft and blade is strong. Spades come in different weights, so choose one to suit you. The 'D-shaped' and 'Y'-shaped-handles are least tiring to use.

3. Digging fork
The fork breaks the soil into small lumps. A digging fork usually has four tines (prongs). As with spades, there are different sizes, weights and types of handle. The tines of a good fork should twang like a tuning fork.

4. Potato fork
Used for lifting potatoes, this will spare the potatoes but let the soil through.

5. Manure fork
Farmyard manure will be difficult to shake off from an ordinary fork when it is to be spread. The answer is a manure fork which has three short, round tines from which the manure slips off.

6. The rake
The rake combs out small stones from the surface of the soil, producing the fine tilth needed for sowing seeds. Rake heads come in various sizes but 23 cm [9″] is good between plants. There are different-shaped heads but those cut from one piece of metal are strongest. A wooden rake is also useful for clearing up garden refuse.

7. Dutch hoe
Hoes loosen the top layer of compacted soil and cut off young weed seedlings. Ideally, you should have a small and large hoe for different row sizes.
The Dutch hoe, which should be the smaller one, is held with the handle low enough to keep the blade nearly parallel with the soil surface, skimming just beneath it to cut or uproot weedlets. Work pushing the blade away from you.

8. Draw hoe
The handle of a draw hoe is held higher than the Dutch hoe, and is worked towards you with an up-and-down chopping movement. This should be the larger hoe. The draw hoe is also used for 'earthing-up' and making seed drills.

9. Five-pronged cultivator
This is a very useful tool that does the same job as the hoes, but covers a larger area more quickly.

10. Hand trowel
The hand trowel is for potting and planting out seedlings. Short-handled types are much less tiring than long-handled ones. Buy a trowel with a tough blade welded or riveted to the handle; pressed steel blades are cheaper but are a false economy.

11. Hand-fork
This complements the hand trowel and can be used for sticky clay soils.

12. Dibber or dibble
The dibber makes clean neat holes for planting seedlings. Metal-tipped or wooden types are available, or you can make your own from the top of an old wooden spade handle.

13. Garden line
The garden line is essential for making straight and parallel drills. You can make it yourself with two sharp sticks, about 30 cm [1′] long and a piece of thick, strong cord a little longer than the rows you are planting.

14. Measuring stick
Some gardeners dispense with this, and guess sowing distances. However, seeds are becoming expensive and it is annoying to find you have some leftover because you misjudged distances. You cannot buy a stick. Also it is cheaper to make your own; use a 2 m [6′] length of lath and mark it with paint or cut notches every 15 cm [6″].

15. Pruning shears
Pruners are essential if you are growing fruit. Only buy the best quality, as blunt blades do irreparable damage.

16. Long-handled pruner
This is used for pruning high branches of fruit trees. It works on a lever system, with a handle at the bottom to move the small hook blade at the top.

17. Pruning saw
For thick branches which pruners will not cut, use a pruning saw. This has a sharp blade which may be slightly curved.

18. Gardener's knife
The gardener's knife has many uses, from pruning small branches to crop harvesting. Buy a good quality knife and always keep it sharp.

19. Syringes and sprayers
Both of these have two functions: to apply liquid insecticides when needed, and also water when moisture is required. The best types have 2 or 3 nozzles, for fine and coarse sprays. The barrel should be of non-corrodible alloy. Sprayers with double-acting pumps give a continuous spray after initial pumping. Syringes are useful for applying small amounts of liquid. Both syringes and sprayers should be washed out with clean water after spraying a chemical.

Improving the soil

The importance of humus
Humus is an organic substance obtained from decayed plant and animal matter. Manure, compost, seaweed, etc. are all humus-supplying materials. Humus is essential to good soil texture and there is seldom enough already in garden soil. It must be added regularly in proportion to the intensity of cultivation.

Types of soil
The basic soils are clay, sand and loam, and these fundamentally differ only in the size of the grains that make up their structure.

Loam is a soil composed of clay, silt, sand and organic matter; it is ideal for the majority of crops – well-drained, warming up quickly and retaining nutrients over a long period, Improvements to other types of soil are made to bring them nearer to the composition of loam.

Clay soil is made up of small particles, which are closely packed. Because of its physical properties, water is held in it and it can become wet and waterlogged. Properly conditioned clay soil can be very fertile because it retains nutrients. To improve a clay soil, add rotting organic, fibrous material and some coarse sand to open up the structure, mixing both well into the top part. You can help break up a clay soil further by adding lime, if it is at all acid or gypsum, if already alkaline, as this has a neutral reaction. Never attempt to work a clay soil when it is wet – it may set like cement and be very difficult to break down subsequently.

Sandy soil is made up of comparatively large particles. Water runs through it rapidly, carrying away plant foods, and it dries very quickly. Properly conditioned, it has the advantage of excellent drainage and easy penetration by plant roots, as well as warming up quickly in spring, making it very suitable for early crops. To improve a sandy soil, again add coarse organic material, to give it sponge-like bulk and hold it together. You can tell, with practice, which kind of soil you have by feeling it when wet. A clay type will be definitely sticky and clinging; a sandy one will feel gritty, and a loam, if squeezed in the hand when moist but not saturated, should fall apart with a gentle tap.

Soil testing
Beyond basic improvement of soil types, the most common problems are highly acid and highly alkaline soils. In a too-acid soil many nutrients dissolve in large quantities, which are damaging to plant roots. In an excessively alkaline one, some plant foods are insoluble so that, although they are present, the plant roots cannot absorb them. The plant then suffers from a deficiency and shows symptoms of illness accordingly.

A simple soil test kit bought from a garden center or garden shop will help assess the soil to determine the degree of acidity or alkalinity – the pH value. Inexpensive soil test kits are based on indicator solutions – colored dyes that change in tint during the test. Precise instructions are given with each type of kit sold, but the principle is that samples of soil are taken from the area in question, shaken up with water and indicator solution and allowed to settle. The color of the resultant solution is then compared to a test card showing varied color bands. The band which matches gives the reading of the pH value of the soil being tested.

Redressing the balance
If the soil is too acid, add lime at the rates suggested in the directions. The addition of lime to a very acid soil not only ensures that plants do not suffer from poisonously great quantities of nutrient, but it also helps a great deal in improving the soil structure of heavy clay soils. Further, some vegetable diseases thrive in acid soils, and lime is a necessity if vulnerable crops are to be grown. Lime also supplies calcium, a necessary nutrient.

There are various types of lime: chalk (calcium carbonate), good for light soils; hydrated lime (air-slaked lime); ground lime, like chalk but slower-acting; quicklime (calcium oxide), caustic (not recommended in the U.S.), gypsum (calcium sulphate), neutral in reaction, and magnesium limestone, containing magnesium.

If the soil is too alkaline, build up the soil depth if possible and add an acid-reacting fertilizer such as sulphate of ammonia and/or organic matter, which buffers the effect of the alkalinity on the soil.

Making a compost heap

Garden compost is a mixture of vegetable waste materials which are collected together in a special container or an enclosed heap and left to rot down. Properly made and well rotted, it can take the place of animal manures and do just as much good when added to the soil. It is always necessary to add some organic matter to the soil to supply plants with nutrients and to give the soil a good structure. Fertilizers will provide food but no humus; only rotted organic matter can supply this substance. It is vital if plants growing in soil are to develop satisfactorily, especially vegetables.

Making your own garden compost
Animal manures and other organic matter are often difficult to obtain and sometimes rather expensive. If you cannot obtain any or want to cut down on expenses, you can make your own compost easily and at almost no cost.
In order to make good compost, certain conditions will be necessary:
1. Air to supply oxygen.
2. Moisture.
3. Warmth, both within and outside the heap.
4. Nitrogen.
All these enable the bacteria which work on the organic matter to live and multiply. A closely compressed heap without air, with too much or too little water, or with not enough warmth or nitrogen will not allow the heap to rot because the bacteria cannot live.

What goes on the heap
You can make the heap of any soft vegetable material: leaves, stems, grass mowings, flowers and so on. All these will supply nitrogen. Large stalks and roots, like those from cauliflowers, Brussels sprouts and similar plants will only rot quickly if they are split in half from top to bottom. If you do not think this worthwhile, leave them out of your heap. Equally, tough woody stems, leathery or evergreen leaves, bark and wood do not rot quickly enough and should not be used. Nor should the heap be regarded as a dump for stones, glass, plastic or any other rubbish. Disease and pest-ridden plants should be burned, as should really bad weeds, any self-propagating rhizomes and all weed

seeds, in case the heap does not heat up sufficiently to kill them. You can also put kitchen vegetable waste on the heap – potato peelings, fruit skins, cabbage leaves, and so on. Crushed egg shells will not rot down but are good to add for their calcium content. Coffee grounds and tea leaves are also excellent additions. Bones, fat, cheese rind or similar waste must not be put on the heap because they will attract rats and mice.
The size of the heap will depend on how much garden material you have. Grass cuttings are best to form the main part of it. The usual size is 90 x 90 x 90 cm [3 x 3 x 3'], which will provide about half a ton of compost. But it can be 1.2 or 1.5 m [4 or 5'] high and the same width and length, or as small as 45 x 45 x 60 cm [1½ x 1½ x 2']. The more quickly the heap is made up the more quickly it will heat up and rot. Heaps made from spring to late summer should be ready for use in about 6-12 weeks; the late autumn ones will not finish breaking down until the following mid-spring or later.

Constructing the heap
When you begin to build the heap you can either contain it with wire netting, corrugated iron or wood, or use one of the commercially sold compost containers. A square container of 5 cm [2"] wire netting supported at each corner with wooden posts is made easily and quickly. The lower 23 cm [9"] of each post should be treated with a wood preservative, and the netting attached by staples. The front posts should be 1.5 m [5'] long, the other two 1.2 m [4']. The heap is built directly onto the soil, but aeration is helped if you make a base about 2.5 cm [1"] deep from woody stems. Build the heap in layers 15-20 cm [6-8"] deep of vegetative material followed by 2.5 cm [1"] of soil with a sprinkling of lime on top of this to prevent the heap becoming too acid. Repeat these layers to the height you have decided on. Cover the heap with a sack each time you finish adding to it. When it is completed, one may cover it with corrugated iron to keep out excess rain. This should be lain on top of the posts and project over the sides by about 10 cm [4"]. The higher front posts

of the heap will give the roof a backward slant so rain will run off. In most climates, however, we need the water. When making the heap tread it a little to get rid of large air pockets and keep the surface even and level, not mounded up in the center and sloping at the sides. If the weather is dry, spray each layer lightly with water. You can also use commercially sold activators to speed up the rotting down process. These are sold as powders which are scattered over the heap as the manufacturers direct on top of each new layer.
The sides of the heap should be turned to the middle occasionally so that the whole heap rots evenly and completely. This will also prevent an unpleasant odor from developing.
When the heap is ready it should consist of dark brown, crumbly material, rather like fibrous soil. If you can still see the shapes of the original plant material, it is not yet fit for use.

Using your garden compost
Garden compost is dug in at the rate of about 5 kg per sq m [10 lb per sq yd] if the soil is very short of humus as with a stony or sandy soil. Otherwise, on a reasonably good soil it can be used at 2.5 kg per sq m [5 lb per sq yd]. As with other kinds of organic matter this is done either in autumn when preparing for vegetables or about a month in advance of planting trees or soft fruit.

Mulches and top-dressings
Garden compost can also be used as a mulch or top-dressing. The mulch is a layer of material spread evenly over the soil surface around the plants, covering the area to which the roots extend. Mulches keep the soil moist and blot out weeds, and are put on in late spring to early summer. This function is distinct from any addition of nutrients. Any material which has not been absorbed by autumn is forked in.
Top-dressings are very similar, but heavier. They are put on in autumn or early spring mainly for the purpose of supplying food and humus. (The term top-dressing is also used in gardening to mean the addition of powdered fertilizer around growing plants.)

Long-term value of a compost heap
To start with, you may find that your garden does not supply sufficient vegetative material for composting to make good the lack of humus in the soil. In this case, farmyard manure or other organic matter is worth buying at first. The quantity of vegetative material from your own cropping will gradually increase, year by year. As the application of compost continues it will build up, and the garden will eventually become more self-supporting.

HOW TO MAKE A SIMPLE HEAP
(see below)

A square container of 5 cm [2″] wire netting supported by wooden posts is quick and easy to make. The lower 23 cm [9″] of the posts should be treated with wood preservative and the netting nailed to the posts. The two front posts should be 1.5 m [5′] high and the two back posts 1.2 m [4′] high. The heap can be built directly on the soil, but a base of woody stems about 2.5 cm [1″] deep laid on top of the soil helps aeration. Build the heap in layers 15-20 cm [6-8″] deep of vegetative material, followed by 2.5 cm [1″] of soil and a sprinkling of lime on top of this. Spray the heap lightly with water if it is dry, and turn it occasionally. Cover the heap with burlap each time you finish adding to it. When it is completed, cover it with a roof of corrugated iron. The higher front posts make the roof slant so that rain runs off. Add extensions as shown below for continuous composting.

Wooden slats make a neat and effective bin. Leave ventilation gaps between slats.

A three-sided brick-walled bin is more permanent and is neat and handy to use.

Poles make an easily constructed bin. Remove poles in turn to reach compost.

A strong circular wire container is well-ventilated and easy to lift away.

Fertilizers

The fertility of garden soils was traditionally maintained by the use of large quantities of farmyard manure. This kept the soil in good physical condition and supplied adequate amounts of mineral nutrients. Today, this is no longer always practical and other methods of feeding have been evolved, using a combination of natural and chemical substances.

A plant's mineral requirements

There are various mineral elements essential to plant growth which must be present in the soil. Three which are required in fairly high quantities are: nitrogen (N), phosphorus (P) and potassium (K). These key elements, NPK, form the basis of plant feeding and constitute most commercial fertilizers. Supplies of magnesium (Mg) are also needed in some instances; calcium (Ca) and sulphur (S) do not, on the whole, need replenishing as most soils contain plenty of these, although calcium is commonly added as lime.

Other mineral foods such as iron, manganese, copper, zinc, boron and molybdenum are classified as trace elements. These are just as important but are only needed in minute quantities by the plant. Some soils contain adequate reserves of these.

Functions of individual elements

Each of these elements has its own role to play in the plant. Nitrogen favors vigorous vegetative growth, while potassium gives sturdiness and encourages flowering and fruiting. Phosphorus is important in all parts of the plant but is of special value for healthy root growth. Magnesium is important for the production of chlorophyll. The roles of the remaining two elements, calcium and sulphur, are more general. The trace elements as a group are involved in many of the key growth processes. Deficiencies of any show up in a variety of ways such as regular yellow patterns, browning, stunting or malformed growth.

Factors affecting plant nutrition

The type of soil can have major affects on the availability of plant foods; all soils contain micro-organisms which break down organic matter such as manure, or garden compost. Regular applications of this type of material will improve the soil structure, thus making it easier for plant roots to grow and absorb as much of the available food as they need.

Most plants are tolerant of fairly wide differences in soil acidity (pH) although they generally do best in soils near neutrality. For this reason the fertility of very acid soils is increased by the addition of lime.

Excessive applications of one plant food can lead to a deficiency of another in the plant. For instance, in the case of potassium, too much will be absorbed at the expense of magnesium, especially with tomatoes.

Weather conditions can affect the intake of nutrients by plants. In cold, frosty weather, there is little or no uptake, so fertilizer applied then will not be of use until spring. Also, the more soluble plant foods may be washed out of the root zone by winter rain. Dressings are therefore best given during the growing season.

Types of fertilizers

Fertilizers are commonly divided into two main types, namely "organic" and "inorganic". They are distinguished by the fact that, generally speaking, the former are obtained from animal or vegetable materials while the latter are either natural minerals or manufactured products.

The most commonly used nitrogenous fertilizers are sulphate of ammonia (21%N), dried blood (12%N) (both quick-acting), and nitrate of soda (15%) (quick-acting). Phosphatic fertilizers consist of: bonemeal (16-32% P_2O_5), very slow-acting even when finely ground; superphosphate of lime (13-18% P_2O_5), quick-responding because of its ready solubility, and basic slag, slow-acting and an industrial by-product which has a variable content of phosphate and also supplies lime. The potash salt generally available to the gardener is sulphate of potash (48-50% K_2O), fairly quick-acting; wood-ash is also good (up to 10% K_2O).

Magnesium is available as Epsom salts (10% Mg) or as Dolomite limestone. The former, although quick-acting, has relatively short persistence, while the latter acts slowly but lasts longer.

Application

It is important that fertilizers should be used at the recommended rate and the dressing applied evenly all over the treated area. Too high a concentration can cause serious damage to roots and may kill off seeds and seedlings.

Fertilizers can be applied either as solids or liquid. The solid fertilizers provide fairly high quantities of plant food which are sufficient for several weeks or months. Liquid feeds supply rather small quantities of immediately available plant food and are valuable for producing quick bursts of growth, as a method of changing the NPK balance at critical stages in the growth of plants and for the correction of minor element deficiencies.

Normally liquid feeds are poured onto the soil but some can be applied as foliar feeds. Very frequent applications are needed for worthwhile effects. This method of application, however, can be of value in cases where root development has been restricted.

It is a legal requirement in the U.S. that the plant food content of a fertilizer be given on the package, the quantity of each nutrient being expressed as a percentage of the total weight.

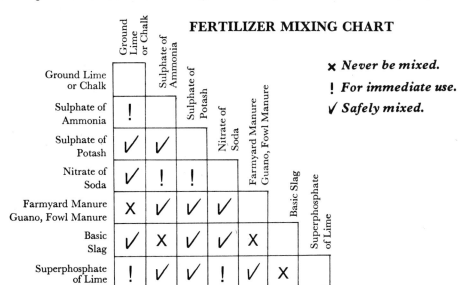

FERTILIZER MIXING CHART

✗ *Never be mixed.*

! *For immediate use.*

✓ *Safely mixed.*

	Ground Lime or Chalk	Sulphate of Ammonia	Sulphate of Potash	Nitrate of Soda	Farmyard Manure Guano, Fowl Manure	Basic Slag	Superphosphate of Lime
Ground Lime or Chalk							
Sulphate of Ammonia	!						
Sulphate of Potash	✓	✓					
Nitrate of Soda	✓	!	!				
Farmyard Manure Guano, Fowl Manure	✗	✓	✓	✓			
Basic Slag	✓	✗	✓	✓	✗		
Superphosphate of Lime	!	✓	✓	!	✓	✗	

Seeds and seed beds

Quality

Buy from reputable seedsmen whenever possible. Their seed will have a minimum germination percentage and most firms date-stamp their packets to prevent old seed being sold. As seeds are seriously affected by storage and age, some firms pack them in sealed humidity-proof packets. Seeds packed in these will remain fresh for several years but once the packets are opened, normal aging begins.

Many seeds are described as F_1 Hybrids, and cost more than the others because the plants which produce them have to be hand-pollinated. However, they are much stronger, or have other worthwhile characteristics. As seeds saved from F_1 Hybrids will not yield plants true to type, buy new seeds yearly.

Saving your own seed

It is sometimes useful to save seed from your own plants but only from 'fixed' species, which will not hybridize with other species. Collect the seed when the plants are ready to shed it, clean it and keep it in a dry, cool place until needed.

Seed separation and germination

Seed should be sown as near the correct time as possible in the year in which it is bought, unless specially packed, otherwise leave the packets unopened in a reasonably steady, cool temperature. Never store in a damp place.

The most suitable germination temperatures for the common outdoor vegetables is from 7 to 16°C [45 to 60°]. If germination is likely to be difficult, soaking the seed overnight will help when the seed has a thick skin or shell, or the skin can be chipped with a razor blade. Seed can be protected with special powder dressings in case of attack from fungi or pests.

'Damping off' is a fungus disease which infects seedlings, so that they turn black at soil level and fall over. Crowded, damp conditions and unsterilized soil encourage it. Prevent or cure it by watering with an approved preventive material.

SOWING UNDER GLASS

Many half-hardy crops are best sown in a greenhouse or frame where the temperature is about 18°C [65°F]. It is more economical to use a propagator for this, consisting of a heated base plate, a plastic tray and clear plastic dome, than to heat the whole greenhouse or frame. Seeds can be sown in trays or pots; the modern plastic trays retain heat and moisture better than the traditional wooden ones. Pots can be made of clay, plastic, peat or other materials. All should have adequate drainage holes.

The soil medium used for the seed should be seed mixture, consisting either of a mixture of sterilized loam, peat and sand, with a little lime and fertilizer added, or mostly of peat.

In seed trays

Fill the seed tray with moist mixture to within 1 cm [½″] of the rim, firm it with the fingers and then level with a board. Water the medium by putting the tray in a shallow container of water and letting it soak upward, then put aside to drain. Sow the seed thinly on the surface, sift a fine layer of mixture over it, and firm gently. Label and date the seed, and cover with black plastic sheet until germination occurs. If you do not need the whole tray for one type of seed, you can divide it into sections with thin wooden slats and sow several types.

In pots

The bigger seeds, and seedlings likely to have sensitive roots, can be sown in pots. Put broken pieces of clay pot in the bottom of clay pots (unnecessary for other kinds), fill with seed mixture to within 1 cm [½″] of the rim, and sow two seeds per pot. When they germinate, remove the weakest. Peat pots are buried whole.

Pricking out and hardening off

Seeds sown in trays will soon outgrow the space available. They must then be pricked out, i.e. transferred to another tray, with a spacing of 5 cm [2″] each way between each seedling. Use potting mixture for this and prick out when two seed leaves have been produced, and the first true leaf is beginning to appear. Lift each seedling gently, holding a leaf, not the stem, and replant, using a seed label as a dibber, so that the stem is buried up to the seed leaves.

As the weather gets warmer, the young plants can be gradually acclimatized to the outside. Put them in a cold frame, leaving the frame light open a little at first during the warm part of the day, but closed otherwise. Gradually increase the exposure before planting out.

SOWING OUTSIDE

An open but sheltered, sunny site is nearly always preferable as it suffers less from waterlogging and warms up earlier in the year than a shaded site.

Preparing the plot

The ground should have been dug for clearing, and limed, if necessary, preferably some months previously. Now break down lumps with a fork, remove large stones and any remaining weeds, and form a reasonably level surface by forking lightly and evenly. Leave the soil to settle for a few weeks, and then sprinkle with superphosphate or a complete fertilizer a few days before sowing, and rake it in.

Choose a day to sow the seed when the weather is mild and calm, and if possible with rain forecast. Seed germinates more quickly in warm soil, so do not be in too much of a hurry to sow the seed early in the season. The soil should be moist, but not wet or sticky. Tread it to firm it, then rake the plot gently to give the surface soil a fine texture, like breadcrumbs. Stand on boards laid alongside each row as you work, and cross-rake the plot. Generally rake to a depth of about 2.5 cm [1″] deeper than the drills need for the seeds.

Sowing procedure

Almost all vegetables are best sown in rows. To help you sow in a straight line, use a garden line (*see* TOOLS) close to the ground. Make a shallow furrow or drill by drawing the corner of the draw hoe along the line of the cord. Lining the drills with moist, granulated peat is often a great help to germination if the soil is sandy, or the weather hot and dry after germination.

Large or pelleted seeds can be sown individually at specific intervals, or stations. Put several together at each station to allow for possible germination failure. Later remove the weakest.

Sow fine seed thinly in a line down the drills; even so, some thinning will always be necessary. Too thick sowing will delay germination and lead to excessive thinning, which can damage the roots of the retained seedlings.

After sowing

Cover the row of seed by drawing the back of your garden rake along the drill. This tips the ridge of soil along each side of the furrow back into the center and levels off the soil. Water the row immediately with a watering can until the soil is quite moist. Light but continuous moisture must be maintained before and after germination. Be sure to label each row clearly.

Cloches and frames

CLOCHES

Cloches are used to protect plants from unfavorable weather. They may be moved around the garden to provide protection when and where necessary. Used intensively, cloches will give year-round benefit, but if two or more crops are to be grown in the same plot in one year, remember to double the amount of organic matter incorporated.

There are a large number of designs used abroad, made either out of glass or plastic glass-substitutes. The simplest

tent cloche

cloche design is the tent type which consists of two sheets of glass held in an inverted V shape. More sophisticated are the T, or flat-topped barn cloche with three sheets, and the pitch-roofed barn cloche with four.

barn shape

Uusually, the glass is made in standard lengths of 60 cm [2'] and the cloches themselves are 23-60 cm [9"-2'] wide. Plastic cloches are made either from thin plastic sheets or from more rigid plastic or PVC. The thinner materials are held in place by half hoops of galvanized wire, dug into the ground for anchorage. The thicker types may be held between metal sections or framed like glass. The lengths of these cloches vary considerably from about 45 cm

plastic sheeting tunnel

[18"] to 90 cm [3']. Widths also vary, but 45 cm [18"] is the most popular.

Choosing which cloche

Plastic cloches are cheap to make, light to handle and easy to store. But they

wire-enforced plastic

lose heat too quickly to help in frosty weather and all but the most expensive deteriorate quicker than glass. Glass cloches give more protection and are better in winter. They are more substantial and easier to use in more exposed gardens but are also more vulnerable to breakage. They can be bought in a greater variety of sizes and some incorporate ventilation panels, for growing a wider range of plants to maturity. Some European cloches are now made with adaptors which raise their height. The cloche is held on wire stilts with the gaps at the sides filled in with two extra sheets of glass.

Use of cloches

Cloches fulfil many useful functions. During wet or cold weather, they can be used to cover soil to keep it warm and dry. This will enable you to sow or plant much earlier than in open beds. They will protect plants and seedlings from cold and wind, extending your growing season significantly and bringing plants through the winter. Ends of rows of cloches should normally be kept sealed

with sheets of glass or plastic to stop the row becoming a wind tunnel.

FRAMES

Frames are more permanent structures than cloches but like them they make use of trapped sun heat. They protect plants on four sides and have removable tops or lights. This enables you to sow earlier than in the open. They can also be used to shelter tender plants during the wetter and colder winter months, to force certain crops out of season and to 'harden off' greenhouse-raised plants.

Types of frame

Many different types of frame are available. Some have brick or concrete bases

square plastic cloche

with glass sides; other have brick, concrete or wooden sides. The top of the frame, the light, may be hinged or sliding and the framework made either of wood or metal. All frames have a deep back and shallow front. The dimensions vary considerably, but there should always be adequate room between the tops of the plants and the light. The Dutch frame has a single light made of a large pane of glass, supported on a wooden frame. The light

Dutch light

slides into grooves in the inside faces of the timber and is secured by a short wooden strip screwed into the base plate of the frame. No putty is used, making it simple to replace broken glass.

English frame

The English type is larger, with several smaller panes of glass supported by longitudinal glazing bars. The latest frame designs use plastics or fiberglass. The former are quite cheap to buy, the

all-glass frame

latter expensive. Plastic sheets may be used instead of glass panes, and require only a light wooden framework. A few designs have clear side and end sections as well; these give good results except in cold weather.

Heated frames

Frames are usually unheated, but the development of safe electric warming cables has made it quite easy to convert cold frames by laying cables in the soil or around the walls. Adding heat increases the versatility of the frame considerably, making it in effect a miniature greenhouse.

Watering

Watering can be a problem in frame gardening, as the soil can dry out quickly in warm weather. The best solution is mist irrigation which involves a rigid plastic water pipe fixed to the frame roof. The pipe has a series of brass nozzles which provide an even, fine mist of water.

Positioning the frame

It is very important to put the frame in the best possible growing position. Ideally it should face the sun, but if this is not possible it must be placed where it is sheltered from cold prevailing winds and will receive maximum sunlight.

Soil preparation

The soil for the frame needs careful preparation. The area should be dug out to a depth of 30-40 cm [12-16″] and the bottom of the hole covered with a 10 cm [4″] layer of small rubble and weathered cinders. If the subsoil is heavy, break it up with a fork before putting in the drainage material. The rest of the hole should be filled with a specially prepared mixture. The formula used depends on whether the frame is for seedlings or for growing plants to maturity. In small frames it is a good idea to use seed trays or pots for seed raising, and to grow plants to maturity in the prepared frame soil.

Watering

Water in the soil

Water not only keeps plants upright (if they lack moisture they will wilt) but also carries with it nutrients from the soil, some of which are used in the leaves for photosynthesis. Thus plants deprived of water cannot grow, but it is equally important that they never become waterlogged. The roots must be able to breathe, which means that some air pockets must always be left in the soil. As water drains from the soil after rainfall it pulls air in behind it, supplying roots with the air they need. Drowning a plant with water will suffocate the roots. All soils have water tables (natural water levels). To ascertain a high water table, dig downward until the bottom of the hole fills with water. The top of the water is the same level as the water table. Generally, water tables rise in winter as there is more rain and less evaporation than in summer. Never plant fruit trees and bushes in ground with high water tables in the winter, as the roots will suffocate.

How much water

Water should be given in large quantities, and only when necessary. Roots follow water, so proper irrigation and heavy rains keep the roots down, searching for water at low soil levels. A daily sprinkle of water is inadvisable as this keeps the surface roots supplied, but leaves the plant prone to real drought in dry conditions. A lot of water every four or five days is the best method. The question of how much and when is more critical for container-grown crops than for those grown in open ground. Water must be given *before* the plants wilt.

When to water

Water should be given very early in the morning and always before the sun is strong. This is because of too great a water loss through evaporation. Evening is another good time to apply water, so that the plants absorb as much as they can hold, ready for the next day's heat.

Watering cans

For the patio and container gardener a watering can is all that is needed. Test for size and weight when full of water before buying. Plastic watering cans are lighter and less expensive than metal types, but become covered in green algae on the inside. A good size for general garden use is a 6-9 L [1½-2 gal] capacity can. This is not too heavy and carries enough to cover quite a lot of ground. Use a fine rose fixed to the spout of the can when watering seeds and young plants.

Sprinklers

Fixed sprinklers are attached to a hose and pipe supply. They have a fast rate of delivery, and need to be moved every 15 minutes. Depending on the water pressure, they will water a circle 3.6-6 m [12-20′] in diameter.
Revolving sprinklers have a fairly even distribution and rate of delivery. They cover a diameter of 7.5 m [25-50′].

Drip irrigation and spray lines

Plastic pipes are fitted with nozzles at regular intervals and water drips slowly and continuously through the nozzles. There are some disadvantages: holes can become clogged, and the pipes are awkward to move. The main advantage is the slow rate of delivery of water, like fine rain. They are particularly suitable for plants which need a good deal of water and have many fine roots such as tomatoes, cucumbers or strawberries. Spray lines are used for large areas of gardens or growing crops. Metal or plastic pipes are pierced with holes at regular intervals.

Soaking the soil

Irrigation ditches are particularly suitable for level beds or small gardens where the gardener wants to avoid sprinkling certain vegetables. It also avoids compacting the whole surface of the garden, saving a lot of cultivation. Dig the ditches before planting, 30 cm [1′] wide, 15 cm [6″] deep, making them as level as possible. Trample bottom of ditches to harden them or line with heavy plastic sheeting. Divide long ditches into 1.8 m [6′] segments on sandy soils and 3.6 m [12′] segments on heavier soils. Use a dam (e.g. a piece of metal, a board or a shovel) to slow the flow of the water and enable it to thoroughly soak that section. (Plants should be only 7-10 cm [3-4″] from the shoulder of the ditch.) Watering basins are a good method for fruit trees. Dig out a shallow basin around the base of the tree – some of the roots may be exposed. Water the basin thoroughly, replace soil, then mulch to help retain the moisture.

The greenhouse

The greenhouse will be a permanent fixture and it is quite a sizable capital asset, so it is worth taking care about the place where it will be erected.

Suitable sites

It should not be too far from the house, otherwise it tends to be neglected, expecially in cold or wet weather. Don't put it where it is likely to be in shade for even part of the day; the glass or plastic alone will cut down the light, even when perfectly clean. So watch for trees, buildings, high walls, or even possible future building on a nearby site.

Put the greenhouse where it is sheltered from strong winds, so that heat is not lost unnecessarily, and if possible align it so that it runs north to south, to get the maximum light. A position handy for a tap or stand-pipe will save a great deal of walking back and forth carrying cans of water; during hot weather you will really need a hose, as it will probably be necessary to water all the plants every day, sometimes twice, and to damp down the inside of the house. Don't put it at the bottom of a slope, however slight, which is backed by a wall or hedge; cold air will collect there, and make it particularly costly to keep the temperature high enough at night.

Easy access to electricity is likewise important, especially if you are planning to heat the greenhouse electrically or install mist propagation (*see* under **Watering** on this page).

A greenhouse is often put to one side or another of a garden; if you do this, make sure there is plenty of room behind the greenhouse for any necessary work.

Choice of greenhouse

When you are choosing a greenhouse there are various pros and cons to be considered, not always obvious if you have never owned one before. For instance, look at the number of ventilators; are they adequate for the size of the house? There should be at least two in the roof and another in one of the sides. The more there are, the more control you will have over the temperature and humidity. Houses with solid walls often have ventilating grids spaced along the walls below the bench level. Houses are sold with hinged or sliding doors; remember that with some sliding doors it is very easy for the door to become jammed with soil at the bottom, and there may be drafts where it does not fit tightly. Make sure the doorway is wide enough for a wheelbarrow.

Various materials are used for the greenhouse structure. Wood needs regular upkeep, besides being treated with preservative, in the form of painting or oiling, but it is much more convenient than metal alloys when hooks, supporting wires and plastic sheeting need to be attached to it. The glazing bars, however, being wider than metal ones, cut down the amount of light available to the plants.

Metal alloys, such as aluminum, make for a very well-lit greenhouse and need no upkeep, but the temperature variations can be greater – they can get very hot very quickly. Aluminum greenhouses are relatively expensive. Concrete is also used; it can make a very heavy-looking structure unless carefully designed, and tends to reduce the light. However, it is extremely long-lasting, needs absolutely no maintenance, and is much more stable.

Plastic walk-in tunnels are cheap and easy to put up, but do not have a very long life, generally two to four years before the plastic deteriorates and the light transmission becomes poor as a result of the sun shining on the plastic. If you want one of these, get the expected life span of the plastic from the manufacturer before you buy, and get a comparison of the light transmission through various kinds of plastic. Decide whether you want to grow plants on benches, in the soil of the greenhouse floor, or a bit of both. There are models which will suit all these. Those with glass down to the ground are best if you will be growing in the soil, but lose more heat, and will need plastic sheet insulation in winter. With brick or wooden half walls, various electric heaters can be used.

If you are going to be away in the daytime, a model with automatic ventilators is well worth considering; besides electrically operated kinds, there are those which rely on a chemical only.

Greenhouse management

It should be possible to manipulate the greenhouse environment so that the plants are always in first-class condition.

Watering

Watering is crucial; never let the plants run short whether in containers or the ground. Do not water late in the day so that there is a damp atmosphere by night, when the temperature is dropping, otherwise disease will thrive. Water container plants only when the soil surface has dried. There are a number of different automatic watering systems on the market. The capillary system involves a feed tank, operated by a ball valve, installed either inside or just outside the greenhouse, connected to the supply. Pipes from the tank feed water gradually into a bed of sand on the benches – commonly using a system of adjustable nozzles. Plants then take up water as and when they need it from the sand. Plastic pots are best. If you find it needed, insert a fiberglass wick into the drainage hole of each pot. The sand is best contained in plastic trays and a depth of 2.5 cm [1"] is needed. A more sophisticated device is the mist propagator, which releases a spray of fine mist from overhead nozzles in response to an automatic device. This is intended to maintain a moist atmosphere.

Heating and ventilation

Increase the ventilation as soon as the temperature goes above 16°C [60°F], and leave one ventilator open a crack all through winter unless the temperature is very low. Try to maintain as even a temperature as possible by manipulating the ventilation. In dull weather keep the house almost closed. When sunny give it plenty of air. Maintain moisture in the atmosphere; if the greenhouse feels comfortable to be in, it will suit the plants as well as you, and keep a good many pests at bay.

In hot weather, spray the paths, benches, soil and walls with water two or three times a day to damp them down.

When heating in winter, try to keep the temperature at 7°C [45°F] or more; low night temperatures in spring especially hold plants back and you will quickly lose the earliness of your crops. A maximum and minimum thermometer is essential, for showing the night temperature, as well as the day.

Heating for greenhouses can be powered by electricity, gas, kerosene, oil or solid fuel, which heats hot water pipes. Whichever you choose, make sure that it will provide the degree of warmth needed for the crops you are growing. In very hot summer weather, shading will be needed, from the simple greenhouse shading paints to the more sophisticated automatic shades, otherwise many plants will be literally scorched. Keep the greenhouse clean at all times, throw out decaying vegetation, and wash down with a sterilizing agent every year.

In a half-wall model, plants are grown on benches;
it is warm but less well lit than an all-glass house.

The all-glass house has panels set in a metal frame.
It admits the maximum amount of light, but loses heat.

The Dutch-light type of house encloses the maximum
floor space in relation to glass, but also loses some heat.

Lean-to models are warmer than free-standing houses,
and may consist of half of any other model.

Plastic stretched over a frame offers some protection;
it is cheaper but less long-lasting than glass.

Multi-angular glass models are good for windy sites.
They offer the maximum ground space and use of light.

Pests and diseases

The first chart, SYMPTOMS AND CAUSES, helps you to pinpoint exactly which pest or disease is affecting your plant. Once you have identified the culprit, look up the suitable treatment. Most often treatment will be given in the A to Z cultivation entry for the plant concerned. Otherwise, treatment is given in the second chart, COMMON TROUBLES. This describes the common pests and diseases that affect many plants and outlines suitable treatment.

SYMPTOMS AND CAUSES

BRASSICAS (except rutabaga and turnip): large-headed broccoli, Brussels sprouts, cabbage, cauliflower, kale, kohlrabi, sprouting broccoli.

Leaves

Large holes in outer leaves, green caterpillars present.	white cabbage butterfly
Large holes in central leaves, some in outer leaves, green caterpillars present.	cabbage moth
Large holes in leaves near ground.	slugs, snails
Large holes in outer leaves, no caterpillars.	birds
Many tiny round holes in seedling leaves and leaves of young plants.	flea beetle
Small white flying insects on undersurface; leaves grayish, sticky, may have black patches.	whitefly
Yellow areas between leaves, dark green bands alongside veins, particularly cauliflowers.	mosaic virus
Lots of small, slowly-moving, gray-blue or greenish insects on leaf undersurface, leaves distorted, plants stunted.	aphids
Leaves of young plants turn gray-green and collapse; roots, swollen and misshapen; white maggots inside when cut open.	cabbage root fly (maggot)
Leaves turn bluish and wilt; roots swollen, turn black and rot, smell unpleasant.	clubroot

Stems

Stems bitten off at or just below soil level, plants collapse – in young plants.	cutworms or slugs
Seedlings: base of stem withers and browns. Seedling dies.	damping off

Flowers

Florets of cauliflower brownish on surface of curd, extending down into stem below.	boron deficiency

LEAFY VEGETABLES (not cabbage family): cardoon, chicory, Chinese cabbage, endive, lettuce, New Zealand spinach, seakale, spinach beet, Swiss chard.

Leaves

Holes in leaves of young plants and sometimes in older ones.	slugs, snails
Leaves pale green or yellow, curled and twisted; tiny green or black insects on undersurface and on stems.	aphids
Tiny rust-colored bumps – spinach beet.	rust
Large, pale green or pale yellow patches on leaves, white mold on leaf under these areas – especially lettuce.	downy mildew
Furry gray mold in spots and patches on leaves – especially lettuce.	gray mold (Botrytis cinerea)
Leaves mottled dark and light green, very crinkled, no heart, plants stunted – lettuce.	mosaic virus
Young leaves, later older ones, yellow, pucker, roll inwards, lie limp on ground; plant dies.	spinach blight virus
Leaves yellow at tips, black leaf veins, black streaks in roots when cut across – seakale.	black rot
Leaves become slimy, turn brown and rot when being forced; also stems – seakale.	soft rot

Stems

Stems of young plants bitten through and plants topple over.	cutworms, slugs
Leaves turn yellow, wither and plant dies; when lifted, purple felt-like growth all over outside of roots – seakale, chicory.	root rot
Leaves poor color and wilt, plants small for no apparent reason, cease growing; dug up plants have small white woolly patches on roots with tiny grayish insects beneath.	root aphid

Roots

Plants stunted and slow-growing; if dug up may have small lumps on roots.	eelworms or nematodes

LEGUMES: asparagus pea, broad bean, bean, lima bean, pea, runner bean, soya bean.

Leaves

Edges eaten into half-moon-shaped holes.	pea/bean weevil
Leaves skeletonized; oval, copper-colored, 16 spotted.	Mexican bean beetle
Large chocolate-colored patches on leaves, stems and pods.	chocolate spot
Covered in small black insects. Leaves curled and pale or yellowed.	aphid
Pinprick holes with brown edges in young leaves. leaves later tattered, growing points blind.	capsid plant bugs
Pale and dark green areas on leaves, which are curled; whole plant stunted.	mosaic virus
Powdery white patches on upper surface of leaves, and on pods – peas.	powdery mildew
Irregular holes in seedlings and young leaves.	slugs
Leaves wilting and becoming gray-green.	Fusarium wilt
Leaves yellowed, curled or crinkled; small green wedge-shaped insects – young crawl sideways, adults fly.	Leaf hopper

Stems

Long, dark brown, sunken patches on stem, leaves wither, pods with reddish-brown spots.	leaf spot (anthracnose)

Pods

Holes in pods; Relatively unknown U.S., to be watched for.	white maggots
Pods torn with holes in them.	birds

STEM VEGETABLES: asparagus, celery, leek, rhubarb.

Leaves

Needle-like leaves completely eaten, small slate-colored grubs present.	asparagus beetle
Pale brown blisters and tunnels in leaves.	celery fly
Leaves yellow and wilt.	onion fly
Leaves yellow and wither or fall, purple felt on outside of roots – asparagus, celery.	root rot
Small or large brown spots on leaves, may spread so that leaf withers; plant stunted.	celery leaf spot
Leaves mottled yellow and green, plant stunted.	mosaic virus
Leaves gray-green, stems thin with swollen bases, crown turns brown internally – rhubarb.	crown rot
Small, powdery, raised, red-brown spots.	rust

Stems

Stems of young plants with holes, or older plants with holes in center.	slugs, snails
Stems in center brown, soft and slimy.	soft rot

ROOT AND TUBER VEGETABLES (except potato): Jerusalem artichoke, beet, carrot, celeriac, Hamburg parsley, onion, parsnip, radish, salsify, scorzonera, shallot, rutabaga, turnip.

Leaves

Pale brown blisters; leaves which shrivel.	celery fly
Leaves curled and stems twisted, small black or green insects on undersurface and on stems.	aphids
Leaves have red tinge then turn yellow, plant grows poorly; pale yellow maggots in roots.	carrot fly
Leaves yellow from tip, wilt and can easily be pulled off bulb; tiny white maggots in bulb.	onion fly
Brown spots on leaves, which wither – celeriac.	celery leaf spot
Mottled yellow and green, plants stunted.	mosaic virus
Grayish-white patches; turn yellow and wilt.	downy mildew
Leaves of young plants distorted and twisted, sometimes swollen; plants small, rot in bulbs.	eelworms or nematodes
Leaves turn yellow and wilt later; white mold on on base of bulb, roots small or non-existent.	onion white rot
Leaves yellowish between veins at first, turning brown later – beet.	speckled yellows
Yellow streaks on leaves or yellow all over, crinkled; plant small – onion, shallot.	shallot virus yellows or yellow dwarf virus
Slight yellowing and stunting; roots with purple felt outside – beet, carrots.	root rot
Dark spots – seedlings and young plants.	onion smut
White patches – salsify and scorzonera.	white blister
Small round holes in leaves of seedlings and young plants; plants may be defoliated.	flea beetle

Roots

Small round tunnels in roots from outside, shiny yellow or brown worms in them or in soil.	wireworms
Bulbs become soft, slimy and smell bad in storage – onions and shallots.	soft rot
Center of root mottled with brown or gray, soft and slimy – rutabaga and turnip.	soft rot
Brown, sunken, elongated, canker-like areas on side of root – rutabaga.	dry rot (Phoma lingam)
Round swellings on upper part of root, with white maggots inside – rutabagas and turnips.	gall weevil
Reddish-brown patches on shoulder – parsnip.	canker
Neck of bulb rots and gray mold appears on it – onion and shallot.	neck rot

FRUITING VEGETABLES (except tomatoes): globe artichoke, cucumber, eggplant, gherkin, squash, okra, peppers, squash and sweet corn. ALSO MELON.

Leaves

Yellow or gray-yellow speckling, webs underneath, leaves wither, plant wilts and ceases to grow.	red spider mite
Young leaves pale green and curling, small green insects on undersurface.	aphid
Yellowing patches on leaves with gray furry mold on top; also on flowers and young fruit.	gray mold (Botrytis cinerea)
Leaves curling and wilting, turning grayish, many tiny white insects beneath, sticky substance on leaves with black patches on it.	whitefly
Pale green or yellowing mottling of leaves, possibly also puckered; plant stunted.	mosaic virus
Powdery white patches on young leaves, later on older ones, growth stunted.	powdery mildew
Leaves wilt, stem becomes dark at base of plant, plant dies.	collar rot
Tiny pale green spots on leaves which spread and and turn gray, then brown, leaf withers.	cucumber leaf blotch

Stems

Holes in stems of young plants.	slugs
Tips of stems eaten, plants blind and stunted – sweet corn. Uncommon U.S.	fruit fly
Corn tassels broken over; pale pinkish worms in stalks or ears.	European corn borer

Kernels eaten by striped green, pink or brown worms in ears.	corn ear worm
Yellow beetles with 3 black stripes or yellowish-green ones with 12 black spots.	cucumber beetles
Leaves and stems wilt as white 'worms' tunnel in stems.	squash vine borer

TOMATOES

Leaves

Yellow areas between veins of leaves, leaf becomes completely yellow and withers.	magnesium deficiency
Top leaves wilt in daytime but recover, then lower leaves, followed by yellowing of lower leaves; finally complete plant wilts permanently; inside stem streaked with brown from base up.	Verticillium wilt
Dark brown blotches on leaves, stems and fruit.	blight
Leaves brown and withered; irregular holes in leaves, leaves may be skeletonized; large green worm with horn at end.	tomato moth hornworm
Leaves grayish-green, limp and curling, sticky with black patches, tiny white flies on undersurface; plants cease to grow.	whitefly
Leaves fern-like, very long and narrow; spotted and streaked with brown; mottled yellow and crinkled; bronze-brown spots.	viruses: fern leaf, streak, mosaic, spotted wilt

Stems

Foliage peppered with small holes; small black hopping beetles.	flea beetle

Fruit

Fruits set but remain size of pinhead, flowers and buds may drop without setting.	dry set
Transparent spots with 'halo' around them.	gray mold (Botrytis cinerea)
Yellow patches on red fruit.	blotchy ripening
Hard, round, sunken, dark brown or black patch on fruit at blossom end.	blossom end rot

Roots

Growth of plants stunted and slow; if dug up may have lumps on roots about the size of a pea, or brown 'cysts' as on potato roots.	root knot eelworm or nematode

POTATOES

Leaves

Dark brown-black patches on leaves; late on stems and tubers.	potato blight
Large irregular holes in leaves, may be skeletonized; reddish-brown caterpillars present; also black and yellow striped beetles.	Colorado beetle
Discolored and yellowing, curled; small green insects on undersurface and shoot tips.	aphid
Leaves rolled inwards, mottled yellow or pale green, or crinkled; plants stunted.	viruses: leaf-roll mosaic, crinkle.
Leaves yellow on occasional plants, stem black at soil level.	black leg
Leaves pale green or yellow, small plants weak and stunted; brown 'cysts' on roots.	potato root eelworm

Tubers

Dark brown or black, rough patches on skin.	scab
Tubers with cauliflower-like growths on them; tubers rot and turn black.	wart disease
Large irregular holes in tubers.	slugs, snails
Small, round tunnel-like holes in tubers.	wireworm
Irregularly-shaped hollow in center.	hollow or black heart
Irregular dark brown or black lines in flesh.	virus disease

MUSHROOMS

Tiny round holes in cap of mushroom.	mushroom fly
Large irregular holes in cap edge and center.	slugs, snails
Mushroom completely misshapen, with white web over cap, smells bad.	bubbles
Stalks with tiny holes, almost hollowed.	mites or spring tails
Casing appears covered in white powder.	plaster molds

STONE FRUITS: apricot, cherry, almond, nectarine, peach, plum.

Leaves

Leaves silvery-white on upper surface, on whole shoots or branches; wood stained internally with irregular purplish color, brown or purple shelf-like growths appear on trunk.	silver leaf
Gray-green withering leaves, minute reddish dots on undersurface.	red spider mite
Irregular holes in leaves, spring and early summer; green or brown caterpillars present.	leaf-eating caterpillars
Small black or green insects appear on undersurface of leaves and at tips of shoots, leaves curled and discolored pale yellow and green.	aphids
Crescent-shaped scars on fruit	curculio
Small brown 'shot holes'; leaves yellow and die, bark cracked and gumming.	bacterial canker
Thickened, wrinkled lighter green patches, later reddish-pink, blister-like, with bloom; leaves drop off; growth checked and stunted.	peach leaf curl
Weakened tree with gum on lower trunk.	peach borer
Chlorosis, leaf fall, failure of fruits to mature. (No real cure. Remove infested parts or whole free.)	yellows diseases (peach yellows, x-diseases cherry, buckskin, little cherry, etc.)
Pale-green speckling in patches on upper surface; small green hopping insects may be seen.	leaf hopper
Pin-prick holes with brown margins in young leaves and tips of shoots, leaves tattered later; tips of shoots blind, growth checked.	capsid plant bugs
Much curled over and twisted at tips of shoots; mass of blue-gray insects on undersurface.	mealy plum aphid

Stems and trunk

Tips of shoots and leaves die, shoot dies back toward parent stem, and turns brown.	die-back
Small brown raised spots on bark of trunk and on stems of shoots; clear sticky substance on leaves on which black patches appear.	scale insects
Patches of brown gum ooze out of bark.	bacterial canker or irregular water supplies

Fruit

Fruitlets have tiny holes, with sticky substance at entrance, and drop in early summer; white maggots feed inside fruit on flesh.	plum sawfly
Patches of brown with white concentric rings of raised spots on them; fruit rots; may drop or mummify.	brown rot
Small dirty-white maggots in ripening flesh.	cherry fruit fly

VINES: grape.

Leaves

Powdery white patches on youngest leaves and tips of vines, growth stunted; spread to fruit.	powdery mildew
Yellow speckling on leaves which wither and fall; minute pink-red insects on undersurface, also webs; growth ceases.	red spider mite
Leaves pale green and curl at shoot tips; small green insects on undersurface, and on stems.	aphids

Gray mold in patches; leaves may fall; mold on young or mature fruit.	gray mold (Botrytis cinerea)
Regular half-circle holes in edges of leaves, top growth becomes poor for no apparent reason, roots infested with white maggots.	vine weevil

Fruit

Berries shrivel without ripening, after stalks have turned brown or black.	shanking
Light brown patches on fruit, which wrinkle and do not ripen.	scalding

Bark

Small dark brown oval or round raised spots on bark, and on skin of shoots; growth is slow; leaves may be gray-green with black patches.	scale insects
Small oval insects with gray-white mealy fluff on upper surface living on bark, moving slowly.	mealy bug

BUSH FRUIT: black, red and white currants, blueberry, gooseberry.

Leaves

Young leaves and tips of shoots tightly curled and twisted over, leaves yellow later, new growth severely stunted; small green insects on undersurface of leaves.	aphids
Irregularly-shaped reddish blisters on upper surface; small cream insects on lower surface.	red currant blister aphid
Pin-prick holes with brown edges on young leaves and in tips of shoots, leaves later much torn; shoots stop growing, may be blind.	capsid
Leaves discolored, fall prematurely; fruit small and poor quality.	red spider mite
Small angular dark brown spots on the leaves, which may wither and fall early; new growth slows, fruits shrivel.	blackcurrant leaf spot
Powdery white patches on undersurface of leaves which curl upward, and later turn brownish, also on fruit and stems where it becomes brown felt; growth stunted.	American gooseberry mildew
Powdery white patches on upper surface of leaves and shoot tips, also on fruit later.	European gooseberry mildew
Leaves very pointed and rather nettle-shaped, fewer main veins than normal, cropping poor.	reversion virus
Leaves severely eaten until only main vein left, from center of bush outwards; green and black caterpillars present.	gooseberry sawfly

Stems

Shoots have dead leaves at tip and along rest of stem from tip downward; stem is dead, tiny red pustules may appear.	die-back

Fruit

Large irregular holes in fruit near ground.	slugs
Large pointed holes in fruit at top of bush.	birds

CANE FRUIT: blackberry, loganberry and other hybrid berries, raspberry.

Leaves

Pin-prick holes with brown edges in leaves at shoot tips and in stems, later much torn; growth checked.	capsid plant bugs

Cabbage club root

Mosaic virus

Pea moth caterpillars

Young leaves curled, may be mottled yellow; small green insects on undersurface. — aphids

Leaves markedly mottled yellow and curled, canes stunted, fruiting poor, sideshoots few. — mosaic virus of raspberry

Leaves rolled up with insect larvae inside. — leaf roller

Leaves chewed irregularly. — Japanese beetle, rose chafer, etc.

Canes

Canes much stunted, develop many blind shoots; leaves may be mottled yellow and distorted. — blackberry dwarf virus

Long silver-gray patches on canes extending from spurs, easily seen in winter; spurs do not produce leaves or sideshoots. — spur blight

Small round purple spots on canes late spring onwards, bark splits; tips of canes often killed. — cane spot

Fruit

Green fruits become brown and remain hard and unripe or may become distorted, white grub inside; ripe fruits misshapen, much less blossom. — raspberry beetle

STRAWBERRY

Leaves

Powdery-white patches on upper surface of leaves, purplish beneath, leaves curl upwards; white powder on berries. — powdery mildew

Small round dark reddish-brown spots on leaves. — leaf spot

Crinkled and reduced in size, or with yellow edges; plants stunted and fruit poorly. — viruses: crinkle, yellow edge

Small, reddish leaves, outer ones brown during growth season; plants small, roots dark brown, with a red center. (No cure. Use resistant varieties). — red stele

Leaves puckered, plant stunted; secondary crowns produced, few flower buds. — eelworm or nematode

Young leaves curled and puckered; small green insects on undersurface, growth checked. — aphids

Fruit

Pale brown patches on pale green fruit; gray furry mold on ripe fruit, often starting from stalk end; also mold on stalks and leaves. — gray mold (Botrytis cinerea)

Flesh eaten on surface, pips removed. — seed or ground beetles

Irregular dry holes in flesh. — slugs, snails or birds

Fruit lopsided and misshapen. — poor pollination or frost damage

Flowers

Petals green and leaf-like. — green petal virus

Black 'eye' in center; will not set fruit. — frost damage

Flower buds and stems lying on ground. — strawberry blossom weevil

Crown

Young plants eaten at soil level any time from autumn to spring, also roots. — cutworms

SEED FRUITS: apples, citrus, fig, mulberry, pear, quince.

Leaves

Black spots and brown marks on upper side of leaf; leaves may fall early; hard black spots on fruit, which crack; 'blisters' on shoot stems. — scab

Leaves turn brown and hairy, vigorous shoot dies quickly, cankers on stems – apple, pear, quince, etc. (No cure. Remove infected area or whole tree if need be.) — fireblight

Powdery white patches on leaves and shoot tips in early spring; flowers creamy-yellow; infected dormant buds gray and pointed, easily seen in winter. — powdery mildew

Large irregular holes, in spring and summer. — leaf-eating caterpillars

Young leaves and shoot tips curled, growth much stunted, small green, red or gray insects on the underside. — aphids

Leaves speckled dull pale yellow or gray-green, wither and fall early, may be webbing; minute pale red insects on undersurface; new growth stunted, tree looks sick and short of water. — red spider mite

Pin-prick holes with brown edges in young leaves and shoot tips; fruitless, very misshapen. — capsid plant bugs

Patches of light green on upper surface. — leaf hopper

Upper surface of leaf has green-yellow or reddish blisters turning black, and leaves fall early; fruit similarly affected. — pear leaf blister mite

Leaves dark brown at edges or sometimes in patches over whole leaf, tattered – pear. — wind damage

Fruit

Holes in side of fruitlets with sticky mess at entrance, ribbon-shaped cork-like scars on skin, fruitlet crops without maturing; white maggot with brown head inside fruit. — apple sawfly

Holes at calyx end, sometimes at side from mid-summer onwards; fruit highly colored and drops early; pale pink caterpillar eats pips. — codling moth

Skin with sunken spots, small brown dots in flesh, flesh bitter – apples. — bitter pit

Holes in mature fruit. — birds

Brown patches on outside of fruit, extending to flesh which rots; later rings of white pustules on brown part; fruit may drop or dry up. — brown rot

Mature fruit are dimpled and pitted on outside, flesh has small hard woody areas without taste or juice – pear. — stony pit virus

Gray furry mold on berries and fruit. — gray mold

Bark

Cracks and splits, breaks off, becomes sunken; shoot or branch encircled by canker dies, leaves gradually become yellow above it. — canker

Small dark brown oval or round raised spots on bark, and on skin of shoots; growth is slow; leaves may be yellow, yellowish-green or gray-green, sticky substance and black patches on them. — scale insect

Masses of white fluff on bark, at forks, junctions and crevices; tiny gray insects underneath; swellings on stems and branches. — woolly aphid

Small oval insects with gray-white mealy fluff on upper surface live on bark, move slowly. — mealy bug

Buds

Buds torn off in winter, no blossom in spring. — birds

Potato blight

Gooseberry sawfly larvae

Pear scab

Cherry black fly

Greenfly (*type of aphid*)

Brown rot on apples

Caterpillar of cabbage white

Wireworms on a carrot

COMMON TROUBLES

Remember that weather conditions, rather than a particular pest or disease, can often be the cause of trouble. Wind can cause leaves to go brown, wither or fall early; frost can produce black centers in blossom; wilting may be the result of drought; cold and drought can cause fruit to crack. A plant dying for no apparent reason may be the result of too wet a soil.

Use as few chemicals as possible but, where necessary, use the least harmful to natural predators, bees and humans, eg. derris, pyrethrum, resmethrin, carbaryl (or Sevin). Alternatively use chemicals that break down quickly, eg. malathion, diazinon.

APHIDS:
Tiny insects 2-3 mm [⅛-1/16″] long, with wings when adult. Grow in stages, molting a skin each time, which remains on plant as a white 'ghost'; green, black, gray, rosy or white in color, depending on species; root aphid and woolly aphid are grayish with fluffy white coating.
Survive winter as tiny black oval eggs. Damage occurs in spring and summer.
Feed by sucking the sap of young leaves, stems and flowers through needle-like mouth parts with which they pierce the plant tissue; root aphids attack roots and live in the soil. They secrete a sticky substance called honeydew, which falls to leaves below and on which sooty mold fungus grows.
Treatment: Finger and thumb; cut off completely heavily infested shoot tips and leaves; wash or wipe off honeydew and sooty mold; keep plants well watered, especially in dry weather; ladybird larvae are predators.
Spray with resmethrin, derris or malathion, or treat winter eggs with a dormant spray, but only if plants are dormant and woody. Treat woolly aphids with denatured alcohol and a stiff brush, and water plants infected with root aphid with malathion or derris.

BIRDS: Peck out fruit buds from late autumn to early spring; peck holes in fruit, including tomatoes when ripening; feed on leaves of brassicas, peck up onion sets, tear off bean flowers, pull out seedlings, eat newly sown seed, feed on peas in pods.
Treatment: Protect with 1.5 cm [½″] netting; spray with harmless but bitter-tasting-to-birds repellants as those containing alum. Put paper bags or nets around individual fruits; crisscross cot-ton above newly sown seeds or use bird scarers such as aluminum foil, scarecrows, mobiles.

BROWN ROT: Fungus disease which infects fruit, either in storage or on the tree. Mummified fruits can serve as a source of infection for the following year. Disease enters through wounds caused by birds, insects, weather, other fungus diseases.
Treatment: Destroy all infected fruit as soon as seen, and do not store diseased or injured fruit.

CAPSID or Plant Bugs: Comparatively large insects to 0.7 cm [¼″], quick-moving, like gigantic aphids, rarely seen as they move fast and drop to the ground when disturbed. Feed like aphids, but as they are much larger, do much more severe mechanical damage. Damage occurs from late spring to end of midsummer to leaves, flowers, fruit.
Treatment: Spray thoroughly with malathion or derris as soon as first pinholes are seen, and spray surrounding ground; repeat as makers instruct.

CATERPILLARS, LEAF-EATING: Green, brown, yellow, black, spotted and/or striped, sometimes hairy, 1.5-4 cm [½-1½″] long; larvae of moths or butterflies.
Treatment: Hand pick; spray with Sevin, malathion, etc.

CATERPILLARS, ROOT-EATING; **WIREWORMS,** ROOT MAGGOTS: Root maggots are white and are found in and around chewed up roots. Cutworms gray, with legs, 3 cm [1¼″] long, usually in a curved position; larvae of the turnip moth, the heart and dart moth, and yellow underwing; all feed at night. Wireworms are yellow, thin, shiny, 1.5 cm [1½″] long and slow moving, the larvae of brown beetles.
Treatment: Hoe regularly to expose to birds; hand pick, keep weeds down, since they provide cover for moths; dust soil with diazinon before planting.

GRAY MOLD: (*Botrytis cinerea*) Fungus disease which infects many plants, entering through injuries caused by pruning, insects feeding, weather conditions, bird and spray damage. Can destroy complete plants, e.g. lettuce, tomatoes, melons, or fruits such as those of eggplant, strawberry, or various others.
Treatment: Disease spreads rapidly in cool, damp, crowded conditions so improve aeration or ventilation and raise temperature. Cut out infected parts on healthy tissues then spray with an approved systemic fungicide, and spray the flowers of fruiting plants mentioned to prevent later fruit infection.

LEAF HOPPERS: *See* APHID for treatment.

LEAF SUCKERS: *See* APHID for treatment.

MILDEW: There are two kinds of this fungus disease, powdery and downy. The former is more common and infects many plants.
Treatment: Cut off seriously affected growth as seen, well back into healthy tissue. Then spray powdery mildew with mildex or sulphur, and downy mildew with maneb or zineb.

RED SPIDER MITE: Minute oval creatures, pale red in color, which need a hand lens to be seen. Found on the undersides of leaves, near the main vein. Fruit tree species spend winter as bright red eggs on bark of trees and hatch in late spring; greenhouse species spend winter as a hibernating adult, emerging to feed during suitably mild spells in winter. Mites feed by sucking sap like aphids and take a month to complete their life cycle.

RODENTS, BIRDS AND SMALL MAMMALS: Eat bark from trees, feed on vegetables, particularly brassicas, lettuce and any others with tender leaves, take ripening fruit, especially strawberries, squashes, okra, cucumbers; eat large seeds; eat fruit and vegetables in storage.
Treatment: Use baits or traps baited with cheese, nuts or fat. Spray repellants as for birds.
Treatment: Maintain humid atmosphere around plants and keep well watered, especially during drought, as mites thrive in hot, dry conditions; spray plants with water daily; spray with derris or malathion.

SCALE INSECTS: Brown, sometimes gray, oval, round or shell-shaped, raised spot-like pests about 2 mm [$\frac{1}{8}''$] long, stationary. Mainly on bark of stems and trunk, but also on undersides of leaves, especially if tough and leathery. Feed by sucking the sap from plants. Container-grown plants may be killed. Because they are immobile and frequently the same color as the bark, these pests are often missed until there are a great many, when they are difficult to control.
Treatment: Scrape off as many as possible with the back of a knife onto paper laid beneath the plants, then spray thoroughly with malathion, and repeat once or twice more at 10-day intervals, depending on the degree of infestation. Sponge off any sooty mold.
SLUGS AND SNAILS: Snails are easily recognized by their shells, but slugs are often mistaken for pebbles at a casual glance. They feed at night and hide during the day.
Treatment: Put rings of gritty material around plants, at least 15 cm [6"] wide; trap in containers of stale beer or sweetened water sunk in soil near plants. Put down poison baits. Eliminate possible hiding places and improve drainage.

SOFT ROT: Bacterial disease which infects roots and centers of plants, and those in storage. Worst in wet seasons.
Treatment: No chemical control, but infected parts should be cut out or plants destroyed. Avoid injury to plants so that bacteria cannot enter; slug damage in particular is dangerous.

ROOT ROT: Fungus disease infecting plant roots.
Treatment: Lift and destroy infected plants, removing all the root. Do not grow any of these plants in the same soil for four years, and keep weeds away, particularly bindweed, dock and dandelion, which are susceptible.

VIRUS: There are many kinds of virus diseases, which become part of the nucleus of the plant cells, hence the difficulty of chemical control. Infection by virus are often easily spread by clothes, tools, hands and sap-sucking insects from infected plants to healthy ones; some are carried by soil-inhabiting pests. Very many plants are attacked. Little or no control, so plants are best destroyed at once. Little knowledge at present, however, new systemic fungicide may offer hope. Do not confuse with nutrient deficiency symptoms, in which discoloration occurs in regular markings and patterns.

WHITEFLY: Adults 1 mm [$\frac{1}{25}''$] long, snow-white, moth-like insects found under leaves; young and eggs flattened, circular, pale green almost transparent, on underside of leaf. Feed by sucking sap from leaves and stems, stationary until adult, then fly moves off to lay eggs on fresh leaves. Plant becomes very messy in bad infestation, especially tomatoes, and can be killed.
Treatment: New insecticide resmethrin gives good results, otherwise whitefly difficult to deal with, because of need for insecticide to penetrate to young through protective scale, and because all stages present all the time. There are several generations in a season.
The simplest effective control: paint cards bright yellow and coat with a sticky substance such as Tack Trap or Tanglefoot. Adults attracted by the color, cannot free themselves from the cards.
WIREWORMS: *See* CATERPILLARS, ROOT-EATING.

Gray mold (Botrytis cinerea)

Mildew on apples

Red spider mite damage

Scale insects (Coccus coryli)

Whitefly damage on tomatoes

Varieties

Each entry lists a number of recommended varieties, indicating their different characteristics and giving, where applicable, the essential information on sowing times, pollination, cropping etc. Where no entry appears for a particular crop, this is an indication that most merchants list only one variety. This applies to the majority of herbs and to a small number of fruit and vegetables.

APPLE

To set a crop, most apples need to be cross-pollinated. Most varieties have plenty of pollen and will pollinate one another, *provided their flowering seasons coincide or overlap.* Some have little pollen they are known as triploid. They need a suitable pollinator to help them set their fruit, but they themselves will not pollinate the other tree. In this case there should be a third variety present (not triploid) to ensure a good crop on all three. A few varieties are self-fertilizing though they crop better with a suitable pollinator.

Baldwin: An old variety, hard, juicy, keeps well and long a favorite. Good for cooking and eating but tends to bear biennially.
Cortland: A winter apple, bears well, well-colored good for both cooking and eating. An improved McIntosh, 2 weeks later.
Delicious: Mild flavored, large, fragrant. Ripens late and keeps well. Good dessert variety.
Early McIntosh: A crisp juicy summer eating and cooking apple. Bears early, hardy, vigorous and annual bearing.
Golden Delicious: Firm, crisp, juicy and golden yellow. A good winter keeper, it bears young and heavily. Eating and cooking.
Jonalicious: A fall eating and cooking apple. Combines many of the qualities of Jonathan and Red Delicious.
Lodi: A new yellow cooking apple of better quality than Yellow Transparent. Vigorous, heavy bearer and hardy. Quality good for summer.
Macoun: Another McIntosh type, of better quality, ripening later and keeping better. Good for eating and cooking.
McIntosh: The standard apple of the Northeast. Vigorous, early bearing, hardy fall ripener. Good for eating and cooking.
Northern Spy: Large, hard, crisp and juicy, it is one of the best keeping winter sorts. Slow to bear.
Red Delicious: Red all over while most apples are still green. Mild and juicy. A winter dessert variety.
Rhode Island Greenery: Vigorous, productive and a good keeper, probably the best cooker of all.
Rome Beauty: Large, deep colored and thick skinned, it stands handling well, bears young.
Stark Earliest: A very early summer apple of the Delicious type.
Summer Delicious: Another early or summer apple. Early bearing, well colored. An eating apple.
Wealthy: A good all-purpose fall apple. An old favorite.
York-A-Red: Winter-keeper type. Flavorful especially for cider, also eating.

CRAB APPLES

Dolgo: Perhaps, the best known. Ornamental, heavy-bearing. Fruits small to medium, deep red. Hardy, bears young. Good for spicing, pickling, jellies, sauce.

APRICOTS

The best Eastern varieties are: *Alfred, Farmingdale, Worley, Peach, Veecot, Goldcot* and *Curtis.*
In the Far West grow: *Royal (Blenheim), Moor Park, Tilton, Perfection, Wenatchee, Blenril* and *Earliril.*

ARTICHOKE, GLOBE

Green Globe: The most widely available.
Grande Beurre: New. Has fleshier heads.

ASPARAGUS

Mary Washington, Paradise: The two most widely grown varieties.

BEETS

Crosby's Egyptian: 56 days. Old, well-known, popular.
Early Wonder: 55 days. Smooth-skinned, semi-globe.
Detroit Dark Red: 60 days. Favorite, all-purpose main crop best.
Red Ball: 60 days. Tasty, sweet, uniform shape and color.
Burpee's Golden: 60 days. Golden flesh does not bleed.
Tendersweet: 55 days. Early. Cylindrical. Exceptionally sweet.
Ruby Queen: 56 days. Ringless. Good in South.
Vermillion: 56 days. New. Highly desirable. Non-bolting.

BLACKBERRY

Bailey: good. Dependable.
Darrow: probably the best of all. New.
Ebony King: a good standard variety.
Eldorado: well-known and good.
Hedrich: good for the East.
Midnight: very dark. Dependable.
Oregon Thornless: Popular in West, Mid-season, medium-size fruit, moderately vigorous.
Smoothstem: grown primarily for clean stem.
Thornfree: Likewise easy picking.
Himalayan Giant: Suitable only in mild climates. Good, medium-size fruit. Late.

BLUEBERRY

Berkeley: Early. Large, sweet, on spreading plant.
Blue Crop: Mid-season. Very reliable, large, good flavor, upright.
Bluette: Early. Variety of good quality.
Blue Ray: Early. One of earliest, vigorous, large, light blue fruits.
Collins: Early—mid-season. A newer, better sort.
Concord: Early, dependable, good bearer.
Coville: Late. Older and smaller but highly flavored.
Darrow: Mid-season. One of the truly superior varieties.
Dixie: Mid-season: Bears truly large, juicy berries.
Earli Blue: Early. One of very earliest, large-fruited, prolific.
Jersey: Late. Tall, vigorous, hardy. High quality, ornamental.
Late Blue: Late. Highly desirable. One of newer sorts.
Weymouth: Early. Weymouth. Hardy, dependable, good quality.

BEANS, FRENCH AND SNAP OR STRING BEAN

Although many people still refer to them as "string" beans, the strings have long been removed and they should properly be referred to as "snap" beans in the U.S. The term "French" applies only to one small group used primarily as dried beans.

Green-Bush Bean:

Bountiful: The most popular flat, green variety.
California Red Kidney: 100 days. Large, red seeds used for drying.
Fava: Can be used fresh or as winter shell bean.
French Horticultural (Haricot): pods splashed with red. A principal shell bean.
Garbanzo (chickpeas of the South): small, round, light brown seeds.

Greencrop: Retain edible condition a long time.
Pinto: Like garbanzo, a staple in the Southwest.
Royalty: purple. Good in colder soils.
Stringless Green Pod: a popular standard round pod.
Tendercrop: resists mosaic and moth virus.
Tenderpod: All-America. Top quality for table, canning, freezing.
Yellow or Wax Bean:
Golden Wax: resists disease and blossoms drop in heat.
Kinghorn Wax: vigorous and productive. Popular for canning, freezing.
Pencil Pod Wax: an old favorite with a long season.
Pole Beans:
Blue Lake: popular commercial variety. Also a good shell bean.
Kentucky Wonder: the favorite climber.
Kentucky Wonder Wax: similar but yellow.
Broadbean:
Broad Windsor Long Pod: large beans in long pods. Hardy. Sow early.
Frostproof: upright, sturdy. Eaten cooked or shelled for winter.
Express: One of the fastest maturing, tender and tasty.
Masterpiece: a good all-round sort, tasty, good grower.

BROCCOLI

Calabrese: another old favorite. Large head with many side heads.
Cleopatra: early-early. Good flavor, uniform, compact heads.
De Cicco: a favorite. Early, high producer of side sprouts.
Green Comet: All-American winner. Very early, single-headed. Resists heat.
Green Mountain: good for short season areas.
Premium crop: All-American winner. Second early, single-headed.
Spartan Early: short, uniform with good-sized, central heads.

BRUSSELS SPROUTS

Early Morn: early, compact, large-sprouted.
Green Pearl: good for early fall. Heavy, uniform bearer.
Jade Cross: very popular. Very heavy bearer of medium, oval sprouts.
Lindo: new. Heavy yielder for late summer and fall.
Long Island Improved: popular market and home sort.
Topscore: late fall. Round, hard, uniform sprouts.

CABBAGE

Early Earliana: one of earliest. Small round, to 5″ and 2 lb.
Emerald Cross: all-America. Compact, 6-9″. Resists bursting.
Golden Acre: good quality, medium size. Few outer leaves.
Stonehead: all-America. Firm, solid, uniform and compact.
Late Fall or Winter:
Baby-Head: miniature, solid-head keeper.
Jumbo (Large Late Drumhead): Seldom under 12lb.
Penn State Ballhead: good for sauerkraut and keeping.
Surehead: uniform, large, flattened head.
Savoy:
Chieftain Savoy: standard commercial sort. Resists bursting.
Savoy King: All-America. Large, uniform, stands heat.

Red:
Red-Acre: deep red, medium head, early-ripener.
Red-Head: All-America. Round, 7″, holds color in cooking.
Buby Ball: All America. Extra-early. Resists bursting.

CARROTS

Danvers Half Long: good, all-around sort. Probably best-known.
Goldinhart: medium length, sweet, coreless.
Gold Pak: smooth, slender, freezes and cans well.
Imperator: large, uniform, cylindrical.
Little Finger: tiny, good for early crop. A gourmet stem.
Royal Chantenay: moderately large, tender, coreless.
Short'n'Sweet: lives up to name. Good for home use.
Spartan Bonus: excellent for canning, slicing, purees.

CAULIFLOWER

Purple Head: flavor like mild broccoli, turns green when cooked. Easier to grow than whites. Freezes well.
Self-Blanching: high quality, well-domed heads, 6-8″, covered by incurved leaves, eliminating tipping.
Snow Crown: all-America. Well rounded, smooth early and of excellent quality. Good in South.
Snow King: all-America. Extremely early, heat and disease-resistant.
Whitehorse: excellent quality. Heads deep, snow white and uniform. Supply limited.

CELERY

Florida 683: bushy, medium green. Very popular for late crop.
Fordhook: tender, crisp and juicy. Use green or blanched. Stores well.
Giant Pascal: good storer. Nutty-flavored, crisp and tender.
Golden Self-Blanching: stalks and heart tender, free from strings. Early.
Improved Utah: early, dark green. Good commercial sort, without pithiness.

CHERRY

Most sweet cherries are infertile to their own pollen. Hence it is of prime importance when selecting varieties to include pollinators.
Bing: red, mid-season to late. One of best known varieties.
Black Tartarian: early. Large, black, meaty. Vigorous and heavy bearing.
Napoleon (Royal Anne): yellow with bright red check. Firm, juicy and very sweet. Good canners. Early.
Schmidts Bigarreau: extra large, deep rich mahogany. Fruits in clusters. Vigorous. Mid-season.
Windsor: one of best quality dark cherries. Rapid, upright grown. Good for eating and canning. Late.
Sour cherries:
Early Richmond: early, red. A popular variety for pies, etc.
Montmammoth: another good red sort, slightly late, ripening.
Montmorency: very popular red sour cherry. Very productive. Self-pollinating.
Hybrid:
Dwarf North Star: a new dwarf (6′), cross between hardy Siberian and English Morello. Stands −25°f. Heavy bearer. Good for eating and cooking.

CHINESE CABBAGE

Michihli: tall, cylindrical (to 18″), dark green, sure heading but does not store well as Springtime.
Pe-tsai: an early introduction. Probably best known and available.
Springtime: a Wang Bok hybrid. But for late spring sowing, for July-August harvest. Stores well.

CUCUMBER
Conventional Varieties:
Burpless Hybrid: crisp, juicy, burpless. For salads or pickled.
Marketer: a fancy, commercial variety. Slender, smooth, crispy.
Ohio M R.17: early pickling sort, for sweet or dill types. Vigorous and productive.
Straight 8: a good dependable, all-around garden sort.
Surecrop Hybrid: all-America. White, crisp, tender, vigorous and disease-resistant.
Victory: all-America. An all-female hybrid. Disease-resistant.
Wisconsin S M R 12: good for dill and larger pickles. Vigorous and productive.
Greenhouse Varieties:
Tosha: seedless, smooth. Highest yielder for winter crop.
Brilliant: outyields all other late spring-summer types.
Pandex: all-female. Stands cold. Good for full-early winter.

EGGPLANT (AUBERGINE)

Black Beauty: early, dark purple, prolific, almost round.
Burpee Hybrid: top quality, medium-sized, oval, keeps cup off ground.
Jersey King: dark purple. Long.

GOOSEBERRY

The European varieties do not do well and culture is relatively limited in the U.S. The following are available only where white pines do not grow: **Chatauqua, Fredonia, Oregon Champion, Pixwell, Poorman, Red Jacket** and **Welcome.**

GRAPE
Labrusca or Eastern Grape:
Concord, Delaware, Fredonia, Niagara, Ontario, Red Amber, Steuben, Van Buren.
Muscadine or Southern Grape:
Burgam, Creek, Eden, Hunt, Scuppernong, Tarheel, Thomas, Wallace.
Vinifera, European or California Grape:
Black Manukka, Cardinal, Muscat Hamburg, Muscat of Alexandria, Ribier, Scarlet, Thompson Seedless.

KALE

Blue-Curled Vates: compact, bluish green. Stands sub-freezing temperatures.
Dwarf Scotch: hardy, finely curled. For salads, garnish, greens.
Dwarf Siberian: low, spreading, leaves frilled at edges only.

Kohl-rabi
Early Purple Vienna
Early White Vienna: no difference except color.

LEEK

Broad London: also sold as Large American Flag.
Elephant: large thick-stalked early that stores well.
Giant Musselburgh: white, tender, standard.

Unique: hardy, long-stemmed, stands cold.

LETTUCE
Heading:
Buttercrunch: compact and heavy. Juicy, crisp, slow-bolting.
Dark Green Boston: popular for quality and reliability.
Minilake: like Pennlake but earlier.
Ithaca: heads very hard, slow maturing.
Great Lakes: a good standard sort for late crop.
Pennlake: popular for early setting-out.
For Hot Weather (Cos or Romaine):
Paris White: vigorous, resists mosaic.
Sweet Midget: small but good and flavorful.
Valmaine: like first but also resists mildew.
Loose-leaf or Non-heading:
Black-seeded Simpson: popular, the most widely used.
Grand Rapids: tender, sweet, crispy; for spring, summer, fall.
Green Ice: new and one of best, slow to bolt.
Oak Leaf: tight rosette with vaguely oak-like leaves.
Salad Bowl: large, crisp, leaves deeply lobed.
Slobolt: resists heat of early summer.

LIMA BEAN
Bush type:
Baby Potato: small, flavorful.
Burpee's Improved: fairly new, superior.
Clark's Green Seeded: delicious; use fresh, can or freeze.
Fordhook Bush: well-known standard.
Henderson Bush: old favorite baby lima.
Jackson Wonder: the "speckled lima", resists heat.
Pole Limas:
Burpee's Best: heavy bearer for fresh use or freezing.
Large Speckled Christmas: large, flat beans, white with markings.
King of the Garden: old favorite fresh or frozen.
Prizetaker: largest beans of all, less to shell.
Sieva: very early, small-seeded, keeps for winter.

LOGANBERRY
The ordinary type and the *Thornless Loganberry* only ones listed.

MARROW (SEE ALSO SQUASH)
Cocozelle: 8 inches, often sold as Italian Marrow.
Fordhook Zucchini: all-America. Tender, best 8-12 inches.
Goldzini: deep butter yellow hybrid.
Vegetable Marrow Bush: a favorite English type.
Zucchini F1 Hybrid: another improved Zucchini.

MELON
Cantaloupe:
Bender's Surprise: an old favorite, widely grown.
Burpee's Ambrosia: new, firm, sweet, edible to rind.
Burpee Hybrid: high quality, 4-4½ lb., flesh orange.
Canada Gem: fruits stand abuse, resists mildew and fusarium.
Delicious: resists fusarium wilt.
Fordhook Gem: has long season, green flesh.
Iroquois: a newer, superior sort.
Mainrock Hybrid: early, good for northern gardens.
Saticoy: hard rind, resists mildew, fusarium, fruit spot.
Honeydew:
Honeydew: very sweet, green-fleshed, juicy.
Honey Mint: a good, all-purpose sort.

Tam-Dew: adapts well to warm climates.
Watermelon:
Black Diamond: largest of all, up to 125 lb., sweet.
Charleston Gray: red, crisp flesh, disease-resistant.
Hybrid Dixie Queen: extra vigorous and productive.
Klondyke: extra/ early, deep red, 25 lb.
Small Sorts:
Market Midget: good keeper, 8 inches long, 25 lb.
New Hampshire Midget: smallest of all, sweet, juicy.
Sugar Baby: 8 lb., thin rind, tender flesh.
Yellow Baby: all-America, yellow-fleshed, thin rind.

NECTARINE
Armking: good home and commercial sort.
Gold Mine: usually dwarf but vigorous and productive.
Nectacrest: New Jersey origination, adapted to East.
Nectarina: genetic dwarf, freestone, golden flesh.
Panamint: scarlet skin, yellow flesh, very productive.
Silver Lode: white-fleshed, freestone.

OKRA
Clemson Spineless: popular in Mid-South.
Dwarf Green Longpod: productive, tender, spineless.
Perkins Mammoth: good northern sort, for canning and soups.
Red Okra: rich red pods, prolific.
Spineless Green Velvet: vigorous, productive, fresh or frozen.

ONION
Bunching:
Beltsville Bunching: best for August harvest.
Evergreen Long White: for fall or wintering over.
Hardy White Bunching: for summer or wintering over.
Sold as Sets:
Golden Mosque: best yellow variety.
Stuttgarter: good for sandy soils.
White Ebenezer: standard white sort.
White Portugal: mild, good pickler.
White Portugal: mild, good pickler.
Yellow Ebenezer: good keeper.
Barletta: very early.
Silver Queen: good early.
For Spring Seeding:
Autumn Spice: for deep muck soils.
Northern Oak: large, late storage type.
Southport Red Globe: strongly flavored.
Storage King: excellent keeper.
Super Elite: large, late storer.
Sweet Spanish Hybrid: large, mild in flavor, yellow.
Yellow Utah: improved Sweet Spanish.
For Fall Planting in Warm Climates:
Bermuda: yellow, Red and White varieties.
Early Harvest: earliest from seed, likes muck soils.
Grainex: mild, yellow, keeper.
Torpedo: a good producer.

PARSLEY
Champion Moss Curled: most popular sort.
Hamburg or *Parsnip-rooted:* grown for parsnip-like roots. *Plain* or *Single* (Italian): flat leaves, rich flavor.

PARSNIP
Harris Model: long, slim-rooted.

Hoolow Crown: the standard sort.
Large Sugar: noted for sweetness.

PEAS
Green Peas:
Alaska: earliest.
Alderman (Telephone): standard, late tall.
Drought-Proof: stands heat.
Fordhook Wonder: good, large-podded.
Freezonian: a good freezer.
Graders: an old favorite.
Little Marvel: small, good producer.
Progress No. 9: resists wilt.
Victory Freezer: All-America.
Wando: stands heat, freezes.
Edible Podded:
Burpee's Sweetpod: 4 feet, early, uniform, productive.
Dwarf Sugar: stands cold well.
Mammoth Melting Sugar: sweet, one of the best.
Table Field Peas:
Black-eyed Pea: dwarf prolific.
Brown Sugar Crowder: eat fresh or dry.
White Sugar: like Brown Sugar but white.

PEACH
Belle of Georgia: white, early.
Bonanza: genetic dwarf
Champion: white early.
Earlihale: yellow early.
Elberts: standard, late yellow.
Hale Haven: yellow, mid-season.
J. H. Hale: yellow, late.
Rio Oso Gem: yellow.
Stark Hal-berta: yellow, very early
Triogem: yellow, very early.
Nectarian: genetic dwarf nectarine.

PEAR
Bartlett: yellow and early. The best known.
Dayenne du Comice: a West Coast favorite.
Kieffer: late. Canner, eater. Resists blight.
Kyle's Sugar: early, yellow, good for fresh use.
Red Anjou: late, red, a home and market type.
Seckel: late, small, a pickling favorite.
Starking Delicious: mid- season, yellow, blight-resistant.

PEPPER
Bell Boy: excellent, productive, maincrop hybrid.
California Wonder: an old, standard variety.
Canada-Cheese: red, firm, ideal for pickle mixes.
Crimson Hot: deep, waxy crimson. For ketchup and pickling.
Golden Bell Hybrid: large, early on compact plants.
Long Red Cayenne: to 5 inches. Often twisted. Easily dried.
Pennbell: good, reliable sort on compact plants.
Stokes Early Hybrid: early, medium-sized, good quality.
Sunnybrook Pimiento: vigorous, productive. Thick, flat fruits.
Sweet Hungarian (Yellow Banana): Sweet, very productive.

PLUM
Abundance: extremely productive, red, Japanese sort.
Beach plum (Prunus maritima): native wild plum, excellent for jams, jellies.
Burbank Elephant Heart: mid-season, red, good in arid areas.
Fellemberg: one of best prunes.
Idaho Prune: good for Far North.
Santa Rosa: red, Japanese. Plant with another.
Superior: large, red, hardy.
Tecumseh: very hardy, red hybrid plum.

Yellow Egg: late, self-fertile, European.

POTATO

Anoka: round, yellow-fleshed, semi-prostrate.
Chippewa; mid-season. Table quality.
Early Gem: for Idaho area, good keeper, resists only scab.
Green Mountain: old standby of good quality.
Irish Cobbler: dependable, standard nearly everywhere.
Katahdin: standard of quality for years.
Redskin: good in South. High yielder. Resistant.
Shoshoni: Idaho type. Good yield but appearance not best.
Teton: for Northeast and Wyoming. Good for cooking and starch.
White Rose: mostly for California and Northwest. Disease-prone.

PUMPKIN

Big Max: reaches 70 inch circumference, 100 lb.
Connecticut Field: standard large variety, 15 to 20 lb.
Jack O'Lantern: 10 to 15 lb.
Small Sugar: favorite pie variety.

QUINCE

Champion: large, yellow and late.
Orange: the standard sort; early, round and orange.
Pineapple: large-fruited, popular in California.

RADISH

Burpee White: round, mild, best when not over 1 inch.
Cherry Belle: round, red. A good greenhouse and muck land sort.
French Breakfast: scarlet with white tip. A favorite.
Scarlet Globe: very early. A favorite.
White Icicle: best white for summer. Long and mild.
White Chinese or *Celestial:* long, white winter radish.

RASPBERRY

Red:
Canby: vigorous, large-fruited, early and thornless.
Durham: good everbearer fresh, canned or frozen.
Earlired: early, productive, good quality.
Tallred: heavy bearing, high quality everbearer.
Latham: standard red, spring cropper.
Newburgh: good early summer bearer.
Taylor: equally good, one-cropper.
Black:
Black Hawk: good new variety, productive and vigorous.
Bristol: productive, almost seedless, disease-resistant.
Cumberland: standard mid-season variety.
Logan: well-known, prolific, dependable.
Morrison: new, giant-fruited, mid-season to late.
Purple:
Amethyst: very early, productive.
Clyde: mid-season. Firm, tart, highly-flavored.
Sodus: long a favorite variety.
Yellow:
Amber: good early summer bearer.
Tallgold: new, tasty, extra-large everbearer.
Golden Queen: very sweet, flavorful, early summer.

RED AND WHITE CURRANTS

Cherry: good, productive.
Red Duchess: reliable, good bearer.
Red Lake: standard red sort, large, prolific.

White Dutch: good but not commonly seen.
White Grape: same as White Dutch.
White Pearl: same as White Dutch.

RHUBARB

Canada Red (Chipman's): currently most widely sold.
MacDonald: good, heavy producer.
Valentine: new, tender, juicy, well-flavoured.
Victoria: an old favorite.

RUTABAGA OR SWEDISH TURNIP

Altasweet: mildest-flavored winter turnip.
Purple-Top Yellow: excellent table sort, good keeper.
The Laurentian: most popular variety.

SPINACH

America: especially good for late spring, early summer.
Avon Hybrid: fast growing, vigorous, slow bolting.
Cold-Resistant Savoy: good for fall, early winter, spring crop.
Hybrid No 8: upright, productive, good in South.
Longstanding Bloomsdale: delicious raw or cooked, slow-bolting.
Winter Bloomsdale: plant early spring for summer or fall for wintering over.

SPROUTING BROCCOLI

Calabrese: large, central, cauliflower-like head.
DeCicco: early, good color, many side sprouts.
Green Comet Hybrid: 12 to 16 inches, medium head, many laterals.
Premium Crop Hybrid: huge central head, no laterals.
Spartan Early: heads small, crisp, early. Plant spring and summer.
Waltham 29: best for fall crop.

SQUASH

Summer:
Aristocrat: all-America, dark green, bush Zucchini type.
Baby Crookneck: early, butter, yellow, 6 inches.
Cocozelle: Italian vegetable marrow.
Patty Pan: early, scalloped, white bush type.
Straightneck: early, creamy yellow, good a long time.
St. Pat. Scallop: all-America, early, vigorous, best small.
Zucchini: very early, dark green, disease-resistant.
Winter:
Acorn: acorn-shaped, family-sized, orange-fleshed.
Blue Hubbard: large, hard-shelled, good keeper.
Butternut: thick-fleshed, flavorful, high yielder.
Table Queen: much like acorn, good keeper.
Turban: high yielder of very ornamental fruits.

STRAWBERRY

Spring-bearing:
Albritton: late season, for North Carolina.
Armore: late mid-season, for Missouri area.
Blakemore; early, Maryland especially.
Catskill: mid-season, Northeast especially.
Florida Ninety: early, for shipping north.
Midway: mid-season, mostly Maryland.
Pocahontas: early, Maryland area.
Shasta: mid-season, Californian.
Sparkle: late, New Jersey and Northeast.
Tennessee Beauty: late, mid-season.
Trumpeter: late, for Minnesota climate.
Everbearing:
Giant Gem: a larger form of old Gem.
Ogallala: from Plains States, very hardy.

Ozark Beauty: medium-sized, good quality.
Streamliner: not widely available but good.
Superfection: same as Gem and Brilliant.
Alpine:
Baron Solemacher: late, good flavor, like a large wild berry, runnerless.

SWEET CORN

Earlivee: extra-early, top quality, 7-inch ear.
Golden Cross Bantam: like Golden Bantam but much better.
Golden Miniature: small plant with small ears.
Honey and Cream: mixed white and yellow, discourages ear worm.
Illinichief: late, extra sweet, especially for North.
Improved Carmelcross: large ears, high quality. Good canner, freezer.
Iochief: very large ears, yellow, drought-resistant, prolific.
Seneca: very high quality, early.
Sugar King: large, late, sweet, good for cool summers.
Pop Corn:
Creme-Puff: yellow hybrid, prolific, pops well.
Strawberry: tiny, red ears, for ornament and popping.

SWISS CHARD

Fordhook Giant: leaves thick, dark, savoyed. Use stalks like asparagus.
Lucullus: the old standby.
Perpetual: bears summer to late fall.
Rhubarb Chard: stems red like rhubarb.
White King: improved Lucullus, for the discriminating.

TOMATO

Beefsteak: large (16 oz.), flat, late.
Big Boy: late, large, smooth, prolific.
Bonny Best: an old standy, medium-sized.
Earliana: early, medium-sized.
Fireball: small to medium, early, heavy cropper.
Golden Giant: large, yellow, late, low-acid.
Golden Queen: large, waxy-yellow, low-acid.
Gulf-State Forcing: for out-of-season crop, indoors or out.
Marglobe: an old favorite, fairly large, late.
Michigan Ohio Forcing: large, uniform fruits on heavy trusses, large plants.
Ohio W. R. 25 Pink Forcing: vigorous, large, wilt-tolerant.
Oxheart: oval, pink, large (18 oz.), very late.
Pixie: tiny, round, very early, good in pots.
Ponderosa: a large, flat, old favorite.
Pritchard: reliable, good quality, not common.
Red Cherry: well-known small, salad, pickling, preserving.
Rutgers: a favorite all-purpose sort.
San Marzano: productive, for paste and canning whole.
Tiny Tim: 8-inch plants with fruits larger than Red Cherry.

TURNIP

Foliage (Shogoin): 30 days for tops, 70 for roots, good.
Just Right: mid-season, white, flat, good quality.
Purple-top Milan: very early, white-fleshed.
Purple-top White Globe: mid-season, good raw or cooked.
Tokyo Cross Hybrid: all-America, extremely early, top quality.

ZUCCHINI

Black Jack: darkest green, smooth, cylindrical.
Goldzini: longest deep yellow of type.
Grayzini: blunt-ended, greenish-gray.
Zucchini Select: good quality, resists mildews.

Glossary

Acid (*soil*): *see* IMPROVING THE SOIL.

Alkaline (*soil*): *see* IMPROVING THE SOIL.

Annual: a plant that completes its life cycle in one year and then dies.

Anther: in the flower, the part of the *stamen* that contains the *pollen* grains.

Axil: the angle formed between a leaf, flower or shoot stem and the parent stem from which any of these arise; usually refers to that formed between the leaf stem and parent stem.

Biennial: a plant that completes its life cycle in two years and then dies. Many vegetables are biennials but are treated as *annuals,* harvested in their first year, before they have had time to flower and seed.

Blanching: the process of excluding light from growing plants to make them white and less bitter.

Bleeding: the loss of sap from plant tissues that have been cut or damaged.

Blind: a seedling or mature plant that has lost its growing tip before it flowers, and so ceases to grow or bloom.

Bloom (*on fruit*): the downy or white waxy covering on grapes, peaches and other fruit.

Brassica: the botanical *genus* to which members of the cabbage family belong.

Budding: a method of propagating a fruit tree by uniting a bud, with a slip of bark attached, to a host plant.

Bulb: storage organ of a plant, composed of fleshy leaf bases wrapped around an embryo shoot, and sometimes also an embryo flower, from which new growth comes.

Bulbil: a miniature bulb, which forms either at the base of a mature bulb or on a stem by a flower head (as in certain onions).

Calyx (*pl. calyces*): the outer series of modified leaves of a flower, made up of sepals, which are usually different in appearance from the petals.

Catch crop: quick maturing crop raised in a plot where a later crop is to be grown.

Chlorosis: the loss of color (usually green) from a plant, often due to a mineral deficiency, resulting in the production of leaves that are yellow, white or mottled.

Clamp: a mound of straw and soil heaped over a pile of harvested roots, such as carrots or potatoes, to preserve them.

Cloane: a group of identical plants obtained by vegetative propagation from a parent.

Compost (*garden*): decayed vegetable matter, forming a valuable organic manure.

Compost (*potting*): a mixture, usually of loam, sand and peat, with the addition of plant foods, used for growing plants in pots and other containers (uncommon in U.S.)

Compositae: the botanical family whose flowers consist of a cluster of many 'florets' in a 'composite' head. The daisy is a typical member; examples are chicory and lettuce.

Cordon: a fruit tree or bush restricted by pruning to form a single main stem.

Cotyledons (*or seed leaves*): the first leaves to appear in a seedling; they usually look quite different from the mature leaves.

Crown: the heart or base of a perennial plant, which grows both roots and shoots.

Cruciferae: the botanical family of plants, the flowers of which have four petals arranged in the form of a cross. Examples are cabbage and radish.

Cross-pollination: the transference of pollen from one flower to another, either on the same plants or between different plants.

Cucurbits: plants of the botanical family *Cucurbitacae*, with tendrils for climbing; examples are squash and cucumber.

Cutting: a small section of a stem, root or leaf cut off the parent plant and given the conditions it needs to produce roots, and become a new plant.

Deciduous: a tree, shrub or other plant whose leaves fall at the end of the season.

Dibber: *see* TOOLS.

Drawn: a term applied to plants which, because they are sown too thickly or in a badly-lit place, become long and sickly.

Drill: a straight furrow, usually shallow, in which seeds are sown.

Earthing-up: the process of drawing soil around a plant to exclude light, as with potatoes and celery. It is also done to protect a plant from frost, or to support it.

Espalier: a type of trained fruit tree in which a vertical trunk has pairs of horizontal, opposite branches arranged in tiers.

Eye: an undeveloped growth bud, used particularly of those on potatoes.

Family: a botanical term for a group of related *genera* of plants.

Fan: a tree or shrub restricted by training to produce a fan-shape.

Fallow: an area in which no plants are grown during a growing season. During this rest period the soil is usually cultivated, to aerate it and to destroy weeds.

Fertilization: the fusion of the pollen of the male plant with the ovule (or undeveloped seed) of the female, to form a seed.

F^1 Hybrid: the first generation of a new hybrid plant produced by cross-pollination.

Foliar Spray: a liquid containing plant nutrients which plants can absorb through their leaves, when sprayed over them.

Forcing: encouraging plants to grow more quickly than normal or at an unnatural time by use of heat.

Friable (*of soil*): crumbly, neither too moist nor too dry; easily worked.

Frame: *see* CLOCHES AND FRAMES.

Fungicide: a chemical to kill fungi.

Gall: an abnormal growth on a plant, caused by insects, bacteria or fungi.

Germination: the first stage in the growth of a new plant from a seed, sprouting.

Genus (*pl. genera*): botanical name for group of closely-related *species* of plants; related genera form a *family*.

Grafting: a method of propagation whereby the stem of one plant is united to a branch or root of another.

Green Manure: growing plants dug into the soil while still green to assist in providing plant food and improving the soil structure.

Hardy: refers to plants able to survive temperatures at or below freezing.

Half-hardy: refers to plants which will grow outdoors in summer but which will not survive temperatures below freezing.

Hardening off: the process of gradual acclimatization of plants that have been grown indoors to outdoor temperatures.

Half-standard: a tree, the stem of which grows vertically to a height of about 1.2 m [4'] before sending out lateral branches.

Haulm: the surplus green parts of a vegetable crop, such as the stems and foliage of potatoes or peas.

Heeling-in: the process of temporarily storing plants by placing their roots in a shallow hole and covering them with soil.

Herbaceous: a plant with tender green stems and foliage as distinct from woody growth. Commonly used of perennials which die down in autumn, forming new growth in spring.

Herbicide: a chemical to kill weeds.

Hotbed: a prepared garden plot, often protected by a frame, in which the temperature is raised by the introduction of heat by the gardener.

Humus: organic matter which has decayed to produce a brown or black substance. One of its most important properties is to improve the soil structure, whether the soil is basically clay or sand. The bacteria which it contains continue to break it down; it therefore has to be replaced constantly.

Hybrid: a plant grown from seed, produced by the pollen of a flower of one plant fertilizing the ovule of the flower on another, usually between two varieties or species.

Intercropping: the practice of growing a quick-growing crop, between rows of slower-growing plants; or of growing two crops in the same plot of ground.

Lateral: a branch or shoot growing from a larger stem.

Leaching: the loss of soluble minerals from the soil through water washing them away.

Leader: a major stem of a plant through which it extends a branching system; the central leader is one which continues growth of the trunk vertically.

Leaf mold: a rich soil formed from decayed or decaying leaves of trees.

Leguminosae: botanically, the plant family to which peas and beans belong.

Light: *see* FRAME.

Lime: a chemical compound supplying calcium to the soil or reducing its acidity.

Loam: *see* IMPROVING THE SOIL.

Maiden: a one-year-old fruit tree or bush ready for training; rooted strawberry runners are also called maidens.

Maincrop: the heaviest yielding crop of the season of a particular fruit or vegetable, as distinct from the early or late crops from specialized varieties.

Manure: originally farm manure, sometimes any bulky material that supplies humus and plant nutrients.

Mulch: any material used to cover the soil to aid cultivation. Organic mulches such as peat, straw and garden compost add food to the soil, help prevent the soil from drying out by reducing evaporation from its surface, keep the soil surface warm in winter and cool in summer and suppress weeds. Inorganic mulches such as plastic sheeting do not add food to the soil, but have all the other advantages of organic ones.

Neutral soil: *see* IMPROVING THE SOIL.

Nitrogen: *see* IMPROVING THE SOIL.

Node: a stem joint from which leaves, buds and sideshoots emerge.

Nodules: tiny round swellings on the roots of leguminous plants, such as peas and beans. They contain bacteria which are able to convert nitrogen gas from the air into nitrogen compounds usable by plants.

Offset: a sideshoot that develops naturally into a young plant, as with many bulbs.

Ovary: botanically, an unripened seedpod.

Ovule: an unfertilized seed in an ovary.

Parthenocarpic: able to bear fruit without pollination.

Peat: a substance formed in bogs and fens from partially decayed organic matter.

Perennial: a plant with an indefinite life-period, longer than two years. Usually applied to herbaceous plants.

Petal Fall: the stage at which fruit trees shed their flower petals.

pH Value: a numerical scale for measuring the acidity or alkalinity of the soil, ranging from 1 to 14. Acid soil has a pH of less than 7, alkaline soil a pH greater than 7, while soil with a pH of 7 is neutral.

Phosphorus: one of the essential plant foods, usually supplied by phosphates these are compounds of phosphorus and other elements.

Pinching out: the removal of the growing point of a plant stem, to encourage it to branch out lower down or form new buds.

Pistil: the female organ of a flower, consisting of an ovary, stigma and style.

Pollen: the male cells of a flower.

Pollination: the transference of pollen from a male flower to the stigma of a female flower. Normally done by bees or other insects but may have to be done by hand.

Potassium: *see* IMPROVING THE SOIL.

Potting on: a term used for removing a plant and the soil around its roots to a larger pot, to allow more space for the roots.

Pricking out: the operation of transferring seedlings from the pots or trays in which they were raised from seed to other containers or to outdoor beds.

Propagation: the increase of plants, by sowing seed, root division, cuttings, grafting or other means.

Propagator: usually applied to a glass-covered container, artificially heated, for promoting the growth of seeds when outside conditions are unfavorable.

Pruning: the cutting back, usually of a tree or bush for various purposes. In winter this is often done to shape; in summer to encourage the development of fruit buds.

Pyramid: a fruit or shade tree, trained to a pyramid shape.

Rhizome: a part of a plant which looks like a root but is actually a creeping, underground stem, as in the weed *Agropyron repens* (couch grass).

Ring culture: a method of growing plants, particularly tomatoes, in which they are made to produce two root systems, one absorbing mainly nutrients and the other water.

Rogue: an alternative name for a mutant, or plant which does not conform to type.

Root-crop: vegetables grown for their roots.

Rootstock: A fruit tree used for its roots alone, onto which a fruit-bearing variety, the scion, is grafted.

Rootstock, dwarfing: a fruit tree rootstock that will produce a smaller tree than is natural to the variety grafted onto it.

Rotation of crops: *see* PLANNING YOUR GARDEN.

Runner: a trailing stem of a plant which produces roots at the *nodes* where they touch the soil and eventually forms a new plant.

Salt: Sodium chloride used as a fertilizer for crops derived from maritime plants. Sold as agricultural salt. Has the property of making insoluble potash already in the soil available to plants. Also a weedkiller.

Scion: the uppermost *variety* of a fruit tree which determines what kind of fruit the tree will bear, grafted onto the stem of the *rootstock* of another variety or *species*.

Scorching: the effect of too much heat, too much sunlight or sometimes dry chemical fertilizer on the foliage of plants. White, brown or shrivelled patches appear.

Seed, pelleted: *see* SEEDS AND SEEDBEDS.

Seed-leaf: *see Cotyledom.*

Selective (of weedkillers): *see* GARDEN HYGIENE.

Self-fertile (*self-fertilizing*): of a plant variety whose flowers produce *pollen* that will pollinate the *ovules* of the same or other flowers borne by plants of that variety. It does not need another variety to act as a pollinator.

Self-sterile: a plant *variety* whose flowers are sterile to their own *pollen;* such a plant needs a different variety nearby to act as a pollinator and so enable it to produce fruit.

Sepal: botanically, the outer layer of modified leaves which comprise a flower, the inner one being made up of the petals. Sepals are often green and protect petals.

Set: of potatoes, those tubers, or parts of them, used as seed and planted; of onions and related crops, small immature *bulbs* in a state of arrested development that are planted to shorten the growing period.

Setting: a term describing the appearance of a young seed or fruit after the *pollination* of a flower.

Soot: a black residue of fuel, resulting from imperfect combustion. It is a source of *nitrogen,* containing up to 6% and also acts as a deterrent to insects and slugs.

Species: botanically, a group of closely-related plants which collectively form a *genus*. Species will breed true from seed.

Spit: the depth to which soil is normally dug with a spade about 23-30 cm [9-12"].

Spur: a short *lateral* twig or branchlet of a fruit-tree which bears a flower and subsequently a fruit. An established spur is one with several fruit buds.

Staging: benches (permanent or portable) on which to place plants in a greenhouse.

Stamen: the complete male organ of a flower, consisting of an *anther,* which is borne on a slender stalk-like filament.

Standard: applied to fruit trees, a standard is a tree with an expanse of bare trunk, below the head of branches; it is produced by *grafting*. Also, a full-sized type.

Station: position for each plant in a row.

Stigma: the tip of the female organ of a flower, producing a sticky fluid when ready for *pollination*.

Stopping: the *pinching out* of the growing point of a stem to encourage branching or the production of more flower buds.

Strig: of currants, one cluster of fruits with their stalks, including the central stalk of the cluster.

Subsoil: the soil beneath the *topsoil* layer, which is derived from it. Usually infertile and badly structured; unsuitable for growing plants.

Sucker: a shoot which emerges from a plant below ground-level, often from the roots.

Succession: the sequence of crops in a garden a matter which requires considerable planning to produce vegetables as they are needed and to avoid waste of space.

Sulphur: an element of which minute quantities are needed by some plants; these are normally obtainable through the sulphates supplied in fertilizers. Also used as a fungicide.

Systemic (*of insecticide or fungicide*): a chemical which, applied to one part of a plant, spreads through all parts of it and, without doing the plant any harm, is lethal to any insects pests or fungus diseases.

Taproot: a root which penetrates directly downwards into the soil and is the main anchor of the plant, such as that of carrot, parsnip and other root crops.

Tender: a plant vulnerable to frost.

Tine: a prong, or spike of a fork or rake.

Tilth: the fine crumbly surface layer of cultivated, or tilled, soil.

Thatch: straw arranged to form a waterproof roof to a storage pile or construction.

Top-dressing: the application of fertilizer to the surface of the soil; or the replacement of the surface layer of soil of a container with new potting mixture.

Topsoil: the uppermost layer of soil in a garden. Varies from 5 cm [2"] to 60 cm [2'9 or more deep.

Training: the art of shaping fruit-trees by pruning, stopping and other means.

Triploid: a plant whose pollen cells contain $1\frac{1}{2}$ times the normal number of chromosomes (microscopic parts of a plant cell that give the plant its characteristics). Such plants have less fertile *pollen* and need extra pollinators.

True leaves: the leaves of a mature plant, which succeed the *cotyledons,* or seed leaves, of the seedlings.

Truss: in some plants, eg tomato, a cluster of flowers or fruit.

Tuber: a storage organ, either a swollen underground stem, as in the potato, or a swollen root, as in the dahlia, by means of which the plant survives a period of drought.

Umbelliferae: a family in which the flowers form a kind of flattened dome, the flower stalks all linking with the main stem at the same point, eg. carrot and parsnip.

Union: the joint where a chosen variety (the *scion*) is grafted into the *rootstock*.

Variety: a subdivision of a *species*. A species has unique characteristics, which are always reproduced by its seedlings, but a variety may not breed true, and may or may not resemble its parents. Strictly speaking, the term now applies to those varieties which have arisen in the wild. Those which have appeared in cultivation, such as in gardens, nurseries or by deliberate breeding, are called cultivars; in gardening, however, the term still includes both kinds.

Virus: an ultramicroscopic organism which invades the nucleus of the plant cell, resulting in irreversible damage to plants.

Index

CREDITS